HISTORY OF THE
GREAT WESTERN RAILWAY

HISTORY
of the
GREAT WESTERN RAILWAY
VolumeThree 1923-1947

O. S. NOCK

LONDON
IAN ALLAN LTD

First published 1967
Reprinted 1982

ISBN 0 7110 0304 1

Published by Ian Allan Ltd, Shepperton, Surrey;
and printed by R. J. Acford, Chichester, Sussex

Contents

VOLUME III

		PAGE
	FOREWORD	ix
	AUTHOR'S PREFACE	xi
I	GROUPING	1
II	A SPLENDID DIVIDEND	13
III	ENGINEERING EMINENCE	23
IV	CO-ORDINATION IN SOUTH WALES	34
V	THE TRAGEDY OF 1926	45
VI	THE 'KING' CLASS LOCOMOTIVES	55
VII	TRAIN SERVICES: 1927–1930	64
VIII	A PARTIAL RECOVERY	75
IX	RELIEF OF UNEMPLOYMENT	86
X	WEATHERING THE STORM	104
XI	CENTENARY OF THE G.W.R.	114
XII	THE LOCOMOTIVE DEPARTMENT: 1930–39	122
XIII	THE ZENITH OF PASSENGER TRAIN SERVICE	135
XIV	THE LAST YEARS OF PEACE	148
XV	THE WAR YEARS: PHASE ONE	159
XVI	THE YEARS OF ENDURANCE: 1940–1	171
XVII	WAR YEARS: THE MIDDLE PHASES	183
XVIII	THE WAR—TO 'VE' DAY	196
XIX	'SOUR APPLE HARVEST'	213
XX	ENGINEERING PROWESS: 1945–1947	224
XXI	THE G.W.R. AND THE NATIONALISED RAILWAYS	233

APPENDICES

I	MAKE-UP OF THE NEW G.W.R.—1923	240
II	DIRECTORATE OF THE NEW G.W.R.—1923	242
III	OBITUARY NOTICE OF VISCOUNT CHURCHILL—1934	243
IV	WHITE PAPER ON RAILWAY CONTROL AGREEMENT—1940	245
V	NEW LINES OPENED 1923–1947	247
VI	NEW STATIONS AND HALTS 1923–1947	248
VII	BRANCH LINES CLOSED 1923–1947	251
VIII	STATIONS AND HALTS CLOSED 1923–1947	252
IX	STANDARD LOCOMOTIVES AS AT DECEMBER 31, 1947	256
X	CHAIRMEN AND CHIEF OFFICERS 1835–1947	257
	INDEX	260

Bibliography

Cook, K. J. The late G. J. Churchward's locomotive development on the Great Western Railway. *Proc. Inst. Loco. Engs.* 1950.

Ell, S. O. Developments in Locomotive Testing. *Proc. Inst. Loco. Engs.* 1953.

G.W.R. Engines. Names, Numbers, Types and Classes. G.W.R. Paddington, 1946.

Knox, Collie. The Unbeaten Track.

MacDermot, E. T. History of the Great Western Railway, Vols. I and II.

Mountford, E. R. Caerphilly Works, 1901–1964.

Nock, O. S. Fifty Years of Western Express Running.

Nock, O. S. Great Western Railway: An Appreciation.

Nock, O. S. Great Western Railway in the 20th Century.

Railway Correspondence and Travel Society. Locomotives of the Great Western Railway.

Railway Gazette. 1922–1948.

Acknowledgements

The Author and Publishers are indebted to the following for permission to reproduce photographs, as under:

E. D. Bruton Esq. for plate 20 bottom, 43 centre
M. W. Earley Esq. for plate 23 lower, 45, and 48 upper
O. S. Nock Esq. for plate 47 upper
The late W. J. Reynolds for plate 32 upper
G. H. Soole Esq. for plate 43 bottom
The Rt. Rev. E. Treacy, Bishop of Pontefract for plate 47 lower
Radio Times Hulton Picture Library for plate 6
Bristol Evening Post for Plate 35
Western Morning News for plate 28 lower
British Transport Docks Board for plates 9 and 41
Westinghouse Brake and Signal Co. Ltd. for plate 15 upper

For the remainder, we are indebted to British Railways, Western Region, and the British Railways Board, Dept. of Chief Engineer, Rolling Stock.

Foreword by

L. W. IBBOTSON

General Manager, Western Region, British Railways

The Railways—and particularly the Great Western Railway—have always been of considerable interest to the public in Great Britain. The level of praise or criticism usually reflects the experience of the last few journeys of the traveller. But whether we are liked or disliked, we remain in the public eye—at any rate judging by the comments in the daily press. I welcome, therefore, a volume which puts the railway scene in perspective.

Readers of this book will find much that is of interest to them, and not a little which is new, however well they know the Great Western Railway. It is only by reading a history of this kind that one can have an objective view of what is happening today.

The period covered by this book is of particular interest to the present day railwayman. Almost from the start of it, the impact of road haulage and the change in the conditions which favoured the build-up of the railways during the Industrial Revolution, were beginning to be felt. In the years before the period here described, the railways were the undisputed masters for the carriage of the raw materials and most of the output of British Industry. By the outbreak of the Second World War, they had lost this pre-eminent position. The full effects were seen after nationalisation, but Mr. Nock gives an interesting account of how the Great Western Board dealt with this increasingly difficult situation.

Mr. Nock's long experience and special knowledge of locomotive matters provides, as one would expect, a very readable and enjoyable account of Great Western locomotive practice, particularly in the working of express passenger trains. No one would want to deny that the 'Castles' and 'Kings' were outstanding examples of the finest era of steam locomotion. This book exemplifies the enthusiasm with which they were regarded both by railwaymen and the public in Great Western territory. And if one would say that too much attention is paid to this feature in this book, I would reply that it is the business of the railway to run trains. The Great Western Railway certainly knew this and I hope that some of their acumen has come down to its successors.

Preface

MacDermot's history of the G.W.R. is one of the great classics of railway literature. Its republication in a modern format was widely welcomed, but I was not a little daunted when Mr. Ian Allan approached me and asked if I would undertake the completion of the history, to the end of the Company's existence in December 1947. For one thing, I had not long previously written two books of my own about the Great Western Railway—not detailed histories, like MacDermot's, but informal causeries similar to those I had written about other railways. The invitation to continue and complete the work of MacDermot was a stirring challenge, and I accepted it gladly; but having done so there was the major question of treatment. I rejected at once the idea of trying to imagine how MacDermot would have written it, had he lived to do so, and to 'ghost', as it were, for him. In any case no railway minute books later than 1923 are yet available to students and historians. On the other hand railway history during the period 1923–1948 is magnificently documented in the files of 'The Railway Gazette' and other periodicals. Furthermore as a regular traveller on the line during the entire period, and one who later came to know many of the chief officers personally, the outlines of the story were in any case a vivid memory.

Seen in retrospect the history of the G.W.R. in the grouping era falls into a series of well-defined phases, and rather than prepare a yearly, or even a month-by-month chronology I have built up the story around these groups of events. The saga that emerges is remarkable, not only in itself but for the astonishing way in which the traits of the old Company, the railway of Brunel and Gooch, of the Armstrongs, Earl Cawdor, and Wilkinson, of Inglis and Churchward recur again and again, to the very end of its existence. It is no part of my task to recall, save for this brief mention, how their successors carried the habits of the G.W.R. into the era of the nationalised British Railways. But carry it they most certainly did!

In preparing this account I have drawn freely upon the files of 'The Railway Gazette' and 'The Railway Magazine'; of 'The Engineer', 'The Railway Engineer' and of the 'Great Western Railway Magazine', as well as upon contemporary newspaper comment upon important events. I am particularly indebted to Mr. B. W. C. Cooke, Editor-in-Chief of 'The Railway Gazette' for his help, and for permission to reproduce certain plans and drawings that have appeared in various publications of the former Tothill group. In studying particularly the files of 'The Railway Gazette' one can only feel a debt of gratitude to that great editor, John Aiton Kay, through whose enterprise contemporary railway history was recorded in such a wealth of detail in his journals. From my friendship with him in post-war years I know that Kay had a great affection for the

G.W.R. and the intimacy of his own friendships with all senior officers of the Company made his chronicling of events exceptionally well informed. Thus although the actual minutes are not yet available there has been the advantage that the contemporary reporting of Great Western affairs was often compiled from access to departmental files, and other sources of unimpeachable authority.

In the preparation of the present book I have enjoyed the most generous help from the Western Region of British Railways, and from the Archivist of British Railways Board. Time did not permit of my seeking out personally all the photographs I needed, but Mr. F. G. Cockman undertook this task for me, and I should like to pay tribute here to the energy and enthusiasm with which he undertook the job, and to acknowledge no less the ready and courteous help that was accorded to him, working on my behalf, by the various railway and dock authorities, and other sources of illustration that he approached.

When Mr. Ian Allan commissions a book he usually wants delivery of the MSS ' the day before yesterday', and the present work was no exception. But in a work like this it was necessary, as in a modern railway timetable, to incorporate some 'recovery time', to say nothing of allowing the family typewriter to cool down occasionally, and giving Olivia my wife a little 'time off' to prepare sustenance for the Author! However, we managed to avoid any 'engine failures' en route, and the MSS was duly delivered 'on time'.

O. S. Nock
May 1967

Silver Cedars
High Bannerdown
Batheaston
BATH

I

Grouping

The year 1923, bringing with it the grouping of the railways of Britain into what one contemporary writer called 'four great soulless combines', dawned upon a world torn and frustrated amid the sour-apple harvest of the Great War. Continental Europe was seething. The bitterness left by the war itself was in many places being exacerbated by the tactics of some of the victors; revolutionary régimes were being set up elsewhere, and the complete withdrawal of the United States of America from an interest in European affairs removed an influence that could have been of immense value. In Great Britain a sustained attempt was being made to rebuild an economy precisely the same as that which had existed before the war—an economy based upon our once-unrivalled position as an exporting nation; but so uncertain were the markets overseas, in the prevailing atmosphere of political confusion, that the greatest difficulties were encountered.

In the meantime the economic situation in Britain gave cause for the greatest anxiety. After a short period of boom after the war stagnation in many industries had set in. The number of unemployed persons was steadily rising; but the world-wide factors that were affecting the home economy were not understood, and in 1923 a Conservative Government proposing to introduce 'protection' in the form of tariffs upon imports, was swept from office, and Britain's first Labour Administration took its place for a short time. As for the railways, 'Grouping' was not generally a popular measure. Unlike nationalisation, 25 years later, railwaymen of the rank and file had no hand in its enactment, and they took little interest in its implementation—in early days at any rate. The Act of 1921 had been produced by Lloyd George's Coalition Government of 1921, that 'chamber of commerce' Parliament returned by the 'khaki election' of 1918. But the process of grouping, which to many seemed no more than a political move imposed upon the railways in 1923, was before long to prove a god-send to some of the smaller concerns whose individuality had disappeared by that most memorable New Year's Day in the railway calendar.

It is sometimes lightly remarked that the Great Western was hardly affected at all. This is very far from the case, and it was a new Great Western Railway that came into being from 1923 onwards. The old company did not absorb the local lines in Wales. Although the old Great Western Railway Company was not wound up the leading Welsh lines came into the new organisation as *constituents*, not absorbed companies, or subsidiaries. The constituent companies of the new group with their respective route mileages were:

1. Alexandra (Newport and South Wales) Docks and Railway
   10¼ miles
2. Barry Railway   68 miles
3. Cambrian Railways   295¼ miles
4. Cardiff Railway   11¾ miles
5. Great Western Railway   3005 miles
6. Rhymney Railway   51 miles
7. Taff Vale Railway   124½ miles

This arrangement set the new organisation off to a splendid start in Wales. Over the years the local lines had achieved immense status and a pride of achievement scarcely equalled elsewhere, and for them to have been swallowed up into the old Great Western would have involved untold loss of *caste* and dignity. To become *constituents* immediately made them full partners in the new enterprise, though at this distance in time it is difficult to appreciate why the Brecon and Merthyr Tydfil Junction Railway should have been excluded from this arrangement. A full list of the subsidiaries, and of the joint lines associated with the new Great Western is given in the Appendix on page 240.

The new directorate, totalling 25, consisted of 19 gentlemen formerly of the Great Western, two of whom had also been on the Board of the Alexandra Docks and Railway; and one each representing the constituent Welsh companies. But it so happened that some of these directors had been on the board of more than one Welsh railway. There were in fact three previously on the Alexandra Docks Board; three on the Rhymney, and two on the Barry Railway board. It was thus only the Taff Vale and the Cardiff that had no more than one of their previous directors on the new board. Viscount Churchill was Chairman, and Sir Ernest Palmer Deputy Chairman. Some of the other directors will perhaps be more familiar to locomotive enthusiasts from their names carried on the various classes of Great Western engines, including Lord Barrymore, Robbins Bolitho, Charles Mortimer, John W. Wilson and Sir Watkin-Wynn; while Lieut. Col. Sir Arthur Yorke was a former Chief Inspecting Officer of Railways at the Board of Trade.

Great importance was attached to co-ordination of the multifarious railway activities in South Wales, and two new organisations were immediately set up. Unlike some products of amalgamation one could recall, that needed amendment after only a few years of their existence, these two Great Western organisations lasted for the entire remaining span of the railway itself. First of all, the dock activities were all brought together under the supervision of a Chief Docks Manager, J. H. Vickery, formerly General Manager of the Alexandra Docks and Railway Company. Secondly, on the railway operating side, a new Cardiff Valleys

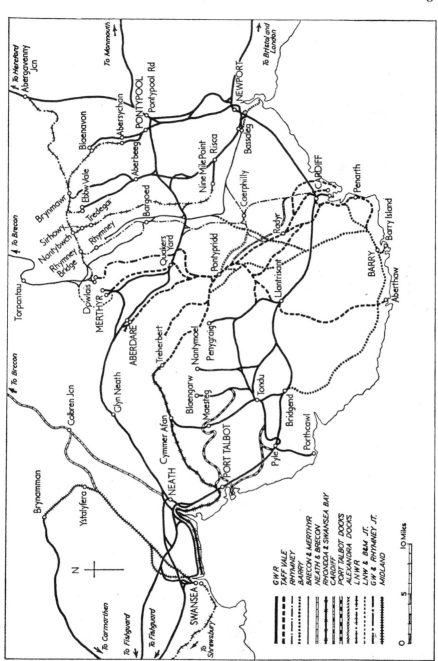

Fig. I. The railways of South Wales showing pre-grouping ownership.

Division was set up, with E. H. Dannatt from the Taff Vale as Divisional Superintendent, and C. T. Hurry Riches from the Rhymney, as Divisional Locomotive Superintendent. Two other appointments of importance in South Wales were W. Waddell, formerly General Manager of the Barry Railway to be Docks Assistant to the Chief Engineer, GWR, and John Auld, Mechanical Engineer, Barry Railway to be Docks Assistant to the Chief Mechanical Engineer, GWR.

Sir Felix Pole, dynamic as ever, immediately turned his attention to the co-ordination of railway facilities in South Wales, and the new year was still comparatively young when a £500,000 scheme was projected to improve coal handling facilities. This included six major points:

1. Additional sidings on the Newport docks lines.
2. Enlargement of Rogerstone marshalling yard.
3. A new junction between the Rhymney and Taff Vale lines at Roath.
4. Additional sidings, Cardiff Docks.
5. Additional sidings at Cadoxton.
6. Additional sidings at Llantrisant.

At that point in history an all-out attempt was being made to rebuild the pre-war export trade in coal from South Wales. Many of the old markets were opening up again, including that of locomotive coal to the Paris, Lyons, and Mediterranean Railway, conveyed to Marseilles in colliers owned by the P.L.M. itself.

Quite apart from the forward-thinking that was so evident from the many-sided enterprises emanating from Paddington the process of grouping had its complications, and two instances may be specially noticed, as occupying the time of certain Great Western officials in the year 1923. On January 1st the legal work involved in the formation of the new company, from its seven constituents and many subsidiaries, was practically complete. But the absorption of two subsidiaries, the Exeter Railway, and the Forest of Dean Central brought some peculiar difficulties. Neither of these companies had come to terms with the Great Western by January 1st 1923, and so, under the provision of the Railways Act, the absorption had to be prepared by the Amalgamation Tribunal.

The Exeter Railway, formerly the Exeter, Teign Valley and Chagford, was originally incorporated in August 1883 for a line from Exeter, St. Thomas's to Chagford. The distance was 18 miles, but only 8 miles of line were constructed, and the concern was leased in perpetuity to the Great Western and worked by them on the basis of 50% of the total receipts. The net revenue in 1913 was £4,370, and the Great Western offered securities in the amalgamated company of an annual value of £4,936. But the Exeter company alleged that there had been considerable improvement in traffic prospects since 1913, and the Great Western offer was declined. There was thus a state of deadlock over this 8 miles of railway at the time of the grouping, and the case was argued before the amalgamation tribunal on Monday May 7th 1923. Although it was, in

Plate 1

The transfers used on coach bodies, with the gartered coat of arms in centre, and the small emblems used to right and left

Plate 2

Viscount Churchill
Chairman 1908-1933

Sir Felix Pole
General Manager 1921-1929

R. H. Nicholls
Superintendent of the Line 1919-1932

C. B. Collett
Chief Mechanical Engineer 1922-1941

perspective, a very small case the decision of the Tribunal is given in full, as indicating the kind of procedure that had to be considered at the time of grouping.

'The net revenue of 1913, plus an allowance for interest on capital, cannot be taken as the sole measure of the revenue-earning capacity of the Exeter Railway for the present purpose. It is necessary to consider its present revenue-earning capacity and also its prospects of maintaining or increasing that revenue.

'It is relevant also, at any rate in view of the probability that the consideration for the transfer may be fixed in securities of the Amalgamated Company, to consider the position and prospects of the Exeter Company in comparison with those of the Amalgamated Company.

'The provision of the Act regarding rates raise questions on which we are not prepared to give a full decision till we have the facts before us, but we consider that in examining the net revenue-earning capacity in 1922, the traffic must be taken as rates at or below those authorised in respect of the line under the statutory provisions in force in the year 1913.' This decision did not, of course, put an end to the argument. It merely provided a basis for further legal wrangling!

If the Exeter case was a minor thorn in the side of what had been, for the most part, a very friendly and co-operative process of amalgamation, the Forest of Dean Central was a classic of legal obscurity, in that the company had no longer any formal existence. There was no board of directors, no offices, and no records! Part of the line was worked by the Great Western between 1865 and 1885 by agreement with the company, and after fruitless negotiations at the end of that period, the Great Western obtained a new lease from the Crown in 1890, the company being no longer a party. The line had been worked throughout at a loss, and the company was indebted to the Great Western for loans to the extent of £22,972. There were various Lloyds' Bonds, amounting to about £12,000 and ordinary shares. Mr. Bischoff submitted that all obligations were long since statute-barred, that the ordinary shares had no value, the Lloyds' Bonds were only to be paid when the Great Western debt had been satisfied, and that, therefore, since the Great Western was obliged by the Railways Act to absorb the undertaking, no consideration should be given.

The tribunal considered that they could prepare the scheme for absorption without the Great Western having to give any consideration at all. There would be a question as to whether the Great Western should take over the liabilities, if any, and on this the parties might confer as to whether it was worth while continuing them formally. But in any case, as an example of the legal proceedings invoked by the Act of 1921 this case could scarcely be bettered.

In the meantime the new Great Western Railway was engaged on many worthwhile and positive new projects. In the realm of passenger train service the acceleration of the 2.30 p.m. express from Cheltenham to Paddington to run the 77.3 miles from Swindon non-stop in 75 minutes was the shape of things to come. This train, making a start-to-stop average speed of 61.8 m.p.h. over a generally favourable road, with no more than a moderate load, was an easy task from the locomotive point of view; but by this acceleration, for the first time since early broad gauge days the Great Western could claim the fastest scheduled start-to-stop run in Great Britain. The superiority over the LNER was no more than marginal, it is true; but it was a beginning, and it was the first stage on the road to the brilliant achievements of the early 1930s, with this same train. It may be recorded that on the inaugural day of the new service, July 9th 1923, the run was made in 72 minutes, 3 minutes inside schedule, by the 2-cylinder 4-6-0 locomotive No. 2915 *Saint Bartholomew*, hauling a 9-coach train of 300 tons.

It was also clear that whatever co-ordinations were intended in other directions as a result of grouping the new Great Western was intent upon pursuing to the utmost its traditional competitive routes, and the restoration of the Irish Mail service via Fishguard and Rosslare on September 17th 1923 was a striking case in point. Traffic between Great Britain and Ireland had, since the war, fallen to a mere shadow of its former volume, because of the political troubles in the south which, by the summer of 1921, had drifted into a situation little short of civil war. This ugly state of affairs was formally ended by the Treaty of 1922, and while outbreaks of violence continued at times, affairs were gradually moving towards a new stability by the summer of 1923. Even so, when the Great Western restored the Fishguard–Rosslare service in September there was some significance in the fact that through carriages were run from Aldershot to Fishguard, presumably to facilitate troop movements, if necessary.

But even more significant of the economic situation in Great Britain itself were the proposals formulated in the summer of 1923 for the construction of certain new lines of railway in Great Western territory. The Government had appealed to the railways in general to undertake as much work as possible for the relief of unemployment, and to overtake arrears in maintenance of track and repairs to locomotives and rolling stock Lord Churchill was able to advise the Minister of Transport on October 15th 1923, that the programme of new works actually authorised amounted to a sum of £4,500,000. But apart from this there was the question of constructing some entirely new lines. During the previous months deputations of local representatives, including several members of Parliament had urged the Great Western to undertake the following new projects:

1. An extension of the Fairford branch westwards to Cirencester, a distance of approximately 8 miles, and estimated to cost £321,000.

2. A new branch line in Pembrokeshire, from a junction with the Fishguard main line at Mathry Road to St. David's. This would have involved about 10 miles of line, and was estimated to cost £350,000.

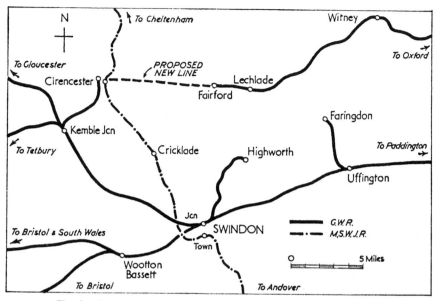

Fig. 2. Proposed new routes. 1: Fairford branch to Cirencester.

3. An extension of the Leominster–New Radnor branch to Trawscoed, in the heart of the mountains of Central Wales, at a cost of £1,750,000. These proposals did not emanate from the Great Western Railway itself, though they were given the most sympathetic consideration by the company. In his letter to the Minister of Transport, Lord Churchill was at pains to point out that while there was no doubt such lines would assist in developing the districts concerned, and after construction would provide a limited amount of permanent employment they could not be justified from a purely commercial standpoint. Lord Churchill's letter continued:

It is recognised, however, that the construction of these new railways calls for consideration, as their provision would not only assist in alleviating present unemployment, but would give permanent employment to a number of men on the railway and in the districts affected. The company, therefore, would be prepared to assist the Government by undertaking the provision of a limited number of new lines, such as those previously mentioned, if financial assistance is forthcoming from the State, similar to that given to local authorities for the construction of roadways under the Roads Act, 1920, and to the Nottingham Corporation for improvement of the Trent Navigation.

Such assistance is essential if the proposed railways are to be constructed as, from the close enquiries which the company have made, there appears to be little prospect for a considerable time to come, of the receipts from the lines being more than sufficient to cover working expenses.

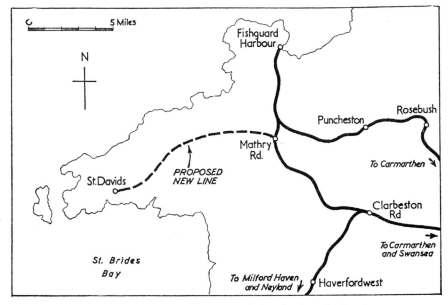

Fig. 3. Proposed new routes. 2: Mathry Road to St. Davids.

Moreover, in two of the cases there would be a loss of revenue owing to the shortening of the railway routes. For example, the Fairford to Cirencester line would give a through railway between Oxford and Gloucester, thus reducing the distance by rail between those cities, with consequent loss of revenue to the company. On the other hand, it is represented by the local authorities that the provision of these railways is vital to the development of the districts where permanent employment for more men could be found in several industries. Another feature to be borne in mind is that the proposed railways would ultimately reduce the expenditure on maintenance of district roads. Any financial assistance given by the State for railway construction should thus be offset to a considerable extent by a reduction in the grants for road maintenance.

If, therefore, the Government are prepared to make a grant on the lines suggested in paragraph (14) of this letter, the Great Western Railway, having regard to the views expressed to them by the deputations referred to and in order to assist the Government in respect of unemployment, will be prepared to undertake the construction of the lines and to maintain and work them when completed.

Being wise after the event it is of course very fortunate that these lines were *not* built. A study of the maps of the districts concerned shows that in the economic conditions that developed, and with the increasing competition from both public and private road transport, they could never have become remunerative to the slightest degree. Before the end of the year however two further lines were added to the list of new projects urged upon the company by local interests, namely a line westwards from Bridgwater running direct to join up with the existing

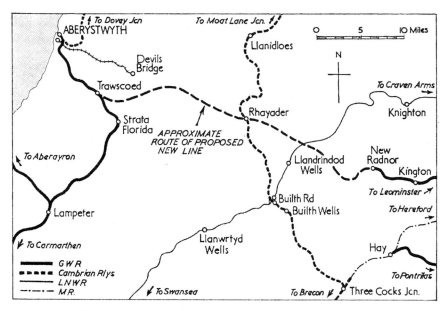

Fig. 4. Proposed new routes. 3: New Radnor to Trawscoed.

Minehead branch at Watchet, and the long contemplated but never fulfilled extension of the Bishops Castle Railway from Lydham Heath to Montgomery. These two projects were estimated to cost £700,000 and £250,000 respectively. The first of these would have provided the very kind of facilities that the Beeching plan sought to eliminate, namely parallel, or duplicate routes, while the Bishops Castle project was perhaps the least likely of all to succeed.

Nevertheless in December 1923 it was announced that the Great Western Railway itself was applying for Parliamentary powers to construct two new lines. One of these, an extension of the one-time Cambrian line from Pwllheli across the Lledr peninsular to Nevin, recalled a grandiose scheme proposed by Brunel, wherein Porth Dinllaen—Morfa Nevin as it is now—was to be the packet station for the Irish Mail service, and terminus of a magnificent broad gauge railway route via Oxford, Ludlow, Montgomery and Dolgelly. It would have been a grandly picturesque express route, through the Welsh mountains; but the Chester and Holyhead route was preferred and the railway to Pwllheli, when it was eventually built, was never of more than secondary importance.

At the end of 1923 the Board had definitely authorised expenditure on new works to the value of £10,000,000, and some of this, such as the placing of orders for carriages, wagons, and locomotive boilers with outside firms certainly cut new ground so far as the old Great Western Railway was concerned. Contracts actually placed included the following:

Reconstruction of Bristol Temple Meads goods station, £556,450; reconstruction of Newton Abbot station, £247,100; new line from Wolverhampton to Kingswinford, £173,000; new locomotive depot at Stourbridge, £119,230; additional sidings for coal shipment at Newport (Mon), Rogerstone, Cardiff, and Barry, £500,000; new locomotive repair depot at Caerphilly, £174,000; station improvements at Oswestry, Aberystwyth and Barmouth, £180,000. A number of smaller schemes which had been or were about to be started amount to an aggregate of £427,674.

Other projects under consideration were:

1. New tunnel at Colwall, 4,800 feet long, under Malvern Hills.
2. Completion of railway between Felin Fran and Pontardawe (Glam).
3. Doubling of line between Welshpool and Forden.
4. New accommodation for milk traffic at Paddington.
5. New locomotive depot at Llanelly.
6. New engine shop at Cardiff.
7. Road bridge under the railway at Ashley Hill, Bristol, for the new road from Stapleton to Ashley Hill (undertaken for the Bristol Corporation).
8. Extensive improvements at the Walsall Street goods depot, Wolverhampton.
9. Electrification of a large number of cranes in the Birmingham district.
10. Cardiff Docks—New power house and improved pumping arrangements.
11. Port Talbot—New Wharf.

The new works in connection with the coal traffic in South Wales will be discussed in more detail in a later chapter; but at this stage it is interesting to note one important development arising out of grouping—the decision to concentrate maintenance of the locomotives working on the South Wales local lines at one works only, Caerphilly. This, of course, was previously the locomotive works of the Rhymney Railway, and was on a site suitable for considerable extension.

Taken all round the Great Western entered the grouping era on a wave of great enterprise and optimism. Although technically the local railways in South Wales were constituents of the new group the Great Western itself was so overwhelmingly the predominant partner that its well-established policies and traditions continued unbrokenly. In this respect it was in a far stronger position to advance than any of the other three groups, all of which had to undergo periods of consolidation, with much jockeying for position between partisans of former companies that had previously been of equal status. The Great Western had none of this, and while the interest and co-operation of the Welsh constituents was secured by the urgent attention given to the co-ordination of facilities for developing the export trade in coal, the more traditional activities of the old Great Western were highlighted by a welcome revival of the old elegance of appearance in the express passenger locomotives and trains.

Engineering prowess is dealt with in more detail in Chapter 3, but the events of the year 1923 cannot be passed over without reference to the introduction of the 'Castle' class locomotives. The high nominal tractive effort of these engines, the greatest of any passenger type then running in Great Britain, was fastened upon in the waging of an intense publicity campaign. But while to connoisseurs of locomotive practice the nominal tractive effort value was not in itself the hallmark of pre-eminence, there was no doubt that these new engines, as a development of the highly successful 'Star' class, were in the very front rank, despite the production of very large Pacific engines just before grouping, by both the Great Northern and North Eastern Railways.

Quite apart from their high nominal tractive effort, however, the 'Castle' class engines marked a return to pre-war standards of painting and adornment. The full lining out, which had been abandoned as a wartime economy was restored, together with brass beading over the splashers, polished brass safety valve bonnets, and polished copper tops to the chimneys. As they went through the shops for overhaul engines of the 'Star', 'Saint' and 'County' classes were similarly restored to their former splendour. Train services had largely been restored to pre-war standards of speed in the autumn of 1921, and the welcome change in the finish of the locomotives together with the reversion to the chocolate and cream style of livery for passenger carriages was symbolical of the final casting off of wartime austerity, and an advance into the new era in full ceremonial dress, as it were.

The effect upon public opinion, both as represented by newspaper comment and the interest of railway enthusiasts, was profound. While unkind things were said and written about the two northern companies, and the southern was attacked right, left and centre, there was a period during which the Great Western seemed able to do nothing wrong! The old company had always been an institution in the life of the West Country, and the fact that the Railways Act, which had overturned and eliminated so many cherished railway traditions elsewhere, left things completely unchanged, merely strengthened the hold the Great Western had upon the bulk of the territory it served. It only needed the production of the *Caerphilly Castle*, the 'most powerful locomotive in Britain', to set the seal upon the company's enlarged prospects and status.

Nevertheless the year 1923 ended in some uncertainty for the country as a whole. The General Election, held in December, saw a great increase in the numerical representation of the Labour Party, but neither Conservatives, Liberals, nor Labour had a clear majority over the combined strength of the other two parties. The Christmas holidays passed in some doubt as to what would happen when Parliament reassembled, and there were many who hoped that the then-considerable voting strength of the Liberals, still led by Mr. Asquith, would be used to retain a Conservative administration in power. The Labour manifesto issued during the election had given a clear hint of some form of public ownership for the railways if that party obtained sufficient power in Parliament. Mr. Baldwin's Government faced the new House of Commons in January 1924, but was immediately defeated and resigned. Mr. Ramsay Macdonald thereupon was called to form the first Labour Government in Britain's history; but being dependent for its survival on Liberal support, no strongly controversial measures, such as railway nationalisation, were brought forward.

II

'A Splendid Dividend'

Despite the political uncertainty that prevailed in the country as a whole the first year of the enlarged Great Western Railway ended in enthusiasm, and a spirit of cautious optimism. The annual general meeting was held on 27th February 1924, and the accounts were such that Lord Churchill was able to announce a dividend of no less than 8% on the ordinary shares. There were several causes for rejoicing at that meeting, not least in the knighthood recently conferred upon Sir Felix Pole. In referring to this in his own speech from the chair, Lord Churchill said:

> I can assure it is an honour of which we all of the Great Western are justly proud, as we knew that the recipient of it has, by sheer hard work, perseverance and outstanding ability, thoroughly earned it, and we wish him many years of health and happiness to enjoy it. We also hope that his working life may always be associated with the Great Western Railway.

Later in the meeting, at question time, Mr. W. J. Stevens, a prominent shareholder, and for some years a spokesman of the British Railway Stockholders Association, fairly let himself go with enthusiasm:

> My Lord, ladies and gentlemen, I am sure this meeting will wish to join with you my Lord, in offering our hearty congratulations to Sir Felix Pole, our General Manager, and to share with you your wish that he may long enjoy the honour conferred upon him, and long to be able to devote his valuable services to this company. I should like to say that the investing public and the people interested in railways generally look to you, my Lord, as the leading exponent of what I may call the higher railway policy, and on this occasion I am quite sure you have not failed us. We have had a splendid report, we hope to get a splendid dividend, and we have certainly had a splendid address, for which we thank you.

I have quoted this extract from the report of the company meeting to show something of the spirit that was prevalent at the time. During the year 1923 rates and fares had been *reduced*, in anticipation of a reduction in expenditure. Traffic originating on the GWR had certainly increased, by a total of 12,600,000 passengers and by 7,800,000 tons of freight. The reduction brought the basic rate for third class passenger travel down to $1\frac{1}{2}d$ a mile. Some of the most interesting parts of the report for the year related to the efforts being made to develop traffic in South Wales, and this, together with other closely associated problems is dealt with in a separate chapter. But while mentioning South Wales, reference must also be made to the promotion of W. Waddell. At the end of the year W. W. Grierson retired from the post of Chief Engineer to the company, and in his place J. C. Lloyd, who was Assistant Engineer, and Waddell were appointed Joint Chief Engineers—the latter having particular responsibility for the South Wales docks.

Three other appointments of great interest were made at the beginning of 1924, namely:

James Milne: Assistant General Manager,
W. A. Stanier: Principal Assistant to the Chief Mechanical Engineer,
John Auld: Docks and Personal Assistant to the Chief Mechanical Engineer.

All three were mechanical engineers born and bred. Milne was trained in the locomotive works, but after drawing office and laboratory experience and taking a University degree at Manchester he transferred to the traffic side of railway work. In 1922 he had been chosen to accompany the Indian Retrenchment Committee, of which Loch Inchcape, a Great Western director was chairman, and for his services he was created a Companion of the Star of India (C.S.I.). The earlier stages of Stanier's career are perhaps not so well known as the later ones, but in addition to his outstanding ability as a mechanical engineer Stanier—'The Black Arrow' as he was nicknamed—was one of the most popular officers in Swindon Works. It is perhaps not generally known that Milne and Stanier had strong family ties since Lady Milne and Lady Stanier, as they afterwards became, were sisters.

The third mechanical engineering appointment of January 1924 brought into a key position a man with a very wide railway experience. Most Great Western officers were born Great Western, and remained Great Western all their lives; but John Auld, coming into the Great Western fold from the Barry Railway had, prior to his last pre-grouping appointment served on three other British railways. His apprenticeship was served on the Glasgow and South Western, and he subsequently held appointments on the Great North of Scotland, and on the London, Tilbury and Southend. He returned to the G&SWR under James Manson to become District Locomotive Superintendent in Glasgow, and then in 1910 he was appointed Locomotive Superintendent of the Barry Railway. In due course he was to succeed Stanier as Principal Assistant to the Chief Mechanical Engineer of the GWR.

An event of the year 1924, which again showed how the Great Western was riding the crest of the wave, was the pleasantly informal Royal visit to Swindon Works on 28th April. This was only the second time that Their Majesties King George V and Queen Mary had visited a locomotive works, the first time having been to Crewe, in 1913. It was appropriate that the Royal Train could, at that time, be worked by a locomotive named *Windsor Castle*, and after the works visit there occurred that event which is so well remembered by locomotive enthusiasts, in which His Majesty drove the train from the works siding to Swindon station. Never before, one would imagine, had so many high officers of the company been together in one engine cab; for in addition to the King and Queen, and the driver and fireman, there were gathered Lord Churchill, Sir Felix Pole, Mr. Collett, and Locomotive Inspector

George Flewellyn. The enginemen were Driver E. Rowe, and Fireman
A. Cook, of Old Oak Common, who were to make history a year later
with their magnificent running on engine No. 4074 *Caldicot Castle* in the
Interchange trials with the London and North Eastern Railway.

The vigorous and clear-sighted management of Sir Felix Pole was
shown in the important changes in train services in the Spring of 1924.
Earlier in that year there had been some considerable loss in revenue
due to labour troubles; and what were regarded as reductions in train
services made from 5th May onward, were generally thought to be clear
attempts to reduce expenditure, and recoup losses, by a reduction of
facilities given to the public. But actually the changes in train service
were the first stages in a long term policy of timetable re-organisation to
meet the changing trends of passenger travel. Pole had, indeed, inaugurated in 1924, the method of passenger travel analysis that has been used
extensively in more recent times. Inspectors were put on to many trains
to count the number of passengers travelling, and where traffic was very
light the trains concerned were withdrawn. As a result of this investigation a daily saving of nearly 4,000 train miles was effected. In some
cases, journeys of branch and other trains were terminated at places
where their serious traffic had, to all intents and purposes, come to an
end; modifications of other trains provided for journey continuations,
thus enabling the former trains to be worked back earlier than heretofore
and thus avoid the necessity for an additional engine and vehicles. In
other instances previously independent trains were combined as far as a
suitable dividing station; alternatively other measures were taken to
provide practically the same travelling facilities as before, without serious
extra journey times, and yet to reduce unremunerative train mileage
and incidentally release engines and sets of vehicles. These objects were
attained in many different ways. Thus, in one instance, a slip-coach
service was replaced by a train following from the previous stopping
station. In another, a slip attached to a main-line train provided a branch
connection where previously a through train was run.

These changes were no more than a prelude to the new timetables of
July 1924, in which the company faced the very difficult and wearisome
task of entirely remodelling its passenger train services. An enormous
amount of detail work was involved. In the first place, the scheme was
undertaken in order to ascertain whether a complete revision of the
passenger services would, in the aggregate, result in a more effective use
of coaching stock and locomotives for the same daily mileage. The
guiding principle was to produce a practical timetable so arranged that
as many sets of coaches as possible would make two trips a day, either
from London to the provinces and back, or vice versa. For various
reasons the old timetable was not always arranged with that end in view.
The timings sometimes allowed a margin that was insufficient for the
stock of an incoming train to be cleaned and used to form the next
return train. Possibly starting a down train 15 minutes earlier and an up

train 15 minutes later might have the effect of saving a set of coaches. It was points such as these that those responsible for the drawing up of the new Great Western timetables had to investigate. It was soon found that comparatively little could be accomplished by piecemeal alterations; remedying one evil might easily cause another elsewhere. In the autumn of 1923, therefore, it was decided to work out in detail a complete new time-table for the whole system, and see what the result would be in comparison with the then-existing arrangements.

The result was a considerable saving in the number of locomotives and coaching stock required to work the same daily passenger mileage as in the summer of 1923. This provided an equally liberal service to the public, with the additional advantage of standardised departure times, which of course could be more easily memorised. 'The Railway Gazette' commented editorially:

There are two extremes in drawing up a passenger time-table, both equally foolish. The one is for the train office to say 'Here is our time-table, now you, the rolling stock superintendent, find the coaching stock, and you the locomotive running superintendent, provide the engines.' There is no team work in such a procedure. The stock and the engines may be provided, but the company's capital is being unremuneratively employed. Similarly, it would be equally foolish to go to the other extreme and design a time-table that might be ideal as regards locomotive and coach working, but with many of the trains running at times very inconvenient to the travelling public. That would not be business. Naturally, the Great Western Company has struck the happy mean.

Of course, the departure times of a number of well-known trains had to be altered, otherwise the scheme would have been spoilt at the outset. Some grumblers there doubtless will be. But when it is realised that there are excellent reasons for the changes we think that little more will be heard of them after a week or two. In passing it may be remarked that Aesop's fable about the old man with the donkey, who in trying to please everybody succeeded in pleasing nobody, might be remembered more than it is in some railway offices. If the departure time of a train is altered from 11 to 11.30, it will probably be more convenient to some travellers and less convenient to others. If it is altered to 10.30 some will be pleased and others cross. But generally speaking, if half-an-hour's alteration either earlier or later means the saving of a set of stock, in our opinion, the stock should have it all the time.

Viewed as a whole, the new time-table was quite as convenient as that which it superseded. With its standardised departure times for the various main line services in regular sequence, it was certainly a more scientific and businesslike structure than the old one—admirable as the latter was as regards the frequency, the high speeds and the number of through coaches. Needless to say, those three features of Great Western practice were retained. From the public point of view the outstanding feature of the new time-table was the introduction of standardised departure times. For the five principal main line services the minutes past the hour at which the trains left Paddington were 0.10 Birmingham and the North; 0.15 Bristol; 0.30 West of England and Weymouth; 0.45 West Midland line; and 0.55 South Wales. Similarly, standard departure times were arranged for the up services; expresses from Birmingham to London leaving at the even hour; from Cardiff at 15 minutes past the hour, and so on. Of course, standard departure times were no new feature in some suburban services, or between adjacent cities such as Liverpool and Manchester; while in America all the Pennsylvania trains between New York and Philadelphia then started at the even hour. Of course there is no inherent economy in standard departure times as such. The Great Western did not undertake the remodelling of its passenger time-table with the standardised timings as the main object in view. The reason behind the alteration was a desire to effect economies in operation by a more scientifically prepared time-table, in substitution for one which had been gradually evolved since the line was first opened. This in any case involved so many alterations that the adoption of the standard timings did not add greatly to the difficulties of the task. In fact, in some respects it made the work easier, as once a standard departure time was decided on for a particular service, the necessity for maintaining the correct sequence made the rest of the task simpler. The intermediate and branch services were built up round the main structure.

The magnitude of this task can be readily realised. In addition to the re-timing of all the main line trains, it necessarily involved the re-timing of hundreds of branch lines working in connection with the main line services. Although to the travelling public the changes might have not seemed very great the alteration of a quarter of an hour in one case, and five minutes in another, involved all sorts of complications, as anyone who has worked in a train office knows. As previously mentioned the main object of the scheme was to secure a better use of rolling stock and locomotives; but when once it was decided that the departure times of trains could be altered, despite the fact that they in some cases had been running at a particular time for many years past, it became a comparatively easy matter to introduce standard departure times.

Making 0.30 past the hour the standard departure time for West of England trains avoided any alteration in the departure time of the Great Western's most famous passenger train, the 'Cornish Riviera Express'. But on another route the new departure times from Paddington of the South Wales trains could be compared with what they were in the previous summer. In the new time-table these trains left at 8.55, 11.55, 1.55, 3.55, 4.55, and 5.55. In the summer of 1923 the corresponding trains left at 8.45, 11.50, 1.10, 3.35, 5.0, and 6.0. As an example, of the standardised timings of the up trains, Cardiff could again be taken. Under the new working the up trains left Cardiff for London at 6.15, 8.15, 10.15, 11.15, 1.15, 3.15, and 5.15. Under the old time-table there was no regularity in the departure times; trains left Cardiff for Paddington at 6.18, 7.45, 10.0, 11.20, 1.20, 3.15 and 5.10.

In certain cases it was not found possible to introduce standardised departure times for all the trains between London and an important provincial station. This was accounted for by the fact that such a place as Bristol might be served by two or more train services, each of which was scheduled for the standard departure time of the service concerned. Thus, the standard departure time from Paddington for Bristol and

Weston-super-Mare trains was 0.15, but some of the West of England trains whose standardised departure time was 0.30 ran via Bristol. Similarly, by two services Bristol was served by a slip carriage off a South Wales train, and the standard departure time on that service was 0.55.

The travelling public got an equally good service to that provided in the previous year, with the additional advantage of standardised and easily memorised departure times for the main line trains. As the plan was put into practice the benefits to the company actually extended far beyond the fact that the complete revision of the time-table effected a considerable saving in the amount of passenger stock and locomotives required to work the same daily mileage as formerly. Under the old system many trains were broken up between trips, and departing trains were frequently made up of coaches from several incoming trains. Under the new system the stock forming particular trains was worked together year in, year out, strengthened according to seasonal requirements. Advantages derived from that practice were numerous. The coaches were cleaned together between trips, and gave main line trains a more uniform and smarter appearance. Moreover, a whole set would go into the shops for repainting at the same time, thus obviating the unattractive appearance of trains in which coaches have been out of the shops for varying periods. Another advantage was a reduction in shunting, as there was less re-marshalling of stock between trips. An analysis showed that the new time-table with the same daily passenger train mileage as in 1923 saved 79 passenger coaches and 32 locomotives.

Quite apart from the standardised ordinary train services, very great care was being taken to rebuild the ocean liner traffic which had been so sadly interrupted by the war. There was little chance of reviving the growing importance of Fishguard as an ocean port. The transfer of the principal Transatlantic services of both the Cunard and the White Star Lines from Liverpool to Southampton killed any such hopes; but from being disappointed over Fishguard the company worked assiduously to build up traffic at Plymouth. Inward bound liners, since the war, had been calling at Cherbourg first, and then crossing to terminate their journeys at Southampton. This not only lengthened the journey for British passengers, but meant that Continental countries received their American mail, by British ships, considerably before we did in Britain itself. The Cunard company was induced to set down passengers and mail by tender, in Plymouth Sound, and in striving to develop this traffic the Great Western certainly provided magnificent transit facilities from Plymouth to London.

The veteran Cunard liner *Mauretania* still held the Blue Riband of the Atlantic crossing, despite increasing competition from Continental rivals, and every eastbound run in the summer and autumn of 1924 was accompanied by a very fast run up from Plymouth by the GWR boat train. These trains had a normal schedule of 4 hours dead, from Millbay Docks to Paddington 226.5 miles, but it was not always possible to get a clear path, owing to the variations in departure time consequent upon the time of arrival of the liners concerned. The Great Western was not only on the crest of the wave so far as its own enterprise and deveploments were concerned; it was getting an excellent press. In the eyes of the daily newspapers it could do little wrong about that time. When the *Mauretania* broke her own record by steaming from New York to Plymouth in 4 days 21 hours 57 minutes, and everyone was full of praise for the achievement 'The Daily Mail' found space to add a eulogistic paragraph headed 'GWR's fine finish'. The boat train certainly did not loiter in running from Millbay Docks to Paddington in 3 hours 57 minutes. The engine was No. 4078 *Pembroke Castle*, but a run very nearly as fast was made when the *Berengaria* made her first call at Plymouth. Despite several checks the journey was completed in 4 hours 3 minutes with engine No. 4034 *Queen Adelaide*.

The Cunard Line was evidently most appreciative of the efforts being made in connection with their fast eastbound runs, and in November 1924 the *Cunard Magazine* had this comment:

The Great Western Railway have deserved congratulations on the admirable way in which they have backed up the record-making runs of the big Cunarders into Plymouth. To complete the journey from Plymouth to London in under four hours is not only gratifying to the railway company concerned, but should set an example in other directions. Coming up from Southampton to London on several occasions recently—a distance of 79 miles—the journey has taken two hours. If accomplished at the same rate as the Great Western boat train, it should have taken under 85 minutes.

It was perhaps a little unfair to compare the achievements of the newly formed Southern Railway with those of the well-established Great Western; but the fact remains, at that time it was just as fashionable to heap odium on the Southern as it was to praise the Great Western!

Still referring to locomotive matters, the year 1924 was notable in witnessing the passing of *The Great Bear*. When constructed at Swindon in 1908 it was the largest and heaviest passenger engine in Great Britain. It attracted a great deal of attention, and was thought to herald a new stage in locomotive development, foreshadowing the general introduction of the 4-6-2 type. It was certainly an experiment on Churchward's part in the design of a very large boiler. Unfortunately the engine was in advance of its time, and the civil engineer would accept its weight only in a very restricted part of the entire Great Western system; in fact only between London and Bristol. With this restriction there was little opportunity of working the locomotive at a level of performance that would really test the steaming capacity of the large boiler, and thus confirm or otherwise the precepts followed in its design.

Despite the limited use that could be made of this great engine it remained for many years a status symbol; a symbol of Great Western pre-eminence. In some countries the engine would undoubtedly have been preserved, because of its historic nature, as the first British 'Pacific' —just as the French have preserved one of the great 4-6-4 compounds of the Nord, which were introduced in 1911, and were very little used. But on the other hand it can well be appreciated that an establishment that scrapped so priceless a relic as the broad gauge 4-2-2 *Lord of the Isles* on the grounds of space would look still less kindly upon so huge an encumbrance as *The Great Bear*. All practical considerations supported the proposal to convert the engine into a 'Castle', though when that conversion became a *fait accomplit* there was consternation among the higher management at Paddington at thus losing their 'status symbol' in the locomotive world; and at Swindon, Churchward is said to have been very upset at the demise of his largest engine. The rebuilt engine retained the old number 111, but was named *Viscount Churchill*.

The year 1924 which for the Great Western had opened on a buoyant and enthusiastic note, ended in misgiving. In national politics the precarious existence of the first Labour administration was ended in the autumn with its defeat in the House of Commons, and the subsequent General Election returned a Conservative Government, with an immense majority. In particular there was general satisfaction on the Great Western Railway that Stanley Baldwin was again Prime Minister. Not only had he himself been a director, prior to taking ministerial office, but his father Alfred Baldwin was Chairman of the company from 1905 to 1908. Despite the resounding triumph of the election however the new Government took office when storm clouds of the most menacing kind were gathering on the horizon of industrial relations, and the railways together with industry and commerce in general were soo nto be engulfed in the most serious internal crisis the nation had yet experienced.

But at the close of 1924 the Great Western, together with the other main line railways of this country were more concerned with a problem that was affecting them seriously for the first time—that of road competition. The war had given a great fillip to the development of the internal combustion engine, and in peacetime the conveyance of goods by road motor lorries was very much on the increase. Railways felt that this new competition was unfair in two ways, and Lord Churchill's address at the Annual General Meeting of the GWR in February 1925 referred to these in some detail. There was first of all the payment of local rates. In 1913 the railways in the Great Western group had paid £970,000 against this charge; in 1924 the figure was £1,570,000. This latter was a huge figure in itself, but the galling thing, so far as railways were concerned, was that a high proportion of it was spent on the upkeep of *roads*. Lord Churchill quoted figures for the country as a whole to show that against the national expenditure of about £45,000,000 on the maintenance of roads only £4,500,000 was recovered in taxation from the owners of heavy lorries.

These heavy lorries were already becoming strong competitors of the railways. What was worse, whereas the railways were by law common carriers, the lorries could pick and choose, and take only those traffics

Plate 3. SOUTH WALES DOCKS

Swansea, a general view

Port Talbot, overall view from entrance

Plate 4. MISCELLANY OF WAGONS

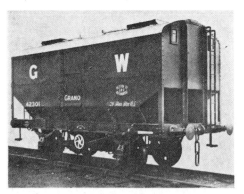

GRANO: 20-ton Hopper grain wagon

Shunting tender

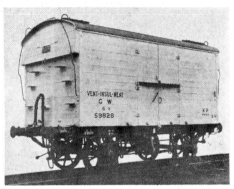

VENT-INSUL-MEAT: 6 ton insulated meat van

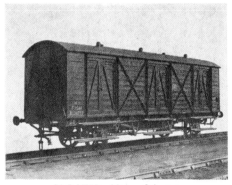

BLOATER: 10-ton fish van

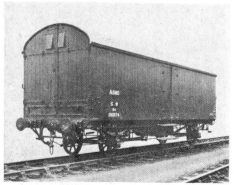

ASMO: 10-ton covered wagon with end opening doors

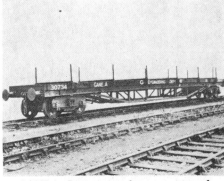

GANE A. Bogie wagon for conveyance of rails and permanent way material

Plate 5

SWINDON WORKS: ROYAL VISIT IN 1924
Her Majesty Queen Mary is walking between Lord Palmer and Mr. Collett:
King George V follows with Viscount Churchill

CAERPHILLY WORKS
The new boiler shop

Plate 6. THE GENERAL STRIKE, 1926

Volunteers unloading milk at Paddington

Delivery van, protected by barbed wire, and driven by a woman volunteer

that were most profitable. Lord Churchill commented:

> They are provided virtually with a free road, and, indeed, with free signalling of the road in the form of a policeman at every corner. Last year the Great Western spent upwards of £4,000,000 on the upkeep and maintenance of our road. If this expenditure had not to be incurred—if we were provided with a free road as are our competitors, as I have already pointed out to you—we could either reduce passenger fares to something about ½d. per mile, or make a substantial reduction in goods rates. Of course, I fully realise that the hypothesis is an impossible one; but I put forward as showing, apart from the unfairness of the position to the railways, that the real interests of the country are not served by diversion of traffic from the railways to the roads.
>
> Whilst I am on the subject of road competition, I should like to sound a word or two of warning in regard to certain branch lines. It is no exaggeration to say that many branch lines do not pay even when allowance is made for their contributive value to the rest of the system. We are considering ways and means of reducing costs of operating branch lines, but the time may come, as I understand is already the case in the United States of America, when branch lines—some branch lines at all events, will have to be closed up, and the places on them served by road vehicles operating from the nearest trunk line station.

It is sometimes argued that the railways were old-fashioned in their outlook, so much so that they did not perceive the difficulties that were encircling them until it was too late. But Lord Churchill's words in February 1925 are enough to show that the Great Western was certainly alive to the danger, but that it was severely restricted by existing legislation. Although the dividend was still as high as 7½% on the ordinary shares already there was talk of increasing the rates, and a hint that steps might be taken to negotiate a general reduction in wages. The storm clouds were already on the horizon, and it is interesting to read once again Lord Churchill's comments in the early spring of that critical year, 1925.

> I need hardly say that personally I should like to see the high standards of pay remain, but in saying this I cannot associate myself with the view which seems to have been accepted by the Government, that before the war railwaymen were badly paid. At that time the railway companies did not fix the wages. They were fixed, if you recollect, by arbitration or by agreement with the duly elected representatives of the men on the Conciliation Boards, and I am confident, as regards the Great Western Railway certainly, that the men who signed the various wage settlements in 1912 were thoroughly satisfied with them. They represented wage rates, particularly in the country districts, which were fairly comparable with the ruling rates in the district. At all events, they were determined by agreement with the men. Today the outstanding criticism of railway wages is that they are out of harmony with the prevailing rates of the locality, more particularly in the agricultural districts. As practical men, we have to deal with the situation as it exists, and not as we would wish it to be, and there has been a strong feeling expressed in public and in various criticisms of the railways that we should endeavour to get some relief from the present high cost of operating. It was whilst this matter was actually under consideration that the National Union of Railwaymen presented the railways with a programme of demands which is estimated to cost a further £45,000,000 per annum on top of the burden we are already bearing. It seems to me quite obvious that it would be impossible to operate railways if such a burden were placed upon them; indeed, as I have already said, we feel that far from adding to the burden, there is every necessity for reduction. Happily, machinery exists to go into and deal in detail with these matters, and in due course our application, together with the men's programme will have to be dealt with by the Central and National Wages Board. As, therefore, the matter is, if I may so describe it, *sub judice*, I do not think I will make any further comment upon it on the present occasion.

The storm actually broke in the coal mines of Britain, just over a year later; but before coming to the events of that tragic year 1926, there are some important matters concerning the Great Western itself to be chronicled which took place in those years of uneasy industrial peace that intervened.

III

Engineering Eminence

At this time, when the enlarged Great Western Railway was just getting into its stride it is appropriate to review the position that the various engineering departments had attained by the year 1924. In speed its express train services generally showed the highest quality of any in Great Britain, while the company had enjoyed the most remarkable immunity from accidents. These two features were in themselves a tribute to the engineering excellence of the rolling stock, track, and lineside equipment, and to the very high sense of responsibility shown by all members of the staff concerned with the working of trains. If this was all that was involved there would be no point in referring any more to the subject in a book of this kind; but there were many points of engineering development in which the Great Western was a pioneer, and in which its practice was a foretaste of things to come generally on the railways of Britain at a later date.

In the second volume of this work, the references to narrow gauge locomotives prepared originally by Mr. A. C. W. Lowe, were necessarily brief, and they concluded with the comment that perhaps the chief new feature adopted during the Churchward régime was superheating. It is certainly true that once he had perfected the Swindon superheater it was applied to the locomotive stock as a whole more rapidly than superheaters of any other kind, on any other railway in Britain. At the time MacDermot's classic work was written perhaps that was a fair assessment of Churchward's work, as seen by an outsider. But in the long run his practice in superheating was the least lasting of his many outstanding developments. In fact the continuance of his practice from the 1930s onwards, in contrast to what was being done elsewhere in Great Britain and abroad, brought Great Western practice into a mild form of disrepute in the early years of railway nationalisation. Churchward's greatest work lay undoubtedly in the magnificent range of boilers he designed, and in his development of modern valve gears. There were also detail features, such as the specialised designs of big ends, and driving axleboxes that contributed to the trouble-free working of Great Western locomotives; but it was the basic design of the boiler, and in the use of long-lap, long-travel valves that the under-lying strength of Great Western locomotive practice was to be found.

There is no doubt that both these fundamental ingredients of success were looked at askance by the engineers of other railways. The Churchward boiler, with its tapered barrel, and the elaborate shaping of the Belpaire firebox, was obviously more expensive in first cost than the far simpler shapes in current use at other celebrated engine-designing centres. But this high first cost was justified over and over again in greatly reduced maintenance charges, quite apart from the inherent reliability in steaming built into the boilers themselves. One of the weaknesses in boilers of the traditional shape fitted with Belpaire fireboxes was the existence of sharp bends in the plates, and abrupt changes of section. Churchward set out to eliminate these sources of weakness, while at the same time so designing the water spaces that circulation would be free and rapid, and thus promote a high evaporation when the boilers were being steamed hard. Design of the boilers was matched in footplate practice by the building up of a tradition in driving and firing that utilised these splendid boilers to the best advantage. On the Great Western the locomotive running inspectors in Churchward's time, and afterwards, were the eyes and ears of the Drawing Office. It was on the reports of these carefully chosen men that the working characteristics of locomotives in everyday service were assessed; and on more than one occasion their reports influenced future design.

This was one of the greatest advantages of the organisation of the Chief Mechanical Engineer's department on the GWR, which remained always on the old pattern that had been usual on all the railways of Great Britain in pre-grouping days—an organisation in which the C.M.E. was responsible not merely for designing building and maintaining the locomotives, but also for running them in service. All the drivers, firemen, shed-staffs, and running inspectors were on the strength of the Chief Mechanical Engineer's department. By the year 1923 the Great Western was the only British railway to retain this arrangement. It ensured that locomotives were used as they were designed to be used; and in those rare cases where the design intentions did not work out in practice some changes to the design were made. One of the most lasting impressions of footplate journeys on all sorts and conditions of Great Western engines in the years 1944 to 1950, over all parts of the line, was the consistent excellence of the firing. I never once encountered the care-free 'slap-happy' fireman, even on some duties when the demands for steam were not high. The firemen worked with just as much diligence and skill as main line men on maximum evaporation jobs, and consequently ran their trains on an exceptionally low consumption of coal and water.

In cylinder and valve gear design the practice of the Great Western Railway was also pre-eminent in 1923; but whereas the Churchward type boiler was good enough to last out steam, not only in Western territory, but on British Railways as a whole, in cylinder and valve design Swindon practice in 1923 represented no more than an intermediate stage. Not for the first time in its history the Great Western inspired others not merely to imitate but to excel it. The design of cylinders and piston valves, with relatively straight and direct passages, ample port openings at minimum running cut-offs, and a free exhaust gave the economy in working that startled the locomotive world in 1924 when

C. B. Collett read his famous paper to the World Power Conference held in that year. The use of the theoretically correct method of steam locomotive working, with regulator wide open, and the valves linked up to the minimum necessary to run the train, was confined, generally, to the four-cylinder 4-6-0 express engines. The two-cylinder engines were generally driven on longer cut-offs and a moderate opening of the regulator. But the point to be emphasised very strongly is that with a good valve gear, and good cylinder and steam chest design this variation from the theoretically correct method made no difference to the economy.

In the years immediately following the grouping a large amount of dynamometer car testing of locomotives took place, as the two northern groups took stock of the varied locomotive studs that came under the unified ownership of the LMSR and LNER. Very little was published about these trials at the time; but subsequent investigation, and the release of official reports to me and other locomotive historians has provided figures for coal consumption, under road service conditions, for a variety of London and North Western, Midland, Lancashire and Yorkshire, Caledonian, Great Northern, North Eastern, and North British designs. These figures did not have the precision that was attained in the test procedures established after nationalisation, but they were enough to give an excellent general impression of engine performance in Great Britain in the years immediately following the grouping. The picture that emerged was that locomotives of good reputation were using anything between 4 and 5 lb of coal per drawbar horsepower hour. Some were showing figures as high as 6 lb, while under very favourable conditions a few were hovering around 4 lb and on individual runs coming a little below 4 lb. Imagine then the consternation among other administrations when C. B. Collett released to the World Power Conference of 1924 a figure of 2.83 lb per d.h.p. hour for the new GWR 4-6-0 engine No. 4074 *Caldicot Castle*. This Swindon figure gave rise to particular concern at Horwich. The Lancashire and Yorkshire Railway had always prided itself on its modern attitude and up-to-date approach to all engineering problems; and the rebuilding of the Hughes 4-cylinder 4-6-0 locomotives had resulted in a reduction of the basic coal consumption from 7 to 5 lb per d.h.p. Intense studies were made at Horwich to try and find some explanation for the fact that the Swindon engine could do its work on roughly *half* the amount of coal needed by their new engine! Here was Great Western pre-eminence displayed to the extent of making other administrations seriously doubt the veracity of the results published by Mr. Collett.

The actual trials that provided the data on which Collett's paper was based, constitute one of the classics of British locomotive performance. Three return trips were made from Swindon to Plymouth, travelling via Badminton, Filton, and the Bristol avoiding line; and on each section of the line the train of empty stock was made up to the maximum permitted with a 'Castle' class engine. At the time of Mr. Collett's paper a very

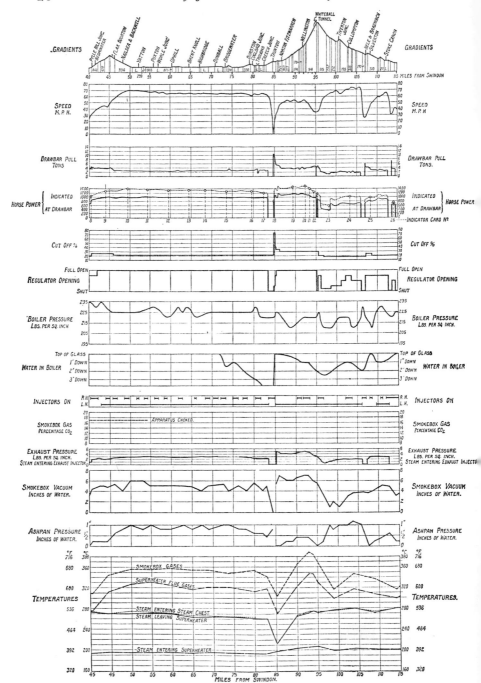

Fig. 5. Curves indicating performance on trial run of 'Castle' Class engine.

comprehensive account of Great Western testing methods was published in 'The Railway Gazette', and details of one particular test as recorded in the dynamometer car, are shown in the accompanying diagram. The actual test figures published were as follows:

Coal burnt	6 tons 10 cwt. 1 qr.
Smokebox ashes (lb)	1,582
Ashpan ashes (lb)	201
Total ashes (lb)	1,783
Smokebox ashes in percentage of coal	10.8
Ashpan ashes in percentage of coal	1.4
Total ashes in percentage of coal	12.2
Water evaporated per lb of coal (equivalent from and at 212°F.)	12.2 lb
Average temperature of water in tender, deg. F. . . .	46.6
Average temperature of water entering boiler, deg. F. . .	176
Mechanical efficiency of engine	74.0%
Calorific value of coal—B.Th.U.	14,780
Coal per i.h.p. hour (lb)	2.10
Water per i.h.p. hour (lb)	20.9
Coal per d.h.p. hour (lb)	2.83
Water per d.h.p. hour (lb)	28.1
Coal per ton mile (lb)	0.101
Coal per sq. ft. of grate area per hour running time . . .	66.1 lb

Thermal efficiency $\dfrac{\text{Work in cylinders}}{\text{Heat in coal}}$ with feed at 50°F., 8.22%

Thermal efficiency of boiler $\dfrac{\text{Heat given to water}}{\text{Heat in coal}}$ 79.8%

Average steam chest pressure with full regulator in percentage of boiler pressure (inside)	92.6
Average steam chest pressure with full regulator in percentage of boiler pressure (outside)	93.6
Oil pints per 100 miles	4.3
Drawbar pull sustained at 71 m.p.h.	2.35 tons

The performance of the 'Castle' engine was undoubtedly very fine, though it was certainly not an all-out effort. As the diagram reproduced shows the sustained speed on level track with a load of 485 tons was 65 m.p.h. with a drawbar pull of 2.3 to 2.4 tons. In maximum working conditions engines of the 'Star' class had sustained speeds up to 68 and 69 m.p.h. on level track with over 500 tons. Nevertheless the object of the trials with the *Caldicot Castle* was to establish basic performance data and to prove the design as a whole. The trials did this admirably. They were made under the general supervision of W. H. Pearce, a leading draughtsman who was a specialist in valve gear design, while the work in the dynamometer car was in charge of C. K. Dumas.

Closely associated with locomotive running were two other engineering fields in which the Great Western was pre-eminent in the years immediately following the grouping. These were the Swindon arrangement of the vacuum brake, and the system of automatic train control. As a stopping agency the vacuum brake by reason of its limited pressure difference cannot, in the ultimate limit, approach the air brake in its power; but in other respects the vacuum has many advantages, and on the Great Western it was developed to a greater extent than on any other railway. Instead of using a small ejector for maintaining the vacuum while running a cross-head pump was used, and this not only made possible the use of a much higher degree of vacuum than on other railways, but made the maintenance of vacuum in the brake system independent of steam pressure in the boiler. Elsewhere cases, leading in one instance to a fatal accident, have occurred in which an engine steaming poorly in adverse conditions eventually lost pressure to the extent that its ejector could no longer create vacuum enough to keep the brakes off. Naturally too, a vacuum of 25 or 26 inches gives a much more powerful brake than the more usual 20 to 21 inches that was used elsewhere on the railways of Britain.

Another Great Western speciality that proved a most important adjunct to the vacuum brake system was the so-called 'direct admission valve'. In its simplest form the vacuum brake was applied throughout the train by admitting air to the train pipe through the driver's brake valve. Tests have shown that on a long train there is a considerable time lag between the time of application of the brakes on the engine and the leading coaches, and the time of application on the rearmost coaches. This time can have an appreciable effect on the stopping distance in emergency, and at Swindon, largely due to C. K. Dumas, the direct admission valve was developed. These were fitted on all vehicles, and they were so designed that a very small reduction in train pipe vacuum was enough to actuate these valves, and allow atmospheric air to enter the brake cylinders on each vehicle directly, instead of through the full length of the train pipe, from the driver's brake valve on the engine. These 'D.A.' valves, as they came to be called, were extremely effective.

The system of automatic train control developed on the Great Western Railway is very well known, and in broad principles it has provided the basis for the British Railways automatic warning system that is being standardised today. Its early introduction was described by MacDermot, but although the extent of its installation had not greatly increased by the time of the grouping, the way in which it was regarded by the Railway Inspectorate of the Board of Trade, and later of the Ministry of Transport had changed profoundly in the ten years elapsing since the serious rear-end collision on the Midland Railway at Aisgill in 1913, and the time of grouping. Colonel J. W. Pringle, who conducted the enquiry into the Aisgill disaster said:

> The principle of cab signalling, in conjunction with audible signalling, has, so far as distant signals are concerned, been adopted by the Great Western at a number of important centres. The object was primarily to meet the difficulties in connection with fog signalling at distant signals. But it cannot be said that the method has yet proved to be efficient, to the extent of meeting adequately the very complicated requirements of traffic on English Railways. It will have to be experimented with much more thoroughly and subjected to further prolonged tests under ordinary working conditions, before it will be possible to recommend it as a panacea for all difficulties.

Fifteen years later when, as Chief Inspecting Officer of Railways, he conducted the enquiry into the Charfield accident on the LMSR it was clear that his views had completely changed, and he was then one of the strongest advocates for the general adoption of the Great Western system.

In signalling generally, Great Western practice included many features that contributed much to the safety of train operation. In 1923–4 semaphores were universal, but the actual arms were very well designed and carefully maintained so that they came off to a good angle and provided an unmistakable indication. But while the standard semaphore signals were all lower quadrant, and remained so for the entire life of the railway, the Great Western was one of the first railways in Britain to experiment with three-position upper quadrant signals. The advanced starting signal on the departure side at Paddington was of this type, and a similar type was used on the Ealing and Shepherds Bush line, which was equipped for electric traction and worked over by the Central London 'tube' trains. When A. T. Blackall was Signal Engineer a number of experimental installations of power signalling were made, including all-electric plants at Didcot and Slough, and the section of automatic lower quadrant semaphores on the main line between Tilehurst and Goring & Streatley.

But so far as signalling control systems were concerned one of the most interesting innovations of the time was the first practical application of the Ferreira–Insell system of route lever working, at Winchester (Cheesehill) on the former Didcot, Newbury and Southampton Railway, absorbed into the GWR at the time of the grouping. This system of working was devised jointly by L. M. G. Ferreira, then chief of the railway signalling branch of Siemens Brothers and Co. Ltd., and R. J. Insell, assistant signal engineer of the GWR, who was to succeed A. T. Blackall as Signal Engineer in June 1923. Although application of the Ferreira–Insell system was to be confined to the Great Western Railway and even then to no more than a limited extent, the point for particular notice is that it was one of the earliest attempts to break away from the conventional methods of signal control, whereby each signal and each pair of points had its own lever. Today with modern push-button panels, route working if not universal, is being adopted for nearly all new installations.

The principle of this method of working is worth recalling in some detail because of the way this Great Western innovation anticipated, with miniature levers, one of the most popular forms of relay interlocking used today. The layout of a particular station or yard was sub-divided into a series of well-defined routes which trains or shunting movements could take, and each of these was provided with a separate route lever. The whole area was track circuited, and the process of setting up a route through the layout was accomplished simply by the pulling of the appropriate lever. In order to provide all the necessary safeguards however, the actual process of pulling the lever went through two intermediate stages in which the clearness or otherwise of the route was proved, and the functions of the various operating members checked. To aid the signalman, to avoid his becoming confused if the final response to his lever movements was not obtained, a series of miniature light indications were provided to cover each stage of the lever-pulling operation. For example, while the lever was normal and no action was being taken by the signalman, a red indication light was shown.

To initiate the setting up of a route, the lever was pulled to the first position and this started an electrical 'search' to ensure that all the track circuits were clear and that no conflicting routes had been set up. This first movement also energised the necessary point motors if any points required to be moved in order to set up the route; and while this was in process a white light was displayed on the indication panel associated with the particular lever. If the route was clear, the points responded, and the switches were thrown and the point detection was proved satisfactorily in the reverse position, the white light beside the lever changed to orange and the signalman was then free to pull the lever past the third position into the fourth position. This pulling of the lever into the fourth position cleared the necessary signals, and when that was done a green light appeared beside the lever.

This method of operation, relying on an ordered sequence of lever positions, provided all the safeguards that are today built in with modern push-button and thumb-switch interlockings. While today, a signalman is free to use the push-button and thumb-switch at any time, and he subsequently obtains some visual indication to confirm that the route is set, with the Ferreira–Insell system he was prevented from completing the lever stroke until each stage of the operation was satisfactorily completed, thus involving a routine for the signalman similar to that customary with ordinary mechanical signalling, operation or power signal operation with one lever per function. As with modern push-button control panels, provision was made in this route-lever frame for the individual operation of points when necessary. There was a separate lever for each pair of points which normally stood in the central position. It was locked in that position when any route setting work was in progress. If it was desired to work any pair of points, in emergency or for maintenance work, or for any other purpose apart from the regular traffic movements it was necessary to reverse the 'King' lever. This locked all the route levers normal and prevented route-lever working taking place in any part of the layout. When the 'King' lever was pulled, the lever for any pair of points could be moved to either normal or reverse. But while the 'King' lever was pulled and route working suspended, the interlocking was such as to prevent any powering of any signal in the layout.

The experimental installation made at Winchester Cheesehill was successful enough for a much larger installation on the same system to be installed at Newport High Street, Monmouthshire, and this installation remained in service for the rest of the existence of the Great Western Railway. It was not until the 1960s that it was replaced by a modern push-button interlocking. Had not the Great Western Railway been in possession of an exceptionally well maintained series of mechanical interlocking at its principal centres and the need for replacement or modernisation not acute, it is likely that the Ferreira–Insell system would have been more widely used. It was a pioneer, but the development that subsequently took place in the field of one-control-switch relay interlocking occurred elsewhere. The association of Mr. Ferreira with this Great Western development was a natural outcome of the long association of Messrs. Siemens Brothers with power signalling on the Great Western Railway. The Siemens system of all-electric signalling had first been introduced on the Great Western Railway at Didcot in 1905, and it was subsequently employed at one of the largest power signal boxes in England, at Birmingham North, which had 224 miniature levers. The application of route working thus followed the more conventional use of individual levers for separate functions.

Although conventional manual block signalling was used over by far the greater proportion of the Company's mileage, much had been done, quite apart from the introduction of the Automatic Train Control system, to provide additional safeguards in working. In two respects the block working was electrically interlocked with the semaphore signals. After the passage of a train a signalman was prevented from sending 'Line Clear' to the box in rear until he had replaced his distant signal lever to danger, and in signalling a train forward he could not lower his starting signal until he had received 'Line Clear' on his block instrument from the box ahead. So far as the actual configuration of the signals were concerned the Great Western always used an elaborate system of route indication 'distants'. This was a practice not universally adopted in Great Britain; but the freedom from accident enjoyed by the company could be regarded as ample justification of the soundness of its operating methods, even though they may have been considered unnecessarily elaborate elsewhere. It should also be emphasised that throughout its last 25 years of existence the company continued to place reliance on the sense of responsibility, judgement, and initiative of individual signalmen. The practice of centralised control, or rather centralised reporting of train movements, was not used to any particular extent.

In this connection a classic story can be told of one particular stretch of line over which locomotives and trains of a 'foreign' railway used to operate. The section included a very heavy gradient, and on this occasion the engine of a passenger train of the 'foreign' company got into such trouble with slipping on the gradient, in one of the short tunnels, that the train ran back slightly and the rear bogie of the rear coach passed through catch points into one of the lengthy sand drags provided on some severe sections of the line. These sand drags are in themselves a remarkably effective safeguard against the effects of a 'run-away'; but having got one bogie of the rear coach in it was found impossible to draw it out clear. The fireman went to the nearby signalbox, and the signalman there, acting on his own initiative, organised immediate assistance by enlisting the aid of the engine of a GWR freight train standing in a goods loop. All the necessary operating precautions were taken, but the joint efforts of *two* engines were not able to draw the coach clear. Again the signalman acted entirely on his own, and telephoned the nearest station-master. The latter promptly arranged for despatch of a second Great Western engine, and eventually the 'foreign' train, then with three engines, was assisted clear, and sent on its way. The signalman had taken immediate steps to advise the large station on the 'foreign' system to which the stranded train was proceeding; but High Authority on the GWR knew nothing of the occurrence until next morning, when they received profuse thanks for the services rendered! The signalman on the spot, and the adjoining station-master had coped promptly and adequately with the situation, and neither had thought it the least amount necessary to advise their own 'Control' of what had taken place.

In the Churchward era carriage design in its basic principles had been complementary to the striking programme of locomotive development. While on the one hand engines of greater power and higher efficiency had been built to work long distance trains at high speed, on a minimum of coal and water consumption, Swindon practice in carriage design had been to build stock that would convey the maximum number of passengers, in comfort, for the minimum tare weight. The outcome had been the famous 70 feet main line stock, which had seated 80 passengers in the 'thirds', for a tare weight of about 33 tons. These were beautiful coaches externally, with their handsome panelling and 'top-light' windows. The underframes were of steel, but the bodies were wood. In 1922–5 however a new range of 70-foot vehicles was introduced, with smooth steel-panelled sides, and slightly bowed ends. In general they were slightly heavier than the Churchward wooden-bodied stock, but nevertheless had a tare weight of only 37 tons for an 80-seater 'corridor third'.

One of the disadvantages of the 70-foot coaches was that they could not be used on all main routes, and a corresponding series of 57-foot coaches had to be constructed for the restricted routes, which included such important cross-country services as those run jointly with the LNWR between Liverpool and Manchester and the West of England, and the Wolverhampton–Penzance service via Stratford-on-Avon. Generally speaking Great Western coach design ceased to have any special distinction after the cessation of 70-foot stock building in 1925. There were some very beautiful special vehicles, like those constructed for the Ocean services between Paddington and Plymouth; but these were representative of isolated, rather than of standard practice. It must also be recorded that in the matter of coach riding the Great Western was certainly *not* pre-eminent. My own early recollections of both the Cornish Riviera Express and of the Cheltenham Flyer are definitely of rough riding. I never attempted to take tea on the latter train, but meal-times in the 70-foot diner of the 'Limited' had their enlivening moments! It could be argued, of course, that the riding reflected as much upon the track as on the design and maintenance of the coaches; indeed, the hapless Civil Engineer usually receives the initial onslaught when anyone writes in and complains about bad riding! However I shall never forget an experience of the mid-1930s when I had occasion, late one evening, to travel from Edinburgh to Glasgow, and entrained in the through GWR coach which then ran from Southampton to Glasgow Queen Street. It was a 57-foot brake composite of 1924 vintage, and the riding was very bad. A walk along the corridor into an adjoining part of the train soon showed that this riding was no fault of the track.

Throughout its existence, following traditions that began at its very inception by adoption of the broad gauge, the Great Western had usually managed to do things differently from everyone else, and in the Grouping Era its permanent way was different by having the chairs secured to the sleepers by through bolts, while everyone else was standardising on screwed spikes. The rail section was $97\frac{1}{2}$ lb per yard, against the more usual 95 lb, and the rail length was 44 feet 6 inches, when standards elsewhere were 45 feet, or 60 feet on the LNWR. Great Western track was in general well-maintained, though taken all round it was not up to the very highest standards to be found elsewhere in Great Britain. In the grouping era the older Great Western standards of track were gradually replaced by the British standard 95 lb rails, either 45 or 60 feet in length; but the bolting of the chairs remained until the end of the company's separate existence.

IV

Co-ordination in South Wales

The railway system of South Wales as it existed in 1922 was typical of the way transport facilities had grown up to meet the immediate needs of trade in local districts, entirely under private enterprise, and without any particular relation to the economic strategy of the country as a whole. I need not recall once again the fascinating and romantic stories of the rise and phenomenal prosperity in Victorian times of concerns like the Taff Vale and Rhymney Railways, nor the traffic situation that led to the inception, and the outstanding success of the Barry Railway. Although the time of exceptional dividends had passed by the early years of the present century the railway industry in South Wales could be still regarded as prosperous in the year 1913, the fateful year on the results of which Government payment for use of the railway during the war years was based.

In 1912 the Barry paid a dividend of 7% on its ordinary shares, the Rhymney $8\frac{3}{4}\%$ and the Taff Vale $3\frac{3}{4}\%$. The latter line had suffered very severely from the results of the Barry 'invasion', and its dividend had dropped from 15% in 1888 to 3% in 1890. It never recovered to more than 4% subsequently. The Brecon and Merthyr, and the Cardiff paid considerably smaller dividends, but were nevertheless comfortably solvent. On the outbreak of war in August 1914 the Government of the day took over the railways and although primary control was vested in a Committee of General Managers that committee existed to carry out Government instructions. But quite apart from the matter of day-to-day operation there was the vital matter of recompense to the railway companies and their shareholders for the use of their property during the national emergency. It was arranged, rather hastily one fears, that payment by the Government should be on the basis of the net receipts of the companies taken over for the year 1913. No account was taken subsequently for the enormous increase in traffic that took place during the war, and still less of the great increase in working expenses that accrued during the period of Government control, because of the increases in wages that were made, nor of the decrease in the working day from 10 to 8 hours.

In South Wales some of the troubles that were to beset the railways were attributed to the Great Western 'take-over'. It was necessary more than once to remind business interests, and other people in South Wales that the amalgamations of 1922 were no result of any Great Western plans of aggrandisement. The grouping was imposed by law; but once legislation was in effect the management of the enlarged Great Western

Railway became very active in promoting a new co-ordination of railway and dock facilities. The extent to which the GWR at once became one of the largest industrial concerns in the area can be judged from the rating position in the City of Cardiff in 1924, when out of a total sum of £86,000 for local rates no less than 11% came from the Great Western Railway. In October 1924 Sir Felix Pole was invited to address the Cardiff Business Club, and while he was anxious to put to the members the position of railways generally it is clear that in South Wales the management of the GWR was looking to the coal industry to continue to provide a huge and lucrative traffic. At that time, too, medium distance road motor coaches and the private motor car had not yet begun to make inroads into the staple passenger traffic of railways, and one of the earliest concerns of the enlarged GWR was to provide improved passenger facilities on the local lines.

Around Cardiff itself there was considerable duplication of some facilities, while other much needed renewals and improvements had not been carried out for lack of capital. The accompanying map of the Cardiff area shows the lines and their ownership before grouping. One of the earliest new projects was a re-arrangement of the tracks at Queen Street, to enable Rhymney trains to run into the Taff Vale station, and to the Taff Vale dock station. The problems of interchange at the main Great Western station had also to be urgently considered. A situation that was just—but only just!—acceptable, where the original Great Western station lay alongside a subsidiary station used by both Taff Vale and Barry trains, could no longer be tolerated when all the tracks were owned, and all the services operated by the same company. In his address to the business men of Cardiff in October 1924, Sir Felix Pole said:

> We have not yet come to a decision in regard to the Great Western station. The problem there is an intensely difficult one, and the situation, I am afraid, will be very costly, but it is fully accepted that the present station is hardly worthy of your City.

The solution was duly worked out; but more than ten years were to pass before the extensive reconstruction was completed. Details of this fine work are described in a later chapter of this book.

It was however of the transport of coal that Sir Felix Pole had most to say to his distinguished audience in Cardiff, and many of the points in his address are of great importance from an historical point of view. During the year ended August 1924 the total amount of coal exported from the Bristol Channel ports was 36,861,000 tons. In the very short time since the amalgamation of railways in South Wales an almost phenomenal reduction had been effected in the railway and dock charges. The actual costs for the 1923–4 export tonnage were £4,684,418, whereas if the charges in force during the year 1920 had prevailed the figure would have been no less than £7,697,375. In 1924 export coal was being sold at 26s or 27s a ton, free on board, and of that price the railway and dock charges amounted to about 2s 6d a ton. At the same time Sir Felix

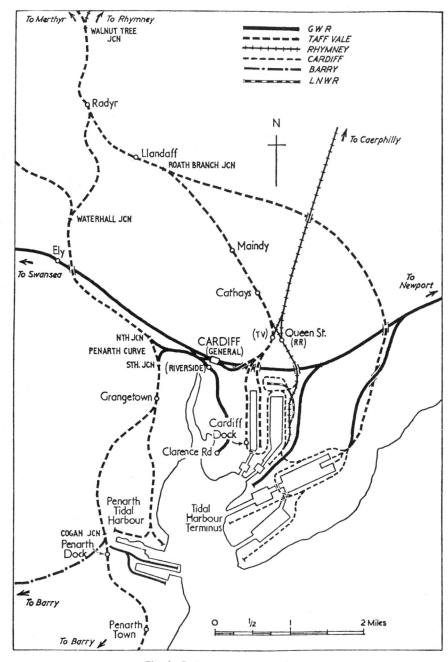

Fig. 6. Railways in the Cardiff area.

An aerial view showing quay used by ocean liner tenders, and station from which boat specials are run

Plate 8. THE 'KING GEORGE V' in U.S.A.

The procession of locomotives at the centenary celebration of the Baltimore and Ohio Railway, with the G.W.R. engine leading

The engine, with Fitter Dando (left) and Chargemen Fitter Williams (both from Swindon 'A' shop)

Plate 9. COAL TRAFFIC AT SOUTH WALES DOCKS

Penarth, in times of export boom

Newport; *importing* American coal, in 1947

Plate 10. CAERPHILLY WORKS MODERNISED

The new erecting shop

The wheel shop

reminded his audience that the Great Western, like other British railways, was not only a very large carrier of coal, but also a very large user. In 1923 the GWR purchased some 2,250,000 tons of locomotive coal, mostly in South Wales, at a price, at the pits, of about £3,000,000. Statistics relating to the year 1913 were still being used as a yardstick more than 10 years later, and Sir Felix emphasised that while coal prices had risen to some 80% above the figure of 6s 8d a ton prevalent in 1913, the railway company had still been able, by improved methods of working, to reduce their rates for its conveyance and handling at the docks.

At the same time, despite the reduction in charges there was not, by any means, general satisfaction with the working at the South Wales ports. In November 1923 the Dutch Shipowners' Association went to the extent of publishing in 'The Times' a complaint alleging inefficient working. As is so often the case with such complaints the delays enumerated were not by any means wholly attributable to the railway working, and a statement issued to the leading Amsterdam newspaper 'De Telegraaf' by the Great Western Railway gave some highly interesting details of dock working in general. It was emphasised that since taking over the South Wales ports the railway company had made extensive improvements at their South Wales docks in connection with the shipment of coal, including:

(a) Large additions to the siding accommodation at Cardiff, Newport, Port Talbot, and Swansea.

(b) The introduction of a complete traffic control system at the Cardiff Docks, involving new telephone installations connecting every coal hoist, shipping berth, as well as the traffic in general offices;

(c) Improved running lines and siding connections.

(d) New hydraulic power plant at Cardiff Docks.

Adaptation of the coal hoists to take wagons of 20-ton capacity had already been commenced, and over £100,000 was being spent on that project alone. The reconstruction or renewal of other remaining hoists and weigh-bridges had already been agreed upon at a total outlay of £1,500,000 to £2,000,000.

There was already siding accommodation at the South Wales docks of the Great Western Company, capable of accommodating 55,000 wagons, apart from the extensive siding accommodation for coal traffic existing at various intermediate points between the collieries and the docks. That accommodation was wholly provided by the company, although the coal was carried in private owners' wagons. There were no wagons of 4-ton to 8-ton capacity then in use in South Wales for coal traffic. The wagons employed were of 10-ton or 12-ton capacity. In order to induce the colliery companies to introduce rapidly wagons of 20-ton capacity the Great Western Company had offered a reduction of 5% on the railway rates in respect of coal carried in fully-laden 20-ton wagons. This was a project of which Sir Felix Pole himself was the principal advocate, and it is referred to in some detail later.

In considering relative rates of shipment then operating at the various ports, regard had to be paid to local conditions. In South Wales the high quality of the coal demanded specially careful treatment to avoid breakage. The mixing of coal to produce certain qualities was an ordinary feature of the South Wales coal trade, and to some extent it reduced the rate of shipment. In years prior to 1923–4 there had been a great development in the South Wales collieries in the construction of washeries by which coals were graded in many varieties, each of which had its particular commercial value. These varieties had to be shunted and sorted at the docks according to grade, and subsequently had to be collected as required for the purpose of shipment. The topography in South Wales was such that at practically every dock the coal reached the ship's side on a level with the water, and had to be hoisted 30 feet, 40 feet, or even 70 feet before shipment.

A few examples of quick loading of colliers at the South Wales ports may be quoted.

CARDIFF

Ship	Commenced loading	Finished loading	Cargo and bunkers: tons
S.S. *Corsenia*	6 p.m. June 25	12 noon June 26	7,385
S.S. *Mokta*	7.10 a.m. Nov. 20	1.30 p.m. Nov. 21	6,638
S.S. *P.L.M.* 25	11 a.m. June 15	12 noon June 16	8,200

NEWPORT

S.S. *S.N.A.* 7*	8.40 a.m. Oct. 11	8.30 p.m. Oct. 11	3,533
S.S. *P.L.M.* 20*	May 31		4,751
S.S. *Polcevera*	May 26	June 6	13,305

PENARTH

S.S. *Gap*	2.45 p.m. Oct. 19	3.25 a.m. Oct. 20	3,286
S.S. *Corcliff**	6 a.m. April 14	12 noon April 14	2,927

* arrived, loaded complete, and sailed same day.

It is interesting to note, among the foregoing, two colliers owned by the Paris, Lyons and Mediterranean Railway, collecting locomotive coal from South Wales.

The campaign for use of 20-ton wagons was waged with great vigour by Sir Felix Pole, but it was not just a case of building the wagons. The transport of coal in South Wales, for export as well as for inland despatches, was almost entirely in private owners' wagons and those owners had to be persuaded to use larger wagons. From the railway point of view a load conveyed in 20-ton wagons occupied much less space on the line than a similar load in 10 or 12 tonners. But in the great majority of collieries in South Wales the wagon handling equipment had been designed to take the old standard length, and great expense would have been entailed in changing it. Sir Felix Pole went to the extent of offering as previously mentioned a 5% reduction in transport and dock charges for all coal conveyed in 20-ton wagons; but while some of the larger mining companies were successfully persuaded by this offer of reduced charges the great majority could not afford the cost of changing their own equipment to accommodate 20-ton wagons. Although coal, by present standards, was still relatively cheap the costs of production were giving rise to acute concern among all the colliery managements, and at that time very few were in a position to consider any appreciable capital expenditure.

Nevertheless Sir Felix Pole kept hammering away at the advantages to be derived from the use of 20-ton wagons, and in his address to the Cardiff Business Club he said:

On the subject of rebate, I was discussing with one of your members the practicability of extending it to apply to the dock charges as well as rail conveyance charges. There appears to be no logical reason why this should not be done and, in accordance with a promise I gave him, the directors of the company will be recommended to give 5% off the dock charges for shipment coal conveyed in fully-loaded 20-ton wagons.

It will perhaps be conceded that to grant a 5% rebate and to contemplate an ultimate expenditure of about £2,000,000 in the reconstruction of tipping appliances alone, needed some little courage on the part of the board of the Great Western Railway.

But we must progress, and the adoption of 20-ton wagons means a saving in the cost of wagon construction and maintenance, and of 35% in siding space, which will enable the railway and the collieries to accommodate a much larger output of coal when occasion demands.

The doubling of the wagon capacity, together with the equipment of more modern tipping appliances, will afford much greater elasticity in the shipping capacity, and from experience already gained it may be taken that under favourable circumstances, when shipments are keen, it will be possible to ship at the rate of about 1,000 tons per hour, as compared with a maximum of 600 to 700 tons with the 10 and 12-ton wagons.

The first train of the new vehicles, 50 in all, arrived at Severn Tunnel Junction in August 1924. The design will be appreciated from the accompanying drawing, which shows the steel framing and wrought iron body. An interesting feature was the provision of a tip door at both ends, to save turning the wagons at the docks. They were, so far as can be traced, the first all-metal wagons to be used for the coal industry in South Wales. By way of a demonstration two trains were made up at

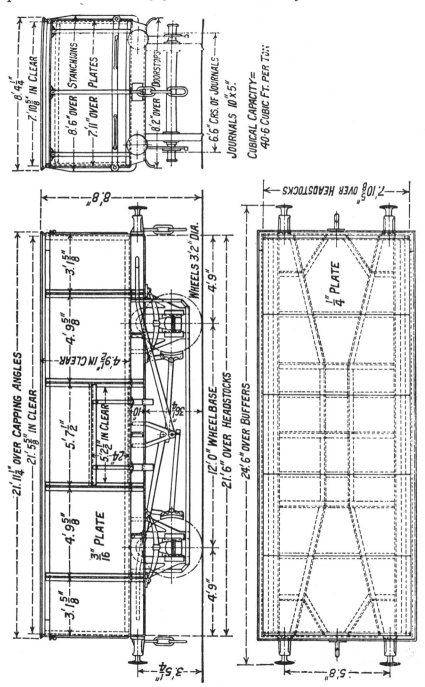

Fig. 7. Drawing of the GWR's 20-ton coal wagon.

Severn Tunnel Junction, each consisting of enough empty wagons to cover a paying load of 500 tons of coal. The train of 25 GWR 20-tonners had a length of 612 feet, whereas the comparison train of 50 mixed wagons, of 12 ton, 10 ton, and still less capacity had a length of 1,009 feet. The tare weight of the new 20-ton all-metal wagons was 9½ tons. Against the formidable total of 110,000 privately-owned coal wagons in South Wales, mostly of 10-ton capacity, this Great Western drive for replacement with 20-ton vehicles certainly showed great enterprise and courage. By August 1924, the GWR had placed orders for 1,000 of them, of which total the contractors were:

(a)	Gloucester Railway Carriage & Wagon Co. Ltd.	250
(b)	Birmingham Railway Carriage & Wagon Co. Ltd.	250
(c)	Bute Works Supply & Co. Ltd.	250
(d)	Stableford & Co. Ltd.	250

In addition to the above, a further 200 were under construction at Swindon. The first users were North's Navigation Collieries, at Maesteg, for shipment of coal at Port Talbot. Other collieries at the western end of the Welsh coalfield began to use the new vehicles, shipped from Swansea (Kings Dock), and their introduction at Newport followed shortly afterwards.

Concurrently with the drive towards modernisation of the docks, and of wagons used in the coal traffic, authority was always given for the first steps towards the improvement of South Wales motive power. Each of the former independent railways had developed a style of its own in locomotive practice; but while the engines themselves looked distinctive enough in their different colours, and smart lining out, the Taff Vale, Rhymney, Brecon and Merthyr, and the Barry all used the 0-6-2 type, and no variations in detail design made a great difference in the performance. After all, provided the boiler would steam adequately it was sheer tractive effort that was needed in the haulage of trains of coal empties up the valleys. The loaded trains were run in the descending direction. In any case, speed was of no consideration.

For general service in South Wales an order was placed with Swindon works for a powerful new design of 0-6-2 tank engine, with inside cylinders. Use was made of the Great Western standard boiler as mounted on the 2-6-2 suburban tank engines of the '51XX' class, but otherwise, so far as wheel arrangement and wheelbase were concerned it was designed to suit local conditions in South Wales. With two cylinders 18 inches diameter by 26 inches stroke; coupled wheels 4 feet 7½ inches diameter, and a boiler pressure of 200 lb per sq. in. these engines had the high nominal tractive effort of 25,800 lb. They had, of course, the standard Swindon arrangement of the Stephenson link motion, with long-lap, long-travel valves. The first order was for 50 locomotives, and by subsequent additions the class, numbered 5600 to 5699, and 6600 to 6699, mustered a total of 200.

Following the introduction of these new engines a policy of standardisation was inaugurated for the locomotives of the smaller constituent companies, and a boiler of Great Western type, with tapered barrel, was designed to suit 0-6-2 engines of the Taff Vale and Rhymney Railways, as and when replacements were necessary. These boilers were somewhat smaller than the existing standard design incorporated in the new engines of the '56XX' class, but larger than those used on the small outside-cylinder 2-6-2 tanks of the '45XX' class. The new 'South Wales' replacement boilers had a total heating surface of 1,247 sq. ft.; a grate area of 17.4 sq. ft. and a superheating surface of 76 sq. ft. These figures may be compared to the corresponding ones for the '56XX' class namely 1,349.1, 20.35, and 82.3 sq. ft. The boiler pressure in both cases was 200 lb per sq. in. The largest pre-grouping 0-6-2s on the Taff Vale, Mr. J. Cameron's 'A' class, had coupled wheels of 5 feet 3 inches diameter, and although primarily designed as general utility machines they had a good turn of speed. On passenger trains they frequently attained speeds of 60 m.p.h. on the level sections of the line. As originally built they had cylinders $18\frac{1}{2}$ inches diameter, and a boiler pressure of 175 lb per sq. in. When fitted with Great Western type boilers and a pressure of 200 lb per sq. in. the cylinders were lined up to $17\frac{1}{2}$ inches diameter.

It was not only in connection with the coal trade that Great Western enterprise was directed towards South Wales in the early years after grouping. One of the most surprising ventures was the provision made, late in 1924, for conveyance of private motor cars through the Severn Tunnel. Until the year 1966 the estuary of the Severn had provided a serious obstacle in the way of road communication between Bristol and the industrial areas of South Wales. Not all motorists were prepared to face the hazards of the ferry service between Aust and Beachley, and in consequence a long journey via Gloucester was necessary. In 1924, with the spectre of road competition looming as a serious drain upon railway revenue, one might have thought that the Great Western would have done everything to emphasise the speed, and other advantages of railway communication between Bristol, Newport, and Cardiff, via the Severn Tunnel; but instead facilities were offered to motorists to have their cars conveyed through the tunnel on carriage trucks kept in readiness at Severn Tunnel Junction, Pilning, and Patchway. They were prepared to attach these carriage trucks, conveying private motor cars, on receipt of 24 hours' notice. While regular travellers would become familiar with the train service, one could, on the other hand, imagine that the facility would not have been much attraction for the chance motorist, who would have the unfamiliar task of looking up a suitable train, and probably finding that by the time he had waited for it he could have made the longer road journey via Gloucester. Nevertheless it was a gesture, typical of the unbounded spirit of enterprise on the GWR during the days of Sir Felix Pole.

While in the neighbourhood of Severn Tunnel Junction mention may also be made of the proposed new station at Chepstow, in 1925. The Great Western Railway had always given admirable service to racegoers, and the special trains run in connection with Newbury and Cheltenham races were always special features of the year's working. At both places special stations were built adjacent to the Race Courses, and at Newbury in particular there are special facilities for stabling many trains during the meeting. As soon as news was received that a new race course was proposed at Chepstow the GWR immediately offered to build a new station alongside the course. Unfortunately however the project was scarcely announced before serious labour troubles began to gather upon the country as a whole, and although the race course was eventually built the station never materialised.

Another enterprise of the mid-20's showed a welcome revival of a pre-war tradition, in the working of day excursions to Ireland. By the year 1925 the political situation had returned so far to normality as to encourage tourist traffic; but while everything was being done to revive something of the pre-war volume of regular holdiay travel via the Fishguard–Rosslare route the day excursions, run mid-week, were at such remarkably low fares as to attract heavy patronage. By way of a first 'feeler' an excursion was run from South Wales stations on the night of August 18th 1925. Killarney was reached at 10.37 a.m. and as the return was not until 6.15 p.m. there was ample time for sightseeing in that beautiful region. It was well patronised, and a fortnight later the first post-war excursion from London was run. The departure from Paddington was 7.50 p.m., five minutes ahead of the regular Irish boat train. This provided the same interval for sightseeing in Killarney, as on the first excursion run from South Wales, and arrival time on the return journey was 9.10 a.m. at Paddington next morning. More than 500 passengers made the trip—a round of nearly 1,000 miles for 24*s*! Several more day excursions to Killarney were made in the early autumn of 1925, and the Irish people were so pleased with the influx of visitors that the Urban District Council of Killarney passed a unanimous vote of thanks to Sir Felix Pole for his enterprise.

Apart from these incidental matters connected with railway working in, and through South Wales, the main emphasis was naturally upon coal, and the Great Western lost no opportunity of furthering its propoganda for the use of 20-ton wagons, but it is perhaps significant that by the commencement of the year 1925 their use had not begun at Cardiff or Penarth. It was reported that they were to be seen in ever-increasing numbers at Newport, Barry, Port Talbot, and Swansea, and even as far west as Milford Haven; and a further inducement to their use was provided by a reduction in the charge for tipping and weighing. Whereas the normal charge in 1925 was $7\frac{1}{4}d$ per ton, for coal conveyed in the new 20-ton wagons the charge was reduced to 6*d* per ton. Nevertheless, despite all the enterprise and hard work put in towards the furthering of coal traffic the latter part of 1924 showed such a serious decline in overall business it became necessary to consider steps to adjust the staff to the diminished requirements of the traffic. The negotiations that took place subsequently with the Sectional Councils of the National Union of Railwaymen, although amicably concluded, were however no more than a symptom of the growing industrial unrest in the country as a whole; and the details of the events leading up to the South Wales dismissals on the GWR are discussed in the next chapter.

V

The Tragedy of 1926

The seeds of the greatest industrial tragedy in recent British history had been well and truly sown before even the year 1925 dawned. It was to involve the Great Western Railway perhaps to a greater extent than any of the other railways of Britain; and ironically enough it was in South Wales, where such assiduous efforts to build up and modernise traffic methods had been made, that the deep rift between the coal-owners and the miners first opened, and where it later widened to catastrophic proportions. Yet for those whose recollections of the GWR mainly centred on its passenger business, and the more spectacular facets at that, 1925 could well be regarded as a vintage year. The seething undercurrents of industrial strife did not, as yet, affect the brilliant running of the West of England and Birmingham expresses. It is impossible to pass towards the year 1926 without some reference to this splendid feather in the cap of the locomotive department. Relative to their size and nominal tractive effort the Churchward 'Star' class 4-cylinder 4-6-0s were doing some almost phenomenal work. It was no more than occasionally that even the new 'Castles' surpassed the maximum efforts of the smaller engines. Morale on the footplate was extraordinarily high, and enginemen never had the slightest qualms about timekeeping if they were required to take an overload.

It was in this spirit that the men of the GWR entered into the cele-brated and controversial locomotive interchange trials with the London and North Eastern Railway at the end of April 1925. The prime mover in what was originally intended to provide a friendly interchange of data and ideas between the technical staffs of the two companies was undoubtedly Sir Felix Pole. With his enthusiasm for all things Great Western one can be fairly sure he hoped for results favourable to Swindon, but the proceedings opened with everything going in the most cordial manner, at any rate at the higher levels. But on the Great Western the rank and file had such supreme confidence in the superiority of their own engines that they frankly disbelieved that any locomotive other than one of their own could work the down Cornish Riviera Express to time with a maximum load train. The disparity in size between the 'Castle' and the Gresley 'Pacific' left them completely unimpressed—rather the reverse; and when the visiting engine and her crew arrived at Old Oak Common prior to the trials they were met by a massive 'build-up' of the difficulties awaiting them from scores of enthusiastic and confident GWR men.

While it is good to record the spirit of the loyalty to their own company that was evidenced by this attitude there is no doubt it had some bearing on the results of the trials. Furthermore, it is clear that some official encouragement was given to the enginemen on No. 4074 *Caldicot Castle* towards making exceptionally fast runs on the first up, and the last down journeys of the Cornish Riviera Express in the test week. Then again the daily newspapers, glad enough to turn to some aspect of railway and industrial life that was not clouded by the gathering labour troubles, gradually built up the trials to the level of a gigantic sporting contest. Crowds flocked to the principal stations to see the rival locomotives, while General Managers and Chief Mechanical Engineers paused from more pressing tasks to come from their offices to the station platforms to witness arrivals and departures of the trains. For the Great Western locomotives the week's running on both the LNER and GWR lines was one long triumph; but the LNER was most unlucky on its own line. The picked engine failed with a hot-box on the first day, and a hurriedly-chosen substitute consistently failed to find top form. On the other hand the Gresley 'Pacific' working on the GWR did very well, keeping good time on all trips; but overall her running was much over-shadowed by the highly spectacular work of *Caldicot Castle*.

When the bare results of the week's running came to be analysed certain impartial observers in the press, and in broadcasting, mindful of the ill-luck experienced by the LNER, tended to construct a defence of the Gresley 'Pacific' design, and to 'water down' the undoubted margin of superiority displayed by the Great Western locomotives. This was not at all to the liking of Sir Felix Pole, and although details of coal consumption and such like were not originally intended to be published, a full account appeared in the 'Great Western Railway Magazine' of June 1925, by way of a reply to the first press 'stories' and the broadcast report. The 'revelations' in the 'GWR Magazine' caused considerable annoyance on the LNER. But from the view-point of scientific data the relative speed and coal consumption on the down Cornish Riviera Express are most interesting to set on record, as representing most probably the highest standards of performance ever attained by the 'Castle' class engines in their original form. The six journeys gave results as follows:

Date	Engine	Average speed London–Plymouth 225.7 miles	Coal consumed lb per mile
27–4–25	L.N.E.R. 4474	54.8 m.p.h.	50
28–4–25	G.W.R. 4074	56.0 m.p.h.	44.1
29–4–25	L.N.E.R. 4474	55.0 m.p.h.	48.8
30–4–25	G.W.R. 4074	55.5 m.p.h.	45.6
1–5–25	L.N.E.R. 4474	54.8 m.p.h.	52.4
2–5–25	G.W.R. 4074	58.4 m.p.h.	46.8

The main point for emphasis is that on the last down journey of the test week, when a spectacular run was made, with an arrival in Plymouth 15 minutes ahead of time, the coal consumption of the 'Castle' engine was less than any registered by her rival, even though the latter was not improving upon the normal schedule. The Great Western Railway had every reason to be proud of the performance of the 'Castle' class engines, though little more than a year was to elapse before they were seen in a less favourable light.

The exhuberance of the Great Western men during these engine trials does not appear to have been affected by the disturbing events in South Wales during the earlier part of the year. The serious falling-off in the coal traffic, and the steps proposed to curtail working expenses to meet the situation were briefly mentioned at the end of the previous chapter. A meeting of the men's representatives on Sectional Councils Nos. 2, 3, and 4 was called and Sir Felix Pole told them that owing to the great reduction in the coal traffic the company were faced with the position of having to consider the following three proposals:

1. The suspension of the guaranteed day and week.
2. Dismissals.
3. Reduction in pay for all grades on a percentage basis.

This of course was a very serious matter; but studying the reports of the various discussions that took place it is evident that the difficulties of the company were appreciated by the men, and negotiations proceeded on a 'give and take' basis. While Sir Felix Pole told them that in 1924 the company had only *earned* a dividend of 3% and that the necessary funds to make this up to $7\frac{1}{2}$% had to come from the reserves, the men had replied that in a time of trade depression it was only fair that the shareholders should also bear the burden, and not expect the employees to bear it alone. Nevertheless the fact that the dividend was made up to $7\frac{1}{2}$% by drawing on the reserves seemed to indicate that the company regarded the period of depression as no more than temporary.

The local difficulties in South Wales seemed at one time likely to spark off a much wider dispute. At an early stage the National Union of Railwaymen made it clear that they would not accept any change to the guaranteed week, nor to a reduction in pay for all grades on a percentage basis. The leaders of both the N.U.R. and of the Associated Society of Locomotive Engineers and Firemen tended to adopt a rather militant attitude, though on the other hand J. H. Thomas, wielding great influence as an N.U.R. leader and a former Cabinet Minister did much to counsel moderation. As a result of the determined stand made by the unions against two of the Great Western proposals for reducing working expenses it was reluctantly decided that the only course to be adopted was that of dismissals. It was agreed between the railway company and the men's representatives that the dismissals should proceed in the following manner: casual, temporary and supernumerary workers to go first. Should reductions be necessary in the appointed staff the juniors should go first, and in cases where temporary work in a lower grade was available this was to be given to men according to seniority. This agreement, which was concluded in May 1925, was subject to review in three months' time. The great point to emphasise was that the men conceded the company's right to reduce working expenses by reduction of staff, and that an agreement *was* reached.

At the same time far more serious trouble was brewing in the mining industry. On the surface it was plainly a dispute between masters and men, but it stemmed from the simple, but unpalatable fact that in the new conditions of the world the industry could not maintain its old scale of employment. Costs were high and rising; output was falling, and the owners demanded precisely the same as the GWR had done in South Wales. This demand was met by an implacable refusal. A. J. Cook, the miners' leader, gave his followers the slogan: 'Not a minute on the day; not a penny off the pay.' The railway unions had mixed views towards the way they would support what seemed an inevitable clash. J. R. Clynes and J. H. Thomas, both ex-Cabinet Ministers, were strong in counselling moderation; John Bromley, of the A.S.L.E.F. was otherwise, and openly warned the railway companies that in the event of a general strike of miners his members would not move a single ton of coal.

The summer of 1925 was one of mounting anxiety. On the Great Western Railway, in the working of the holiday express trains to South Devon and Cornwall it was veritably a golden age, and it was a sobering thought to reflect that at any moment the life-blood of the service—the choice Welsh coals that made such sparkling performance possible—might suddenly be cut off. It was then that the Prime Minister, Stanley Baldwin, made his bid for lasting peace in the coal industry. By granting yet a further period of subsidy to the owners he forestalled the cuts in working expenses that were threatened, and at the same time set up a Royal Commission to examine the state of the industry as a whole and make recommendations for its future wage structure. To the 'man in the street' to whom the magnitude of the crisis had at last been brought home, the affair was 'settled'; but Baldwin had done no more than gain time. The President of the Mining Association told him bluntly that by dating the end of the new subsidy he was dating the commencement of the strike. While the Royal Commission examined the situation it seemed clear to many onlookers that both sides in the industry were spoiling for a fight, and it was not altogether a surprise that when the Royal Commission published its terms the owners reluctantly accepted them, and the men contemptuously refused them.

Baldwin had certainly gained a breathing space. If a miners' strike occurred it had seemed certain to the Government that other industries would be involved sooner or later. The railway unions had given clear warning of their attitude, and the intervening months had given time to organise the distribution of essential supplies in case of a general stoppage

of transport. How the railwaymen became engulfed in the general
debâcle is easy to understand. Among trade unionists there was a great
wave of sympathy for the miners, and this sympathy led the Trade
Union Congress to take a step that was both injudicious and fatal for its
interest. The calling of a General Strike could have been very serious,
but in their eagerness to support the miners the bulk of trade unionists
completely overlooked the legal aspects of their precipitate action.
Looking back on that exciting spring of 1926, to those who lived away
from the coalfields, and whose way of life was little affected by the
shortage of fuel that followed, the General Strike was of far greater
significance than the prolonged and disastrous coal strike; but both had
far-reaching effects upon railways, and particularly upon the Great
Western in its close association with South Wales.

On Saturday afternoon, 1st May 1926, the London evening newspapers
had placards reading: 'General Strike—Date.' It was timed to commence
at midnight on Monday 3rd May, and on 2nd May, Sir Felix Pole made
his bid to avoid the worst on the GWR. He sent a message to all stations
and departments on the railway, worded as follows:

> The National Union of Railwaymen have intimated that railwaymen have been
> asked to strike without notice tomorrow night. Each Great Western man has to decide
> his course of action, but I appeal to all of you to hesitate before you break your contracts
> of service with the old company, before you inflict grave injury upon the railway industry
> and before you arouse ill-feeling in the railway service which will take years to remove.
> Railway companies and railwaymen have demonstrated that they can settle their
> disputes by direct negotiations. The mining industry should be advised to do the same.
>
> Remember that your means of living and your personal interests are involved, and
> that Great Western men are trusted to be loyal to their conditions of service in the same
> manner as they expect the company to carry out their obligations and agreements.

At first there was a fairly general cessation of traffic; indeed despite the
undertaking given by the N.U.R. and A.S.L.E.F. to run food trains,
large quantities of fish were held up at Milford Haven without means
of rail or road transport, resulting in 2,000 women workers being thrown
out of employment, unless the fish were removed. The Great Western
took the matter immediately in hand. In the London area some stopping
trains were worked on the main line on the first day, one from Oxford
to Paddington stopping at all stations. The Irish Mail from Fishguard
started at 3.20 a.m. and worked through to London, stopping at principal
and many other stations. A steady stream of volunteers presented themselves for work on the railway and were allotted duties wherever possible.

From that start, transport facilities rapidly improved, with the aid of
volunteers, and a number of company's men who remained loyal. On
the railways as a whole, a good number of steam operated suburban
routes on all lines had trains, while the nucleus of main-line facilities
was generally built up from the Wednesday onwards with improvement
day by day, including many branch line trains. Further, while volunteer
labour was a very big item, increasing numbers of railwaymen came
back, so that quite early in the strike it was estimated that, including

those who did not go out, upwards of 100,000 railwaymen were at work. But, as with the volunteers, many of these required training before they could be utilised for operating duties. Volunteer labour was throughout very plentiful, and, although there was in many cases a demand greater than the supply for enginemen and signalmen, large numbers of the offers of assistance could not be utilised. An interesting feature was that on several lines the services of students from engineering colleges and other institutions were recruited; their technical knowledge enabled them to adapt themselves to their new duties rapidly and readily. At the start of the strike it was decided to keep to simplified operating methods, and this eventually became the limiting factor in the number of trains that could be run. To extend railway services to any great extent would have involved many of the complications of standard railway working. Even so, as the volunteers became more and more familiar with the work, it was found possible to add very considerably to the numbers of passenger trains run, and gradually to increase to a substantial degree the number of goods trains operated.

On the Great Western the extent to which emergency services were organised can be appreciated from the following numbers of trains run:

Date	Number of trains
May 4	194
,, 5	250
,, 6	300
,, 7	479
,, 8	500
,, 9	520
,, 10	908
,, 11	1025
,, 12	1297
,, 13	1385
,, 14	1517

One remarkable feature of strike working on the Great Western Railway was its ability, not only to deal with the normal ocean passenger and mails business through Plymouth, but to handle additional calls and landings diverted into that port. Twenty boats called to land 3,000 passengers and seven special trains were run to London. In other cases the two trains regularly run at 9.25 a.m. and 12.30 p.m. to Paddington were used. When the strike broke out the dock lines were badly congested with goods wagons; but volunteer labour was eventually able to clear the running lines to enable the boat passengers to entrain alongside the docks waiting rooms as usual for the direct run thence to Paddington. In addition to the inwards traffic three embarkations were arranged, including a special call of the P. & O. Company's *Kaiser-i-Hind* for which a restaurant car special was run from Paddington.

In addition to what might be termed the more 'glamorous' jobs for volunteers, such as engine driving and firing, and the manning of signal boxes, men and women of every estate buckled to on every kind of humdrum job, such as goods and passenger porters, ticket collectors, van drivers and such like. The amount of sheer physical work done by volunteers in handling food, milk, eggs, and urgent parcels was prodigious; while the part played by women, including several titled ladies, in tending the large stables at Paddington is a reminder of the extent to which the GWR relied upon horse-drawn lorries for delivery of goods in the London area. Elderly railwaymen, long since retired, turned out to help, and a former station-master of Paddington acted as a volunteer guard on the Minehead branch.

On 11th May, the following circular was issued by Sir Felix Pole:

A stage has now been reached in the strike when it can be said with confidence that railway services are improving each day, and I should like to offer my very hearty congratulations and thanks to all the officers, loyal staff and volunteers who have risen so splendidly to the occasion and who are responsible for this satisfactory state of affairs.

At the same time another circular of a different kind was also issued by Sir Felix Pole:

The word 'victimisation' has often been used in connection with strikes. In the experience of the Great Western Railway it has usually been imported at the end of a strike, the trade unions invariably asking that there should be no victimisation. The present strike not only differs from previous strikes in that it is not associated with any dispute or labour question affecting the company, but because of the fact that victimisation started with the strike, the victim in this case being the Great Western Railway Company. It is indeed true to say that the country as a whole is being victimised by a strike which is the blackest spot in the history of Labour in this country. That thousands of men with no grievance against their employers should have been 'instructed' to leave work, and that so many of them should have done so, passes all comprehension. It can only be explained on the ground that there was a deep conspiracy against the State. Thank God such a conspiracy cannot succeed and can only result in the discrediting of its promoters and the disillusionment of those who have been used as pawns in the game.

The same evening the Prime Minister broadcast to the nation. I well remember listening to that broadcast, through headphones attached to a primitive 'crystal set'. Broadcasting was then in its infancy, and many people like myself were probably hearing Stanley Baldwin's deep resonant voice for the first time. Earlier in the day Mr. Justice Astbury had declared the strike illegal, and the next morning a deputation from the Trades Union Council waited upon the Prime Minister to tell him of their decision to call off the strike, unconditionally. There was nevertheless a certain hesitancy on the part of the railwaymen to return to work at once, and on Thursday and Friday 12th and 14th of May, there were long meetings between Union leaders and the railway managers. Eventually a settlement was signed in the afternoon of 14th May, the terms of which were as quoted on the following page.

So ended the strike so far as the railways were concerned, and for industry in general. The public heaved a sigh of relief, and affairs quickly reverted to normal, except, of course, that a settlement of the coal dispute was as far off as ever. Train services, as first restored, were far from normal. On the Great Western many crack expresses were temporarily

TERMS OF SETTLEMENT AS BETWEEN THE RAILWAY COMPANIES ON THE ONE HAND AND THE NATIONAL UNION OF RAILWAYMEN, ASSOCIATED SOCIETY OF LOCOMOTIVE ENGINEERS AND FIREMEN, AND THE RAILWAY CLERKS' ASSOCIATION ON THE OTHER.

1. Those employees of the Railway Companies who have gone out on strike to be taken back to work as soon as traffic offers and work can be found for them. The principle to be followed in reinstating to be seniority in each grade at each station, depot or office.

2. The Trade Unions admit that in calling a strike they committed a wrongful act against the Companies, and agree that the Companies do not by reinstatement surrender their legal rights to claim damages arising out of the strike from strikers and others responsible.

3. The Unions undertake:—

    (a)   not again to instruct their members to strike without previous negotiations with the Companies.

    (b)   to give no support of any kind to their members who take any unauthorised action.

    (c)   not to encourage Supervisory employees in the Special Class to take part in any strike.

4. The Companies intimated that arising out of the strike it may be necessary to remove certain persons to other positions, but no such person's salary or wages will be reduced. Each Company will notify the Unions within one week the names of men whom they propose to transfer and will afford each man an opportunity of having an advocate to present his case to the General Manager.

5. The settlement shall not extend to persons who have been guilty of violence or intimidation.

On behalf of the
General Manager's Conference:—

On behalf of the
Railway Trade Unions:—

FELIX J. C. POLE
H. G. BURGESS
H. A. WALKER
R. L. WEDGWOOD
R. H. SELBIE

J. H. THOMAS ⎫ National Union
C. T. CRAMP ⎭ of Railwaymen.

J. BROMLEY: Associated Society
of Locomotive
Engineers and
Firemen.

A. G. WALKEN: Railway Clerks'
Association.

DATED THIS FOURTEENTH DAY OF MAY, NINETEEN HUNDRED AND TWENTY-SIX.

withdrawn, and long distance trains made many intermediate stops to avoid running feeder services and using additional coal. Supplies of foreign fuel were obtained however, and as spring was followed by summer, and the holiday season approached the full express service was restored, though not to the additional lavish extent of a normal summer season. Instead, the duplication of ordinary services was resorted to at peak week-ends, and it is on record that on one Saturday the Cornish Riviera Express was run in *five* portions. Even amid the difficulties of a season that was so far from normal the innate sense of publicity traditional of

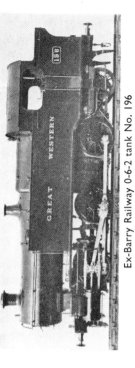

New standard 0-6-2 '56xx' class

Ex-Barry Railway 0-6-2 tank No. 196

Ex-Brecon & Merthyr 0-6-2 tank No. 11

Ex-Taff Vale 0-6-2 'A' class No. 299

Ex-Barry Railway 0-6-4 tank No. 1349

G.W.R. 2-8-0 formerly '52xx' class, as modified to 2-8-2 type, '72xx' class

Plate 12. GREAT WESTERN BUSES

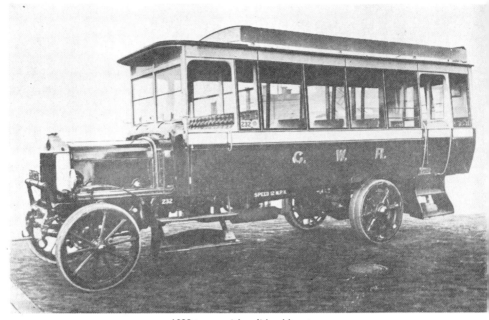

1923 type, with solid rubber tyres

1925 type, with pneumatic tyres

Plate 13. RAILWAY AIR SERVICES

A D.H.84 Dragon, one of the earlier aircraft used by Railway Air Services

A D.H.89 Dragon Rapide, specially named *City of Birmingham* for G.W.R. services

Plate 14. REBUILDING AT BRISTOL

View from Totterdown at an early stage in the reconstruction works

Inside the old station, during the platform remodelling

the GWR was not absent. The engines for the five sections of that famous train were sent from Old Oak Common to Paddington coupled together, and press photographers were invited to witness and record the cavalcade.

The coal strike continued throughout the summer, with little signs of conciliation on either side. Railways, and particularly the Great Western were inconvenienced by the poor quality of the continental coal it was possible to import. On some railways locomotives were temporarily converted to burn oil, but this was not done on the Great Western. All in all, the principal express services were run remarkably well; but the recorders of locomotive performance could detect on main lines the symptoms of shortage of steam, and in certain sections of the railway press unfavourable comparisons were drawn between the behaviour of the 'Castle' class engines, in these conditions, and that of their rivals in the 1925 Interchange trials—the LNER Gresley 'Pacifics'. It was claimed that while in the veritably ideal conditions of the 1925 trials, the Swindon boiler and firebox design had shown a marked superiority, that superiority was not sustained in adverse conditions. Certain individual runs published in the autumn of 1926 appeared to bear this out; but in my own experience the argument could not be sustained. Some examples of very bad steaming by Gresley 'Pacifics' also came to my personal notice.

But engine steaming or not the prolongation of the coal strike into the autumn and early winter was, economically as well as socially a national disaster. The industry based upon the country's greatest source of indigenous wealth, the very foundation of her industrial supremacy in former years, virtually committed suicide. And South Wales, whose livelihood depended almost entirely upon the one great industry, was utterly ruined. The huge overseas markets to serve which the railways and dock facilities of the Bristol Channel ports had been built up were lost for ever, and with them foundered all the hopes and ambitions that had been cherished by the Great Western Railway for co-ordinating and modernising the varied resources of the former independent railways of South Wales. The attitude of the coal-owners in the dispute has been apostrophised by one writer as one of 'avarice and greed'; that of the men's leaders as mere 'stupidity'. The statesmanship of the Prime Minister was never shown to greater advantage than in his handling of the General Strike and its aftermath; but all his statesmanship could not bring masters and men in the coal industry together until ruin had encompassed them both.

Although the coal strike had taken some toll of Great Western locomotive performance, and by the publicising of certain failures brought Swindon practice into a more critical light than it had been subjected to for many years past, the melancholy year brought back a gleam of the old prestige in the unexpected appeal for technical assistance that came from the London Midland and Scottish Railway in the autumn. On that railway there was disagreement in high quarters as to the most suitable type of locomotive for future construction. The Chief Mechanical

Engineer favoured a 4-cylinder compound 'Pacific', whereas the Operating Department considered that a 4-6-0 would be adequate. Arrangements were therefore made to borrow a Great Western 'Castle', and accordingly engine No. 5000 *Launceston Castle* was subjected to extended trials between Euston and Carlisle. The results were so favourable that the LMSR approached the Great Western with a view to the purchase of 50 'Castle' engines. But this request, and the subsequent one for a complete set of drawings were declined, and the LMSR went elsewhere for assistance. But the trials themselves, and the subsequent approach were enough to enhance the reputation of Swindon practice in general, and of the 'Castle' class engines in particular.

VI

The 'King' Class Locomotive

In a book of this kind one would not ordinarily dwell upon the details of locomotive engine design. With an able Chief Mechanical Engineer, and an excellent staff one could assume that the needs of the traffic would be competently met, and that recommendations for enhanced power made as circumstances required it. In the history of a railway company the work of the locomotive department only steps out of its appointed niche in cases of crisis, as at the close of the Webb era on the London and North Western Railway, or in the unhappy case of the 'River' class 4-6-os on the Highland. Swindon was so very much 'a house in order', with an illustrious record, and a succession of first class engineers constantly coming forward to take the posts of major responsibility, that the stability and efficiency of the locomotive department could be taken as something for granted.

Yet in 1926 outside circumstances caused the Locomotive Committee of the Board to view the situation at Swindon in rather broader perspective. The results of the Interchange Trials with the L.N.E.R. has naturally caused immense satisfaction, however subsequent recriminations over publicity may have clouded relations between the two companies for the time being. But the performances of the 'Castle' class engines in 1926, when using imported coal, had been less satisfactory, and despite the further fillip created by the good work of *Launceston Castle* on the L.M.S.R. in the autumn of 1926, it was generally felt that the 'Castle' was not the ultimate answer to Great Western traffic needs, if the pattern of train loading was to remain in the form it had in 1925–6. A further blow to Great Western prestige in locomotive matters was the construction of the Southern Railway 4-cylinder 4-6-o *Lord Nelson*, in 1926, with a nominal tractive effort exceeding that of the 'Castle', and thus robbing the latter of its claim to be the most powerful passenger locomotive in the country. Prestige may not seem a vital matter in the practical business of running a railway; but it meant a good deal to a General Manager like Sir Felix Pole. Thus, when the Chairman of the Locomotive Committee Sir Aubrey Brocklebank, told him of some of the shortcomings of the 'Castles' he took the matter very seriously.

In view of the wonderful subsequent record of the 'Castle' class as a whole it may seem a little odd to talk of shortcomings so early in its history as the year 1926. One must give due weight to the very impressive displays put up by the engines engaged in the 1925 Interchange Trials, and to certain individual feats of performance on the G.W.R. when the loco-motives were under special observation, as for example when Cecil J. Allen rode on the footplate of the engine working the down Cornish Riviera Express in the autumn of 1924. But distinguished locomotive engineers have more than once referred to the symposium of engine performance represented by the monthly feature 'British Locomotive Practice and Performance' in 'The Railway Magazine', and strange to say the early record of the 'Castles' as shown under that particular spotlight was not too good. Up to the end of the year 1926 Allen had published details of 14 runs with engines of this class, apart from logs of the running during the 1925 Interchange Trials, and of these 14 no fewer than four had shown loss of time to be booked against the engine. To this may be added my own personal record of 753 miles of travel behind them on five separate journeys. Three out of the five showed loss of time to engine, and while two of these failures could be attributed to imported fuel during the summer of 1926 the third took place at midsummer of 1925, in what were generally thought to be halcyon days for the locomotive department of the G.W.R.

Larger and more powerful engines seemed desirable; but the design staff at Swindon were hampered in any investigations towards greater power output by the continuing restriction of a maximum axle load of 20 tons. To a remarkable extent the civil and mechanical engineering departments of the G.W.R. remained very much in isolation from each other. In the early years of the present century there had been a very serious clash of opinion on organisational policy between Churchward and Sir James Inglis, the General Manager who had formerly been Chief Engineer. Although Churchward had fought off the elements of control that Inglis sought to impose upon him the controversy had been bitter, and there had subsequently been no more contract between the two departments than was absolutely essential. When Sir Aubrey Brocklebank discussed with Collett the possibility of larger engines the latter could only point to the weight restriction imposed upon him. But when details of the *Lord Nelson* were published, and it was seen that the Chief Mechanical Engineer of the Southern had been permitted to use an axle-load of 20¾ tons Sir Aubrey took up the question of Great Western maximum axle-loading with Sir Felix Pole. In his usual vigorous and incisive way Pole immediately set to work to untie some of the knots.

The Chief Engineer, J. C. Lloyd, was sent for, and it then transpired that not only had his department provided for a maximum axle-load of 22 tons in all new bridge work on main lines, but on the West of England main line such had been the programme of repair and strengthening of existing structures that in the winter of 1926 only four bridges remained subject to the 20-ton maximum axle-load. With this information to hand Sir Felix Pole immediately issued two directives: to the Chief Engineer to have the four remaining bridges brought up to the new standards as quickly as possible; to the Chief Mechanical Engineer to design a new class of express passenger locomotive, of maximum power, having a maximum axle-load of 22 tons. He was assured that authorisation for the construction would quickly be forthcoming, so that some at least of the new engines would be available for the summer traffic of 1927. As usual with any project that Sir Felix Pole thought worthwhile, the heat was on in earnest from the moment that conference closed. Circumstances were quickly to arise to make the pace hotter still for the locomotive department.

Following construction of the *Lord Nelson* engine at the Eastleigh Works of the Southern Railway, which for a few months held the distinction of of having the highest nominal tractive effort of any British passenger locomotive, there ensued a general competition among the 'Big Four' in powerful engine building. Following the trials of the *Launceston Castle* on the L.M.S.R. in the autumn of 1926 it was known that a powerful new 4-6-0 was under construction at the works of the North British Locomotive Company, while experiments with higher boiler pressures were known to be pending on the L.N.E.R. On the Great Western, once the question of axle loading had been cleared Sir Felix Pole wanted a 'super' locomotive. C. B. Collett and his staff at Swindon found that they could produce such a locomotive entirely in the Churchward tradition, by taking the salient features of the 'Star' and 'Castle' classes, and enlarging them to the limit of weight, and structure gauge. To obtain the final increment of tractive effort, and push the nominal value above 40,000 lb. however, a departure was made from the standard wheel diameter used on all Swindon express passenger engines since the turn of the century, namely 6ft. 8½in. The new engines had 6ft. 6in. diameter coupled wheels. The other dimensions contributing to the increase in tractive effort over the 'Castles' were cylinders 16¼in. diameter by 28 in. stroke, against 16 in. by 26 in., and by raising the boiler pressure from 220 to 250 lb. per sq. in.

The cylinders, piston valves, and general layout of the machinery were all quite traditional of Swindon practice, and the really critical feature of the new locomotive was the design of the boiler. While the general trend of design abroad, and in England too on the London and North Eastern Railway, was towards huge boilers, with wide fireboxes, requiring carrying wheels at the rear end and use of the 4-6-2 or 4-8-2 wheel arrangement, it was thought extraordinary at the time that the Great Western should provide a locomotive of 40,300 lb. tractive effort with a relatively small boiler, and narrow firebox having a grate area of only 34 sq. ft. There were some commentators who felt that the lessons of 1926 had not been learned at Swindon and when one of the earliest performances to be published showed loss of boiler pressure on account of inferior coal that particular criticism of the design seemed to gain weight. Before coming to this however there are some remarkable events to be chronicled. By way of further preliminaries it need only be added at this stage, that following a series of locomotives named after 'Courts', 'Abbeys', and 'Castles' it was the original intention to name the 'Super-Castles' as they were sometimes referred to, after Cathedrals. This class-name was an open secret in the West Country in the early spring of 1927, and was freely used by Great Western men, and others having friends or relatives in Swindon Works.

Other circumstances arose to cause a complete change of class-name.

In the year 1927 the large American railroad, the Baltimore and Ohio, was due to celebrate its centenary. Its management wanted to do the thing in style, and the President, Daniel Willard, commissioned a noted railway enthusiast and writer, Edward Hungerford, to co-ordinate the collection of data and ideas. The decision to organise a mammoth celebration was made some years before the actual date, in order to give plenty of time for preparation, and with the British railway centenary falling two years before that of the Baltimore and Ohio, Hungerford naturally journeyed to England to witness the Centenary celebrations at Darlington in 1925. In the course of his visit to this country he met Sir Felix Pole, and put forward the suggestion that a British engine should be exhibited at their own celebrations in 1927. Pole, doubtless with the idea that such an exhibition could bring some useful publicity for the G.W.R., agreed readily enough. Nevertheless, the acute difficulties of the year 1926 had tended to thrust any such idea into the background. In any case, at the time the suggestion was first made Pole was probably thinking that a 'Castle' class engine would form an entirely suitable exhibit. After all, first *Caerphilly Castle* and then *Pendennis Castle* had brought some magnificent publicity for the G.W.R. at the British Empire Exhibition at Wembley, in 1924 and 1925.

When the time of the Baltimore and Ohio centenary drew nearer however the project of the new 'Super-Castle' had been well and truly launched, and after consultation with Collett, Sir Felix decided that it was one of the new engines that should be sent to the U.S.A. This not only necessitated a considerable speed-up in the production at Swindon, but a change in the class-name. The engine would not only represent the G.W.R. in this great American event; it would, willy-nilly, represent the railways of Great Britain. Whether the other British railways looked upon this Swindon engine as representing them, as well as its owners is another matter. But in the U.S.A. the engine would undoubtedly be looked upon as a national exhibit, and no one was more conscious of this than Sir Felix Pole. With this in mind, and with the gracious consent of His Majesty, the first engine of the new class was named *King George V*, and the class as a whole then became known as the 'Kings'. It was another master stroke of Great Western publicity. The organisation at Paddington which had produced those attractive little books: 'The 10.30 Limited', 'Caerphilly Castle', and so on, could continue in tremendous style with ' "The King" of Railway Locomotives', and such terms as 'might and majesty' came naturally from the publicists.

In popular esteem Great Western prestige rose to its very zenith in the summer and autumn of 1927. The question as to which railway had the most powerful express passenger engine locomotive had, in the popular view, been settled decisively by the production of the *King George V*. The Southern *Lord Nelson*, which had temporarily stolen the Great Western thunder was put completely in the shade; the L.M.S.R. *Royal Scot*, which appeared about a month after the 'King' was nowhere in the picture, and even the fitting of a boiler carrying a pressure of 220 lb. per sq. in. to one of the Gresley 'Pacifics' only brought the nominal tractive effort of that engine to 36,465 lb., and a long way below the 40,300 lb. of the *King George V*. Once again Sir Felix Pole had led the Great Western into a position of out-stripping all its rivals. On the paper facts of basic dimensions, and in the magnificent appearance of the new engine it was a triumph, and many thousands of Great Western men, women and children, and other well-wishers were able to feel this natural glow of pride when the engine was exhibited at a number of centres on the line early in July. The receipts from the small entrance fee charged at these exhibitions were put to the G.W.R. 'Helping Hand' fund, that was so appreciated by the members of the staff in time of need.

If the high strategy of Sir Felix Pole, in the production of the engine, had been brilliantly timed those responsible for its detailed design and construction deserved a special word of praise; for the whole project had been a tremendous race against time. Quite apart from the actual manufacturing processes many new patterns and tools had to be made, and the fact that there were practically no teething troubles reflects the greatest credit upon F. W. Hawksworth, who not long previously had been appointed Chief Locomotive Draughtsman, and R. A. G. Hannington, the Locomotive Works Manager. There was comfortable time to run the engine in, send her on a round of exhibition appearances, make a very successful maiden trip on the Cornish Riviera Express on 20th July 1927, and then to ship her from Roath Dock, Cardiff, on 3rd August. If the publicity in England had been in the classic Great Western style, the welcoming hand from America was stretched out even before the SS *City of Chicago* had weighed anchor. The *New York Herald Tribune* printed this interesting article:

A DISTINGUISHED ENVOY

The Great Western Railway of England will send as an exhibit to the Baltimore and Ohio centenary this fall the first of its new 'King' class of locomotives. Breathes there a man with soul so dead that he doesn't thrill a little at such news? Especially when he learns that this engine, now under construction will be capable of a speed of eighty miles an hour, the most powerful locomotive ever built for an English railway.

Somewhere in the breast of every normal *homo sapiens* there stretches a chord that vibrates only to the sight of a fine locomotive. Even now, with airplanes and motors to bid against it in its own field of romantic interest, the steam locomotive retains its fascination. There are probably a number of reasons for this. We can think of at least two— its unusually demonstrative nature and its extraordinary beauty.

Man has devised no other machine that expresses its feelings so frankly and unmistakably. A locomotive sighs, it pants, it coughs, it barks; it emits empassioned shrieks and mournful toots; it puts forth powerful staccato protests at hauling a heavy load or climbing a steep grade; it purrs ecstatically as it romps along the rails at a mile a minute; it can hiss and throb and snort and tinkle. And in addition to all these auditory forms of expression it has its visual signs, its plumes of steam spelling surplus energy, its belchings of black smoke denoting determination, its sparks at night registering passion.

This new English locomotive that is coming over, the first of its race to pay us a visit since the Chicago World's Fair in 1893, will bear the name *King George V* and be one of twenty, each bearing the name of an English monarch.

It is really no exaggeration to say that the engine created a sensation in the U.S.A. Its fine colouring, beautiful finish, and the quietness of its running brought forth a positive chorus of panegyrics, and the fact that the exhaust was always clear astonished American locomotive men, who were accustomed to see a steady stream of black smoke issuing from the chimneys of steam locomotives. In the meantime the remaining five engines of the first batch were in regular service on the West of England main line, and although they were immediately acknowledged to be immensely powerful machines there were reports almost at once of rolling at high speed. This was something new for Great Western 4-cylinder 4-6-0s, all of which had hitherto been notably steady. One might get a lurch or an isolated roll; but the new 'Kings' seemed to have a more alarming action, and on August 10, 1927, barely a week after the SS. *City of Chicago* had sailed with the *King George V* on board, the authorities at Paddington, shortly after 11.30 a.m. were concerned to hear that the down Limited was off the road near Midgham. I well remember a lunch time conversation between two friends of mine, who were then in the General Manager's office, and how one said : 'Great Scott, we shall have to keep this quiet!', and how the other replied: 'My dear chap, whatever we do it'll be in the Midday editions.' And so it was.

Fortunately the derailment was confined to the bogie of the engine, and although the train was travelling at 60 m.p.h. when it occurred the rest of the engine wheels and the whole of the train kept the road, and no harm was done except to the peace of mind of all the senior officers concerned. It was perhaps no more than natural that in the first investigations into the affair the Civil Engineer blamed the engine, and the Chief Mechanical Engineer blamed the track. But the reports of rough riding with the 'King' class engines set going a full-scale enquiry at Swindon, and Collett cabled Stanier, who was with the *King George V* in America, telling him not to allow the engine to do any main-line running until permission was sent from England. The investigation revealed that the springing of the bogie was not satisfactory, and a fairly simple alteration made the riding safe enough for authority to be given to run No. 6000 in America, after certain changes had been made. The Great Western Railway earned the reputation of being fortunate in its freedom from serious accidents in the twentieth century. This was in large measure due to the excellence of its engineering, and the diligence of the staff; but at the same time when mishaps did occur the luck was on the side of safety. It was certainly so at Midgham on August 10, 1927. The bogie became derailed on plain, straight track; if there had been points or crossings nothing could have saved a major disaster.

As it was, from the public point of view the incident was quickly forgotten, and it only needed the highly-coloured stories of the exploits of the *King George V* in America to consolidate the popular impression of these engines, as things of almost legendary might. The story that delighted English enthusiasts when it was 'splashed' in the popular press emanated from the very successful dynamometer car trial run made on the Baltimore and Ohio Railroad on 17th October, 1927. The story that went the rounds concerned a spell of fast running when the engine was making about 75 m.p.h. The newspaper told how the American railway people were so unused to this kind of speed that they grew alarmed, and instructions were given from the dynamometer car to slow down. At home everyone enjoyed the story. Even Cecil J. Allen repeated it in 'The Railway Magazine', and when eventually Stanier gave the facts at a meeting of the Western Branch of the Institution of Mechanical Engineers early in 1928, the revelation was made to such a limited audience as to do little to counteract the immense popular satisfaction that had arisen from the original garbled version. What actually happened was that the American pilotman had forgotten to warn the Great Western driver that they were nearing a curve round which a 30 m.p.h. restriction was in force; and the warning was given from the dynamometer car, when the train was drawing dangerously near to the curve. Far from being anything to cause gratification in the sense originally conveyed, the only real cause for gratification was in yet another lucky escape!

At home the prowess of the new locomotives was being exploited to the full. On 26th September, 1927, the non-stop run of the down Cornish Riviera Express was accelerated, from 4hr. 7 min. to the level 4 hr., with appropriate publicity, and then on Thursday 3rd November, 1927, there was inaugurated a most novel and successful piece of combined advertising and revenue earning. A week previous to this event a special excursion from London to Swindon Works was announced, including fast runs in each direction, and a conducted tour round the 'birthplace', as it was termed, of the *King George V*—all for 5s. The bookings were so heavy that the sale of tickets had to be suspended two days before the trip, and no fewer than 700 passengers were conveyed. So keen was the disappointment felt by many who could not obtain tickets that another trip was organised a week later; and this second excursion, on 10th November, required *two* trains. The original advertisement had guaranteed that the trains to and from Swindon would be hauled by 'King' class engines, and as at that time the *King George V* had not returned from America, on 10th November, two engines out of the five available were engaged in running these special excursions.

They were not by any means an occasion for youthful 'railfans'. Photographs taken of the excursionists walking from the station to the works show a preponderance of middle-aged men, with bowler hats and smart attire much in evidence. Railwaymen from other lines were included, and I know of a number of engineers, in middle status, who were sent by their firms, to observe what they could of production methods at Swindon. The visit commenced with an inspection of the carriage-building shops, the various operations employed in preparing the upholstery work, French polishing, and so on, being noted, followed by a tour through the body shop and wood-working machine shop and sawmill. The party was then conducted across the main lines to the locomotive works, and entered the foundry, where the casting of various locomotive detail parts was observed with interest, while attention was also attracted by a number of cylinder castings for new engines of the 'King' class. In order to add to the general interest various parts were labelled with their proper descriptions, and the words 'for the "King" class engine' displayed upon cards or boards.

After the party had passed through the foundry, the locomotive testing plant, on which 4-6-0 locomotive No. 4092, *Dunraven Castle*, of the 'Castle' class, was being steamed, attracted much attention. In the erecting shop the oxygen flame-cutting apparatus received considerable attention, and a firebox for one of the new 'King' class engines was seen nearing completion. A number of tank engines were noted under construction, and the ease with which the completed engine was handled by the overhead crane and on the traverser was remarked upon by many of the visitors. The tour concluded with a visit to the footplate of the engine *King Edward VII* standing outside the shop.

Care was taken also to provide the special trains with a clear road so that some fast running could be included in the day's outing; and the working on 10th November, certainly gave a most impressive display in this respect. At that time the 2.30 p.m. express from Cheltenham to Paddington was still the fastest train on the line, with its allowance of 75 min. for the run of 77.3 miles from Swindon to Paddington. On 10th November, 1927, with 10-coach restaurant car trains the following times were made:

Train, Paddington dep.	Engine No.	Overall time
12.20 p.m.	6001	76
12.40 p.m.	6003	76½

Train Swindon dep.	Engine No.	Overall time
5.11 p.m.	6003	75
5.34 p.m.	6001	68½

In passing it may be mentioned that engine No. 6003 *King George IV* was the one concerned in the Midgham derailment; but by November of course the trouble with the bogie had long since been diagnosed and put right.

On 24th November, 1927, the *King George V* was landed at Cardiff Docks on return from the triumphant American visit, and its return to traffic on the G.W.R. was marked by the fixing of two souvenirs, presented by the Baltimore and Ohio Railroad. For the celebrated dynamometer car test run in America the engine had fixed to it a regulation bell, which was duly tolled as required during the run. This was retained, and carried by the engine for the rest of its working life. In addition two medals were fixed to the cab sides, commemorating its participation in the Baltimore and Ohio centenary celebrations. More splendid publicity! It did indeed seem as though the G.W.R. could not put a foot wrong in this period of its life. Yet in that same December of 1927 'The Railway Magazine' contained the first description of a run on the footplate of one of the 'King' class engines, working a maximum load, on the accelerated 4-hour schedule of the Cornish Riviera Express. Considerable trouble with steaming was experienced due to inferior coal, and the publication of this account started a long correspondence in the columns of 'British Locomotive Practice and Performance' on the merits and demerits of the boiler, as compared with the wide firebox type favoured on the L.N.E.R. On this published run the situation that developed on the footplate was very carefully handled, and the train brought through to destination several minutes ahead of time; but to the most critical of observers the details published were enough to show that the 'Kings' had their susceptibilities, like all other engines. Nevertheless, the year 1927 will be for ever memorable in Great Western history for the sustained and astonishingly successful use made of publicity for a new locomotive. While some of this was, at the time regarded as publicity pure and simple, time was to show that the 'King' class locomotives were a really great design, though this final and lasting appraisal was not to come until very many years later.

VII

Train Services

1927-1930

From the autumn of 1927 the high speed express train services of the Great Western Railway began to partake of a new pattern. The new form was shown by the acceleration of the down Cornish Riviera Express from its time-honoured 4 hr. 7 min. for the non-stop London-Plymouth run to the level four hours. It was but one step towards the systematic clipping of minutes off fast train schedules, edging the start-to-stop average speeds higher and higher, and steadily increasing the aggregate of high speed mileage. It was exhilarating to the train speed statisticians, if for nothing else than the contrast it afforded to the policies then being pursued by the northern lines. In the summer of 1927 the record for maximum length of daily non-stop run passed from the Great Western after they had held it for 23 years. Against the 225.7 miles of the Cornish Riviera Express, from Paddington to Plymouth, the L.N.E.R. clocked up 268.3 miles from Kings Cross to Newcastle, and the L.M.S.R. 236 miles from Euston to Carnforth. With lower average speed on the L.N.E.R. and with double-heading throughout on the L.M.S.R. these marathon Anglo-Scottish express non-stop runs were still far below the Cornish Riviera Express in the demands they made upon locomotive power; but the plain fact remained, that the Great Western length of non-stop run had been surpassed, and it was difficult to see how the latter could be extended while retaining economic railway working.

While some mild consideration was given possible *riposte*, in the form of a London–Truro non-stop as a feature of some future summer timetable the L.M.S.R. in their winter timetable of 1927 gave any such ideas the complete *coup de grace* by scheduling the 'Royal Scot' non-stop in each direction over the 299.1 miles between Euston and Carlisle. The L.N.E.R. followed this, in the summer of 1928 by the ever-memorable Kings Cross–Edinburgh non-stop. Shorn of the glamour of having the world's record non-stop run the Great Western then gave consideration as to whether the London–Plymouth run was really an economic proposition, as all-the-year-round performance. But before coming to consider the developments of the express train service, as from 1927 onwards, it is important to review the general standards of travel that obtained in that year, as compared with those prevailing in 1914, before the onset of war caused such disruption. The following table shows the relative position, in regard to eight provincial centres, which between them indicate the general position on the West of England, South Wales, and the Birmingham and North route.

FASTEST TIMES FROM LONDON: IN 1914 and 1927

STATION	Distance miles	Fastest times		Speed* July 1927 m.p.h.	Increase (+) OR Decrease (−) 1914–1927 per cent.
		July 1914 min.	July 1927 min.		
Birmingham	110.6	120	120	55.3	NIL
Bristol	118.3	120	120	59.2	NIL
Cardiff	145.1	170	160	54.3	- 5.9
Chester	195.2	253	248	47.2	- 2.0
Exeter	173.7	180	180	57.8	NIL
Penzance	305.2	395	390	46.9	- 1.3
Plymouth	225.7	247	247	54.7	NIL
Torquay	199.7	218	215	55.7	- 1.4

* Inclusive of intermediate stops in most cases

The foregoing table indicates a slight improvement in maximum facilities; but against this must be recorded the case of Worcester, which in 1914 had three non-stop runs to and from London, of which the fastest was made at an average speed of 55.7 m.p.h. After the war non-stop running to Worcester was not resumed, while in the summer of 1914 there was a non-stop run of 101.2 miles from Paddington to Frome by the second section of the Cornish Riviera Express, leaving at 10.35 a.m. and making the run at an average speed of 56.7 m.p.h.

The statistics for long-distance non-stop running for 1914 and 1927 show that the tendency was to reduce the length of run, by inserting stops at important intermediate stations, often within the same overall times as previously. On the Birmingham route, for example, in 1914 there were four non-stops over the full distance of 110.6 miles. In 1927 only two non-stops remained, but seven other trains ran between Paddington and Birmingham, or vice versa, in two hours while making one intermediate stop. It was, of course, the need for insertion of stops at Oxford and elsewhere on the West Midland line that precluded any non-stop service between Paddington and Worcester. In addition to Oxford, a town like Leamington received a much better service than in pre-war years. The standard of long-distance express running in 1927 is well illustrated by the following list of 100-mile non-stop runs.

So far as the locomotive work is concerned some of the above runs are duplicated. For example two of the Bath non-stops, including the fastest one, were made up by slip coach off trains also running non-stop from Paddington to Bristol; the same applies to the fastest of the Taunton runs, made by slip coach off one of the Paddington–Exeter non-stops, and the Exeter–Reading run, by a slip coach off a corresponding up West of England express running non-stop from Exeter to Paddington. The standard of speed was high for the period. At that time it had not become customary to decelerate express train services at week-ends in the peak period of summer traffic; but with the running of many extra trains it was the practice to extend slightly the length of non-stop run of the first sections of the regular trains. With the Cornish Riviera Express, for example, on Saturdays the first section conveyed passengers only for Truro and beyond, and to avoid occupancy of valuable platform space at Plymouth North Road, engines were changed at Devonport Junction, involving a non-stop run from Paddington of 226.9 miles. Far from showing any deceleration the time allowance for this longer run was actually 3 min. less than the normal run to North Road station. In a similar way the first section of the 'Torbay Limited' was booked non-stop from Paddington to Paignton, 201.8 miles, and there was an up non-stop run of 209.4 miles from Brent to Paddington.

DAILY NON-STOP RUNS : 100 MILES, OR MORE, 1927

Section	Distance miles	Number of runs	Av. Speed of fastest m.p.h.
Paddington–Plymouth	225.7	2	54.8
Paddington–Torquay	199.7	2	55.7
Paddington–Exeter	173.7	3	57.8
Paddington–Taunton	142.9	4	57.9*
Exeter–Reading	137.7	1*	57.8
Paddington–Newport	133.4	6	57.2
Paddington–Bristol via Bath	118.3	2	59.2
Bristol–Paddington via Badminton	117.6	2	58.8
Paddington–Birmingham	110.6	2	55.3
Paddington–Bath	106.9	5	61.1*
Reading–Taunton	106.9	2	56.9*
Stroud–Paddington	102.2	1	57.3
Badminton–Paddington	100.0	1	56.1

* By slip coach

While these runs were no doubt scheduled for operating convenience one must take leave to question how often they really were made non-stop on summer Saturdays. At peak periods the Cornish Riviera Express frequently had to take an assistant engine over the heavy gradients of the South Devon line, involving a stop at Newton Abbot, and sometimes at Brent also to put the leading engine off; while in my own experience in two successive summers the first part of the Torbay Limited was so delayed as to be more than half an hour late in arrival at Paignton. On one of these journeys indeed, the train was stopped by signal four times before reaching Newton Abbot, and having passed Torquay in exactly 4 hours from Paddington—25 min. late—was so blocked as to take 33 min. to cover the last 2 miles! The siding and running-line facilities in the West of England were quite inadequate to deal with the enormous volume of traffic that piled up on a summer Saturday. It was the general experience that in the case of expresses from London, via Westbury, a good run would be obtained until Taunton was neared; but then the confluence of the two streams upon the Taunton 'bottleneck' began to set up congestion, and the complete absence, then, of siding accommodation at Paignton set up reactions back to Newton Abbot and Exeter. The situation was further complicated by the fact that 4-6-0 express locomotives were not permitted to run beyond Paignton, and that such trains as were proceeding to Kingswear were required to change engines at Paignton, thereby adding to the difficulties.

Reverting to the ordinary, as distinct from the weekend services, the total number of daily 100-mile non-stop runs showed a total of 28 for 1927, as against 33 in 1914, and a great reduction in the number of slip coach services. In 1914 there had been no fewer than 70 cases of arrival by slip coach, whereas in 1927 this number was 44. The 1927 list was:

SLIP COACH ARRIVALS

Number detached daily.	Station at which detached
9	Reading
4	Westbury
3	Banbury Bridgwater
2	Bath Bicester Chippenham Leamington Stoke Gifford (for Bristol) Swindon Taplow Wellington (Salop)
1	Didcot Exeter Maidenhead Moreton-in-Marsh Newbury Princes Risborough Taunton Twyford Yatton

The slip coach services in 1927 in many cases provided continuation, by through carriage, to branch lines, or stations further along the main line. The Westbury and Taunton slip coaches on the West of England expresses, for example, were continued to Weymouth on the one hand, and to Ilfracombe and Minehead on the other. The Twyford slip provided a service to Henley-on-Thames, while the Chippenham slips off Bristol expresses were conveyed forward to Bath, attached to rail motors to

provide through services to Corsham, Box, and Bathampton. The Stoke
Gifford slips were detached from the 8.55 a.m. and 7.55 p.m. South
Wales expresses from Paddington, and in the former case provided a fast
and most acceptable alternative service to Bristol to the semi-fast 9.15 a.m.
from Paddington, via Bath. Despite this still extensive use of slip coach
services the Great Western never adopted the London and North Western
and Midland practice of having vestibuled connections to the slip carriages,
and consequently passengers travelling therein, sometimes for as long as
three hours, were cut off from restaurant cars, and other amenities of the
main part of the trains concerned.

The winter service of 1927 saw the acceleration of the Cornish Riviera
Express to a 4 hr. non-stop run to Plymouth, raising the average speed to
56.4 m.p.h. while in the summer of 1928 this was paralleled by the
Torquay non-stop of the down 'Torbay Limited' in $3\frac{1}{2}$ hr. at an average
speed of 57.1 m.p.h. These West of England accelerations brought an
addition to the then-small number of 60 m.p.h. services, because the
Westbury slip coach off the down Cornish Riviera Express was booked to
arrive at 12.4 p.m.—94 min. for the 95.6 miles from Paddington. A fine
new service of 1928 was the run of the 8 a.m. from Cheltenham to Paddington, which was booked to run non-stop from Kemble 91 miles, at an
average speed of exactly 60 m.p.h. While the Cheltenham Flyer still
remained nominally the Company's fastest train, with its start-to-stop
average of 61.8 m.p.h. from Swindon to Paddington, the acceleration of
the late-afternoon Plymouth express, via Bristol, to a departure at 4.30 p.m.
brought another slip-coach 60 m.p.h. run, whereby the Chippenham

G.W.R. Journeys Timed at over 58 m.p.h. start-to-stop

Train	From	To	Distance miles	Time min.	Speed m.p.h.
5.55 p.m.	Swindon	Chippenham	16.7	16*	62.6
3.45 p.m.	Swindon	Paddington	77.3	75	61.8
11.15 p.m. ⎫ 1.15 p.m. ⎬	Paddington	Bath	106.9	105*	61.6
5.55 p.m.	Swindon	Bath	29.6	29	61.2
12 noon	Paddington	Exeter	173.7	175	59.6
11.15 a.m. ⎫ 1.15 p.m. ⎬	Paddington	Bristol via Bath	118.3	120	59.2
10.30 a.m.	Paddington	Taunton	142.9	145*	59.1
11.45 a.m. ⎫ 5.15 p.m. ⎬	Bristol	Paddington via Badminton	117.6	120	58.8
9.42 a.m.	High Wycombe	Leamington	41.0	42*	58.6
10.30 a.m. ⎫ 3.30 p.m. ⎬	Paddington	Westbury	95.6	98*	58.5
4.10 p.m.	Paddington	Leamington	87.3	90	58.2
5.0 p.m.	Paddington	Kemble	91.0	94	58.1
2.18 p.m.	Evesham Kingham -Worcester		35.8	37	58.1
1.10 p.m.	Swindon	Paddington	77.3	80	58.0

* arrival by slip coach

Plate 15. MODERN SIGNAL ASSEMBLIES

Searchlight type colour light signals at Cardiff East

Typical group of semaphores at Reading West Main, looking towards London

Plate 16

Viscount Horne
Chairman 1934-1940

Sir James Milne
General Manager 1929-1947

J. C. Lloyd
Joint Chief Engineer 1924-5
Chief Engineer 1926-1929

Raymond Carpmael
Chief Engineer 1929-1940

Plate 17. REBUILDING AT TAUNTON

View, showing beginning of new work at West End, with original Brunel roof still in existence

The new station, looking towards Bristol

Plate 18. THE CENTENARY FILM

The first train arrives at 'Maidenhead'

General view of the *North Star* replica train, and 'period' passengers

arrival was booked in no more than 16 min. from Swindon start, 16.7 miles. It is to be doubted however if this 62.6 m.p.h. start-to-stop run for the slip coach was often strictly maintained, because the run of the main train from Swindon to Bath did not require running approaching this degree of vigour.

The express train services of the Great Western came in for some favourable comparison with the best then obtaining on the continent of Europe in the winter of 1927–1928.

In 'The Railway Gazette' of 2nd March, 1928, comparison of the previous table made with current working on the Northern Railway of France:

C. de F. du NORD: JOURNEYS TIMED AT OVER 58 m.p.h.
start-to-stop

From	To	Distance miles	Time min.	Speed m.p.h.
Paris	St. Quentin	95.2	94	60.7
Paris	Aulnoye	134.0	135	59.5
Paris	Abbeville	109.1	110	59.4
Paris	Arras	119.4	121	59.2
Paris } Jeumont }	Jeumont } Paris }	147.8	150	59.1
Paris	Étaples	140.8	143	59.1
Paris	Compiegne	52.0	53	58.8
Arras	Longueau	41.1	42	58.7
Étaples	Amiens	59.5	61	58.5
Aulnoye	St. Quentin	38.8	40	58.2
Paris } Calais }	Calais } Paris }	184.3	190	58.2

From the viewpoint of length of journey and scheduled speed the comparison is very close; but it must be recorded that in the following summer French speeds began to draw ahead, and it must also be added that in general the loads conveyed in France were very much heavier than on the Great Western. Nevertheless in speed of service it was a fine record, the more so that a remarkably high standard of safety, with high speed, had been established. Since 1905 there had been no mishap on the G.W.R. to a passenger train involving loss of life.

There was nevertheless a considerable disparity between the speeds of the fastest trains on most routes and many of the other services. This was particularly noticeable to and from Bristol. The two-hour non-stops, with their Bath slip-coaches in the down direction made excellent time; but there were trains like the 9.15 a.m. from Paddington, with stops at Ealing Broadway, Reading, Didcot, Swindon, Chippenham and Bath which barely needed to exceed 60 m.p.h. at any point in the journey. The 10.45 a.m. to Cheltenham was another very leisurely train. There was nevertheless a reason for the slow running of these trains, and for the inordinate length of stop at intermediate stations. The Great Western prided itself on its personal service to the rural community, and was always ready to attach horseboxes, or other four-wheeled vehicles to passenger trains. When such vehicles were included in the make-up trains were not desired to exceed 60 m.p.h., and these moderately-timed passenger trains were used for the conveyance of such loads. The station stops allowed for attaching or detaching at intermediate points. Such factors were nevertheless not likely to be appreciated by the traveller who was in a hurry, and I well remember a railway-carriage argument between one such exasperated individual, on the 9.15 a.m. from Paddington, and a staunch upholder of the G.W.R. In answer to allegations of dilatoriness the 'staunch upholder' instanced the running of the Cornish Riviera Express. 'But' countered the other 'I don't want to go to Penzance! Never did. I want to get to Swindon, but not at the speed of a funeral.'

The most uniform speed was to be seen on the Birmingham route, on which the principal expresses—and there were plenty of them—all completed the journey between Paddington and Snow Hill in two hours, or 2 hr. 5 min. The stimulus of competition with the L.M.S.R. undoubtedly played its part in the framing of this section of the timetable, whereas on the journeys to and from South Wales, where the Great Western had a monopoly, the average speeds were not so high. The South Wales trains were mostly heavy and the negotiation of the awkward section through the Severn Tunnel presented its difficulties. In the period between 1927 and 1930 many of the most important trains to and from South Wales were still worked by the 'Saint' class 2-cylinder 4-6-0 locomotives, and consideration had to be given to the class of motive power available when framing schedules for the heavy business expresses.

Although in overall speed and in point-to-point running they fell a good way below the London trains, great importance was attached to the cross-country services. That worked via the Severn Tunnel jointly with the former L.N.E.R. included a number of well-equipped if not very speedy trains. Most of the trains on this service were heavy and included sections from the Torquay line and from Plymouth for both Liverpool and Manchester. Some were worked to and from Penzance, and a full restaurant car service was usually available for all sections of the trains throughout between Newton Abbot and Crewe. Additional through carriages were conveyed on some trains to and from Birkenhead—detached at Shrewsbury—while on other trains there were through carriages to and from Glasgow Central. There was nothing in the way of long non-stop runs on these trains. It was usual to call at Teignmouth, Dawlish, Exeter, Taunton, Bridgwater, Weston-super-Mare, Bristol, Pontypool Road, and Hereford. The longest non-stop run was over the 51 miles from Hereford to Shrewsbury. On certain services some of the stops were omitted particularly in the relief workings at weekends. These trains were almost entirely confined to haulage by the older Churchward 4-6-0 locomotives, and in relation to the heavy loads taken some hard work was involved, particularly between Bristol and Shrewsbury. On some services the loading was even heavier between Crewe and Pontypool Road, by the conveyance of through carriages for the South Wales towns from Liverpool and Manchester.

Another cross-country service of great importance was that between Wolverhampton, Birmingham, and the West of England via Stratford-upon-Avon and Cheltenham. This route had been opened up in strong competition to the West of England main line of the Midland Railway, between Birmingham and Bristol, and in addition to developing the rural traffic by a series of halts between Stratford-upon-Avon and Cheltenham, a good service of through expresses was operated between Wolverhampton, the Torquay line, and Penzance. Some of these trains were given preferential treatment on the main line between Bristol and Newton Abbot, including non-stop runs between Bristol and Exeter. North of Bristol also, Gloucester was by-passed, and regular non-stop running made between Bristol and Cheltenham (Malvern Road), using the Gloucester avoiding line. The start-to-stop average speeds bore no comparison with the spectacular express working from Paddington to the West of England, and to Birmingham; but on the line between Bristol and Wolverhampton in particular, the time-tabling had to have in mind the motive power available. For many years the L.M.S.R. authorities would permit no larger engines than the Churchward 4-4-0 'County' class over the section of line between Standish Junction and Yate, over which the Great Western exercised running powers.

The year 1929 saw some further accelerations on the high speed routes. The fastest time between London and Exeter had come down to 2 hr. 53 min.; Penzance was reached in 6 hr. 20 min., and the time to Torquay was the level 3½ hours. An innovation during the summer service was the introduction of an all-Pullman express to Torquay and Paignton, on Mondays and Fridays, leaving Paddington at 11 a.m. and running the 193.9 miles to Newton Abbot non-stop in 205 min. The overall time to Torquay was 3 hr. 40 min., against the 3½ hours non-stop of the Torbay Limited. An 8-coach train was run, but it did not prove a success. There appeared to be little call for a luxury service at higher fares, and at slightly lower speed than the very popular ordinary train. But the principal feature of the summer service of 1929 was the acceleration of the Cheltenham Flyer to run the 77.3 miles from Swindon to Paddington non-stop in 70 min.— an unprecedented start-to-stop average speed of 66.3 m.p.h. That it was easily possible had already been shown on several previous occasions, when lost time was regained on the former 75 min. schedule. The fastest fully authenticated time up to then had been one of 66 min. 12 sec., with an engine of the 'Star' class. Nevertheless the new schedule was widely and justifiably acclaimed as a notable achievement, and at the time it was the fastest start-to-stop run anywhere in the world.

One very noteworthy feature of Great Western operation at that time was the gradual acceleration of express freight train services. Some of these, running through the night, made lengthy non-stop runs, and three, with mileages over the '100' may be specially mentioned:

NIGHT EXPRESS GOODS TRAINS

Time	Route	Distance miles	Time min.	Av. Speed m.p.h.
10.30 p.m.	Greenford-Shrewsbury	145.1	223	39.0
12 midnight	Newbury Racecourse to Newton Abbot	141.5	221	38.4
11.35 p.m.	Bristol East Depot–Acton	112.7	197	34.3

These trains were mostly worked by the '47XX' class 5 ft. 8 in. 2-8-0s, working through between London and Plymouth and London and Chester. Many of the regular goods trains on the G.W.R. had nicknames, dating in some cases from broad gauge days, just as certain express passenger trains had nicknames among the staff. At the time of which I am now writing the 1.30 p.m. from Paddington to Penzance was always known as the 'Dutchman', and the 3 p.m. from Birmingham to Paddington was the 'Zulu'—originating from the old 'Northern Zulu' to distinguish the latter from the broad gauge West of England express of the same name. But in 1929 it became a matter of official policy to name many of the express goods trains, and in a pamphlet issued to traders entitled 'How to send and how to save' a list was given of the officially adopted nicknames for no fewer than 75 regular goods services. These names were as follows:

1.5 a.m.	(Acton to Bristol) *The High Flyer*
7.40 p.m.	(Acton to Cardiff) *The Early Bird.*
9.25 p.m.	(Acton to Llanelly) *The Leek*
3.40 a.m.	(Banbury Jc. to Bristol) *The Competitor.*
2.10 a.m.	(Basingstoke to Wolverhampton) *The Cherbourg.*
9.35 p.m.	(Basingstoke to Wolverhampton) *The B.B.C.*
	(Basingstoke, Birmingham, Crewe).
3.55 p.m.	(Birkenhead to Smithfield) *The Meat.*
6.5 p.m.	(Birkenhead to Pontypool Rd.) *The Feeder.*
8.20 p.m.	(Birkenhead to Paddington) *The General.*
9.5 p.m.	(Birkenhead to Cardiff) *The Mersey.*
10.50 p.m.	(Birkenhead to Bordesley Jc.) *The Birmingham Market*
11.35 p.m.	(Birkenhead to Oswestry) *The Cambrian Pioneer.*
11.0 p.m.	(Birmingham to Paddington) *The Pedlar.*
9.10 p.m.	(Bordesley Jc. to Birkenhead) *The Shipper.*
10.10 p.m.	(Bordesley Jc. to Swansea) *The Hardware.*
6.50 p.m.	(Bristol to Birkenhead) *The Farmer's Boy.*
7.40 p.m.	(Bristol to Paddington) *The 'Bacca'.*
9.20 p.m.	(Bristol to Wolverhampton) *The Western Docker.*
10.5 p.m.	(Bristol to Leamington) *Spa.*
10.5 p.m.	(Bristol to Paddington) *The Cocoa.*
10.55 p.m.	(Bristol to Laira) *The Drake.*
12.25 a.m.	(Bristol to Carmarthen Jc.) *The Bristolian.*
3.50 p.m.	(Cardiff to Hanwell Br. Sdgs.) *The Stock.*
9.45 p.m.	(Cardiff to Saltney) *The Spud.*
11.10 p.m.	(Cardiff to Paddington) *The Ironmonger.*
12.55 a.m.	(Cardiff to Swansea) *Port to Port.*
7.30 p.m.	(Carmarthen to Paddington) *The Up Welshman.*

8.35 p.m.	(Carmarthen to Bristol) *The Open.*
11.0 a.m.	(Exeter to Pontypool Rd.) *The Ponty.*
4.0 p.m.	(Exeter to Old Oak Common) *The Flying Pig.*
12.5 a.m.	(Gloucester to Cardiff) *The Bacon.*
7.50 p.m.	(Gloucester to Paddington) *The Cotswold.*
11.0 p.m.	(Handsworth to Acton) *The Queen's Head.*
8.20 p.m.	(Kidderminster to Paddington) *The Carpet.*
7.45 p.m.	(Manchester to Bristol) *The 'Mon'.*
8.25 p.m.	(Manchester to Wolverhampton) *The Early Riser.*
4.58 p.m.	(Marazion to Bristol) *The Tre Pol and Pen Flyer.*
10.25 p.m.	(Margam to Bordesley) *The Tinman.*
5.30 p.m.	(Newton Abbot to Paddington) *The Hackney.*
9.32 p.m.	(Old Oak Common to Penzance) *The Cornishman.*
8.5 p.m.	(Paddington to Bristol) *The Shopper.*
9.10 p.m.	(Paddington to Birkenhead) *Northern Flash.*
9.35 p.m.	(Paddington to Carmarthen Jc.) *The Welshman.*
10.10 p.m.	(Paddington to Laira) *The Tamar.*
10.30 p.m.	(Paddington to Cardiff) *South Wales Borderer.*
10.50 p.m.	(Paddington to Weymouth) *The Jersey.*
11.5 p.m.	(Paddington to Wolverhampton) *The Hampton.*
11.15 p.m.	(Paddington to Bristol) *The Western General.*
11.35 p.m.	(Paddington to Newton Abbot) *The Devonshireman.*
12.5 a.m.	(Paddington to Worcester) *The Sauce.*
12.15 a.m.	(Paddington to Fishguard) *Irishman.*
12.30 a.m.	(Paddington to Bristol) *The Mopper Up.*
12.10 a.m.	(Park Royal to Stourbridge Jc.) *The Stour.*
2.50 p.m.	(Penzance to Paddington) *The Searchlight.*
7.20 p.m.	(Penzance to Plymouth) *The Pasty.*
5.40 a.m.	(Pontypool Rd. to Newton Abbot) *The Laira.*
10.30 p.m.	(Reading to Laira) *The Biscuit.*
11.40 a.m.	(Southall to Crewe) *The Grocer.*
3.50 p.m.	(Swindon to Tavistock Jc.) *The Rasher.*
7.10 p.m.	(Victoria Basin to Basingstoke) *The Cargo.*
4.20 a.m.	(Westbury to Wolverhampton) *The Moonraker.*
7.35 p.m.	(Westbury to Manchester) *The Lancashire Lad.*
9.55 p.m.	(Westbury to Penzance) *Western Flash.*
10.50 p.m.	(Westbury to Pontypool Rd.) *The Northern.*
7.22 p.m.	(West Drayton to Wolverhampton) *The Drayton.*
6.35 p.m.	(Weymouth to Paddington) *The Up Jersey.*
1.30 p.m.	(Wolverhampton to Basingstoke) *The Southern Docker.*
2.10 a.m.	(Wolverhampton to Basingstoke) *The Southerner.*
2.45 a.m.	(Wolverhampton to Birkenhead) *The Northern Docker.*
4.0 a.m.	(Wolverhampton to Crewe) *The Northern Exchange.*
8.15 p.m.	(Wolverhampton to Paddington) *The Racer.*
10.15 p.m.	(Wolverhampton to Westbury) *The Crosser.*
12.45 a.m.	(Wolverhampton to Birkenhead) *The Flying Skipper.*
6.45 p.m.	(Worcester to Cardiff) *The Worcester Fruit.*
8.35 p.m.	(Worcester to Crewe) *The 'Sparagras'.*

No survey of train service facilities at this time would be complete without mention of the many race specials run during the season. Particular attention was always given to race meetings at Cheltenham and Newbury, and for the latter the 'Members and First Class' special was given V.I.P. treatment from the operating and locomotive point of view. Engines were specially selected, and it was usual for a locomotive running inspector to travel on the footplate. The working of the Cheltenham race specials was the reason for Old Oak Common Running Shed having one isolated turn of duty to Gloucester; the 10.45 a.m. down from Paddington returning with the Cheltenham Flyer. The inclusion of this duty among the top link turns at Old Oak meant that there were always drivers available in London who could work the Cheltenham race specials without the necessity of having to provide pilotmen.

The most remarkable enterprise in connection with race meetings was launched in 1927, when it was decided to compete for the special traffic in connection with the Grand National, at Aintree. This may have seemed somewhat venturesome, seeing that the Great Western could convey its patrons only as far as Birkenhead, while its rivals could take their passengers right to the course. Nevertheless the Great Western, in partnership with Pickfords Ltd., ran two excursion trains on 25th March, 1927; a third class special leaving Paddington at 7.50 a.m., calling at Ealing Broadway, and running thence non-stop to Birkenhead in 4 hr. The first class special left Paddington at 8.25 a.m. and ran non-stop to Birkenhead in 4 hr. The road journey thence to Aintree was arranged by Pickfords. While naturally this service could not compare for speed with that of the most direct route, from Euston, it provided considerably later departure time from London than those of the L.N.E.R. specials from Marylebone, and Kings Cross, despite the road journey at the Liverpool end. The Marylebone departures were at 7.8 and 7.45 a.m., and those from Kings Cross at 7.30 and 7.45 a.m. On the Great Western, the inclusive return fares including all meals on the trains were £2-14-6 first class, and £1-17-0 third class.

Although no intermediate stops were scheduled, between Ealing Broadway and Birkenhead in the one case, and Paddington and Birkenhead in the other, actually both trains called at Shrewsbury to change engines. As in the case of Newbury and Cheltenham race meetings preferential treatment was given to the working of these Grand National specials. The first train arrived at Birkenhead 9 min. early and the second 10 min. early. It is interesting to record the engines concerned:

GRAND NATIONAL SPECIALS: MARCH 25, 1927.
LOCOMOTIVES USED

Train, Paddington dep.	7.50 a.m.	8.25 a.m.
London—Shrewsbury	4081 *Warwick Castle*	4097 *Kenilworth Castle*
Shrewsbury—Birkenhead	2952 *Twineham Court*	2948 *Stackpole Court*
Overall average speed, including stops: m.p.h.	53.7	55.9

VIII

A Partial Recovery

From consideration of individual items of equipment and working it is now necessary to turn again to the affairs of the Company as a whole. As might be expected, the year 1926 was a bad one financially, with the General Strike in May, and the prolongation of the coal strike practically down to the end of the year. During 1926 the Company carried 21 million fewer passengers than in 1925, while the coal traffic receipts were down by £2,300,000, or 36 per cent. as compared with 1925. Faced with this situation the management instituted the most stringent and widespread measures to reduce working expenses, and among other items there was a saving of some 15 million engine miles. But despite everything that was done the balance of income over expenditure allowed for the payment of no more than 3 per cent. dividend on the ordinary stock. Lord Churchill, in presenting the balance sheet to the proprietors at the Annual General meeting held on February 23, 1927, said in conclusion:

> Well, Ladies and Gentlemen, all I can say is that I trust it may never again fall to my lot, nor to any of my successors, to have to submit to you accounts showing such adverse results. The dividend which has been declared on your ordinary stock is sufficient to maintain the full trustee character of our pre-ordinary stocks, and I think I an entitled to emphasise that the results now put before you have only been made possible by the prudence with which your financial affairs have been looked after in past years—a policy which, if I may so, has now been proved to be not only judicious, but wise; and whilst nobody regrets more than I do the hardship which the drastic reduction in the rate of dividend will cause to the very large number of small proprietors in the company, we have the consolation of knowing that it is in the main due to an entirely abnormal state of affairs.

The Great Western, in common with the other three major railway companies of Great Britain was constantly concerned with policy towards road competition, towards rating and valuation, and towards the ever-mounting cost of running the railway—cost of supplies, locomotive fuel and so on, and needless to say, the wage bill. In 1928 two events took place which had a considerable bearing on the welfare of the G.W.R., in common with other railways. In his budget speech of 1928 Mr. Winston Churchill, as he was then, Chancellor of the Exchequer, foreshadowed measures to relieve the burden of local rates, and when the Rating and Valuation (Apportionment) Bill was introduced in the House of Commons in May of that year its provisions included the prospect of some relief to railways. In the Act which received the Royal Assent on August 3, 1928, a sum of £4,000,000 was apportioned to the railways for reduction of the effect of local rates. This relief was to be passed on by the railways in the shape of rebates on their carriage charges in the case of certain selected commodities. It was part of a scheme for assisting the depressed industries, principally iron, coal, steel, and agriculture. The railways themselves would not directly benefit, except that they could reduce rates on certain traffics, and possibly receive additional business on that account. But the larger measure that was promised by Mr. Baldwin's Government, whereby the whole basis on which railways were rated was to be brought up to date was unfortunately crowded out of the Parliament Session of 1928–9; and with the defeat of the Government in the General Election of 1929 it did not materialise at all.

In the year 1928 the Great Western was undoubtedly in a far better position, financially than the other British railways, and the results from 1927 were good enough to justify the payment of a 7 per cent. dividend. But the industry as a whole was suffering from loss of traffic from the effects of road competition, and other adverse factors, and the companies were seeking means of reducing one of the heaviest items of expenditure, the wage bill. The managements of the four main line railways, and the Metropolitan, therefore, in 1928 approached the three railway unions with a proposal to:

1. Eliminate the remaining war bonus for conciliation staff.
2. Cancel enhanced payments, for night duty, Sunday duty, and overtime.
3. Suspend the guaranteed day and week.

Such proposals, which of course amounted to reduction in earnings for very many men, coming only three years after the deadlock in the coal industry which led to the General Strike, opened up some delicate ground. For it was on precisely the same formula, though differing considerably in detail, that the coal owners and the miners had come into such implacable opposition. The railwaymen were being approached, in plain language, to help their industry by taking less money.

As in the negotiations with the unions following the General Strike Sir Felix Pole took a leading part in the long discussions that ensued. He had with him Sir Herbert Walker of the Southern, and Sir Ralph Wedgwood of the L.N.E.R., and they met in conference such prominent trade unionists as J. H. Thomas and C. T. Cramp of the N.U.R.; A. G. Walkden, of the Railway Clerks Association, and John Bromley, of the Associated Society of Locomotive Engineers and Firemen. The negotiations could be described as a model of co-operative and sympathetic action by both sides of a great industry. There was a good deal of hard bargaining, but it was carried out with a definite will to agree. The original proposals of the companies were not adopted, and instead the simple, but very far reaching alternative was agreed upon, that an all-round reduction of wages and salaries to an amount of 2½ per cent. should take place. This would apply to everyone on the railways, from the highest executive officers downwards, and once the terms of the agreement was published it was announced also that all railway directors intended to participate in the scheme and accept a reduction of 2½ per cent. in their fees.

The amicable nature of the agreement attained is underlined by some of the comments of trade union leaders afterwards. Mr. G. N. Barnes, for example, a former General Secretary of the then-Amalgamated Society of Engineers said:

> It is creditable to the men's leaders that they have recognised solid facts, and creditable to their moral courage that they have accepted the implications and recommended the agreement to the men.

Mr. Frank Hodges, formerly General Secretary of the Miners' Federation and a prominent participant in some unhappy industrial disputes prior to the major troubles of 1925–6 said:

> The railwaymen and railway leaders must be complimented on their quick effort to rehabilitate the industry.

Sir Felix Pole was naturally delighted. He said:

> I regard the agreement as highly satisfactory and as demonstrating the true spirit of the co-operation that happily exists between the trade unions representing the railwaymen and the companies.
> Unquestionably, it will be of great assistance to the companies in enabling them to meet the difficulties due to the fall in traffic.

Although the Great Western had not begun to experience the effects of trade depression to the same extent as the other companies were already doing they were to need that spirit of co-operation from the men to the utmost extent in the years that were soon to follow. But in the meantime 1927 had proved a surprisingly good year financially; it had witnessed a remarkable recovery from the heavy setback of 1926. It was found possible to pass a dividend of 7 per cent. on the ordinary shares, but as usual Lord Churchill warned the shareholders, at the Annual General Meeting held on 29th February, 1928, of the growing seriousness of the competition from road transport. He said:

> Ladies and gentlemen, this is neither the time nor place for discoursing on the services which the railway companies have rendered to the country, not only in times of peace but whenever a national emergency had arisen. The need for keeping the network of railway systems in this country up to a high standard of efficiency is obviously so necessary that I need not labour the point. Whatever developments may occur in road transport, I cannot bring myself to believe that that form of transport will ever supersede the railways from a strategic point of view, or as common carriers, and if the country is still to be served efficiently by the railways in these two important respects the railway companies must have just and fair treatment. As I remarked just now, all we ask is to be given common justice; let common justice be given to us so that we may be placed in the same position as other ratepayers, and have the right to meet competition on an equal footing. The zealous watch which hitherto has been kept on the operations of the railway companies should now be directed to the position of their shareholders. The many hundreds of millions of capital which have been sunk into the construction and equipment of our railways have been subscribed by investors attracted by the very modest degree of prosperity which has attended the development of the undertakings. It would be a national calamity if that attraction were diminished, through hesitancy to give railway shareholders fair play.

The excellent financial results justifiably gave the impression that the country as a whole and the Great Western Railway in particular was

57

8 787

777777

through the worst, after the tragedy of 1926. In respect of traffic prospects Lord Churchill said:

> Before I sit down I should just like to allude to the extremely difficult times through which we are still passing. Trade in South Wales, with which our own prosperity is so closely allied, was probably affected more severely than any other district by the long coal dispute in 1926, but it is some consolation to know that in the past year there has been a slow but gradual recovery, and the task of regaining our trade, built up so laboriously in preceding years, has been undertaken with courage and determination. Foreign competition was stimulated by that regrettable dispute, alternative modes of heating, lighting and propulsion were given new impetus, with the result that many markets were lost, and these have had to be, and are being, recovered.
>
> Although the traffic figures for the current year to date are not quite as favourable as last year, this is mainly due to the abnormal conditions which followed the termination of the dispute in the coal industry. I am glad to say, however, that the latest Board of Trade returns indicate a gradual improvement in trade, and if South Wales obtains its normal share I see no reason why we should not look forward to a satisfactory revenue during the current year from both our passenger and goods traffic.
>
> One thing I can say with certainty, and that is, that the will to succeed is the foremost consideration not only with the Board but with the bulk of our staff, and I am confident that they will not be found wanting in playing their part in helping the revival of trade, of which we see such encouraging signs.

That encouraging view was echoed by one of the shareholders, who in the ensuing discussion, said that among the junior stocks on British railways, there was only one safe investment at the present time, and that was 'Great Western ordinary.'

The year 1928 witnessed a diversity of interesting and enterprising developments, and rather than take them in strict chronological order I have grouped them thus:

1. The use of road transport for collection and delivery of goods in rural areas.
2. Branch lines and feeder services.
3. The drive for increased business in South Wales.
4. Main line express passenger developments.

The Great Western was one of the first railways to develop the co-ordination of rail and road transport in rural areas. Although the railway network in the West Country was comprehensive it was, even in the heyday of branch lines, easy to find comparatively wide areas with large villages and scattered farms and residences with no regular and reliable means of transport for goods and parcels to and from the nearest station. In these days when the ownership of motor cars, or estate wagons is a commonplace it is perhaps a little difficult to appreciate how inconvenient rural conditions could be, some 50 years ago. Many years earlier than that, indeed, in the early 1900s the Great Western inaugurated country motor lorry services, between Llandyssul and New Quay, and between Haverfordwest and St. David's to provide accommodation for parcels and goods traffic which was proving too heavy for the roofs of the ordinary railway omnibuses. These facilities were later extended to railheads at Montgomery, St. Clears, Penzance, Helston, and St. Austell, and were outstanding in that the lorries ran to regular daily services, and not as and when traffic offered.

At the time of which I am now writing, when the threat of independent road services was growing ever more serious, the Great Western rapidly increased the number of centres from which road motor transport for goods and parcels was regularly operated. The extent to which the railway strove to fight off local competition is indicated by the growth of the railway operated lorries, since 1925:

Services established up to December 1925	.	. .	8
,, ,, ,, ,, June 1926	.	. . .	12
,, ., ,, ,, December 1926	.	. . .	19
,, ,, ,, ,, June 1927	.	. . .	29
,, ,, ,, ,, December 1927	.	. . .	45

Although primarily intended to feed traffic on to the railway and to develop business in country districts, the rates were fixed so that the operation should earn a small profit in each area. The way in which the new facility was received differed considerably from centre to centre. In many places farmers and shopkeepers were enthusiastic, because the rates charged by G.W.R. lorry were much below those of the local private hauliers; elsewhere there was criticism that the rates were too high. The rail-centres from which the lorry services were run were in many areas quite close together, as in North Wiltshire, where the stations acting as rail-head distributional points in 1928 were Chippenham, Devizes, Lavington, Melksham, Swindon, Warminster, Westbury and Wootton Bassett. Others just over the Wiltshire boundary to the west were Badminton, Frome, and Radstock. Well equipped and well maintained railway lorries greatly improved the speed and efficiency of the collection and distribution of traffic.

During the summer seasons the Great Western management, appreciating that there was everything to be gained by an efficient co-ordination of road and rail services organised some excellent combined rail and road excursions, made particularly attractive for tourists from overseas. One such excursion, run daily from London during the summer embraced a conducted road tour of the Shakespeare country. At this same time the 'Shakespeare Express' ran daily between Paddington and Stratford-upon-Avon; but on the combined tour passengers de-trained at Leamington. They were then taken by coach to Guy's Cliff, Kenilworth, and Warwick, where a halt was made to visit the castle, and have lunch; then the tour continued to Stratford-upon-Avon, with a short extension to Shottery. Participants in the tour were then conveyed back by coach to Leamington to join the up 'Shakespeare Express' for London. It was a very full day's sightseeing, lasting in all 11 hours. It was no less an excellent advertisement for the Great Western Railway, particularly for the American visitors. At that time American railways were renowned neither for their speed nor their smoothness of travel. I found it an amusing and exhilarating experience to tour one's own country in the company of a positive swarm of Transatlantic visitors and their comments on the fast, smooth and punctual running between Paddington and Leamington brought a glow of pride to an Englishman and an ardent supporter of the Great Western.

Another extraordinary enterprise of that period was an organised excursion from Aberystwyth to the top of Plynlimmon. This was an all-road trip, because no one at that time had evidently thought to include the Vale of Rheidol narrow gauge line, to make a combined rail and road trip. The route involved about three miles of rough track, bog and grass with the occasional necessity of fording a pool or stream, and in view of the character of the ground traversed, the steep gradients, and the conditions generally, a six-wheeled coach of Morris design was used. It was fitted with a caterpillar track for use when necessary. Owing to the high winds, and the need for having an unobstructed view all the time the coach body was of the open type. The ascent from Aberystwyth to the summit took about 50 min. and the descent 35 min.

Attention was still being devoted on an extensive scale to the fostering of traffic in local country areas, and each year down to and including 1929 brought long lists of new stations and halts brought into service. In 1929, for example, 25 new halts were opened. The halt had the attraction that it needed no staffing. As originally introduced, before World War I, the function of a halt, or 'halte' as the name was at first spelt, was to work in conjunction with rail motor cars, and the platform lengths were constructed to accommodate no more than three or four bogie coaches. Sometimes halts were built relatively close to existing stations, and for passenger traffic were more convenient than the original fully equipped and staffed installation. A case in point was that of Box Mill Lane, which was only a few minutes' walk from the centre of Box village, whereas Box station proper was situated adjacent to where the Bath Road crossed the railway nearly a mile from the village. In recent times practically all passengers used Mill Lane halt, and with the stopping of six and seven-coach 'Parliamentary' trains it was frequently necessary to draw up twice. But the point for emphasis in this connection is that down to 1930 the Great Western was opening stations, rather than closing them.

In the winter services of 1929, the Great Western, in company with the the L.M.S.R. and the L.N.E.R. introduced third class sleeping cars for the first time. At first the G.W.R. put these new vehicles on to one service only, the popular 9.50 p.m. from Paddington to Penzance, and its corresponding eastbound working, the 8.35 p.m. up from Penzance. These cars were run seven days a week; the only variation on Sundays being the departure time of the up train from Penzance, at 9.50 p.m. instead of the weekday 8.35 p.m. The new Great Western cars, built at Swindon, were 60 ft. long by 9 ft. wide, and had three sleeping, five ordinary and two lavatory compartments. It was intended that the third class cars should be marshalled next to the existing first class sleeping cars run on those trains, so that a single attendant could look after the needs of all passengers. It was evidently thought that the demand for sleeping berths would not be very great since the vehicles were composites, having some ordinary and some sleeping compartments. The latter had four berths, two upper and two lower. The bottom berths were fixed, but the top ones could be tilted up and secured at an angle of 45 degrees, thus providing ample room for four persons to sit on the lower berths for a portion of the journey if they so desired. The charge for a third class sleeping berth was 6s. between any two stations en route. These cars at once proved very popular, and from March 1929 they were provided on the 9.25 p.m. from Paddington to Neyland, and the corresponding up service, and from May 1929 on the midnight service from Paddington to Plymouth and Truro. The further cars built at Swindon for these latter services were the same as the original ones of 1928, having only four-berth sleeping compartments. At the time they were considered to be rather dear at 6s. a berth for the facilities provided.

Despite the enterprising developments made in 1928 it proved a disappointing year, with the dividend down to 5 per cent. on the ordinary stock. In his review of events, at the Annual General Meeting held on 27th February, 1929, Lord Churchill gave his usual masterly summing up of the situation, and in respect of South Wales in particular he said:

The slight improvement in the trade outlook which took place in the early part of the year was not maintained, and as the year wore on it became obvious that we should have to reconcile ourselves to the task of combating the consequences of severe depression in those branches of industry upon which we rely for so much of our traffic, namely, the coal, iron and steel industries.

You will recollect that so far as the Great Western Company was concerned, the principal feature of the grouping brought about by the Railways Act of 1921 was the amalgamation of all the railways and docks in South Wales with the Great Western, and as it is these portions of the undertaking which have suffered most severely by the regrettable conditions existing in the heavy industries, we have naturally felt the burden more acutely than would have been the case if the receipts from coal traffic had not been such a very important constituent of our revenue.

You will appreciate the difficult situation in which we found ourselves when I tell you that whereas the tonnage of exports at our six principal ports in South Wales was approximately thirty-one and a half millions in 1927, the figure for last year dropped to about 29 million seven hundred thousand tons, being a decrease of one million tons, and an aggregate decrease, taking both exports and imports together, of very nearly three million tons, which meant a loss to us of nearly £300,000 in revenue at the docks alone, and in addition to this we also lost revenue on the railways, through the traffic not passing.

The bulk of the loss is represented by coal and coke shipments, which accounted for a decrease of approximately one and a half million tons. To illustrate still further how seriously our revenues were affected by the depression in the coal trade, I may say that whereas the coal exports in South Wales for 1913 aggregated thirty-nine million tons, this figure fell to about twenty-six and a half million last year, and was much less than 1923, the best post-war year, when we shipped nearly thirty-six and a half million tons of coal from the ports.

It was given out officially by the Secretary for Mines in July last that since 1923 no less than 117 pits in Wales, employing 11,800 men, have been notified as abandoned, but it is a consolation to know that some of the other pits temporarily closed have recently been re-opened. Apart from the loss attributable to domestic troubles in the coal industry the output has been very seriously affected by the depression and the supersession of coal by oil. We sincerely hope that some of these causes are only of temporary duration, and the one bright spot that emerges from the set-back which the coal industry has experienced in recent years is that it has led to more extensive research being made into practicability of utilising coal products for other purposes. Moreover, the measures of relief which circumstances have compelled the Government to introduce in aid of the industry, and the steps that the colliery owners are themselves taking for the protection of their own interest, will, I sincerely hope, have beneficial results, and I am glad to say that since the beginning of this year our coal traffic has shown an improvement.

The disappointments in South Wales were certainly not for lack of trying, nor of any slackness of effort as the trade depression gradually deepened over the whole industrial network of the country. The records of the years 1927, 1928 and 1929, show very determined attempts to utilise the various docks for traffic other than export coal, and some interesting developments took place. The equipment of the docks, throughout the coast from Newport to Swansea had all been installed to deal almost exclusively with coal, and indeed the traffic was so great and the congestion at times so severe that there would have been little chance of handling anything else. Since 1926 however various items of equipment had been added, such as the 125-ton floating crane at Cardiff, and new cranes at Roath Dock. Some excellent working was recorded from time to time, particularly in the rapid unloading of incoming cargoes of iron ore. Of the South Wales docks Swansea perhaps suffered least, because there quickly developed a diversity of traffic through the port, as well as a continuing demand for export anthracite. Swansea benefitted as being a port for discharging of oil tankers, and for the export of tin plate.

In 1929 also, there was much discussion on the possibility of Bute Docks, Cardiff, being developed as a Transatlantic liner port, as an alternative to Southampton, Liverpool and London. Ships of the United States Line, of the Canadian Pacific Railway, and of the Cunard line made frequent calls during the summer of that year. But the traffic was largely of a second class nature, including the conveyance of large parties of emigrants from this country, who, sadly affected by the widespread unemployment, were seeking better fortune in Canada and the U.S.A. Nevertheless, the Great Western did all that was possible in co-operating with the shipping companies in handling this traffic, and the special boat trains were run non-stop between Paddington and the dock side.

The continued pressure brought upon the Government of the day to provide legislation that would enable the railways to complete on more level terms with their new-found rivals, the road hauliers, led, in 1929, to the setting up of a Royal Commission on Transport, under the Chairmanship of Sir Arthur Griffith-Boscawen. The terms of reference were:

To consider the problems arising out of the growth of road traffic, and with a view to securing the employment of the available means of transport in Great Britain to the greatest public advantage, to consider and report what measures, if any, should be adopted for their better regulation and control, and, so far as is desirable in the public interest, to promote their co-ordinated working and development.

Already, however, in August 1928 a Great Western Bill to provide for extended powers in road transport had received the Royal Assent, and in consequence discussions were at once opened with private companies operating road services in Devon and Cornwall. As a result the Western National Omnibus Co. Ltd. was formed, with the Great Western Railway, and the former National Omnibus and Transport Co. Ltd. contributing

A Partial Recovery — 83

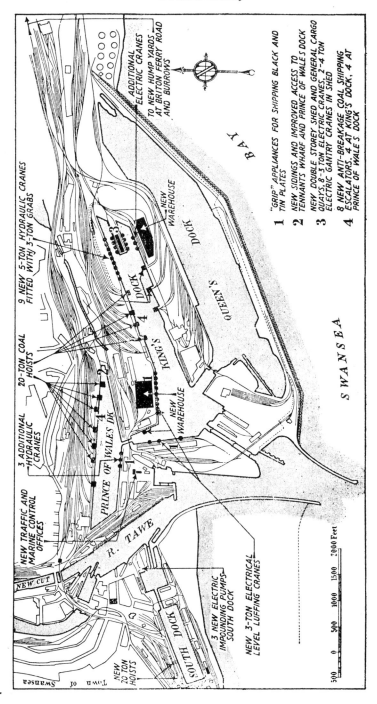

Fig. 8. Swansea docks showing the principal works completed in 1934.

assets or money of the same total value so as to give both an equal interest in the new company with equal representation on the Board. A similar arrangement was made with the South Wales Commercial Motors Ltd. By these arrangements a great deal was done to avoid wasteful competition in the wide areas served.

The year 1929 was notable in the field of express passenger train services for the introduction of all-Pullman expresses, both for the Ocean Liner specials, and of the Torquay Pullman, as referred to in Chapter Seven. But the resounding success of the year, which brought lasting fame to the Great Western Railway and its locomotives, was the acceleration of the Cheltenham Flyer. This development, which provided much the highest start-to-stop average speed that had ever been regularly scheduled on any British railway up to that time, $66\frac{1}{4}$ m.p.h., could be regarded as the last 'throw' of Sir Felix Pole in his sustained endeavour to keep the Great Western ahead of all its rivals. For the accelerated Cheltenham Flyer went into service almost simultaneously with unexpected news of Sir Felix's resignation from the General Managership. It can nevertheless be fairly said that until a relatively short time before it was actually announced nothing was further from his mind than any thoughts of resignation. In answer to what at first seemed to be a chance question from Sir Guy Granet he had, indeed, said that he had never thought of leaving the Great Western, and he never would. It was then however that Sir Guy made the first tentative move towards inviting Sir Felix Pole to take the Chairmanship of Associated Electrical Industries, and eventually he was persuaded to do so. And so, on 6th July, 1929, he retired from the Great Western Railway.

The Great Western Railway, more perhaps than any other of the British main line companies was one in which the character and quality of individual officers far surpassed what could be called the 'terms of reference' of their actual positions. In the twentieth century one thinks immediately of men like Churchward and Inglis, to say nothing of the Chairman himself, Lord Churchill. In this distinguished company Sir Felix Pole was outstanding, and at the time of his resignation 'The Railway Gazette' interpreted this sentiment in the following felicitous appreciation:

The resignation of Sir Felix J. C. Pole from his position as General Manager of the Great Western Railway must be regarded as the close of another chapter in the life of one of the most remarkable men amongst the present generation of railway officers.

From the very early days of his career he was always regarded by his colleagues as having a distinct personality. Like all railwaymen who commence at the bottom of the ladder, he had a pretty stiff fight for position during the first twenty years of his service, but his ability, thoroughness and well-nigh limitless capacity for work marked him down for high office quite early in his career.

His first real step forward was in connection with the Great Western Company's staff arbitration proceedings which followed the setting up in 1908 of the first Railway Conciliation Boards. At this period he held a somewhat minor position on the staff of the General Manager of that day, but to him was entrusted a considerable section of the work in connection with the preparation of the company's case for arbitration. So successful in this task that as a reward he was made head of the Labour Section of the office, and this was followed in February, 1912, by his appointment as Secretary of the Company's side of the new Conciliation Boards.

Plate 19. WOLVERHAMPTON WORKS

General view of new shops

The new erecting shop

Plate 20. DIESEL RAILCARS

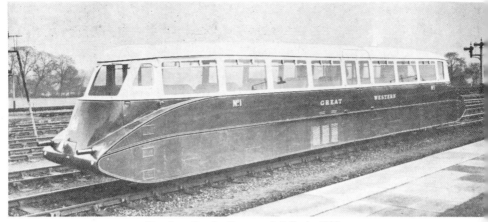

The first diesel railcar, ex A.E.C., in 1933

Railcar No. 19, built A.E.C. 1936

3-car set, with car No. 35 leading and trailer car between two power cars at Reading West

Plate 21. STATION REBUILDINGS

Newton Abbot, looking towards Plymouth

Bristol Temple Meads interior, during platform remodelling

Plate 22. LOCOS OF THE 'THIRTIES'

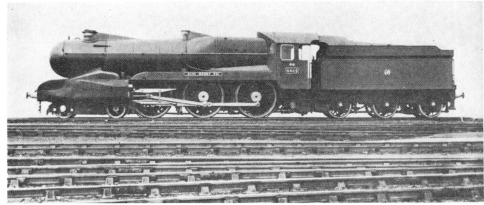

No. 6014 *King Henry VII*, with experimental streamlined fareings (1935)

No. 5005 *Manorbier Castle*, similarly treated (1935)

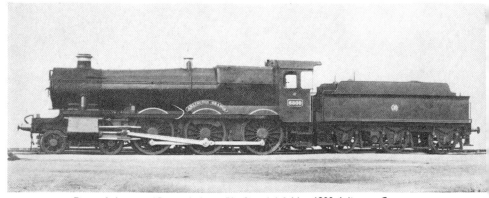

First of the new 'Grange' class; 5ft. 8in. 4-6-0 No. 6800 *Arlington Grange*

In connection with labour matters he soon came to be regarded as a power in the railway world, being closely identified with all the intricate questions of that time. His success in this sphere of railway affairs led to his appointment, in 1913, as Chief Clerk to the General Manager. In this capacity he rendered invaluable assistance during the war, when extraordinary demands had to be met and unexampled difficulties had to be overcome. When Mr. Charles Aldington was appointed General Manager of the company in 1919 there was no question whatever as to who should be his Assistant, and it may be safely stated that there was then no matter connected with the policy or working of the company in which Sir Felix Pole did not play a strong hand. The unfortunate breakdown in the health of Mr. Charles Aldington in 1921 rendered necessary the appointment of another General Manager. By that time so great a factor had Sir Felix become in the affairs of the company that the appointment to the highest executive position a railwayman can achieve—that of General Manager—in July, 1921, occasioned little surprise.

The eight years of his term of office in that position have been productive of many changes in the railway world, but undoubtedly the outstanding problem has been the translation of the terms of the Railways Act, 1921 into actual practice. The intricate negotiations connected with the many amalgamations and absorptions rendered necessary by that comprehensive Act were carried through by Sir Felix with great skill and marked ability. An interesting feature of these negotiations was that alone amongst the four great railway groups created by that Act the Great Western Railway retained, and still retains, its old name and its old traditions.

An example of his remarkable prescience is to be found in his endorsement of the desirability of the use of higher-capacity wagons, a policy which the Great Western Railway has been steadily following since 1923.

Many instances could be quoted of difficulties encountered and conquered during his term of office, but they would only serve to accentuate his remarkable perception of eventualities and his sound judgement and great tact.

The outstanding characteristics of Sir Felix Pole are his infinite capacity for hard work, his unrivalled knowledge of detail, his remarkable memory, and his accessibility to all classes, whether peer or porter, and his careful consideration and courteous treatment of the numerous requests made to him by the staff of the railway.

Finally, he will take into his new sphere the good wishes of the whole of the Great Western staff, and they will watch the next chapter in his career with the keenest possible interest.

While his resignation could definitely be regarded as the close of a chapter in his own life and career, it equally, and most decidedly marked the end of an era on the Great Western Railway. Happily, too, the last year in which Sir Felix was associated with the Company was an exceptionally good one, in which the total receipts from railway and ancilliary business rose by £656,509 over those of 1928 to reach £36,184,053. One of the most important factors contributing to this result was the increase in freight traffic. The tonnages in excess of those carried in 1928 were 1,250,000 in general merchandise, and 5,250,000 in coal. There were very positive signs of a general revival in railway business, though the results on the Great Western were very much better than those being currently achieved by the other main line railways of Great Britain. The shareholders of the G.W.R. had every reason to be very satisfied with their lot, and while it is perhaps invidious to make comparisons, such a comparison is nevertheless justified in order to present the general railway position at the time.

The extension to the luxury-class hotel at St. Ives, the 'Tregenna Castle', carried out in 1929, and the opening of the new Manor House Hotel at Moretonhampstead were both signs of continuing faith in a first class clientele, though in the same year there came the first proposals for closing unremunerative branch lines and certain stations too.

While the departure of Sir Felix Pole closely marked the end of an era in railway prosperity, and of an unceasing drive to sustain Great Western supremacy, in other respects the change in General Managers could have passed almost unnoticed. The succession had been assured and James Milne stepped up into Pole's place with the very minimum of interruption in the command. The organisation in every department of the railway remained completely unchanged, and it continued so until the life of the Company itself was brought to an end by nationalisation of the railways. Amid all the political influences of the present time, when changes in organisation are frequent and those changes seem inevitably to bring disruption of career and disappointment to many men who have given long years of faithful service to railways, one can look back somewhat wistfully to the days of the 1920s and 1930s on the Great Western. The financial position may have given cause frequently for the utmost anxiety and the fight for traffic seemed often to be a losing battle; but the tranquility in management and stability of organisation sustained a very high degree of loyalty to the 'firm', and of pride in the job. In the areas it served it was 'something' to have a job on 'the Western', whether that job happened to be a chargehand in Swindon Works, a porter at a country station, or a chief executive officer. On succeeding Sir Felix Pole, Milne maintained that happy and profitable state of affairs for another 18 years, through the tremendous stresses and strains of the second world war, and through the agonising period of uncertainty and apprehension that intervened between the end of the war, the result of the General Election of 1945, and the vesting date for the nationalisation of the British railways.

RAILWAY DIVIDENDS: PER CENT.

Year	1927	1928	1929
G.W.R. ordinary	7	5	$7\frac{1}{2}$
L.M.S.R. ordinary	$4\frac{3}{4}$	$3\frac{1}{2}$	$4\frac{1}{2}$
L.N.E.R. Preferred ordinary Deferred ordinary	$\frac{3}{8}$ NIL	$\frac{1}{4}$ NIL	3 NIL
Southern Preferred ordinary Deferred ordinary	5 2	5 2	5 $2\frac{1}{2}$

IX

Relief of Unemployment

At the time the Labour Government took office after the General Election of 1929 there were in Great Britain more than a million men out of work. Alleviation of this grave position had been promised in election manifestoes, and Ramsay McDonald's new administration at once began to initiate vigorous action. On Tuesday 16th July, the House of Commons considered in committee the following motion:

That it is expedient . . .

(1) To authorise the Treasury, after consultation with a committee appointed by them, to guarantee at any time within the period of three years from the thirty-first day of August, nineteen hundred and twenty-nine, the payment of the principal of and the interest on any loans to be raised for the purpose of meeting capital expenditure to be incurred under schemes for development, reconstruction, or re-equipment in connection with public utility undertakings in Great Britain carried on under statutory powers by bodies of persons other than local authorities or such statutory bodies as are mentioned in paragraph (3) of this resolution (including loans the proceeds of which may be applied in part towards the payment of interest on the loans during a limited period), and to charge on the Consolidated Fund any moneys required to fulfil any guarantees given under this provision:—

Provided that the aggregate capital amount of the loans so guaranteed shall not exceed such amount as is sufficient to raise the sum of twenty-five million pounds;

(2) To authorise the Treasury, with the concurrence of the appropriate Government department and after consultation with the committee aforesaid, to make at any time within the period aforesaid grants for the purpose of assisting persons carrying on any public utility undertakings as are mentioned in paragraph (1) of this resolution in defraying, during a period not exceeding fifteen years from the raising of the loan, the interest payable on any loan (not being a loan in respect of which a guarantee has been given under the said paragraph (1) to be raised for such purpose as is mentioned in the said paragraph (1)).

J. H. Thomas, as Lord Privy Seal, piloted the motion for the Government, and as a former railwayman he naturally looked to the railways for maximum support in the efforts to relieve unemployment. When the plan was developed in detail it became clear that the railways were providing the solid backbone for the entire edifice. To realise this one had only to try and imagine the programme with the railway schemes left out. As 'The Railway Gazette' commented editorially:

No matter what may be the political complexion of the Government of the day, whether Conservative, Liberal, Labour or Coalition, whenever they find themselves in a practical difficulty, equally in war and in peace, they turn to the railways to help them out, and, be it added, they are never disappointed. Mr. Thomas, who is himself a railwayman, clearly recognised this, and stated in his speech that, so far as the railway companies are concerned, they have never hesitated to respond to the appeals made to them.

In the House of Commons on 16th July nevertheless he was careful to explain how the measure then in consideration could help the railways with their proposals. No railway company, for example, could accept the provisions of paragraph 1, in the motion previously quoted. The borrowing powers of railway companies were limited by their legislation to a certain proportion of their share capital, and in 1929 all of them had exercised those powers up to the limits prescribed. Thomas told the House of Commons that when he discussed it with them they all told him a loan was no good, but paragraph 2 was another matter. By its provisions the Government could guarantee and pay the interest for two, three or four years on the capital expended on a scheme of development, and the railway companies welcomed it. The measure eventually received the Royal Assent, as the Loans and Guarantees (1929) Act, and the Great Western Railway was one of the first to come forward with schemes for authorisation. By the late autumn of 1929 proposals had been made for capital expenditure of £4,500,000 affording direct employment for 200,000 man months. In November the following programme was announced:

1. Paddington Station—Lengthening of platforms and roofing to accommodate longer trains; provision of a commodious depot for handling parcels business away from the passenger station platforms; enlargement of station buildings; development of concourse. Enlargement of Bishop's Road station with longer platforms to facilitate working of suburban traffic.

2. Bristol—Enlargement of Temple Meads passenger station to facilitate the working of traffic to and from the West of England. Quadrupling of the line between Temple Meads station and Portishead Junction. Reconstruction and enlargement of Locomotive Depot. Provision of additional siding accommodation, &c.

3. Cardiff—Enlargement of the General Station, including provision of longer platforms, additional lines, widening of the lines between Newtown and Cardiff Station, 2¼ miles, and thence to Ely Paper Mills.

4. Olton to Rowington Junction—Extension of the quadrupling of 9½ miles of line between Birmingham and Olton to Rowington Junction.

5. Taunton—Quadrupling of the line from the junction of the Bristol and London direct lines at Cogload to Norton Fitzwarren 7 miles, to facilitate the working of traffic to and from Devon and Cornwall, including the reconstruction of Taunton passenger station, the remodelling and enlargement of the Taunton goods station and locomotive depot, &c.

6. Westbury and Frome—Deviation of the railway on a straighter alignment to avoid present restriction of speed, and so improve the working of West of England express trains.

7. Wolverhampton—Reconstruction and modernisation of locomotive repair shops.

8. Wolverhampton—Reconstruction of Herbert Street Goods Depot; provision of a three-floor warehouse, and installation of electrical appliances.

9. Banbury—Construction of an extensive 'gravitation' yard for expediting the transit of freight traffic.

10. Severn Tunnel Junction—Enlargement of freight marshalling yard.

11. Rogerstone—Englargement of freight marshalling yard.

12. Swindon—Modernisation of engine repair shop and spring shops.

13. Paignton—New goods depot and improvement of the passenger station.

14. Bugle to Goonbarrow Junction—Doubling of the line.

15. Scorrier to Redruth—Doubling of the line 2 miles.

16. Cardiff (Cathays)—Provision of new carriage and wagon repair shop. New locomotive depots, engine sheds, &c., at Pantyffynnon, Landore, Cardiff East Dock, Radyr, Duffryn Yard, Port Talbot, Treherbert.

It is interesting to see that nearly all the largest works undertaken at this time were towards the improvement of facilities for handling passenger traffic. It is true that at many of the large centres the track layouts and the station facilities had grown up piece-meal, and various improvised methods of working had grown up over the years to alleviate in some ways the cramped and inadequate conditions that prevailed. It would seem that the major policy dictating the scale of the works undertaken was based on the biggest possible development of passenger traffic, and particularly that to and from the West of England. While the greatest intensity of this traffic was centred upon the summer holiday period the G.W.R. was still endeavouring to attract, by every means possible, an 'all-the-year-round' first class clientele to the holiday resorts of South Devon and Cornwall. While the winter traffic had not been affected to any serious extent by the inconvenience that occurred at stations like Bristol, Taunton, Exeter and Plymouth, and the very poor accommodation available for stabling empty stock at stations on the Torquay line, these inadequacies led to very serious delays when the traffic was at its height; and one had therefore the undesirable situation, that when most people were using the G.W.R. service to the West of England the service itself, and its punctuality were at their worst.

At that time the competition from long-distance road coaches was beginning to become quite considerable. The main roads of this country were, as yet, relatively free from congestion and there was a certain attraction for holiday-makers anxious to spend as little as possible on fares, using road coaches instead of the railways. Even though the scheduled times on the railways were faster, the delays—very often to the principal expresses—were so severe on Saturdays, as to nullify much of the time-table advantage. Furthermore a train that gets held up for 10 or 15 mins. at a time, creates a very bad impression. Passengers who travel only a very few times in the year inevitably get the idea that railway travel is always like this, and consequently many came to prefer road transport at a cheaper rate, even though conditions in the coaches were more confined, and overall speed lower. In view of this, looking at the programme one can be sure that the Great Western Board was making very sound decisions in selecting among its works for the relief of unemployment important schemes that would benefit the working of the holiday traffic at peak periods. At the same time one notes the continued attention being given to the freight traffic of South Wales, in the improvements proposed to the marshalling yards at Rogerstone and Severn Tunnel Junction, and of the many new engine sheds on the former independent railways in South Wales, incorporating Great Western standard practice.

One of the first tasks to be undertaken was the construction of the Westbury and Frome avoiding lines. The original announcement of the work stated that the purpose of these straighter alignments was to provide better running of the West of England express trains. But of course in the elimination of speed restrictions to 30 m.p.h. it was not only time that would be saved. Slowing down, and re-accelerating heavy trains involves an increase in coal consumption, as well as extra wear and tear in the machinery. On the other hand, in 1929, except for the period of the summer service there were only three down and four up expresses running through Westbury without stopping, though no West of England expresses then called at Frome. On the face of it these avoiding lines might have seemed expensive works for the advantages they would prove, though in the case of Westbury the benefits extended to far more than the West of England trains. The station was a veritable railway cross-roads in Wessex, and as the tracks existed in 1929 West of England expresses followed the least favourable alignment of any route passing through. From the traffic point of view the crack express trains to and from the West were always given the utmost priority, and in the course of many runs I cannot recall a single check at Westbury or Frome.

The West of England main line was perhaps the least busy route through Westbury. By far the heaviest flow of traffic was that between Bristol, Bath and Salisbury, including the constant succession of coal trains from South Wales to stations on the Southern Railway. This latter route was indeed chosen as one of the freight train test routes in the Locomotive Interchange Trials of 1948. The diversion of the high-priority, non-stopping express passenger trains, clear of the station and of the busy junctions at the north and south end, avoided the holding up of heavy coal trains to give 'line clear' to through expresses, and additionally improved the working of the passenger service between Bristol, Southampton and Portsmouth. The accompanying plans show the location of the avoiding lines. The four junctions were laid out to permit of unlimited speed over the new lines, while the re-alignment shortened the distance from Paddington to Castle Cary and beyond by 0.2 miles. Travelling in the down direction the Westbury by-pass was entered at Heywood Road Junction, and the old line rejoined at Fairwood Junction just before Westbury troughs were reached. As will be seen from the plan the Westbury by-pass included much curvature; but the Frome line, entered at Clink Road Junction, was practically straight. It ended at Blatchbridge Junction.

One result of the diverting of trains like the Cornish Riviera Express clear of Westbury station was that slip portions providing through carriages to stations on the Weymouth line had to be detached at a point some distance short of Heywood Road Junction, and hauled subsequently into Westbury station by another engine. So far as the working of through express passenger trains were concerned there was a great improvement, not only in the elimination of the speed restrictions themselves but in the avoidance of the need for recovery of speed in the down direction from Westbury up the steep gradient leading to Clink Road. The contract for the work was placed with Messrs. Logan and Hemingway, of Doncaster, in 1930, and it was then estimated that the total cost for the two avoiding lines, providing 4¼ miles of additional double line railway, would be about £220,000. They were brought into service in March 1933. So far as the

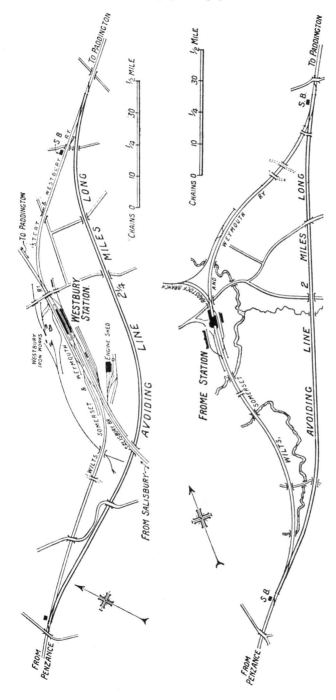

Fig. 9. Plans of the Westbury and Frome avoiding lines as originally announced. As constructed the signal box at the London end of the Westbury cut off was built adjacent to the actual junction and not as shown.

saving time on through runs was concerned, examples of typical running before and after, in both the down and up directions may be quoted as follows:

RUNS THROUGH WESTBURY AND FROME
TIMES BETWEEN EDINGTON AND WITHAM

Direction	Before by-passes were built	After by-passes were built
	m. s.	m. s.
Down	18 25	15 15
Up	17 55	14 50

The distance by the old route is 15.2 miles, and by the new, 15.0. In round figures there was a saving of roughly 3 min. in each direction with average speeds over this distance increased from 49½ to 59½ m.p.h. in the down direction, and from 51 to 61 m.p.h. in the up. This was thus a very worthwhile improvement in the running of through express trains alone, quite apart from the improved operation of cross-country made possible at Westbury.

The next big scheme to be authorised was that centred upon Taunton. The main objective was the removal of the 'bottleneck' that existed between Cogload Junction and Norton Fitzwarren, a distance of 7½ miles. Short though this length was, it actually constituted the key to the West of England. At Cogload traffic from London on the one hand, and Bristol on the other funnelled into a double line section, while at Taunton itself there were only two through passenger running lines through an old-style 'broadgauge' station with an all-over roof. Through the 'key' section had to pass the whole of the Great Western passenger and freight services to and from London, Bristol, Swansea, Birmingham, Birkenhead, Bradford, the North and Aberdeen. Taunton itself was the junction from which radiated the branches to Minehead, Ilfracombe and Chard, and in the confines of the old, out-dated station, with its two main and eight bay platforms there was always a heavy interchange of passengers and freight between local and through trains. On summer Saturdays congestion was intense, though some relief was provided—albeit by a very slow and restricted route—by diverting non-stopping passenger trains via the through goods lines to the south of the station.

In the summer of 1930 a contract was placed with Messrs. Scott and Middleton Ltd., of London, for the quadrupling of the line. This involved

Fig. 10. Map showing the extent of the installation of Automatic Train Control in 1930.

Existing
372 track miles

New
1758 track miles

the construction or reconstruction of 16 bridges, numerous culverts and the removal of some 140,000 cu. yd. of earthworks. One of the most important features of the work was the complete reconstruction of Cogload Junction to avoid a surface crossing between the up London and the down Bristol lines, by provision of a 'fly-over'. Between Cogload and Taunton the four new roads, reading from left to right looking towards the west became: Down Bristol; Down London; Up London; Up Bristol. At Cogload Junction however a system of crossover roads enabled trains to be switched from one to the other, as required. Taunton station itself required almost complete rebuilding, to consist of four main line through platforms, three of which were to be 1200 ft. long, and the longest 1400 ft. Only the old down through platform remained virtually unchanged, though it was considerably lengthened. Norton Fitzwarren station, the actual junction point for the Minehead and Barnstaple branches was to be completely rebuilt with four platforms instead of two. The total cost of this excellent scheme of railway improvement was in the region of £360,000.

Viewed in the light of modern railway traffic control methods this reconstructed layout between Cogload and Norton Fitzwarren would seem ideal for the installation of a central signal box, with remote control systems for the outlying junctions so that the entire area and its traffic would be depicted upon a single illuminated diagram. Such projects were then being actively studied and developed elsewhere in Great Britain even at that early date; but the Great Western remained faithful to its traditional signalling methods and the whole of the reconstructed line between Cogload and Norton Fitzwarren was signalled mechanically with standard block working arrangements from box to box. The majority of the distant signal arms were electrically operated, and the very effective Great Western arrangements of track circuit locking, and interlocking of the signal controls with the block circuits were included. In the distance between Cogload and Norton Fitzwarren no fewer than seven signal boxes were concerned in the main line working, namely Cogload, Creech Junction, Taunton East Junction, Taunton Station West, Taunton West Junction, Silkmill Crossing, and Norton Fitzwarren.

A very important development associated with standard signalling practice, but not enumerated among the schemes specifically undertaken for the relief of unemployment, was the decision to extend the installation of Automatic Train Control to cover practically all fast running main lines on the entire system. In 1930 the total mileage equipped was 372, and 334 locomotives were fitted. It extended only from Paddington to Swindon; from Old Oak Common to High Wycombe; from Didcot to Oxford, and on the two branches where much of the original experimental work was done, namely from Twyford to Henley-on-Thames, and from Oxford to Fairford. But experience on the fast running main line had enabled the system to be virtually perfected, and in 1930 the Board authorised the

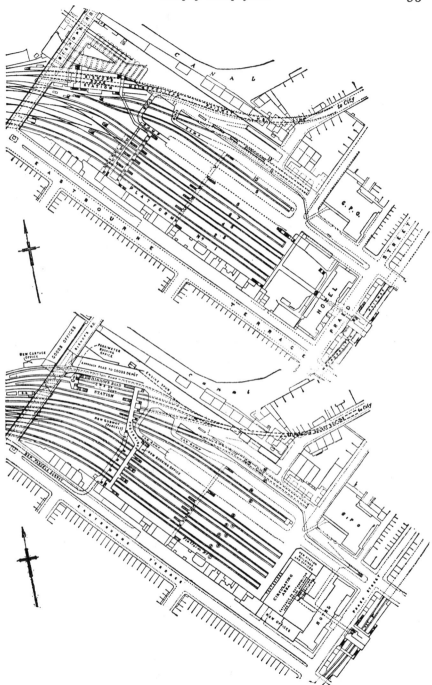

Fig. 11. Plans of Paddington Station before (above) and after (below) modernisation

equipment of a further 1758 miles of track, and 200 locomotives, at a cost of £208,000. The lines to be equipped under the 1930 authorisation were:

(a) Swindon to Plymouth, Weymouth and Swansea,
(b) Oxford to Wolverhampton, via Worcester,
(c) High Wycombe to Wolverhampton via Bicester,
(d) Worcester to Hereford and Newport,
(e) Birmingham to Gloucester (via Stratford-upon-Avon),
(f) Swindon to Gloucester and Newport.

The full extent of this installation will be appreciated from the accompanying map. This work, taken in conjunction with the various elaborations upon the basic block system used, still further enhanced the safeguards in train operation that undoubtedly assisted in maintaining the very high reputation for safety enjoyed by the G.W.R., despite the fact that its express train services were, taken all round, the fastest in Great Britain at the time.

The station reconstructions at Paddington, Bristol Temple Meads and at Cardiff all involved very large works. At Paddington, although the number of platforms in the main part of the station was not increased the majority were greatly improved. For example, in the old station the area between the buffer stops and the Great Western Royal Hotel—always known as 'The Lawn', was used for parcel traffic. Business had greatly extended beyond what could be comfortably handled in that area, and in any case there was very limited space for passenger circulation around the platform ends. There had existed however, beyond the main line departure platform No. 1, the old 'A' platform, used for excursion trains, and its platform line formed a berth for incoming trains of empty stock for platforms 1 and 2. It was a very long platform extending to beyond Westbourne Bridge, and being open to the public formed a favourite promenade for railway enthusiasts, for observation, and for photographing the departing trains—all of which, main line express, and suburban alike left on the one down running line. At that time Bishops Road station was concerned only with trains to and from the Metropolitan, some which worked between Great Western suburban stations and the City, changing from steam to electric traction at Bishops Road.

Reverting to platform A, in the scheme of modernisation this was converting for handling parcels traffic, together with provision for efficient depots for receipts of parcels and ample arrangements for cartage. This change involved the closing of the platform to the public, and from the time of completion of this scheme the platform line always seemed to be occupied, so that its old rôle, as a grandstand for train-watching enthusiasts would have been ended in any case. But the removal of parcel traffic from The Lawn enabled that area to be re-constructed as a spacious and handsomely-styled circulating area for passengers, and with the provision of new office buildings, with refreshment rooms and other offices, the dingy area at the head of the platforms was transformed into a dignified concourse that befitted the historic position of Paddington as one of the oldest and greatest of the London terminal stations. All the main line platforms, except No. 1, were lengthened, so that their outward ends extended at least to Bishops Road bridge, and the track layout on the approach lines was modified to suit. At the same time Bishops Road station was completely rebuilt so as to provide a terminal point for Great Western suburban trains as well as through platforms for trains to and from the Metropolitan line. This provided easy interchange between electric trains on the Hammersmith and City line and steam hauled suburban trains of the G.W.R.

The alterations at Bishops Road involved the building of new goods and cab approaches, and these were works of considerable engineering magnitude. The old tunnel leading to the Metropolitan had to be demolished for part of its length, to provide the necessary widening for four platform roads, and the enlarged entrance was built in the form of a covered way. This reconstruction involved the installation of what was then the heaviest plate girder in Great Britain, having a length of 133 ft. and weighing 126 tons. It supports an area of 4502 sq. ft. of the goods and cab approaches, and made possible a clear space underneath for the much enlarged Bishops Road station. With the reconstruction however, the name 'Bishops Road' was discontinued, and the four platforms in the new arrangement were designated Nos. 13 to 16, in Paddington station proper. Included with these very intensive reconstructions in Paddington station and its approaches was complete resignalling with power-worked points, and colour light signals of the searchlight type. The system of colour light signalling adopted on the G.W.R., not only for Paddington but for the equally large reconstructions at Bristol and Cardiff is discussed later.

The station reconstruction works at Temple Meads and Cardiff General involved in both cases the provision of extra platforms and improved running facilities. At Bristol in particular, all the platforms dealing with West of England traffic had previously been accommodated under the all-over roof, and to provide running lines in some small way commensurate with the traffic some of the platforms themselves were very narrow. The addition of many new platforms outside the original confines of the station enabled excellent circulating space to be provided, and the main platforms under the old roof were widened, and equipped with rebuilt offices and facilities appropriate to the station which was frequently referred to as the 'hub' of the entire Great Western Railway. At Cardiff the work not only involved track remodelling to facilitate interchange working between main line trains and those running on the former Taff Vale and Barry lines, but complete rebuilding of the long-outdated station buildings and frontage.

Turning now to the new signalling works, the Great Western Railway was one of the first in Great Britain to experiment with signals showing more than two aspects, and for many years the advanced starting signal on the down departure line at Paddington was a three-position electrically-operated semaphore showing the indications that at one time were very

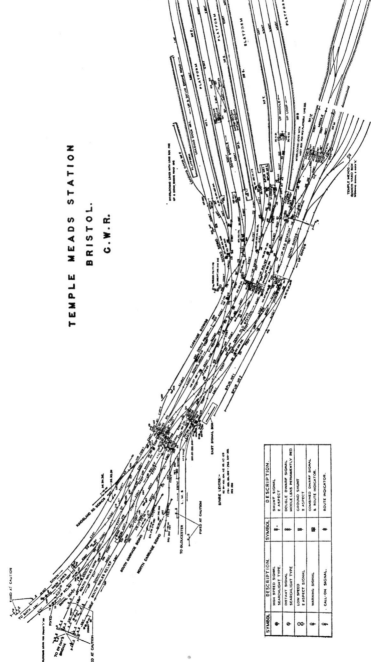

Fig. 12. Bristol Temple Meads. New layout and signalling, east end.

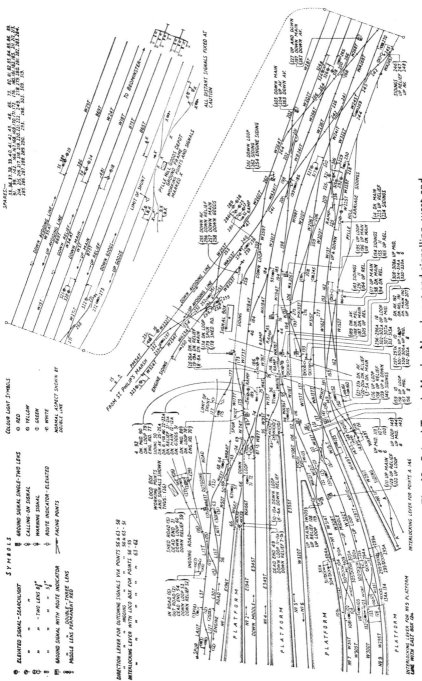

Fig. 13. Bristol Temple Meads. New layout and signalling, west end.

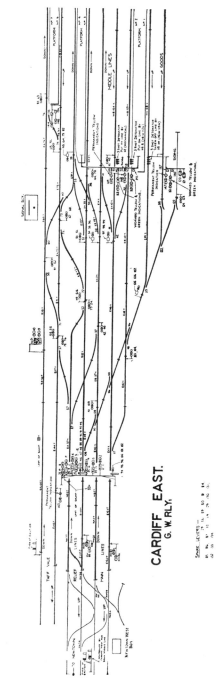

Fig. 14. Cardiff general reconstruction.

Plate 23. MODERN SIGNAL BOXES

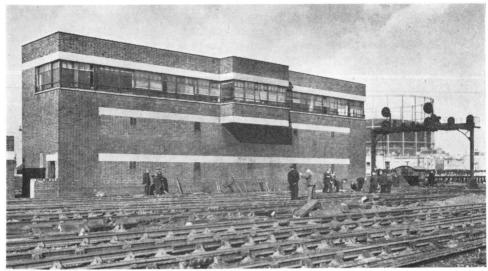

The new power box at Bristol Temple Meads East

Typical mechanical apparatus Reading West Main Box

Plate 24. THE TREND IN STATION ARCHITECTURE

The facade at Newport (Mon.)

Leamington Spa completed 1939

Plate 25. TANK ENGINE VARIETY

Vale of Rheidol, new design built at Swindon 1923

Vale of Rheidol Narrow Gauge 2-6-2 tank original type

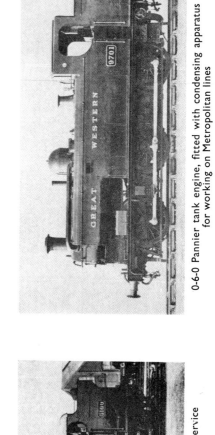

0-6-0 Pannier tank engine, fitted with condensing apparatus for working on Metropolitan lines

Standard 2-6-2 passenger tank for fast suburban service '51xx' class

Plate 26

Caerphilly Works: scene in heavy machine shop

Wolverhampton Works: stamp shop, with heat treatment furnaces

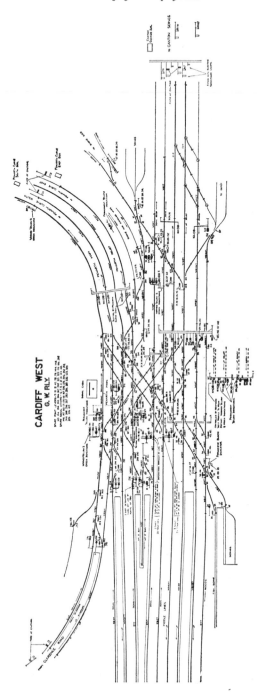

Fig. 15. Cardiff general reconstruction.

popular on the railways of the U.S.A., namely the arm horizontal for 'Stop'; inclined upwards at 45 degrees for 'Caution', and vertically upwards for 'Clear'. This type of signalling was also installed on the electrified Ealing and Shepherd's Bush line, over which 'tube' trains of the Central London Railway operated. Between the commissioning of this latter installation and the time when the rebuilding of Paddington, Bristol Temple Meads, and Cardiff stations were authorised, an established code of colour light signalling had firmly taken root in this country, and installations using not only three, but four aspects had been made on the London Midland and Scottish, and on the Southern Railways. In addition, extensive installations of three-indication signals were in course of construction on the London and North Eastern Railway. There was general agreement that where multi-aspect signalling was installed, with the use of signals displaying more than two indications, there should be a complete break with traditional semaphore practice, and the spacing of the signals according to the traditional location of block posts along the line should be superseded by location of signals at intervals to suit the running of the trains, rather than located in relation to physical features of the route.

On the Great Western Railway, however, the principle of multi-aspect signalling had not been accepted by the early 1930s. It was considered that the existing principles of manual block, with the special Great Western refinements, coupled with the use of A.T.C., still provided everything that was needed for safe and efficient working of the traffic. Great store was set upon maintaining the tradition of personal responsibility vested in all grades of the railway service who were concerned with the running of the trains, and it was felt that this could best be maintained by continuance, with all modern adjuncts, of manual block working. At the same time the Great Western had also been a pioneer in the use of power signalling, and when the extensive rebuilding of the three large stations was decided upon, and very extensive track alterations were also required it was no more than logical to enhance the equipment of those stations by using power signalling of the latest type. In several respects however, the installations carried out at Paddington, Bristol and Cardiff stood completely apart from the general trend of signal development that was taking place both in this country and overseas.

It was considered that there was no case for changing the basic signal aspects displayed to the drivers of trains; and although colour light signalling was to be used, the system worked out was unique in that the new signals displayed precisely the same indications that would have been seen from semaphore signals at night: in other words, the practice of using 'stop' and 'distant' signals was continued, with the 'stop' signals displaying appropriately red or green, and the 'distant' signals green or amber. The new signals were of the so-called searchlight type, and in many cases two of these units were mounted on a single mast to provide the indications of a semaphore slotted 'home and distant' assembly. As a result, Great Western drivers working into the areas of colour light signalling had no new code of aspects to learn. They saw by day exactly the same aspects that they were familiar with at night in semaphore territory; and in the extension of colour light signalling on the main line as far west as Southall exactly the same practice was used. At each interlocking there would be distant, home and starting signals just as in semaphore territory.

While power signalling with complete track circuiting on all lines concerned was used to facilitate control, and to provide the additional safeguard of track circuit locking, the overall method of operation remained traditionally manual. Normal block working was used at all the new power boxes, with miniature block instruments specially designed to be accommodated on the new interlocking frames. The number of actual signal boxes, particulary in the large layouts at Bristol and Cardiff was notably reduced, but this in its train brought certain complications, and one had the extreme case of Temple Meads East Box, which contained no less than 23 different bells, each differing in tone slightly from the rest, to accommodate the block working on the numerous approach lines to the station from the eastern side. In passing, however, I must add that on my visits to this particular box, and in talking to the signalmen on duty there, I formed the impression that experience taught these men quite readily to distinguish, by ear, the various block bells concerned and to turn without the slightest hesitation to the instrument concerned in response to a ring on one of the bells. The magnitude of the installations concerned with some locking frames of more than 300 levers can well be appreciated; but in connection with the block working it must be added that although there were two large power signal boxes at each end of Temple Meads station there was, nevertheless, block working between these two boxes.

The signalling principles adopted in all these installations was the same, but the work was divided between different contractors, and in consequence, the actual interlocking machines differed. At Paddington, and its approaches, and at Bristol Temple Meads, the locking frames were of the General Railway Signal Company type, with pull-out slides instead of orthodox levers, and incorporating the principles of 'dynamic indication'. With power signalling in the ordinary way the lever cannot be pulled to its fullest extent of its stroke, and the interlocking released thereby, until there is confirmation, by means of the electric detection, that the function operated, either the clearing of a signal, or the movement of a pair of points has actually been completed, the facing point lock must be proved correctly inserted. With the orthodox type of lever frame, completion of the stroke is delayed at the check lock position until this indication is received. In the G.R.S. frame, however, the signalman himself did not have to wait to pull the lever for the last fraction of the stroke himself. Once the indication was received, a small solenoid moved the lever to the completion of the stroke. In contrast to these G.R.S. type frames, at Cardiff, the large new power signal boxes were equipped with the Westinghouse type of miniature lever frame with electric interlocking between the levers.

X

Weathering the Storm

The great economic slump, which was becoming world wide, struck the Great Western badly in 1931. The effects, even so, were not so severe as they might have been because prudent and farsighted management had some time previously initiated many measures of economy, and the reduction in working expenses had been a notable feature of successive annual reports. During 1930, for example, the gross expenditure on railway and ancillary businesses, amounting to £28,226,477, showed a reduction of no less than £982,314 on that of the previous year, and this reduction was more than 50 per cent. of the reduction in the gross revenue. The serious falling off in traffic receipts made a reduction in the dividend inevitable; but it was remarkable in a year of such deepening depression that the results were such as to justify payment of 5½ per cent. on the ordinary shares. So far as actual measures of economy were concerned, the profitability or otherwise of many branch and secondary lines had been under close scrutiny for the past two or three years, together with the traffic at a number of intermediate stations. By the end of 1930 these studies had resulted in the closing entirely of 26 stations and halts, while a further 60 stations had been closed to passenger traffic. No time was wasted in deciding the fate of certain experimental innovations. The trial of Pullman cars, both on the Ocean specials from Plymouth, and in the all-Pullman service to the Torquay line proved a failure, and all the Pullman cars were withdrawn from Great Western routes as from September 1930.

Despite the severe recession in all kinds of traffic considerable enterprise continued to be displayed in the provision of new facilities. Reference has been made in earlier chapters to the use of 20-ton coal wagons in South Wales. In 1931 two new types of 20-ton wagon were introduced. One redeeming feature of the freight business in South Wales was the tin-plate trade in the Swansea district, and to effect economies in transport of local short hauls of iron a new series of 20-ton wagons was introduced. These set a problem in design, as it was desirable that they should not exceed the length of the standard 12-ton wagons, and thus be accommodated in sidings, turntables, loading banks, gantries, and curves at the works at the various firms concerned, The new wagons were similar in appearance to ordinary open wagons, and had wooden bodies with steel underframes. To protect the inside of the body at the ends, plates 1 ft. 6 in. deep and ½ in. thick were fitted into the end sheeting for the full width of the wagon.

The second type of 20-ton van introduced in 1930 was a high-capacity covered vehicle for general merchandise. This was an interesting design, in that it was a four-wheeler having the exceptional length, for a British railway, of 33 ft. over buffers. Long-wheelbase four-wheelers had been popular on the Continent of Europe for many years previously, and the bulk of the fast freight traffic of today is still so conveyed; but on the Great Western, as elsewhere in Great Britain, smaller vehicles had been favoured, as being more suitable to the small consignments characteristic of British railway goods business. The new 20-tonners, of which 100 were built at Swindon in 1930, were allocated to work mainly on sections of the line where the traffic passing daily was such as to justify the use of wagons larger than the standard size. The new wagons which had a cubic capacity of 1640 cu. ft. were given the code name 'Mink G'; they had a tare weight of $10\frac{3}{4}$ tons, and the wheelbase was 19 ft. 6 in. They were fitted with the vacuum brake, but instead of having screw couplings they had three-link couplings of which the centre one was of the 'Instanter' type. This was so proportioned as to permit of a buffer-to-buffer coupling-up to be rapidly made when marshalling, and to avoid the clashing of buffers when a train is decelerating, and coupling snatches when accelerating.

The year 1930 was also marked by the retirement of the Chief Goods Manager of the Company, Mr. Elias Ford, after a railway career of 45 years. He had joined the Great Western at Plymouth, in 1886, and at the early age of 20 years he was attached to the Chief Goods Manager's office at Paddington to work on matters affecting goods traffic in connection with the forthcoming abolition of the broad gauge in the West of England. In various subsequent appointments he gained an intimate experience of railway working in South Wales, where so much of the most remunerative of the Great Western freight traffic used to originate; and in 1924 he was appointed Chief Goods Manager. He was succeeded by Mr. Alexander Maynard, all of whose earlier experience had been obtained outside railway service. Until the age of 27 he had been entirely engaged in shipping and Continental trade; but in the year 1909 he was appointed G.W.R. Agent at Nantes. Two years later he was transferred to Paddington to take charge of the Company's Continental Department. From that time onwards he was closely associated with many important developments in freight traffic, and when Mr. Ford was appointed Chief Goods Manager in 1924, Mr. Maynard was appointed Assistant Chief Goods Manager and Development Agent. His activities were prominently associated with overseas business, and a notable phase of his work was in 1925 when he was responsible for re-organising the Company's representation in Canada and in the U.S.A.

As might be expected the results from the year 1931 showed a serious worsening of the traffic position. As compared with 1930 the percentage reduction in traffic receipts from the various classes of business were:

Passengers	9.22 per cent.
Ordinary merchandise	7.22 „

Minerals and heavy merchandise   12.85 per cent
Coal and coke   11.75   ,,
Livestock   13.36   ,,
Docks receipts   17.56   ,,

Taking the receipts as a whole, the average worked out at 9.34 per cent. This result reflected the unprecedented depression in the trade of the country during the whole year, but as if this were not enough there was a coal strike in South Wales in January which in itself caused a loss in revenue to the G.W.R. of about £180,000. The decline in receipts was to a remarkable extent offset however by a decrease of no less than £2,173,493 in gross expenditure on railway and ancillary businesses, and this amounted to no less than 68 per cent. of the fall in revenue.

In his speech at the Annual General Meeting of the Company on 24th February, 1932, Lord Churchill said, in respect particularly of heavy traffics:

The total decrease in our gross receipts since 1929 is £5,000,000 in round figures, of which approximately one-half is accounted for by the decrease in our revenue from coal, mineral and heavy merchandise traffic, and the higher classes of merchandise traffic.

The total quantity of coal shipped from our South Wales docks has fallen from 30,000,000 tons in 1929 to 22,000,000 tons last year, a decrease of 8,000,000 tons or 26 per cent., and apart from an increase which we anticipate in our exports of anthracite to Canada, I am afraid we cannot expect any substantial improvement in our coal shipments until conditions abroad become more stabilised. At present nearly every country in the world is endeavouring to curtail its exports, and although the depreciation of sterling was expected to assist British coal sales in certain foreign markets, particularly in France and Italy, little benefit has yet been experienced owing to the increased tariffs and other restrictive measures which have been imposed by the countries in question. The French Government have recently intimated that the 15 per cent. surtax on British coal is to be withdrawn, but under the quota system we are still only entitled to export to that country 64 per cent. of the average of the years 1928, 1929 and 1930. If (as is hoped) this quota is increased before long, it will be of material advantage to South Wales.

The plight of the iron and steel industry, to which I referred last year, has become even worse. The imports of foreign iron and steel at our South Wales ports have increased from 721,000 tons in 1929 to 887,000 tons last year, an increase of 166,000 tons, or 23 per cent., whereas our exports of iron and steel have declined by 306,000 tons or 52 per cent., and our exports of tin plate by 166,000 tons, or 28 per cent. It is estimated that for every ton of manufactured iron and steel the railways carry at least 6 or 7 tons of constituents in the shape of coal, iron ore, limestone &c. This decrease therefore represents a loss of nearly 3,000,000 tons of railway traffic based on the 1929 export figures, and in addition there is a further loss of passenger traffic attributable to the unemployment resulting from this loss of trade.

Nevertheless, despite these very abnormal conditions it was still found possible to pay a dividend of 3 per cent. on the ordinary shares, and by so doing the Great Western remained the only one of the four amalgamated companies whose stocks retained full trustee status in both England and Scotland. The financial position remained strong, and future prospects had been improved by the replacement of the Labour administration in the autumn of 1931 by a National Government, under the Premiership of Ramsay McDonald. Although at the time of the Great Western meeting in February 1932, little in the way of tangible results could be discerned from the urgent measures the new Government was taking to revive trade

Lord Churchill emphasised to the shareholders the fact that the Great Western had never been better equipped to deal with increases in traffic. A source of much pride and gratification, in what was otherwise a melancholy year, was the acceleration of the Cheltenham Flyer to a 67-min. run from Swindon to Paddington, thus regaining for the Great Western, and Britain, the distinction of making the world's fastest daily start-to-stop run. That the timing of 67 min. was very far below the utmost that engines of the 'Castle' class could achieve was shown by the running of this train on the first three days of the accelerated service when the overall times for the 77.3 miles from Swindon to Paddington were successively 59½, 58½, and 58¼ min. in each case with engine No. 5000 *Launceston Castle*.

The Annual General Meeting of February 1932 was notable for the first official mention that the directors were considering alternatives to steam traction. Under the heading: 'Electrification and the Diesel Engine' Lord Churchill said:

First, as regards railway electrification, you will no doubt recollect that the Weir Committee reported to the Minister of Transport in March, 1931, on the question of main line electrification. The Committee made no recommendation, but it was quite clear from their report that the heavy expenditure involved could not be justified on commercial grounds, and I need hardly add that we have no intention of embarking upon a project which at best could only be regarded as a highly speculative venture. The question of electrifying particular sections of our line has been investigated on more than one occasion during recent years, but in all cases the probable financial return was considered inadequate to justify the capital expenditure involved. There is no doubt that the electrification of suburban lines where there is a dense traffic is an attractive proposition, but until the position in regard to road competition becomes more stabilised, it is not possible to forecast the probable results of any electrification scheme.

As a possible alternative to electrification we are keeping in close touch with developments now taking place in regard to Diesel and Diesel-Electric locomotives. At the present time the initial cost of these types of locomotives is very high indeed compared with that of steam locomotives, and we are not satisfied that sufficient economy in the cost of maintenance and operation can be secured to warrant our purchase of either Diesel locomotives or railcars.

The Great Western was indeed one of the first English companies to consider diesel traction, and some very interesting developments were to follow in a year's time.

The outstanding developments of the year 1932 however was not on rails at all. In 1929 the four main line railway companies obtained Parliamentary powers enabling them to operate air services, but an announcement by the Great Western Railway of its intention to commence an air service on 12th April, 1931 was the first step taken by any of the groups to exercise those air powers. The service was arranged to operate between the municipal aerodrome at Cardiff and Haldon aerodrome, to serve Teignmouth and Torquay. It was operated by the Great Western Railway in conjunction with Imperial Airways Limited, which latter provided a three-engined six-seater Westland Wessex plane, together with the pilot and the necessary ground staff. The plane was painted appropriately in the railway coaching stock colours of chocolate and cream, and the interior *décor* of the saloon was similar to that of a standard first class railway carriage. At the start it was planned to run two trips daily, at a single fare of £3 and a return fare of £5. The route chosen for the service was extremely suitable for the experiment, as it was possible for the plane to cross the Bristol Channel and perform the journey in about 50 minutes as compared with nearly four hours for the 140 miles by train, due to the necessity for travelling via the Severn Tunnel and Bristol. The service gave direct connection between a thickly populated industrial area and one of the most popular holiday coasts in the country. The terminal services were performed by the railway company by means of motor omnibuses, and passengers were given the additional facility of having their heavy baggage collected, conveyed by rail, and delivered at destination without any extra charge.

The service was successfully inaugurated through to Plymouth and in view of its historic nature the full timetable and fares are quoted as follows:

		First Service		Second Service	
		a.m.	a.m.	p.m.	p.m.
Cardiff General Station ..	dep. by 'Bus	9.00	—	1.30	—
Cardiff Air Port	arr. by 'Bus	9.10	—	1.40	—
Cardiff Air Port	dep. by 'Plane	—	9.15	—	1.45
Haldon Aerodrome ..	arr. by 'Plane	—	10.05	—	2.35
Haldon Aerodrome ..	dep. by 'Plane	—	10.10	—	2.40
Roborough Aerodrome ..	arr. by 'Plane	—	10.35	—	3.05
Plymouth North Road Station	arr. by 'Bus	10.55	—	3.25	—

		a.m.	a.m.	a.m.	p.m.
Plymouth North Road Station	dep. by 'Bus	11.00	—	3.30	—
Roborough Aerodrome ..	arr. by 'Bus	11.20	—	3.50	—
Roborough Aerodrome ..	dep. by 'Plane	—	11.25	—	3.55
Haldon Aerodrome ..	arr. by 'Plane	—	11.50	—	4.20
			noon		
Haldon Aerodrome ..	dep. by 'Plane	—	12.00	—	4.30
		p.m.	p.m.		
Cardiff Air Port	arr. by 'Plane	—	12.50	—	5.20
Cardiff General Station ..	arr. by 'Bus	1.00	—	5.30	—

There was also a special bus service between Haldon Aerodrome, Teignmouth and Torquay which gave connections each way on all services. The fares charged were as follows:—

	Single £ s. d.			Return £ s. d.		
Cardiff—Teignmouth .. .. Torquay	3	0	0	5	0	0
Cardiff—Plymouth	3	10	0	6	0	0
Plymouth—Torquay .. .. Teignmouth	1	5	0	2	0	0

On 22nd May, 1932, the service was extended to Birmingham, with one flight each way daily, including Sundays. The effect of this development can be seen from the following comparison of distances, journey times and fares:

Journey Time			Fares		
By Rail between Stations	By Air between Aerodromes	Between Birmingham and	By Rail	By Air	
			1st single	single	return
170 mins.	70 mins.	Cardiff	22/6	40/-	75/-
298 ,,	140 ,,	Torquay	39/10	50/-	90/-
320 ,,	170 ,,	Plymouth	45/3	60/-	110/-

The actual timetable, with the bus connections was:

Birmingham Snow Hill station	dep.	9.00 a.m.
CASTLE BROMWICH AERODROME	dep.	9.30 a.m.
Cardiff General station	dep.	10.30 a.m.
CARDIFF AIR PORT	arr.	10.40 a.m.
Cardiff General station	arr.	10.55 a.m.
CARDIFF AIR PORT	dep.	11.00 a.m.
Torquay Vaughan Parade	dep.	10.55 a.m.
Teignmouth enquiry bureau	dep.	11.25 a.m.
HALDON AERODROME	arr.	11.50 a.m.
HALDON AERODROME	dep.	11.55 a.m.
Teignmouth enquiry bureau	arr.	12.10 p.m.
Torquay Vaughan Parade	arr.	12.40 p.m.
ROBOROUGH AERODROME	arr.	12.20 p.m.
Plymouth North Road station	arr.	12.40 p.m.
Plymouth North Road station	dep.	3.30 p.m.
ROBOROUGH AERODROME	dep.	4.00 p.m.
Torquay Vaughan Parade	dep.	3.30 p.m.
Teignmouth enquiry bureau	dep.	4.00 p.m.
HALDON AERODROME	arr.	4.25 p.m.
HALDON AERODROME	dep.	4.30 p.m.
Teignmouth enquiry bureau	arr.	4.45 p.m.
Torquay Vaughan Parade	arr.	5.15 p.m.
Cardiff General station	dep.	5.10 p.m.
CARDIFF AIR PORT	arr.	5.20 p.m.
Cardiff General station	arr.	5.35 p.m.
CARDIFF AIR PORT	dep.	5.40 p.m.
CASTLE BROMWICH AERODROME	arr.	6.40 p.m.
Birmingham Snow Hill station	arr.	7.20 p.m.

The financial results for the year 1932 showed a continuing decline in traffic. The receipts from railway and ancillary business were £28,462,343 as compared with £31,139,630 in 1931; but economy measures had once again been successful, and the effects of the depression were not so serious as they might otherwise have been. Nevertheless the results by themselves were not enough to support a reasonable dividend, and a sum of £1,100,000 was withdrawn from the free reserves. This caused some adverse comment in financial circles, and Lord Churchill referred to it at some length in his speech at the Annual General Meeting on 22nd February, 1933, as follows:

The decision of the Board to recommend the payment of a dividend at the rate of 3 per cent. for the year on the consolidated ordinary stock of the company, I can assure you, was only arrived at after a careful review of the whole position, and it was not governed primarily by the desirability of maintaining the full trustee status of the prior stocks as I notice has been suggested in some quarters.

Prior to the close of the past year, the total of the General Reserve and Contingency Funds was £3,400,000. These are free reserves which were built up for use in abnormal times to be available amongst other purposes for supplementing dividends on the ordinary stock, and to a large extent they represent undistributed profits of previous years or moneys set aside to provide for contingencies which have not eventuated.

The experience of the last two years has certainly been abnormal, and as trade must ultimately revive if the whole world is to go on, I see no reason for any lack of confidence in the future of our undertaking. The Board therefore felt that it would not be right to withhold from the stockholders the benefit of these free reserves in this period of widespread stringency especially as on the return to more prosperous times the proprietors will doubtless be asked again to agree to the resumption of the policy of building up reserves for the future.

In reviewing the position the Board have also taken into consideration many representations made by many proprietors of very limited means whose savings are invested in the company and who have seen the market value of their investment depreciate to a very serious extent in recent years. Many appeals have been received by the Directors to bear in mind the serious position in which a large number of shareholders would be placed in the event of failure on the part of the company to maintain the same rate of dividend as was paid last year, and I am sure you will agree that they are deserving of sympathy.

Taking all the circumstances into account, therefore, the Directors believe that the course they have adopted is the best one in the interests of the proprietors as a whole. They fully recognise that drawing on free reserves cannot continue indefinitely, but in their opinion it would not be a wise policy to allow the prior stocks to lose their full trustee status just at the very time when there are at last some signs of returning confidence and of a slight, however slight, improvement in trade. The steps taken by the Government to restore the country's credit have been successful, and while many international problems still remain to be solved before any marked recovery in the export trade can be expected, there is little doubt that prospects have improved materially during the last twelve months. The policy which the Directors are recommending will at any rate find favour with those who hold the view that it is in the national interest at the present time to aid those with limited means whose spending power is appreciably affected by a dramatic drop in income, and it is common knowledge, as I have already said, that a large percentage of railway shareholders fall within this category.

I may add that the Board are satisfied that notwithstanding the withdrawal of the sum of £1,100,000 from the free reserves, the financial position of the company remains very strong. Ample resources are available to cover the expenditure on all the new works which the company have in contemplation.

New Year's Day 1933 saw Mr. H. L. Wilkinson taking office as Superintendent of the Line, in succession to Mr. R. H. Nicholls, who had retired. The Great Western was the last of the British Railways to retain the historic title 'Superintendent of the Line', one of the highest and most important executive offices on the railway. Nicholls had filled the post since 1919, when he succeeded Charles Aldington on that gentleman's appointment as General Manager. Nicholls had joined the G.W.R. in 1884, at the age of 16, and from the very outset of his long career he was in the department of which he eventually became the head. He was no different from any other of the long-service officers of the company in that the Great Western Railway was to him the very breath of life. The affection in which he was held was aptly expressed by Lord Churchill at the Annual General Meeting on 22nd February, 1933, when he referred to him as 'our dear old friend.' H. L. Wilkinson, who succeeded him, had already served the Great Western for 42 years when he took office. He came of an old railway family, his father having been Chief Goods Manager from 1896 to 1904. The latter held office at the time of Sir Joseph Wilkinson's General Managership. They were not relations, and to avoid any confusion with his superior officer the Chief Goods Manager took the name of 'Maiden' while in office. H. L. Wilkinson enjoyed no more than a short spell as Superintendent of the Line, because ill-health compelled his retirement in the summer of 1936, when he was succeeded by Mr. F. R. Potter, himself the son of a celebrated Great Western officer, Frank Potter, who was General Manager from 1912 to 1919. These appointments, and the outstanding success with which the officers concerned fulfilled them are important as indicating something of the tradition, and spirit inherent in service with the Great Western Railway.

While tradition continued on the traffic side of the railway the year 1932 had marked the departure of Mr. W. A. Stanier from the post of Principal Assistant to the Chief Mechanical Engineer. The offer that came to him, to become Chief Mechanical Engineer of the London Midland and Scottish Railway, was the highest possible expression of the esteem in which Great Western mechanical engineering practice was held on other railways, and Stanier's outstanding qualities as an engineer combined with his vigorous and charming personality soon had a profound and lasting effect upon L.M.S.R. locomotive practice. It was through Stanier that the precepts of Churchward, particularly in boiler design, were so remarkably demonstrated throughout the length and breadth of the L.M.S.R. system, that the men who became his closest assistants had no hesitation in perpetuating that practice when it came to them to provide locomotives for the nationalised British Railways after 1948. At Swindon itself, as if to sever yet another link with the past, there came in December 1933 the tragic death of Churchward at the age of 77, killed on the line by an express train on a foggy morning. John Auld, formerly of the Barry Railway, was appointed to succeed Stanier as Principal Assistant to the Chief Mechanical Engineer.

The year 1933 saw the first introduction of diesel traction on the G.W.R. in the form of the experimental railcar No. 1. This was a lightweight streamlined vehicle with mechanical transmission, built by A.E.C. Ltd. of Southall. It was put on to local services between Paddington, Slough, Reading, and Didcot, and proved very popular, carrying over 10,300 passengers in the first month's working. In May 1934 its sphere of operation was extended to Oxford, and after three months of service the aggregate number of passengers conveyed had exceeded 40,000. Rail motor cars had always been popular units with the Great Western operating department; but the original steam cars were rather slow, and could not successfully compete in an age when local road transport offered so many attractive alternatives. But the diesel railcar was a very speedy vehicle, and was justly popular on that account. It was powered by a single four-stroke engine of the same type then in regular use on the standard London buses, and developed 130 b.h.p. Its regular duty had involved running 240 miles a day, with 75 stops. Experience with this car was so favourable that as early as February 1934 the G.W.R. decided to order six more, for a totally different class of duty.

On 9th July, 1934, an entirely new service, worked by diesel railcars, was put on between Birmingham and Cardiff, primarily for the use of business men. This was a real express service making intermediate stops only at Gloucester and Newport. The six cars designed and built specially for this service were considerably larger than the No. 1 unit used on local services in the Thames Valley, and powered by two standard A.E.C. 'London bus' engines they had a maximum speed of 75 to 80 m.p.h. Speeds of that order were necessary to maintain the fast schedules, which included running the 60¾ miles between Birmingham Snow Hill, via Stratford-upon-Avon, and Gloucester in 72 min. Seating accommodation was provided for 120 passengers. The cars were third class only, but the accommodation was of a very superior type, and as the tickets issued were limited to the seating capacity of the car every passenger booked was sure of a seat. The accommodation included an attractively styled buffet, which immediately proved very popular.

As the first express diesel railcars in Britain the interior *décor* is worth recalling in full. The passenger saloons were fitted with fixed seats with removable tables between, and the seats and tables were in weathered oak. The former were upholstered with green horsehair, and the panels and pelmets were of light oak covered in gold-brown Rexine. Tubular lights with two bulbs were fitted on the side panels above each seat, and the same type of lamp was also fitted down the centre of the roof, where it was interspersed with ventilators. Sliding ventilators were placed above the windows. Entrance to the car was in the middle through double doors opening into a vestibule which led to the two long centre-gangway saloons.

The timetable inaugurated on 9th July, 1934, was as follows:

WESTBOUND:

Dist. miles			a.m.	p.m.
0	Birmingham	dep.	9.05	3.40
60¾	Gloucester	arr.	10.17	4.52
		dep.	10.19	4.54
105	Newport	arr.	11.10	5.52
116¾	Cardiff	arr.	11.27	6.10

NORTHBOUND:

Dist. miles			a.m.	p.m.
0	Cardiff	dep.	9.10	4.50
11¾	Newport	dep.	9.29	5.06
56	Gloucester	arr.	10.21	5.55
116¾	Birmingham	arr.	11.35	7.15

The times were thus very attractive to business men, providing ample opportunity for a long day's work at either end. In consideration of the speed and amenities offered a very modest supplement of 2s. 6d. over the third class fare was charged for the full journey from Cardiff to Birmingham, or vice-versa. Local passengers were not conveyed on these fast rail car services between Newport and Cardiff.

What proved to be the last year of Lord Churchill's Chairmanship also marked the beginning of the end of the great depression. The anticipation which he expressed regarded the trade outlook, in February 1933, proved to be correct though the tangible signs of improvement did not appear quite so early in the year as had been hoped. Nevertheless there was a welcome increase in receipts during the latter half of the year. Heartened by this the Board decided there was an adequate justification for taking the same course as taken on the results for 1932, and paying a dividend of 3 per cent. on the ordinary stock. Even after the withdrawal of the necessary sum from the contingency fund, the latter still stood at £1,822,057. One of the most disappointing features of the year 1933 was in respect of the dock business. Shipments of coal from the G.W.R. ports in South Wales declined from 29,985,000 tons, in 1929 to 20,249,000 tons in 1933, a decrease of 32 per cent. Compared with 1913—a yardstick year—the decrease was no less than 48 per cent. Although as the result of the Ottawa Agreement shipments of anthracite coal to Canada showed that satisfactory increase of 669,000 tons compared with 1929, the coal shipment to France during the same period declined by 1,920,000 tons, and those to Italy by 1,039,000 tons; to Brazil by 1,016,000 tons; to the Argentine Republic by 921,000 tons; and to Egypt by 776,000 tons. There had also been losses on a similar scale to many other countries. While it was recognised that exports had been adversely affected by the world depression, and by the substitution of fuel oil for coal, there is no doubt that they also suffered severely by the operation of quotas, international trade agreements and currency restrictions, which then, as now, are matters that can only be dealt with by the Government. Incidentally, it was not generally realised that trade agreements favourable to one part of the country many have embarrassing repercussions on other districts. For example, in 1933 certain trade agreements made by the Government with Scandinavian countries, whereby the coal trade of the North East Coast of England had benefitted, adversely affected South Wales by driving Polish coal into Mediterranean markets in competition with Welsh coal. There were, however, certain factors in operation which it was hoped would favourably affect the internal coal consumption in South Wales. For one thing, the iron and steel trade, which is the sister of the coal industry, showed distinct signs of improvement. Great Western transportation of general merchandise and minerals in 1933 was 528,000 tons in excess of the previous year, due largely to the improvement which had taken place in the iron and steel industry. The quantity of pig iron and steel produced in South Wales and Monmouthshire during 1933 was 519,600 tons, or 30 per cent. in excess of 1932; and as each ton of steel produced meant 6 or 7 tons of traffic to the railways it was matter of considerable importance to the G.W.R. that the steel industry should be prosperous. And on that note of guarded optimism the last year in which Lord Churchill was Chairman of the Company drew to a close.

XI

Centenary of the G.W.R.

From the summer of 1925, when the hundredth anniversary of the opening of the Stockton and Darlington Railway was celebrated, several railway centenaries had been observed, with appropriate pageantry, and a welter of speech-making. The Great Western had already participated in three very notable events. Its locomotives and carriages were prominent at *the* Railway Centenary, in 1925: the centenary of *all* public passenger carrying railways, when a great parade was staged at Darlington. It has already been told, in an earlier chapter of this book, how the *King George V* locomotive crossed the Atlantic to take part in another great gathering in celebration of the centenary of the Baltimore and Ohio Railroad. In 1927 indeed the latter was the oldest railway in the world to bear its original name, and when its management decided to celebrate the centenary with a great exhibition and pageant it is easy to appreciate how readily the invitation to participate was taken up on a railway so mindful of its past heritage as the Great Western. The third centenary celebration was that of the Liverpool and Manchester Railway in 1930, to which the Great Western sent one of its latest express locomotives, No. 6029 *King Stephen*.

But as far as Great Britain was concerned the approach of the year 1935 had an added significance. Of all the old railway companies the Great Western was the only one that had not been wound up at the time of grouping, and so the forthcoming centenary was not merely the anniversary of the incorporation of the original railway, it marked a hundred years of corporate life of the one railway company. Centenaries are inevitably a time for reflection and reminiscence, but in the present chapter one needs to do more than suggest to the reader that he turns back through the closely documented pages of 'MacDermot', to get a glimpse of some of the events that had marked the first hundred years of the G.W.R. At the same time, in approaching the time of the centenary one can feel a little sad that some of the greatest men who ever served the old railway were no longer in its ranks. The earlier chapters of the present book will have given some impression of the strength of the great partnership between Lord Churchill and Sir Felix Pole, and of the part they had jointly played in steering the G.W.R. through the immense difficulties of the 1920s. It would have been both delightful and appropriate if both had been able to play a major part in the centenary celebrations; but as told earlier Sir Felix had resigned from railway work in 1929 to go into the City, and here I must record that Lord Churchill died, still in harness, in January 1934.

It is indeed unfortunate that no biography of this remarkable man has ever been written, because his span as Chairman of the company not only extended to nearly 26 years, and covered the times of no fewer than five General Managers, but embraced such times of change, of internal stress, of world war, of grievous industrial unrest, and finally the worst trade depression the world had ever known. His own memories must have been monumental. Could one imagine, for example, a greater difference between the times of Sir James Inglis, and the celebrated feud between him and Churchward, the period of the General strike, so resolutely handled from the Great Western viewpoint by Sir Felix Pole, and the grievous days of the great slump. Lord Churchill had lived through the days when the chief officers looked to him as their 'boss', rather than the General Manager, and when Churchward had openly flouted Pole's wishes, and said 'When my Chairman tells me to do so, I'll do it; but not before.' The succession of General Managers who had served him—Inglis, Potter, Aldington, Pole, and finally James Milne— in the very diversity of their natures show the manner of man Lord Churchill was; for he got the finest out of them all, and constantly moved with the times. When he succeeded Alfred Baldwin as Chairman, in 1908, few could have foreseen the circumstances in which the Great Western was to be involved in the ensuing years; but amid all that befell, each successive crisis seemed to secure Lord Churchill ever more firmly in the saddle at Paddington. Although he was turned 68 years of age when at the Annual General Meeting in 1933 he reviewed for the last time the previous year's working, he was still full of vigour and drive; and despite the serious financial position, which permitted the payment of no larger dividend than 3 per cent. on the ordinary stock, he was, as ever, full of optimism for the future. As recorded in the previous paragraph, he died suddenly on January 3, 1934. He was succeeded as Chairman by Sir Robert Horne, afterwards Viscount Horne, a man of immense stature in business circles, who had been Chancellor of the Exchequer in the first Baldwin Government.

So we come to the year of grace 1935. It was a year of celebration; the first in 38 years in which a Royal Jubilee had been celebrated—the Silver Jubilee of His Majesty King George V. It was certainly fitting in view of the Company's long association with Royalty that the centenary should have fallen in so auspicious a year. The Great Western Railway Bill received the Royal Assent on 31st August, 1835, and 100 years to the day there was great celebration in Bristol where, virtually the Company had its birth. *The Railway Gazette* of 6th September, 1935, happily summed up the general sentiments in one of its leading articles thus:

Among the many pleasant features of the G.W.R. centenary celebration last week-end was the full recognition not only by the participants but also by the press, of the unique nature of the event. Never before in the history of the railways of Great Britain—the birthplace of this means of locomotion—has a main line railway company attained to the dignity of a full hundred years of corporate life. There are, of course, older railways than the G.W.R. but the process of amalgamation (almost as ancient as railways themselves) has always resulted in a loss of identity long before ten decades of life were run. Nor is the G.W.R. record in this respect likely to be challenged within living memory, as the Railways Act of 1921 left only the G.W.R. of all the main line companies to continue operating under the original charter. In its long life under the familiar title the G.W.R. has deservedly gathered a wide circle of friends, and Lord Greenwood expressed this sentiment happily in a letter which Sir Robert Horne quoted at Bristol on Saturday when he said: 'All England seems to have a friendly family feeling for the Great Western'.

The day was a kind of dress rehearsal for the new high-speed 'Bristolian' express, introduced on 9th September, 1935. The London party proceeding to the great celebration Lunch, in the Great Hall of Bristol University, were conveyed in a special express leaving Paddington at 10 a.m. the time fixed for the new high-speed service; and while the down journey was sedately run in nothing faster than two-hours non-stop, the return working was in precisely the path of the new 'flyer'—4.30 p.m. from Temple Meads and 6.15 p.m. arriving in Paddington. On the down journey crowds gathered at the lineside to see the train, and at Swindon it seemed that the entire strength of the works had assembled to give the train a cheer as it ran past. This was very much a family occasion for the Great Western. The guests were principally civic dignitaries of Bristol and the representatives of commercial and industrial interests of Bristol and district. After the Lord Mayor of Bristol had proposed the toast of 'The Great Western Railway Company', Sir Robert Horne replied, and some paragraphs from his speech are worth quoting once again, in full. He said:

The occasion which brings us together here is one which is worthy to stir the memory and to inspire the imagination. The Centenary of one of our great railways, whose span of life is practically coterminous with the invention and development of railway transport in this country, inevitably sets agoing in our minds a certain train of reflections. Who is there amongst us at this moment that can help thinking of the revolution that was caused in commercial and industrial life by adoption, one hundred years ago, of this new mode of conveyance, and who is there who can forget the vast changes which it has brought about in the conduct of human affairs through out the civilised world? It is indeed no casual or random or haphazard episode that we are celebrating here today, but an event which takes its essential place in the movement of historical significance and of world-wide importance.

There are some who deprecate the holding of centenaries, but although today may be but the continuation of yesterday and the flow of time an unbroken stream, yet there are definite and significant periods when we reach a fuller realisation of events—when we seem to halt for a space and look both forward and back; when we reflect upon the past and take account of the future; and when the just pride in a record of long and honourable achievement may afford a heartening encouragement to new energy and a powerful stimulus to achievement. Such points of time are charged with vital elements of new strengths and provide the driving power of the years to come. It is in this attitude of mind and spirit that we find ourselves today, in Bristol, cheerfully conscious of a hundred years of strenuous effort and substantial accomplishment behind us, and deriving fresh inspiration from a community of people whose far-seeing forebears initiated our railways, which was to become the source of a mighty river of traffic, fed by a multitude of tributaries.

Bristol was in truth the *fons et origo* of the Great Western Railway. Can I say anything more complimentary than as is sometimes hopefully said of a bride and bridegroom, that Bristol and the Great Western Railway are worthy of each other. A hundred years ago Bristol was already one of the most important centres of business in the United Kingdom. She had an enterprising population and carried on many important industries. From her crowded havens, her seafaring men, like the Venetians of old, sailed into all the known seas. Nor was this eminent position a thing of recent or sudden acquisition. She was the first town outside of London to receive the status of a County—and that was as early as the days of Edward the Third. It was from Bristol that John Cabot sailed in 1497 to anticipate Christopher Columbus in the discovery of America. From the earliest time

The Locomotive Testing Plant at Swindon, during reconstruction in 1935. Air compressor for absorbing power just discarded, but belts not yet removed. Engine No. 2931 *Arlington Court* on test

Plate 28. OCEAN TRAFFIC

An early view of Fishguard when attempts were being made to attract calls from Transatlantic liners

The *Queen Mary* in Plymouth Sound: passengers being landed by Great Western tender *Sir Richard Grenville*

Plate 29. STATION REBUILDINGS

Swansea High Street, 1926

Newton Abbot, 1927

Plate 30. THE SQUARE DEAL CAMPAIGN

Posters and streamers at Paddington

and onwards, Bristol has been a city of enterprise and activity as well as of character and dignity. When we think of Bristol, we of the Great Western Railway are proud of our origin.

The special conveying the guests back to London consisted of six of the saloons built for the ocean liner traffic from Plymouth, and a kitchen car, and it was hauled by the *King George V*. Strangely enough, although none but the most carping critic could say that time was lost on the new schedule —the actual overall time was 105 min. 29 sec.—it was a poorly judged piece of locomotive running. The train was a minute down on schedule as early as Badminton, and although any attempt at record-breaking had been officially vetoed one could have certainly expected a higher speed than $80\frac{1}{2}$ m.p.h. at Little Somerford, and a descent through the Vale of the White Horse, at no more than $77\frac{1}{2}$ m.p.h., with the train falling still further behind time. It was only when Southall was passed, $1\frac{1}{2}$ min. late, that those on the footplate seemed to realise that they were cutting things very fine, and there came a tremendous acceleration to 88 m.p.h. between Acton and Old Oak Common. When the Bristolian express went into regular service 'King' class engines were used, and detailed logs seemed to indicate that the drivers were finding difficulty in maintaining a steady pace—in striking contrast to the 'Castles' working on the 'Cheltenham Flyer'. Certain commentators went as far as to suggest that the 'Kings' were unsuitable for the job! What was happening, as I saw for myself on the footplate many years later, was that use of the main regulator in conjunction with minimum working cut-off produced too great a gain on time, and first valve was not quite enough. So that drivers were alternating between one and the other adjustment, with the speed fluctuating somewhat. But I must leave the subject of locomotive running for the rest of the Centenary celebrations which culminated in the Banquet held at the Grosvenor House, London, on 30th October, 1935.

At this great gathering, which totalled more than a thousand persons, H.R.H. The Duke of Windsor, then the Prince of Wales and afterwards King Edward VIII, proposed the toast of 'The Great Western Railway Company'. He recalled how, from its earliest days the G.W.R. had been a link between the Sovereign and the Government. He referred to the constant coming and going of distinguished personages, prime ministers, would-be prime ministers, members of the Cabinet, and others between London and Windsor in the days of Queen Victoria. 'Indeed', he said, 'your company, your great company, deserves its name of 'The Royal Road' if only for the fact that it was on your wheels that Queen Victoria first experienced railroad travel, and because it was on your lines that she was borne on her last journey home.

'Ladies and gentlemen', the Prince continued, 'I have a personal association with the Great Western Railway because it serves the West of England. Your tracks pass through the counties of Somerset, Devon, and Cornwall, where, as Duke of Cornwall, I have many tenants dependent on your services. You carry their produce from the West Country to their chief market, and, which is as important, you bring them holiday-makers and tourists who in the summer season rejoice to be able to visit some of the most beautiful parts of the British Isles.

So it is not only as a traveller, but as a landowner, and indeed a customer of the line, that I have the pleasure of accepting your hospitality tonight. I wish, therefore, to pay my tribute to all that the Great Western Railway has done for the West Country during the century of its existence. Speed, comfort, convenience, flexibility, have all been keynotes of your administration. It can never be said that the Great Western Railway has not moved with the times. It is a fact that your company was the first railway company to establish, a few years ago, a regular daily air service. You have held the balance fairly between competing interests. You have discharged your duty to the public with loyalty. You are a venerable, honourable, institution in our native land.

It was not his intention, the Prince continued, to exalt the Great Western above all other railways, but this was the company's night out, and it was entitled to have its own trumpet blown, and he was very happy to have the opportunity of giving it a hearty and resounding blast.

The Prince then referred to the way in which the Great Western Railway had preserved the continuity of its traditions, and the fact that so many families had remained in its service for generation after generation. For many years the company had paid special attention to the welfare of its staff, and to the preservation of the good will of all ranks and grades of its employees, of whom he was glad to see so many present that evening. The company offered not only employment, but a career to those who served it well. Its staff had established a very high standard of efficiency and courtesy.

Many difficulties and anxieties had beset the administration of our railways in the last few years, and new problems lay ahead. If those connected with the administration of that great company continued worthily to uphold the traditions of their predecessors, they would surmount those difficulties and long continue to discharge a public trust with honour to themselves and with great benefit to their fellow countrymen.

The Prince coupled with the toast the name of Sir Robert Horne.

I know, that he is so well known to you that he needs no introduction from myself, and I may say this, that I first had the pleaure of meeting him and making his acquaintance when I was very new to this kind of game. It was just after the war when he was in the Cabinet; we sat next to each other on several occasions, and he was always kind to me, and I might say that he gave me an almost fatherly confidence at this time. He is one of the most important public men in this country, and I am very proud to be especially his guest.

The Prince of Wales certainly set the speeches of the evening off to a gay, friendly start, and Sir Robert Horne, in responding, continued in the same vein, when he began by saying that he felt the greatest possible diffidence in replying to the witty and charming speech that had just been delivered. The Prince of Wales, he said, had blown them a blast from a great trumpet, and he was sorry that he could reply only with a very feeble horn. Lord Palmer, Deputy Chairman, in proposing the toast of 'The Guests' referred to the Chairmanship of Alfred Baldwin, who had preceded the long reign of Lord Churchill. He said that but for the pending General Election his son Stanley Baldwin, the Prime Minister, would have been there; but instead they welcomed Mrs. Baldwin. She responded, on behalf of the guests, with one of the most amusing speeches of the evening. After having said that her husband still entertained the deepest regard for the company, she went on to tell of an occasion very long ago when she tried to impress upon her family the great dignity to which their grand-father had been raised by his appointment as Chairman of the company. She was interrupted by a small voice inquiring whether the Chairman was the person who carried their luggage when they went to the seaside; whereupon another voice chimed in with the remark 'No, stupid, he's the man who blows the whistle'.

The Centenary was naturally the subject of much comment, of all kinds, in the Press of the day; but perhaps the shrewdest, and most strangely prophetic was that of *The Times*:

> One hundred years ago today, almost exactly ten years after the opening of the first public railway in the world to be worked by steam, which was the railway between Stockton and Darlington, the Royal Assent was given to a Bill for the making of the Great Western Railway. The very lively centenarian is doubtless keeping the anniversary on its own account. The contribution of this journal to the celebration is the Great Western Centenary Number presented with *The Times* this morning. In that Number an effort has been made to exhibit its subject in every one of the many aspects, in which, first, this great railway itself, and, next, railways in general occupy the thoughts and emotions of men. From the days when the railway was a new and mysterious birth—to some minds a child of hell, to others an angel of light— down to the present time, when the long periods of success and of failure, of dominance and of subservience, have brought the English railway to a moment in which some see the twilight of their decline and others the dawn of a new day, the story of the Great Western Railway is followed in engineering, mechanics, geographical growth, commerce, war, social usage, and a score of other fields. Of all those fields one must needs be of supreme national interest at the present time. The railways played a capital part in the industrial success of Great Britain. How to maintain and how to improve so much as is left of that success is now a problem that keeps statesmen and others awake at nights. Meanwhile the supremacy of one of the strongest elements in it, the railways, has given way to a struggle against other forms of transport.

The Centenary was inevitably a time for reminiscence and reflection upon the amazing early history of the G.W.R., and one delightful piece of fantasy was printed on the Scrap Heap page of *The Railway Gazette*, in the form of a letter to the Editor:

> Being in London recently and desirous of making a call on the Publicity Department of the Great Western Railway, I arrived at Paddington at about 1.30 p.m. As I had not been to the station since the completion of the extensive alterations there, I was glad to find my objective over the entrance to the Metropolitan Railway without much trouble. The young lady at the enquiry office upstairs, to whom I stated my business, directed me to the fourth door on the left, and I went along, and knocked, and opened the door, only to find the office empty. Reflecting that it was the luncheon hour, I decided to await the return of the man I wanted, and sat down. Really I *was* rather tired, for it was one of those close and muggy days of which we have had so many of late.
>
> Perhaps I ought to explain that the object of my call was to make enquiries as to the early days of the Great Western Railway, so shortly to be celebrating its centenary. Well, as I have said, I sat down, and found myself gazing from the office window at the various departure and arrival platforms, thronged with passengers and about their business.
>
> Watching this animated scene for a minute or so, I am afraid—no doubt owing to the fact that I had recently lunched and that the air was close—I nearly dozed. But, even if I did, and I am not admitting anything of the kind—let's get this right, at the start,— I was very soon awakened by a brisk step along the passage outside, and at the same time caught the aroma of a fine cigar. The footsteps stopped outside the door, and someone coughed once or twice, and then knocked on the door, which, by the way, is marked "Private", and came quietly in.

Seeing me there, the newcomer apologised very graciously for his intrusion, and asked if I minded smoking. Then, without giving me an opportunity to reply, he placed a well-filled cigar case on the desk and invited me to help myself.

The cigar was, well, full-flavoured, and as I was lighting it, the donor coughed again, explaining that some years ago he had inadvertently swallowed half-a-sovereign which there had been some difficulty in removing, and as a result his throat was affected. The thought occurred to me that his trouble was probably enhanced by his partiality for strong cigars.

He moved closer to the office window the better to look out, and I had an opportunity of observing his appearance, and his peculiar attire. He was smallish, well set-up with a high forehead and side whiskers, and was carrying curiously enough, a high old-fashioned 'stove-pipe' hat, which he had removed on entering. He wore a huge black necktie, swathed once or twice round his throat, and rather badly creased trousers of the 'pepper-and-salt' variety, held underneath his boots by straps.

He was quite friendly and even inclined to gaiety, and the strange thing was that, in spite of the century-old style of dress, it did not seem to me in any way incongruous that he should be there and dressed as he was.

The visitor beckoned to me to stand by him at the window, and after a short silence he suddenly began to speak rather slowly. I thought at first he was addressing me, but it was fairly clear, after a minute or so, that he was talking to himself.

'A hundred years ago', he repeated, once or twice. Then looking up into the roof of the station, ejaculated, 'Excellent', adding, after a pause, 'But those are not *my* columns, though they are holding up *my* roof'. He counted up the number of platforms and appeared pleased. Because he was now apparently quite unconscious of my presence, as he continued talking to himself, I returned quietly to my chair and whilst listening as well as I could to what he was saying, glanced at the leather cigar case and tried to decipher the well-worn initials on the corner. Beyond the fact that the middle of the three letters appeared to be a 'K', I could make nothing of them.

It is not, of course, easy to recall precise words spoken, but I felt impelled to write down some of his remarks. 'Dear old Paddington—eighty years old. Wharncliffe viaduct, they've widened that. Maidenhead bridge has *not* fallen down!' He smiled. 'They've widened it, too, and according to my design. Sonning cutting, much as it was, but with four roads. Reading, Swindon, Box tunnel.' At the last word, he chuckled, adding, 'That opened their eyes!' ; then, Bath, Bristol, all as level as a—'— I missed the conclusion. Then, exultantly, 'Glorious Saltash, they can't beat *that*'.

Suddenly he caught sight of the far end of the station, and stared hard up in the roof. I looked out, but could see nothing exceptional. Presently he ejaculated 'Heavens! they've taken away my scrolls.' Whatever he saw seemed to affect him deeply, for murmuring to himself he turned on his heel and abruptly left the office. I called to tell him he had left his cigar case behind, but he didn't seem to hear me and the last I saw was his extraordinary figure as he ran, coat tails flying, across the 'Lawn' and along the side of No. 8 Platform. Opening the window I tried to call him, but my voice somehow refused to function. I tried again, and the effort to shout seemed to rouse me, for I found myself in the chair, gazing at a framed portrait in colour on the office wall. Curiously enough, the features were those of my recent visitor, and as Mr.———, whom I called to see, then returned, I asked whom the portrait represented. "Oh, that is the famous first engineer of the Great Western Railway—Isambard Kingdom Brunel. He built the station just 80 years ago."

Well, if anyone had told me this story I should have put the whole experience down to some vivid kind of dream. But how was I to explain the large black cigar I was smoking? As to the cigar case, that seemed to have vanished, with its owner, but I wish I had made *quite* sure about those initials.

I ought to explain, perhaps, that I have the habit of holding my pencil in my mouth, and when I removed the 'cigar' I found it was a pencil—but if anyone doubts any part of this story I still have the pencil—to prove it.

Once the celebrations were over those with the keenest perception would probably agree that the old Company was steaming into its second century without some of the gusto that had distinguished equally the days of Brunel and the days of Sir Felix Pole. In the spectacular matter of express train speed its thunder, once on a pinnacle of pre-eminence, had been completely stolen by the brilliant achievements of the L.N.E.R. Silver

Jubilee express, and while the institution of the high-speed 'Bristolian' was a move away from old traditions, in providing a very fast morning service out of London its departure time at 10 a.m. was rather too late for a businessman anxious to make the most use of a day's visit to Bristol. The old traditions of English business life persisted. London remained the grand central clearing house, and while there were excellent fast trains from all provincial centres arriving in London between 10 and 11 a.m. there were then no corresponding services out of London. In general policy, as well as in train service the Great Western remained traditional, and its plans for the future were mainly in the form of renewing and consolidating the old, rather than striking out into new fields. There were some surprises to come in the four years remaining between the centenary celebrations and the outbreak of war in 1939. But real progress on the G.W.R. was covert in those last years of peace, and the fruits of it were scarcely revealed before the company itself was ended, in 1948.

The final gesture, in Centenary year, was the building of some entirely new coaching stock for the Cornish Riviera Express. In the summer service of that year the historic name of the '10.30 Limited' was changed to 'Cornish Riviera Limited', and it was followed, at 10.35 a.m. by a new named train, 'The Cornishman'. It must be recorded however that these names did not last very long; but the 'Centenary Riviera' stock, as it became known, had some interesting features. It was built exclusively for the service, and it was perhaps characteristic of the Great Western Railway to take advantage of the wider loading gauge existing on the former broad gauge lines to build these new coaches to an extreme width of 9 ft. 7 in. As a consequence of this they could not be used on any service working to other railways. Their route availability was indeed quite limited; but for the Paddington and Cornwall trains they certainly provided spacious and luxurious travel. The overall length of the coaches was 60 ft. and the full train of 13 vehicles provided seating for 84 first class and 336 third class passengers, with an additional seating accommodation for 88 in the dining cars. The tare weight was 420 tons.

XII

The Locomotive Department

1930-1939

With the production of the 'King' class 4-cylinder 4-6-0 in 1927 it is generally considered that the Great Western Railway reached its climax in locomotive design, and that having out-stripped all other British railways in the matter of nominal tractive effort affairs at Swindon tended to stagnate. Nothing is further from the truth. Certainly in the last decade before World War II no major new designs were produced. The 'Grange' and the 'Manor' class 4-6-0s were merely variations on the basic 2-cylinder 4-6-0, and the light branch 0-6-0 of the '22xx' was to some extent a synthesis of existing standard items. Inevitably of course the apparent inactivity at Swindon, so far as major new designs were concerned, could be contrasted with the spectacular developments on the L.M.S.R. and the L.N.E.R., followed in both cases by almost sensational increases in both maximum and scheduled average speeds. This situation was to some extent a reflection upon the extent to which the Great Western had been ahead of the other companies in the years leading up to 1930, and that with such express passenger locomotives as the 'Castles' and the 'Kings' at their disposal nothing further was needed.

In two very important respects however the 1930s were a time of notable development at Swindon. The work of a locomotive department extends inherently to far more than the production of designs that are basically sound and which can produce outstandingly good work in favourable conditions. Coal consumption is not measured by the performance on a few specially favoured and closely watched duties; it is the coal bill for the entire stud. The same applies to repair costs. To some extent the two are interlinked, since an engine that is kept in a good state of repair will perform its allotted duties on a lower coal consumption than one that is beset by leaks, and other defects. By the year 1930 the 'Castles' and 'Kings'—to quote the outstanding members of the express passenger stud—were established beyond any doubt in their basic economy. The entire stud of 2-cylinder simple engines, tender and tank, derived from the historic Churchward design of 1901, was equally beyond reproach, by the standards of 1930; and the problem became one of endeavouring to hold that economy, with a minimum of deterioration, during the entire period from one works overhaul to the next. The standard of workmanship at Swindon was very high and undoubtedly contributed to the excellent performance of engines newly outshopped; but under the direction of C. B. Collett a new conception of locomotive erection and repair was developed.

In the machinery of a locomotive, axle bearings, crank pins, big ends, slide bars, and all the moving parts of the valve gear, clearances have to be allowed to permit of free working; but to some extent the amount of clearance to be provided for is governed by the accuracy to which the chassis of the locomotive is built. It goes without saying that the frames should be truly 'square', and that the centre lines of the cylinders should be exactly parallel to them. In engineering construction however the terms 'square' and 'parallel' can be relative, and practical tolerances have to be laid down, permitting slight deviations from the mathematically precise values. The wider the tolerances, the greater the clearances that have to be provided in the working parts. There is another aspect also to be taken into account. A bearing that has a liberal amount of clearance, besides being noisy in operation will tend to develop wear and consequent slogger more quickly than one that is a more nearly perfect fit. In the machinery of a locomotive slogger in the pin joints of a valve gear results in a loss of accuracy in the steam distribution, and inequality in the amount of work at each end of the cylinders. This in turn leads to inequalities in the loads on the crank pins and big ends. The factor of 'clearance' can therefore work up into a vicious circle: each item accentuating and aggravating another, which in turn react back and start the chain of consequences moving further, with increasing ill-effects. One comes back, therefore, to the foundation on which the machinery is assembled—the main frames.

On the German State Railways use was being made in the 1930s of Zeiss precision optical gear for lining up locomotive frames, and the experience of that administration was that the time of lining up was cut to between one quarter and one third of that previously taken. Furthermore a locomotive so treated would run a greater mileage between repairs than previously. This method was studied by the engineers of the Great Western Railway, and after modification of the Zeiss apparatus to suit production methods at Swindon it was adopted as standard practice for all new and repaired locomotives.

The basis of the apparatus was a telescope mounted within a tube, arranged so that it could be pivoted in vertical or horizontal planes by two dials. When these dials were both set at zero, the telescope was in exact central alignment with its external tube—which was set with a self-centring spider—in the front bell mouth of one cylinder, and by an adaptor in the stuffing box at the back of the cylinder. A spirit level ensured that the vertical and horizontal axes were correct, and a measuring surface set level with the front cylinder face by a straight edge provided zero for distance. The overall width across each pair of horns was measured by a vernier, after which a sighting scale was clamped to each horn in turn and the scale read through the telescope. The sighting scale was similar to a surveyor's staff and the reading gave the distance of the cylinder axis to the outside edge of the horn. This distance plus half the width over that pair of horns gave the distance to the theoretical centre line of the engine. If that sum did not amount to the same total at each horn, the cylinder axis was not parallel with the centre line of the line. A certain tolerance could be allowed there and the telescope pivoted horizontally until its centre was parallel with the engine centre line, but if the correction would have been beyond the allowed limit it would have been necessary to cut down some stiffeners or cross stays and reset the frames.

Assuming that the telescope was set parallel with the theoretical centre line of the engine, the sighting scale was removed and a collimator, clamped to a tube in such a way that it was dead at right angles to the axis of the tube, was supported at the driving horn, the tube being right across the frame between both driving horns. The tube was held in a stand, the top of which could be moved vertically or horizontally to or from the cylinder, and through an angle horizontally. The collimator was an optical apparatus carrying two sets of cross scales illuminated by an electric lamp, and had the property of accepting at zero on its infinite scale only rays parallel with the telescope. If on sighting from the telescope the telescope cross lines cut the horizontal and vertical lines of the infinite scale of the collimator at zero, then the telescope and the collimator were truly parallel, although not necessarily in the same plane. How much they were out of plane could be read by focussing the telescope on the finite scale of the collimator and reading the graduations. The horizontal, vertical and angular adjustments provided for in the collimator stand allowed the latter to be brought easily into alignment with the telescope. As the collimator was then parallel with the telescope and was fixed accurately at right angles to the collimator cross tube, it followed that the cross tube was then between the driving horns at right angles to the cylinder axis.

A dial indicator was used to obtain the distance of each horn cheek from the collimator cross tube, and the latter was traversed longitudinally until it was central between the driving horns. A length gauge with dial indicator from locating points on the telescope tube and the collimator tube gave a direct reading of the distance from the cylinder face to the centre of the driving horn, and from the collimator cross tube a locating stud on each frame was set at a definite distance from the horn centre. Length gauges enabled further locating studs to be set at each of the other horns, i.e., 'leading', 'intermediate' and 'trailing', and from those similar measurements could be made to each of the corresponding horn cheeks. By means of the accurate rods and the dial indicator, all those measurements could easily be read to within a thousandth of an inch, although the total length between the leading and trailing horn centres might have been as much as 20 ft.

Thus a very accurate survey of the salient points of a locomotive frame could be made expeditiously, and from this decisions taken as to the amount of corrections to be made. I have dwelt on the process at some length because it proved the very cornerstone of Swindon constructional practice. It enabled valve gear parts to be made with precision, with an absolute minimum of clearance when new, so that newly outshopped locomotives ran with the quietness of sewing machines. Such was the tightening up of clearances possible as a result that the situation became one that was vividly described by one ex-Great Western man, after nationalisation, when the differing practices of other famous locomotive manufactories came under review. This engineer said: 'We scrap at the amount of clearance they start with'! After nationalisation, the precision methods of erection so assiduously developed at Swindon in the 1930s were applied with notable success at other railway works. Equal precision was applied in the rebuilding of locomotives after heavy repair, so that after a heavy general overhaul a locomotive took the road again as good as new.

As with the frames and cylinders so also with boilers the practice of the Great Western Railway was constantly being improved. The standard design of boiler used on all the larger types of locomotive, having tapered barrel and Belpaire firebox had, over the years, been highly developed in all its detail. But apart from design the maintenance of boilers always presented one of the greatest problems with which locomotive engineers had to deal. The gradual development of boiler repair methods, always under such constant scrutiny at Swindon, continued to yield quite outstanding results. In recalling developments of the period around 1930–5 it is interesting and gratifying to see how the precepts of Churchward were still followed by those who succeeded him. He was always keenly aware of developments in locomotive design and constructional practice taking place elsewhere, and if such developments could be to the advantage of the G.W.R. he adopted them, or adapted them to his own needs. His successor adopted with great success a German method of optical lining-up of frames and cylinders; equally he took a French device, and adapted it to Swindon requirements for tube expanding, drilling, reaming, and tapping of locomotive boilers. Portable machines of a type designed by Constructions Électriques Wageor, of Paris and St. Étienne, as shown in the accompanying diagram were installed for the expeditious carrying out of jobs such as drilling out old staybolts, drilling throat plates and crown plates, reaming and tapping staybolt holes, fitting new stays, and perhaps most interesting of all, the method of automatic tube expanding. Some remarkable results of high productivity were achieved with this apparatus.

The application of modern methods of layout and production were not confined to Swindon works. The most careful attention was also given to Wolverhampton and Caerphilly. Brief reference has already been made to the selection of the latter as the works for maintenance of the locomotives used in South Wales, and more detailed reference to the development there will follow. But so far as Wolverhampton was concerned, since their original erection in 1858 the works at Stafford Road had been extended from time to time, with the result that the general layout of the plant, which had spread on each side of the main road and at two different levels had latterly become inconvenient to operate. Advantage was taken therefore of the financial assistance afforded by the Development (Loan Guarantees and Grants) Act of 1929, to undertake the complete re-organisation of the works. The task was commenced as early as November 1929,

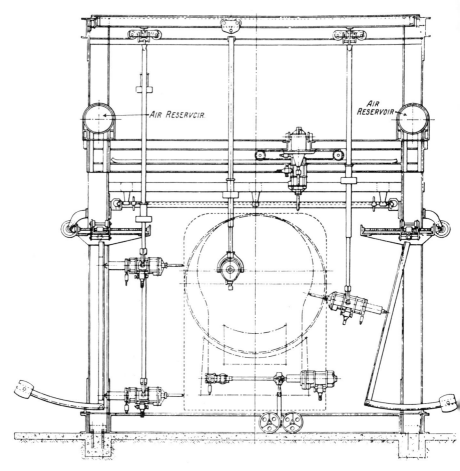

Fig. 16. Diagram of the Wageor boiler drilling rig.

and it was completed within 3 years. The accompanying plan shows the new layout, but a study of it also brings out the difficulties and restrictions of the particular site, intersected as it is by public highways, main railway routes of both the G.W.R. and the L.M.S.R. and adjoining property. At this works no new building of locomotives was undertaken, the work being that entirely of repair. The locomotives dealt with were for the most part of the lightest types; but a number of 'King' class locomotives were stationed at Wolverhampton for the London expresses, and the equipment was adequate for dealing with light or intermediate tasks on these large engines.

In the reconstruction, an entirely new building, incorporating erecting, machine and wheel shops, was built. This was indeed of impressive proportions being 450 ft. long, by 196 ft. wide. It was arranged in three bays, two forming the erecting shop, and the third the machine and wheel shop. Engines for repair, on arrival at Stafford Road were put into the sidings until such time as they could be brought into the repair shop, where they were dealt with in accordance with a routing system which was classified into either light, intermediate or general repairs. The engines were sent from the various stations throughout the line to the works on receipt of an advice from Swindon, and all classes were dealt with, with the exception of the large express passenger engines. The engines came in at the south end of the shop, where the necessary stripping was carried out, and in the case of a general repair, where the boiler was removed from the frame and sent direct to the boiler shop located on the south side of the Victoria goods line, where a special track was laid for the purpose. The general layout plan shows also the large running sheds from which, due to the restrictions of space, there is a somewhat circuitous exit for locomotives on to the main line.

The re-organisation at Caerphilly arose from different circumstances from those at Wolverhampton. It was begun soon after grouping, which had as one of its principal objects the cutting out of redundant services and facilities. It was a process extending over the various phases of railway operating, and one of the consequences was this disestablishment of certain smaller repair centres and the grouping and centralising of work at larger ones. Of outstanding interest in this connection was the case of the railways in South Wales. Dotted about the various systems were several small repair works, in which also a certain amount of new work was undertaken; and in conformity with the general principle of amalgamating these interests and economising in respect of plant and labour, it was decided that the relatively modern workshops established in the year 1901 at Caerphilly, near Cardiff, and utilised for the upkeep of locomotives, carriages and wagons owned by the Rhymney Railway would, with suitable extensions and improvements, provide a convenient centre at which operations on a larger scale could be carried out.

This involved repairs to the many different classes of locomotives previously maintained by the constituent companies at their own works,

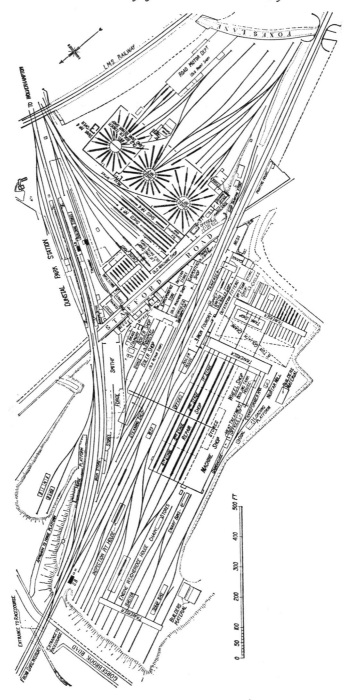

Fig. 17. Wolverhampton Works. Layout of shops and running sheds as modernised

but on lines which would make possible the more rapid completion of work performed under conditions of more modern character. This decision having been taken, plans were prepared for the building of a large erecting shop laid out in three bays, and supplied with electric overhead cranes, a traverser, and so on, and second only in respect of size and capacity to the much larger erecting shops at the principal railway works elsewhere. At the same time the re-organisation of the older shops was taken in hand bringing them into line with a general scheme of scheduled operations aiming at a larger output of repaired locomotives in a given time and the closing down, or greatly restricted use, of older and smaller shops located at different points on the South Wales railway systems.

This meant bringing to Caerphilly a number of workmen previously employed at the other centres and concentrating there activities which before had been widely scattered. The Caerphilly Works, as re-organised, represented what may be termed an ideal, self-contained factory in which tank locomotives of various sizes, types and weights were completely overhauled. The work was carried out in accordance with a very carefully organised plan of operations, in which a definite time was set for each different kind of work on the various parts of the locomotives. That system achieved a steady flow of work through the shops instead of peak periods and slack periods following one another, thus making sure of uniformity in the number of locomotives under repair and in service at a given time. As a result of this a steady improvement was made in output of repaired locomotives. In 1927, 87 heavy and 74 light overhauls were completed, whilst in the corresponding period of the following year the figures were 153 heavy and 67 light. In 1929, 213 heavy and 38 light engine repairs were completed, and the general tendency at the works was to concentrate on heavy repairs and reduce the number of light ones.

The most interesting work undertaken at Caerphilly in the early days of the re-organisation was the rebuilding of engines of the constituent companies with standard Great Western boilers, and the repair of the new standard heavy South Wales 0-6-2 tank engines of the '56xx' class. Around 1930–1 under the leadership of the Works Manager, S. R. Jones, some astonishingly rapid feats of productivity in repair were achieved, to some extent due to keen competition between the distinct groups of men in the erecting shop. E. R. Mountford, in his book on Caerphilly Works, has quoted details of what is known to be the all-time record for a heavy repair to one of the '56xx' class 0-6-2 tank engines, and the complete details are set out below. The normal time for repair to one of these engines was 18 days.

Engine No. 5664 Group 'B'.

Stripping commenced at	7.45 a.m.	28.1.31
Tanks off by	9.30 a.m.	28.1.31
Cab off by	9.30 a.m.	28.1.31
Boiler out of frame by	1.30 p.m.	28.1.31
Motion plate out of frame by	2.45 p.m.	28.1.31

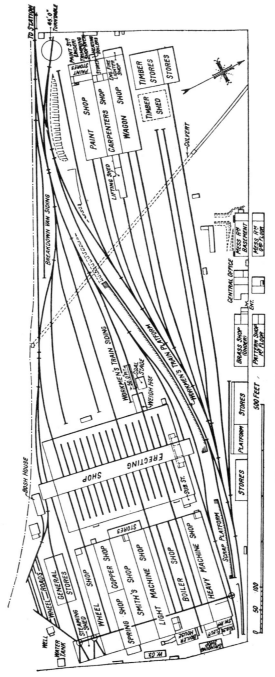

Fig. 18. Caerphilly Works. Layout of shops as modernised.

Wheels out of frame by	4.00 p.m.	28.1.31
Frames cleaned and painted by	10.15 a.m.	29.1.31
Valve boring started at	10.00 a.m.	29.1.31
Back cylinder covers faced by	10.30 a.m.	29.1.31
Cylinder boring started at	10.45 a.m.	29.1.31
Boiler back in frame by	3.00 p.m.	29.1.31
Tanks back on by	3.45 p.m.	29.1.31
Cylinder and valve boring finished by	3.00 p.m.	30.1.31
Motion bars set by	3.30 p.m.	30.1.31
Axle boxes fitted by	4.15 p.m.	30.1.31
Engine wheeled by	10.45 a.m.	31.1.31
Brakegear, pipework, general		31.1.31
finishing off and painting	and	2.2.31
Valve setting started at	4.30 p.m.	2.2.31
Valve setting finished and engine ready by	11.00 a.m.	3.2.31

Unfortunately the traffic on the line ceased to demand such productivity from the re-organised work, and from the middle of July 1931 many men had to be discharged, and the remainder put on short time. Normal working was not in fact resumed until October 1936. The general layout of the works, as re-organised, is shown in the accompanying plan.

Reverting now to Swindon Works, there was a steady programme of new engine construction in the years at present under review, and for express passenger working over the entire line the 'Castle' class was standardised. Ten new engines of the class were built in each of the years 1932, 1934 and 1935; 15 in 1936, and 10 each in 1937, 1938 and 1939. Furthermore, at various times during 1938 and 1939 ten engines of the 'Abbey' series of 'Stars' were renewed as 'Castles'. By the end of 1939 this very successful class, including various converted 'Stars', and the replacement for the 4-6-2 engine *The Great Bear* totalled 121 engines. Other standard 4-6-os were the 2-cylinder 'Hall' class with 6 ft. 0 in. diameter coupled wheels totalling 187 in 1939; the similar 'Grange' class, with 5 ft. 8 in. coupled wheels totalling 80 engines, and the scaled-down lightweight 4-6-os of the 'Manor 'class, introduced in 1938 and totalling 20. Extensive building of the very useful 0-6-0 pannier tank engines took place during the period, and a new series of standard 2-8-0 mineral engines of the '28xx'' class was commenced, having the more recent type of cab. It is not appropriate here to attempt to chronicle all locomotive constructional activities in detail; but mention must be made of the conversion of some of the South Wales 2-8-0 tank mineral engines to the 2-8-2T type. The provision of much enlarged coal bunkers enabled these engines to undertake main line coal traffic workings, and some were used on the cross-country route from Bristol to Salisbury. The first of these conversions was made in 1934. This chapter is concerned only with steam. The introduction of the diesel railcars has already been referred to in Chapter 10.

At Swindon works itself a very important development, and one that was to have a considerable influence upon the steam locomotive practice of the nationalised British Railways in later years, concerned the old Churchward stationary testing plant. One of its original functions had been to obviate the necessity of sending new and repaired locomotives out on the line for trial trips, and the fact that the plant itself was not capable of absorbing more than about 500 h.p. was of no particular consequence. It had never been used for measuring the maximum output of of any particular class of locomotive. On the other hand Sir Nigel Gresley, Chief Mechanical Engineer of the L.N.E.R., had for some years been strongly advocating the setting up of a national testing laboratory, and to emphasise the lack of it, in the most public manner possible he had arranged for his 2-8-2 locomotive the *Cock o' the North*, to be sent to France for testing on the Vitry plant. The authorities of the L.M.S.R. were solidly behind Gresley in his desire for a British testing plant, but with the bulk of Southern motive power activities directed towards electrification little support could be expected from that quarter.

There remained the Great Western. So far as the outside world was concerned activities inside Swindon works were cloaked in some secrecy, and engineers from other railways rarely, if ever, visited the establishment. At the time Stanier left, to join the L.M.S.R., the stationary testing plant was unchanged from Churchward's day; but much had happened since, and when a joint approach was made to the Great Western to join with the L.M.S.R. and the L.N.E.R. in the setting up of a national testing plant of modern design, Swindon was able to demonstrate, on a modernised plant, the 2-cylinder 4-6-0 No. 2931 *Arlington Court* developing maximum power. The plant as modernised was indeed capable of absorbing a great deal more than the maximum output of which a 'Saint' class engine was capable, and was later used for very high output trials of one of the 'Kings', and still later of the British standard 3-cylinder 4-6-2 engine No. 71000. At this stage however it is necessary to do no more than record the modernisation of the plant. How it came to form an integral part of a new conception of locomotive testing belongs to the last days of Great Western history —between the end of World War II, and the nationalisation of the British railways.

No reference to the work of the Locomotive Department in the 1930's would be complete without an account of the proceedings on that historic afternoon of June 6, 1932, when a deliberate and successful attempt was made to secure the world speed record for a start-to-stop journey, by a specially staged performance of the 'Cheltenham Flyer'. Not only this, but as the daily performance of that train had been criticised on account of the journey being made over a route that is 'all downhill', it was arranged to run the down Cheltenham Spa Express also at high speed. As a result the 3.48 p.m. up ran from Swindon to Paddington in 56 min. 47 sec., and the 5 p.m. down arrived at Swindon in 60 min. 1 sec. from Paddington. The latter was not a regularly scheduled stop, but was made for demonstration purposes on this special occasion. Two very experienced observers of locomotive running, Mr. Cecil J. Allen and Mr. Humphrey Baker, of Bath, were invited to accompany these special runs, and to round off the day, and return the observers from Swindon to Paddington as soon as possible, the 5.15 p.m. up 2-hour Bristol express was stopped at

Plate 31. GREAT WESTERN STEAMERS

The *St. Julien* leaving Weymouth for the Channel Islands, 1929

The new *St. Patrick*, 1948

Plate 32. 'KING' CLASS LOCOMOTIVES

Engine No. 6004 *King George III* in original peacetime livery

Engine No. 6029 *King Edward VIII* in plain green, wartime austerity style

Plate 33

Cardiff Docks: 60-ton self-propelled floating crane

Plate 34. AIR RAID PRECAUTIONS

Emergency ambulance at Paddington during gas drill

Home Guard and Civil Defence Parade at Cardiff, 1943

Swindon instead of slipping a coach. Despite the intermediate stop, and two incidental checks, the latter train still arrived in Paddington $2\frac{1}{2}$ min. ahead of time.

The two special runs provide classic examples of the working of the 'Castle' class locomotives, and detailed logs are tabulated herewith. These are supplemented by a speed chart of both runs, superimposed upon the gradient profile of the line. The two locomotives concerned were worked in the text-book manner, with regulator full open and short cut-offs, as follows:

UP JOURNEY   Engine No. 5006 *Tregenna Castle*
                            Driver Ruddock; Fireman Thorp

Regulator gradually opened to full by Shrivenham

Cut-offs:

Shrivenham to Goring	17 per cent.
Goring to Maidenhead	18 per cent.
Maidenhead to Southall	17 per cent.
Southall to Milepost 2	18 per cent.

DOWN JOURNEY: Engine No. 5005 *Manorbier Castle*
                              Driver Burgess; Fireman Gibson

Regulator gradually opened to full by Ealing

Cut-offs:

Ealing to Southall	23 per cent.
Southall to Slough	20 per cent.
Slough to Reading	19 per cent.
Reading to Goring	20 per cent.
Goring to Didcot	19 per cent.
Didcot to Uffington	20 per cent.
Uffington to Highworth Junction	21 per cent.

The afternoon's proceedings were aptly summed up by Cecil J. Allen writing in 'The Railway Magazine' of July 1932:

'The remembrances of the day still leave me breathless, but at the same time happy to have been a personal witness of all that transpired and proud of the fact that British railways, and locomotives, and men were exclusively responsible. For a record of this character is not merely the private possession of one single railway and its staff; it is a national triumph and a national asset.'

One point not generally appreciated is that the 'stage management' had to extend to several trains other than the two with which the records were made. Ordinarily the Cornish Riviera Express was due in Paddington at 4.45 p.m.—10 min. ahead of the 'Cheltenham Flyer'; but on this occasion it was run specially hard to keep well clear, and arrived at 4.38 p.m.—7 min. early, and approximately the same amount ahead of the world record-breaker. In the down direction a possible obstruction would have been the 4.45 p.m. Worcester express, a heavy train calling first at Oxford. The down Cheltenham Spa Express passed Didcot at $5.41\frac{1}{2}$ p.m., without a vestige of a check, so that the 4.45 p.m. departure from Paddington, with a load of over 400 tons must have covered the initial 53 miles of its run in about 'even-time' to keep clear.

THE WORLD'S RECORD RUN

3.48 p.m. SWINDON—PADDINGTON: JUNE 6, 1932

Load: 6 coaches, 186 tons tare, 195 tons full
Engine: 4-6-0 No. 5006 *Tregenna Castle*

Dist. miles		Actual m. s.		Speeds m.p.h.
0.00	SWINDON	0	00	–
5.75	Shrivenham	6	15	$81\frac{1}{2}$
10.75	Uffington	9	51	$85\frac{1}{2}$
13.41	Challow	11	42	$87\frac{1}{2}$
16.90	Wantage Road	14	05	89
20.77	Steventon	16	40	90
24.17	DIDCOT	18	55	$91\frac{1}{2}$
28.84	Cholsey	21	59	$91\frac{1}{2}$
32.55	Goring	24	25	92
35.76	Pangbourne	26	33	$90\frac{1}{2}$
38.66	Tilehurst	28	28	92
41.30	READING	30	11	$91\frac{1}{4}$
46.30	Twyford	33	31	88
53.06	Maidenhead	38	08	87
58.85	SLOUGH	42	10	$86\frac{1}{2}$
64.07	West Drayton	45	51	84
68.22	Southall	48	51	$81\frac{1}{2}$
71.60	Ealing	51	17	$84\frac{1}{2}$
75.30	*Milepost 2*	53	56	$82\frac{1}{2}$
76.05	Westbourne Park	54	40	
77.30	PADDINGTON	56	47	

Average speed 81.6 m.p.h. start-to-stop

THE DOWN RECORD RUN

5 p.m. PADDINGTON—SWINDON: JUNE 6, 1932

Load: 6 coaches, 199 tons tare, 210 tons full
Engine: 4-6-0 No. 5005 *Manorbier Castle*

Dist. miles		Actual m. s.		Speeds m.p.h.
0.00	PADDINGTON	0	00	
1.25	Westbourne Park	2	34	
5.70	Ealing	6	52	73
9.08	Southall	9	25	$80\frac{1}{2}$
13.23	West Drayton	12	26	$84\frac{1}{4}$
18.45	SLOUGH	16	03	$86\frac{1}{2}$
24.24	Maidenhead	20	14	$82\frac{1}{2}$
31.00	Twyford	25	$17\frac{1}{2}$	$78\frac{1}{2}$
36.00	READING	29	$02\frac{1}{2}$	82
38.64	Tilehurst	30	58	$83\frac{1}{2}$
41.54	Pangbourne	33	01	$82\frac{1}{2}$
44.75	Goring	35	23	$82\frac{1}{4}$
48.46	Cholsey	38	03	84
53.13	DIDCOT	41	25	$85\frac{1}{4}$
56.53	Steventon	43	47	$83\frac{1}{2}$
60.40	Wantage Road	46	35	$81\frac{3}{4}$
63.89	Challow	49	13	$80\frac{1}{2}$
66.54	Uffington	51	13	$78\frac{1}{2}/77\frac{1}{2}$
71.55	Shrivenham	54	59	$81\frac{1}{2}$
76.00	*Milepost 76*	58	$15\frac{1}{2}$	$83\frac{1}{2}$
77.3	SWINDON	60	01	

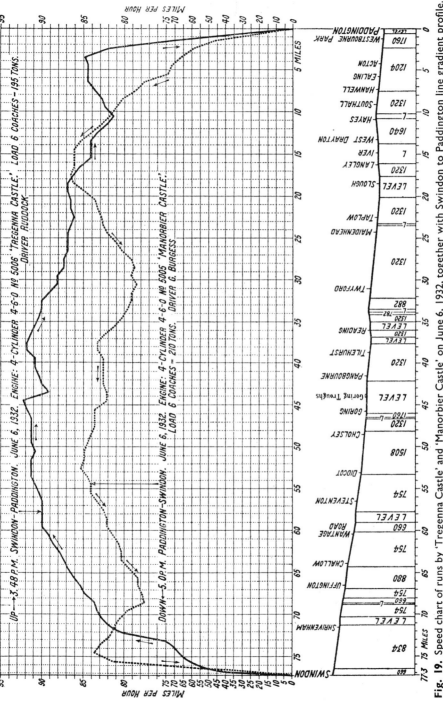

Fig. 19. Speed chart of runs by 'Tregenna Castle' and 'Manorbier Castle' on June 6, 1932, together with Swindon to Paddington line gradient profile.

XIII

The Zenith of Passenger Train Service

In the last few chapters numerous aspects of the railway have been discussed, all of which are of great interest to different sections of the railway staff, to the proprietors, and to outside enthusiasts. Railways in their privately-owned days were run for the benefit of the shareholders, but in order that a degree of profitability should be maintained it was, of course, highly necessary to ensure that services to the public were of the highest standards, particularly in the case of a railway so proud of its traditions and its prestige as the Great Western. This chapter is therefore a summary and appraisal of the service to the public offered by its express passenger trains at a time when the line reached what was probably the zenith of its efficiency. To illustrate this I have chosen the summer service of 1938, operated at a time when the International situation on the continent of Europe had certainly become ominous, but before it had deteriorated sufficiently to cause definite interference with internal transport in Great Britain. I have tried to present an overall picture, not only high-lighting the performance of the more spectacular services, but including the service from London and elsewhere to important towns and cities on the system that from one cause or another lay apart from the most spectacular high speed routes. When one comes to analyse the results it is a rather sobering reflection upon the unevenness of the service. The disparity is even more so when one comes to compare the speed of transit between the important provincial cities as compared with the service provided from the same cities to and from London.

In studying, and inevitably criticising the overall result it must nevertheless be appreciated that it is good railway business to guide, or try to guide, passengers and freight on to the routes that can be operated to the best advantage. The Great Western was consciously, or unconsciously trimming its services to suit the geography and other physical characteristics of its main line network in much the same way as the much-publicised Beeching Plan tried to do for the railways of Britain as a whole. On the Great Western in 1938, as always, there was the over-riding fact that in England the pattern of passenger travel has always been drawn towards London. It is only on certain well defined cross-country routes that any attempt has been made to develop high speed service. This point has already been stressed in this book, when discussing train services of a decade earlier. It became even more apparent in later years. Nevertheless, although the overall picture, in common with that of other British railways does not present such a brilliant picture as the achievements of the crack

EXPRESS TRAINS TIMED AT 58 M.P.H. OR MORE
START TO STOP
SUMMER SERVICE—1938

From	To	Departure Time	Distance miles	Time min.	Aver. Speed m.p.h.
Swindon	Paddington	3.55 p.m.	77.3	65	71.4
Paddington	Bristol (b)	10.00 a.m.	118.3	105	67.6
Bristol (c)	Paddington	4.30 p.m.	117.6	105	67.2
Oxford	Paddington	(10.10 a.m.)	63.5	60	63.5
		(5.35 p.m.)			
Swindon	Reading	5.40 p.m.	41.3	39	63.5
Chippenham	Paddington	8.28 a.m.	94.0	89	63.4
Kemble	Paddington	9.03½ a.m.	91.0	86½	63.1
Paddington	Bath	(11.15 a.m.)	106.9	102	62.9
		(1.15 p.m.)			
Paddington	Bath	5.05 p.m.	106.9	103	62.3
Westbury	Paddington	10.18 a.m.	95.6	92	62.3
High Wycombe	Leamington	9.44 a.m. (a)	60.8	59	61.8
Paddington	Exeter	12 noon	173.5	169	61.6
Paddington	Exeter	11.10 a.m.	173.5	170	61.2
Swindon	Paddington	1.14 p.m.	77.3	76	61.0
Paddington	Kemble	5.00 p.m.	91.0	90	60.7
Westbury	Reading	5.09 p.m.	59.6	59	60.6
Moreton-in-Marsh	Oxford	9.35 a.m.	28.3	28	60.6
Oxford	Paddington	3.17 p.m.	63.5	63	60.5
Paddington	Westbury	3.30 p.m.	95.6	95	60.4
Paddington	Taunton	11.35 a.m.	142.7	142	60.2
Paddington	Newton Abbot (d)	10.30 a.m.	193.7	193	60.3
Swindon	Paddington	4.18 p.m.	77.3	77	60.2
Didcot	Paddington	9.24 a.m.	53.1	53	60.1
Westbury	Taunton	5.09 p.m.	47.1	47	60.1
Exeter	Paddington	12.41 p.m.	173.5	174	59.8
Paddington	Swindon	2.30 a.m. (g)	77.3	78	59.5
Bath	Paddington	9.17 a.m.	106.9	108	59.4
Reading	Frome	9.50 a.m.	65.3	66	59.4
Frome	Taunton	10.59 a.m.	41.6	42	59.4
Swindon	Bath	3.52 a.m. (g)	29.6	30	59.2
Swindon	Reading	7.20 p.m.	41.3	42	59.0
Taunton	Westbury	(9.28 a.m.)	47.1	48	58.9
		(3.28 p.m.)			
Exeter	Paddington	1.30 p.m.	173.5	177	58.8
Bristol (c)	Paddington	(11.45 a.m.)	171.6	120	58.8
		(5.15 p.m.)			
Castle Cary	Westbury	11.06 a.m. (f)	19.6	20	58.8
High Wycombe	Birmingham	9.44 a.m.	84.1	86	58.7
Reading	Westbury	2.23 p.m.	59.6	61	58.6
Paddington	Newport	(1.20 a.m. (g))	133.4	137	58.4
		(6.55 p.m.)			
Reading	Paddington	6.23 p.m.	36.0	37	58.4
Newton Abbot (d)	Paddington	1.20 p.m.	193.7	200	58.1
Newbury	Paddington	9.55 a.m.	53.1	55	58.0
Newbury	Lavington	1.43 p.m.	33.8	35	58.0

(a) by slip coach (b) via Bath (c) via Badminton (d) locomotive stop (f) diesel railcar
(g) Newspaper train.

trains might lead one to expect, it would be graceless not to give the utmost prominence to the 'neonlights' display, and equally to note a fine acceleration to Swansea and Fishguard, which was the principal factor in cutting the time from Paddington to Waterford and Cork by the direct steamer service by a full hour. The time from Paddington to Swansea, a level 3¾ hr., was the fastest ever scheduled up to that time.

Pride of place therefore in this chapter comes a list of 46 start-to-stop runs made at an average speed of 58 m.p.h. or more. The aggregate mileage involved, namely 4144, represented a very fine standard of speed on main routes, but an analysis of the routes involved gives this result:

Paddington–Bristol, including runs to Oxford and Kemble	22
Worcester line	1
West of England via Westbury	19
South Wales, from Paddington	2
Birmingham line, via Bicester	2

The Worcester line run was by the 9 a.m. up express, which made a 28-min. run from Moreton-in-Marsh to Oxford, 28.3 miles, while the South Wales runs were two Paddington–Newport non-stops, by the 1.20 a.m. newspaper train, and by the 6.55 p.m. Irish boat express previously mentioned: 133.4 miles in 137 min. in both cases. The two Birmingham line runs were made by the same train, which ran the 84.1 miles from High Wycombe to Snow Hill in 86 min. (58.7 m.p.h.) and detached its Leamington slip coach in 59 min. from the start, 60.8 miles. It is interesting to note that slip coach services were featuring less and less in Great Western time-tables, as the years went by.

We are left therefore with 41 out of the 46 runs made on two routes only—the Bristol main line, with its offshoots to Kemble for 2 runs, and Oxford for 3, and the West of England main line via Westbury. This is not to suggest that fine running was not performed elsewhere, and the Birmingham line as always demanded some hard work from its locomotives; but the highest average speeds were to be seen on the Bristol and West of England lines. Detailed reference is made later to an interesting analysis of engine performance on the Birmingham line in relation to an investigation made towards a higher standard of speed; but the difficulties in the way were merely high-lighted by this investigation. Before passing on to a detailed consideration of some of the runs made at average speeds of 58 m.p.h. and more, it is only natural for the reader to enquire how the Great Western statistics in this respect compared with those of the other railway groups, and the figures are tabulated both in relation to the total route mileage, and to the total passenger train mileage, as shown in the table on the following page.

The proportion of high speed running was thus greater, in relation to the total passenger train mileage, on the Great Western than on any other company, though in relation to route mileage the Company took second place to the L.M.S.R. The latter had a greater proportion of fast running lines. The very high total of passenger train miles run on the Southern is of course explained by the intense electrically-worked services around London. Taken broadly, the Great Western figure was a very satisfactory one, and although the year 1938 was one of severely declining traffic the service offered to the public was if anything enhanced rather than reduced.

Referring now to individual fast runs, there were some fine schedules between Paddington and Swindon, in addition to that of the 'Cheltenham Flyer', including the 63.5 m.p.h. run of the 5.40 p.m. up, to Reading, and the 59.5 m.p.h. run of the 2.30 a.m. down newspaper express. Over

Railway	G.W.R.	L.M.S.R.	L.N.E.R.	S.R.
Total route mileage	3781	6845	6349	2156
Passenger train mileage	43,515,942	104,366,896	70,307,099	64,833,831
Mileage at 58 m.p.h. start to stop average or more	4144	8934	4497	318
58 m.p.h. average per route mile	1.095	1.305	0.707	0.147
58 m.p.h. average per million train miles run.	95.3	86.0	64.0	4.9

this same route will also be noted the fast runs of the up morning Bristol expresses: 63.4 m.p.h. by the 8.28 a.m. up from Chippenham and 59.4 m.p.h. by the 9.17 a.m. from Bath. Two trains ran from Oxford to Paddington in the even hour, and another 63 m.p.h. run was that of the 9.03½ a.m. from Kemble—91 miles in 86½ min. Apart from the Bristolian, which followed the 'Cheltenham Flyer' in descending order of speed, there were 5 trains running between Paddington and Bristol in the level 2 hours. The two up expresses were non-stop, but all three down trains included a stop at Bath, and this non-stop run of 106.9 miles involved average speeds of 62.9 and 62.3 m.p.h. Why the 5.5 p.m. was given one minute more to Bath than the other was not clear. It is notable also that many of these very fast trains on the Bristol and Oxford routes were hauled by engines of the 'Star' class, and the individual engine performance was exceedingly fine. The 5.15 p.m. up 2-hour express from Bristol detached slip coaches at both Swindon and Reading, and the latter involved a severe reduction in speed to pass through the platform road.

On the West of England road the standard of service between Paddington and Exeter was very high, with two trains in each direction falling into the '58 m.p.h. and over' category. The long runs of the Cornish Riviera

Express during the summer season, neither down nor up, were of any benefit to the citizens of Newton Abbot because the stops were made purely for locomotive purposes. During the summer the load of that famous train for Plymouth and beyond was too great even for the 'King' class locomotives to take unassisted over the South Devon line. Slip coach services on the West of England line had virtually disappeared, and none were carried either by the Cornish Riviera Express or the 3.30 p.m. down. The latter train made two successive 60 m.p.h. start-to-stop runs: Paddington to Westbury, at 60.4 m.p.h., and Westbury to Taunton at 60.1 m.p.h. Note must also be taken of what might be called a rather 'unlikely' high speed run, that of the 11.6 a.m. from Castle Cary to Westbury. It was unlikely, in that the route is heavily graded, and the distance short. Actually it was made by diesel railcar, and was 2 min. *slower* than that scheduled in the previous summer. Certainly 18 min. start to stop for a distance of 19.6 miles, giving an average speed of 65.3 m.p.h. was a highly enterprising run. The deceleration rather suggests it was a little too enterprising to be maintained. I have never seen a detailed log of the trip.

In discussing the 58 m.p.h. runs of the 1938 summer season the disappearance of the once-substantial lead of the Great Western over all other companies in the matter of aggregate mileage must be noted. In relation to the total train miles, run as previously mentioned and tabulated the Great Western still had the best record; and the loss of its one-time lead was a measure of the way in which the northern companies had caught up rather than of any falling off in standards on the part of the G.W.R. itself. The figures for the years 1936, 1937 and 1938 were:

AGGREGATE DAILY MILEAGE BOOKED AT 58 M.P.H. AND OVER

Year	1936	1937	1938
G.W.R.	3729	3857	4144
L.M.S.R.	2964	7694	8934
L.N.E.R.	2219	3401	4497
S.R.	204	318	318

Once again, as on so many previous occasions, the Great Western had by its own enterprise and achievement stirred other administrations to excel it.

Before leaving the subject of high speed running by individual trains more than a passing reference is needed to the agitation that took place in the winter of 1937–8 for some acceleration of the Birmingham service. The introduction of the high-speed Bristolian express in the Centenary year went some way towards making a counterblast to the L.N.E.R. high-speed streamlined service to Darlington and Newcastle; but there was no

Great Western counterpart, in the Coronation year of 1937, to the additional streamlined services of the L.N.E.R. nor to the Coronation Scot of the L.M.S.R. With a 1¾-hour service existing between London and Bristol there was a weighty concensus of public opinion that a 1¾-hour service over the shorter distance between Paddington and Birmingham ought to be possible. One gathers however, from correspondence in 'The Railway Gazette' and elsewhere, that there was some strong resistance inside the G.W.R. to any acceleration over that route. It was suggested that those who advocated acceleration over this route were not entirely acquainted with its physical difficulties, both in regard to gradients and speed restrictions. The latter certainly occurred at points where a reduction of speed hampered the subsequent climbing of severe gradients, as at High Wycombe and Leamington, while some of the less severe restrictions such as those at Ashendon and Aynho junctions interrupted what could have been unbroken stretches of sustained fast running.

For many years the standards of individual engine performance over that route had been very high; in fact certain very experienced observers of locomotive running considered that for many years the finest daily work in the British Isles was to be seen on the two-hour expresses between Paddington and Birmingham. There is little doubt however that the various speed restrictions were not always accurately observed, and when the high-speed streamlined services were introduced on the L.N.E.R. insistence was rightly placed upon the very strict observance of all speed restrictions, permanent or temporary, imposed by the civil engineer, and the locomotives were fitted with speed recording apparatus on which a graphic record of every journey was taken, and subsequently examined by the locomotive running department officers. Thus, when consideration came to be given to possible acceleration over the Birmingham route of the G.W.R. the route was examined very carefully in the locomotive drawing office at Swindon, and all its physical features were related to the capacity of the 'King' class locomotives. The investigation set out to determine the maximum load that could be conveyed on a non-stop run of 1¾ hours over the 110.6 miles from Paddington to Snow Hill. For the purpose of the exercise an overall maximum speed limit of 80 m.p.h. was taken, though in ordinary daily running speeds up to 85 m.p.h. were of regular occurrence. In addition, speed curves were drawn to show the working required with a 400-ton train on the existing two-hour schedule, with a 3-min. intermediate stop at Leamington on both the down and up runs.

The investigation showed that to permit of a reasonable recovery margin in the case of temporary engineering restrictions the maximum load that could be conveyed on a 1¾-hour schedule was 300 tons. This was surprisingly good, having regard to the physical conditions to be encountered, but contemporary comment suggested that some of the old Great Western enterprise was missing. There was reference to the

300-ton maximum in rather apologetic terms, as the best that could be done if there was a public demand for such a service. In the past the Great Western management had not waited for 'public demand' before it had put on improved services. The Cornish Riviera Express, the Ocean Mail specials and other innovations were not the result of public demands; they were offered to the public with appropriate publicity, and the public welcomed them. 'The Silver Jubilee' of the L.N.E.R. was not the result of public demand; it was a brain-child of Sir Nigel Gresley's, but it brought good financial results and immense prestige to the railway. If the Bristolian was limited to a 7-coach train was there any need to carry more on a service of high-speed trains between Paddington and Birmingham? As it was, it was left to the L.M.S.R. to cut the London–Birmingham below the time-honoured two hours—by no more than 5 min. it is true, but by a longer route. The fact that this move evoked no response from the G.W.R. suggested that a more placid contemplation of competitive services had taken root at Paddington. Certainly one could not have imagined such a challenge going unanswered in the days of Sir Felix Pole! The running diagrams prepared in the Swindon drawing office are reproduced herewith, and are extremely interesting as evidence of the scientific study of engine performance then in progress. It was this study that eventually evolved the systems of locomotive testing that were to be adopted as a national standard after 1948.

The publication of the charts together with the somewhat apologetic and defensive tone of the accompanying article led to a lively correspondence in 'The Railway Gazette' from which three salient points emerged:

1. That there would be a wide popular welcome for a $1\frac{3}{4}$-hour service, particularly if it were not confined, as in the case of Bristol, to a single high-speed train in each direction.

2. That the difficulties of working, from the locomotive point of view, were being greatly exaggerated.

3. That it was more necessary to bring up the general average of train services over the G.W.R. system rather than put on 'star' trains over specially favourable routes.

For many years the Great Western had held the world record for length of non-stop run; by the summer of 1937 the Paddington–Plymouth run had dropped back into 11th place, and it was then made by the 12.50 a.m. newspaper train, and not by the Cornish Riviera Express, which, as the table on page 137 shows ran non-stop only between Paddington and Newton Abbot in each direction. The long runs ahead of the 1937 Great Western maximum of 225.5 miles including one American and two French, but all the rest were British on either the L.M.S.R. or the L.N.E.R. In view of the one-time ascendancy of the G.W.R. in this respect, the details of journeys being regularly made non-stop, down to, and including the Paddington—Newton Abbot runs of the Cornish Riviera Express, are tabulated herewith:

THE WORLD'S LONGEST NON-STOP RUNS—1937.

Country	Railway	Distance miles	Between	Fastest av speed m.p.h.	Fastest train	Traction
G.B.	L.N.E.R.	392.7	Kings Cross and Edinburgh	56.1	Flying Scotman	Steam
G.B.	L.M.S.R.	299.1	Euston and Carlisle	63.4	Coronation Scot	Steam
G.B.	L.N.E.R.	268.3	Newcastle and Kings Cross	67.9	Coronation	Steam
G.B.	L.M.S.R.	263.6	Euston and Holyhead	51.9	Irish Mail	Steam
U.S.A.	Burlington	254.4	Denver and McCook	73.4	Denver Zephyr	Diesel
France	P.O.Midi	249.1	Paris and Limoges	60.2	Barcelona Express	Electric
G.B.	L.M.S.R.	243.2	Glasgow and Crewe	47.9	Night Scot	Steam
G.B.	L.M.S.R.	234.2	Euston and Morecambe	55.8	Ulster Express	Steam
G.B.	L.N.E.R.	232.3	Kings Cross and Darlington	70.4	Silver Jubilee	Steam
France	Nord	226.7	Paris and Liège	57.6	Nord Express	Steam
G.B.	G.W.R.	225.5	Paddington and Plymouth	56.4	12.50 a.m. Newspaper	Steam
France	Est	219.0	Paris and Nancy	62.3	9.9 a.m. Up	Steam
G.B.	L.M.S.R.	214.6	Crewe and Carstairs	48.8	Royal Highlander	Steam
G.B.	L.N.E.R.	205.5	York and Edinburgh	61.7	Coronation	Steam
G.B.	L.M.S.R.	205.5	Euston and Prestatyn	53.6	Welshman	Steam
Germany	State	204.7	Berlin and Breslau	76.8	8.6 p.m. Down	Diesel
Germany	State	200.1	Leipzig and Nuremberg	56.4	Fliegende Münchener	Diesel
Italy	State	196.5	Rome and Florence	62.1	(no name)	Electric
G.B.	G.W.R.	193.7	Paddington and Newton Abbot	60.2	Cornish Riviera	Steam

From the criticisms made by certain correspondents to 'The Railway Gazette' following the London–Birmingham $1\frac{3}{4}$-hour investigation, it is a natural step to review the express service as a whole. I have prepared a table showing the services from London to fifty-two provincial centres during the summer service of 1938. This table not only sets out the fastest trains over the route but the average service provided by all the

EXPRESS SERVICES FROM LONDON
SUMMER SEASON 1938

Station	Dist. miles	Fastest time	Av. Speed m.p.h.	Number of Fast Trains Down	Up	Average time Min. Down	Up
WEST OF ENGLAND							
Westbury	95.6	95	60.3	5	6	106	116
Yeovil	141.4	147	57.8	4	4	159	173
Weymouth	168.8	185	54.7	4	4	203	214
Taunton	142.7	140	61.2	5	4	146	155
Exeter	173.5	175	59.5	6	4	189	184
Dawlish	185.7	198	56.2	4	4	226	242
Newton Abbot	193.6	215	54.0	5	6	228	244
Torquay	199.5	210	57.0	4	5	241	252
Plymouth	225.5	245	55.2	3	3	275	270
Looe	242.2	355	40.9	3	3	388	382
Newquay	281.3	370	45.6	2	3	430	410
Truro	279.2	336	50.0	3	4	380	379
Falmouth	291.2	378	46.2	3	4	430	420
St. Ives	303.7	395	46.1	4	4	462	443
Penzance	305.0	390	46.9	3	4	434	436
BRISTOL etc.							
Swindon	77.3	65	71.4	7	8	89	83
Chippenham	94.0	89	63.4	7	6	115	114
Bath	106.9	102	62.8	8	7	112	119
Bristol	188.3	105	67.7	10	9	138	140
Weston-super-Mare	137.4	152	54.2	8	7	181	181
Bridgwater	151.5	163	55.7	7	6	212	226
WEST MIDLAND							
Oxford	63.4	60	63.4	11	11	82½	75
Evesham	106.6	118	54.2	3	3	126	121
Worcester	120.4	130	55.5	3	3	139	140
Hereford	149.7	205	43.9	3	3	205	215
SOUTH WALES							
Newport	133.4	132	60.7	7	8	145	159
Cardiff	145.1	152	57.3	7	8	168	179
Bridgend	165.4	187	52.9	5	3	209	206
Port Talbot	177.5	212	50.2	5	5	220	223
Neath	183.1	223	49.3	5	5	235	233
Swansea	190.9	225	50.9	7	7	241	247
Llanelly	200.1	254	47.3	6	5	272	281
Carmarthen	220.5	280	47.3	6	4	305	324
Tenby	249.5	368	40.7	3	3	380	411
Pembroke Dock	261.0	390	40.1	3	3	415	430
Haverfordwest	251.1	357	42.2	3	3	371	417
Milford Haven	259.5	378	41.3	3	3	402	428
Fishguard	261.4	350	44.7	3	4	371	380
Barry	176.9	213	49.8	7	8	218	228
GLOUCESTER etc.							
Gloucester	114.1	122	56.1	9	7	170	148
Cheltenham	120.9	140	57.8	10	8	188	174
Ross-on-Wye	130.2	205	31.8	3	3	219	254
BIRMINGHAM & NORTH							
Banbury	67.4	69	58.6	5	4	84	82
Leamington	87.3	90	58.3	6	7	92	100
Birmingham	110.6	120	55.3	6	8	122	127
Wolverhampton	123.0	145	50.9	6	7	148	157
Wellington	142.6	170	50.3	5	5	181	194
Shrewsbury	152.9	184	49.9	6	7	195	207
Oswestry	181.5	221	49.2	5	5	234	248
Chester	195.2	259	45.3	5	5	265	283
Birkenhead	210.4	287	44.0	5	5	310	316
Stratford-on-Avon	103.4	127	48.9	5	4	133	149

fast trains scheduled each week-day. This gives a better idea of the general standard of service than consideration of no more than the star trains. Taking a few places of intermediate size, as first examples there is, for instance, Weston-super-Mare; the fastest time was 152 min. but the average time, equally by 8 down and 7 up trains was 181 min., representing average speeds of 54.2 m.p.h. and 45.5 m.p.h. An industrial centre like Port Talbot fared better, for while its fastest train took 212 min. to cover the 177½ miles from Paddington, the average times of 5 down and 5 up expresses were 220 and 223 min. respectively. There was, of course, a great disparity between fastest and average in the case of Bristol, for against the 105-min. run of the Bristolian the average of ten fast trains in the down direction—including the Bristolian—was only 138 min. The difference between fastest and average in the down direction was thus one of 67.7 against 51.5 m.p.h.

The fastest average speeds naturally became slower as one proceeded farther from London, and the falling became most rapid on lines where the initial speed was highest. Thus on the West of England main line while Westbury, Taunton and Exeter had services at, or only a shade under 60 m.p.h. the best average dropped to 55 m.p.h. to Plymouth, 50 m.p.h. to Truro, and 46.9 m.p.h. to Penzance. This of course is understandable in view of the severity of the gradients. But on the Birmingham and North line it was the frequency of intermediate stops that lowered the averages: 58.2 m.p.h. to Leamington; 55.3 m.p.h. to Birmingham; 50.9 m.p.h. to Wolverhampton; 50.3 m.p.h. to Wellington; 49.8 m.p.h. to Shrewsbury; 45.2 m.p.h. to Chester; and 44 m.p.h. to Birkenhead. On the South Wales main line the Newport and Cardiff spurts of the 7.55 p.m. down Irish boat express rather stood apart from the average standards of the South Wales services. But west of Cardiff the averages tailed off much more gradually from 52.9 m.p.h. to Bridgend, to 47.3 m.p.h. to Carmarthen and 44.7 m.p.h. to Fishguard. The fastest averages fell off rapidly if there were branch line connections to be made, even by through carriages, and one finds the fastest trains of 1938 averaging only 46.2 m.p.h. to Falmouth, 40.8 m.p.h. to Looe, 45.5 m.p.h. to Newquay and 46.2 m.p.h. to St. Ives. All these fastest services were, as would be expected, by connection off the Cornish Riviera Express. The Weymouth line had some excellent trains, with a fastest average of 57.8 m.p.h. to Yeovil and 54.7 m.p.h. throughout to Weymouth, by connection and through carriage off the 3.30 p.m. from Paddington.

One of the finest average services in the Great Western timetable of 1938 was that to and from Bath, with eight down expresses averaging no more than 112 min. (57.3 m.p.h.) and seven up expresses averaging 119 min. (54 m.p.h.). This was distinctly better than the Bristol average, and so far as average train time then prevailing one could reach Bath in quicker time than Chippenham, to which the average time of seven down expresses was as much as 115 min. for 94 miles. Chippenham was no more than slightly better than Bath in the up direction, with an average time of 114 min. against 119 min. By far the greatest uniformity of service was on the Birmingham route, where six down expresses averaged 122 min. against a fastest time of 120 min., and eight up expresses averaged 127 min. against the standard fastest time of 120 min. Taking all round the services to and from London were good, and the fastest, even to remote branch line termini like Looe, Pembroke Dock, and Milford Haven still measured up to Professor Foxwell's one-time standard of speed for qualification as an 'express train'—an overall average speed of 40 m.p.h.

FASTEST TIMES BETWEEN PROVINCIAL TOWNS

From	To	Distance miles	Time min.	Average Speed m.p.h.
Birmingham	Birkenhead	99.8	162	37.0
,,	Bristol	98.8	128	46.2
,,	Cardiff	117.1	150	47.8
,,	Cheltenham	54.1	60	54.1
,,	Gloucester	60.9	73	50.1
,,	Penzance	305.6	485	37.8
,,	Plymouth	226.1	332	40.8
,,	Torquay	200.1	300	40.0
Bristol	Cardiff	38.0	54	42.1
,,	Cheltenham	44.7	58	46.3
,,	Exeter	75.6	95	47.8
,,	Plymouth	127.6	187	40.8
Cardiff	Plymouth	165.6	297	33.5
,,	Swansea	45.8	61	45.2
Liverpool	Bristol	187.8	310	36.3
,,	Cardiff	162.5	251	38.8
,,	Plymouth	279.8	517	32.5
,,	Torquay	253.8	463	32.9

One sees the other side of the 'coin' when it comes to examining the train service between important provincial towns, and in a further table I have set out the running of the fastest trains from Liverpool, from Birmingham, from Bristol and from Cardiff, to certain other large centres. Where the service over the West to North route via the Severn Tunnel is concerned I have extended the journeys to Liverpool, because the L.M.S.R. continued the same kind of treatment to its cross-country passengers north of Shrewsbury. The results are really rather shocking! It is extraordinary to recall that the very fastest train between Bristol and Exeter averaged no more than 47.8 m.p.h., while the best average from Bristol to Plymouth was only 40.8 m.p.h. The fast times between Birmingham, Cheltenham and Gloucester were made by the South Wales railcars, and not the Wolverhampton–Penzance expresses, and the overall average speeds by this latter service of 40.8 m.p.h. from Birmingham to

Plymouth, 40.0 m.p.h. to Torquay and 37.8 m.p.h. to Penzance make a vivid contrast to the corresponding average speeds of the best trains from London to those places. Speeds along the same main line were poor, as for example, only 45.2 m.p.h. from Cardiff to Swansea, and 37 m.p.h. from Birmingham to Birkenhead. One can only assume that better services were not called for.

XIV

The Last Years of Peace

Until the year 1938 the Great Western Railway had never paid a dividend of less than 3 per cent. on the ordinary shares, and it was a source of great pride to the management that its full trustee status should have been preserved through such difficult times as those of the 1930s. In 1937 indeed, things had improved sufficiently for a 4 per cent. dividend to be paid. All the time nevertheless it had been a fight against odds: odds of varying and severe nature, but none more frustrating than the manifestly unfair conditions in which railways as a whole were compelled to compete against road haulage. Reference to this had been made each year at the annual general meeting since the late 1920s, and the railway agitation had received a sufficiently sympathetic hearing from Mr. Baldwin's Government of 1925–9 to secure the setting up of a Royal Commission on Transport. Unfortunately, economic conditions over the country as a whole so absorbed the attentions of the Labour Government that followed, and the National Government that followed it in the autumn of 1931 that the railway industry did not get the attention it needed.

In February 1932, however, the immediate national financial crisis having been surmounted, the four main line railway companies combined to start a campaign for the revision of the age-old legislation that so hampered them in competition with the road hauliers. Winston Churchill, when Chancellor of the Exchequer, had said in the House of Commons on April 24, 1928: 'It is the duty of the State to hold the balance even between road and rail,' and with this statement as its basis the railways issued a booklet under the title 'Fair Play for the Railways'. The case was admirably summarised by the Chairman of the G.W.R., Viscount Churchill, in his statement to the shareholders, at the Annual General Meeting of the Company on February 24, 1932, thus:

Ladies and Gentlemen, it is not in the public interest that railway revenue should continue to be depleted by road competition, which in many cases is rendered possible only by the inequality of treatment accorded to the road and rail industries. Representations on this subject have again been made to the Ministry of Transport by the four main-line railway companies, and I sincerely hope they will receive the immediate attention of the Government, and that steps will be taken forthwith to adjust the balance fairly between the two competing industries. When all relevant costs have been taken into consideration, conveyance by rail still remains the most economical form of transport in the country and while I fully recognise that the development of motor transport has been of great benefit to the country, it is not right that public funds should be used to aid one form of transport at the expense of another. The road motor industry claims that the licence and import petrol duties constitute an adequate contribution towards the cost of the roads, but until Parliament has decided what proportion of the licence and import petrol duties should be earmarked as a sumptuary tax on private cars and as a tax on a foreign product used in competition with the country's coal supplies, it is not possible to

Plate 35. WARTIME AT BRISTOL

Children being evacuated February, 1941

Damaged coaches outside Temple Meads after an air raid

Plate 36. PADDINGTON BOMBED

The general offices, facing Eastbourne Terrace, after a direct hit, April 1941

The scene in the cab approach after the raid

Plate 37. AIR RAID DAMAGE

Birmingham Snow Hill, November 1940

The booking offices, Temple Meads, January 1941

Plate 38. AMERICAN LOCOMOTIVES ARRIVE

Unloading an Austerity 2-8-0 at Cardiff, November 1942

Unloading a 0-6-0T shunter at Cardiff, December 1943

ascertain the actual amount contributed by road transport towards the cost of the roadways and its apportionment among the different classes of road users.

It may interest you to know, however, that in the case of large omnibus companies the total amount paid annually for licence and import duties represents only about 11½ per cent. of their gross receipts. Approximately 15 per cent. of the gross receipts of the Great Western Railway Company go in maintaining and signalling our permanent way alone, but this figure is increased to 33 per cent. of the gross receipts when allowance is made for a return of even a modest 4 per cent. on the capital expended on the construction of our lines.

Our position in regard to local rates also compares unfavourably with that of our road competitors. We have to pay local rates in every district through which the railway runs, whereas road hauliers have no similar burden. The railway companies (although they are themselves probably the largest road users in the country when their extensive interests in omnibus companies are borne in mind) submit that in the national interest the ratepayer and the taxpayer should be relieved from the whole cost of providing, maintaining and policing roads, and that all future expenditure should be borne by the road users as such and apportioned between them upon an equitable basis. Apart from the question of road costs, road transport companies enjoy the further advantage of not being subject to the same legal regulations as the railway companies, and this applies particularly in the case of freight charges to which I will refer later.

The Road Traffic Act, 1930, provides that the Traffic Commissioners, when fixing the passenger fares to be charged by road undertakings, shall have regard to the fares charged by other forms of transport. It appears to have been the intention of Parliament that the Traffic Commissioners should thus regulate competition between road and rail, and whilst the railway companies appreciate the way in which the Traffic Commissioners are carrying out their difficult duties, it is obviously impossible for them to deal satisfactorily with competing industries while those industries operate under unequal conditions. The Act also contains provision in regard to speed limits and hours of duty, but these are openly disregarded by the owners of both passenger and goods vehicles, as is shown by the flagrant instances which have been brought to the notice of the Minister of Transport and the Home Office. The weight limits prescribed by the Motor Vehicles Regulations 1931 are also freely ignored.

With regard to merchandise traffic, the road hauliers have the great advantage of being able to select their traffic, and they are under no obligation in regard to the charges they make for the traffic they convey. It is well known that in many cases their charges for return loads bear no relation to the cost of transport, and while individual traders may derive temporary benefit from this state of things, it is obvious that if the practice is not checked it must ultimately lead to a chaotic position which will be detrimental to the general interest.

The dangers of unregulated road competition are referred to in the following extract from the final Report of the Royal Commission on Transport. The Report says: 'The growth of road traffic, however, has been so rapid during the past decade that an entirely new situation has developed. At first regarded as complementary, road transport soon became highly competitive with rail transport, and this, accentuated by the depression in the heavy basic industries and the stable textile trades—an unfortunate feature of recent years—has created problems not peculiar to this country alone. If allowed to continue unchecked or uncontrolled, the evil results of this competition will become even more serious, and will not only adversely affect the financial stability of those who provide transport facilities, but will also hamper the development of trade and the economic progress of the nation.'

To summarise the position, we think it is essential both in the interests of the railway companies and of the nation that the Government should take immediate action to adjust the balance fairly between the competing road and rail interests.

There can be no disputing the fact that an efficient railway system is a national necessity, and I have no hesitation in saying that the British railways are the finest and the most efficient in the world. We are making every effort further to improve our facilities and services, and are quite prepared to meet any road competition which may arise provided it is conducted on an equitable basis. If, however, we are forced to reduce unduly the charges on traffic in the higher classes it will ultimately be necessary for us to make good our losses by an increase in our charges for low-grade traffic. This means that the basic industries of the country would be penalised as the result of reductions made in other charges to meet unfair and subsidised competition. I earnestly ask all our shareholders to support the representations which we have made and which have been published in the press. The matter is essentially one for Parliament to deal with, and we are hopeful that Parliament will recognise that the merits of our case justify immediate action being taken.

Six anxious years were to follow, during which an enormous amount of 'back-stage' work was done, and when Lord Horne addressed the shareholders in February 1938 the prospects were hopeful. But by then the International situation was assuming the utmost gravity. Following the Nazi coup in Austria the early summer passed with the threat to Czechoslovakia growing stronger every week, and much of the immediate attention of railway managements was given over to the working out of arrangements to be put into effect in emergency. These preparations are referred to in some detail later. But the mounting International tension, and the strain it inevitably put upon all members of the Government, led to something of a pause in the pressing of the railway case for new legislation. But when the now-notorious Munich Conference took place, in which the Prime Minister, Mr. Neville Chamberlain, met the French, German and Italian leaders and reached agreement, the tension, if not the suspicion was relieved, and on November 23, 1938 a deputation of railway chairmen waited upon the Minister of Transport to present a memorandum stressing the case for a revision of legislation on the methods of charging rates for merchandise traffic. They proposed abolition of the existing merchandise classification and the repeal of publication requirements and undue preference legislation. At the same time a vigorous campaign was inaugurated in the Press, and by posters and streamers demanding 'A Square Deal Now.'

This campaign was of course common to all the railways, and not confined to the Great Western; but it formed so large and vital a part of all railway management considerations at that time that its inauguration and progress must inevitably loom large in the history of any railway company at that period. Very soon however it was evident that the appeal for a square deal was having a somewhat mixed reception. This is clearly indicated in some contemporary press comments. 'The Daily Telegraph' was firmly on the side of the railways, thus:

With the demand for parity with the road hauliers there can be no quarrel in principle, for it is beyond doubt that the unilateral restriction upon the freedom of the railways in fixing their charges operates unfairly in favour of the road hauliers. . . .

It is of the first importance to realise that the railways perform an indispensable function, and that the community therefore has the inescapable obligation of ensuring them such conditions as will enable them to pay their way.

'The News Chronicle', while agreeing with the fairness of the railways' case gave a clear hint towards some form of national control, if not necessarily national ownership:

The railway companies' claim must be carefully weighed and treated as a matter of urgency. But it may well be that the problem will prove insoluble until there is a nation-wide organisation of transport in which there will be established a community of interest between road and rail—both working in co-operation on a public or semi-public utility basis.

'The Daily Express' was definitely hostile:

The railways are asking for something that the public will never concede to them. They are asking that they should be granted the power to fix privately the charges and conditions for the conveyance of merchandise . . .

If we conferred that right upon the railways, there would be two rates, one for the rich and another for the poor.

I have the clearest recollections of the period, both as a season-ticket holder, and frequent traveller, and I have vivid memories of many conversations overheard in trains and on the stations. It is to be feared that the poster and streamers campaign made very little impression upon the public. Very few ordinary travellers were affected by what was the heart and soul of the campaign—the fixing of freight charges. Occasions of late running during the winter months are always the subject for grumbles, and during the winter of 1938–9 one not infrequently heard the comment that it was the railways who should give their passengers a square deal! The brutal fact was that an overwhelming majority of passengers had no other interest in railways other than getting from point A to point B, and the appeal, so far as the public was concerned, fell largely upon deaf ears. And then, the new year of 1939 was not many weeks old before further Hitlerian aggression in Europe reopened all the wounds of 1938, and showed clearly that a major war could not long be averted.

Nevertheless it must be recorded that the reports of the Transport Advisory Council, which had been set up by the Minister of Transport to examine the 'Square Deal' campaign, issued on May 19, 1939, had all the ingredients of a settlement, recommending a general relaxation of statutory rates control in favour of extensive transport co-ordination. Controversy did not end however with the publication of the report. The Minister of Transport, then Capt. Euan Wallace, had a rough passage in the House of Commons, because the contents of the report were made public before being laid before Parliament. A month earlier 'The Railway Gazette', well informed as usual as to the likely contents of the report, had an amusing leader under the heading of 'War and Peace':

It is becoming increasingly apparent that a large section of the daily press loves the sabre-rattling species of news items. Whether their clients as a whole are equally enamoured of this tendency to foster bellicosity and war psychosis is a moot point, although soaring circulations compel our grudging admission that publicists' poison is still multitudinous readers' meat. An eminent railway chieftain, addressing his very friendly enemies in their own camp, was emboldened to say that wars, controversies and disagreements invariably filled columns, whereas, when peace, concord and harmony reigned, there was 'nothing to report'; allowing for a modicum of rhetorical hyperbole, we concur with the illustrious speaker. Wherefore, we trust, fervently, that, if rail and road, their differences satisfactorily composed, lie down and bask contentedly together in the genial warmth of co-ordination, such a felicitous event will ignite at least a 'scintilla' of journalistic comment. No less fervently do we trust that the furnaces of the press will refrain from roaring, if the railways' antagonists, intransigent to the last, maintain that a modified rating structure is a 'violation of the status quo,' that carrying competitive merchandise is an 'act of aggression,' and that in short the envisaged 'square deal' is (with due respect to geometricians) nothing more than economic 'encirclement.'

Light-hearted as one would like to be however the times were becoming desperately serious, and so, in the face of International crisis, the last bid of the old railway companies of Great Britain for a modernisation of their 'terms of reference' had to be laid aside. When the war did come, in September 1939, they were brought immediately under Government control, and ultimately after six years of the most fearful years of their history they were released only to be nationalised. The whole period of severe competition from road haulage, of the 'Square Deal' campaign, and of subsequent control and legislation left feeling of deep disappointment and resentment among railway stockholders and senior management alike; but the odds against the privately owned railways had become too great, and the General Election of 1945 only hastened their disappearance.

Against this sombre background the Great Western Railway had, in those last years of peace, an interesting record of achievement. One of the most remarkable projects was that launched in February 1938, when the well-known firm of electrical consultants, Messrs. Merz and McLellan, was commissioned to prepare a scheme for the electrification of all lines west of Taunton. This move came as a tremendous surprise, because although the Company was making increased use of diesel railcars for main line working, the Great Western was always considered to be essentially a steam line. But the price of locomotive coal was ever on the increase, and that used west of Taunton was subject to considerable haul, from South Wales. The project was referred to at some length in Lord Horne's address to the shareholders at the Annual General Meeting in February 1938. After saying that they had been watching the upward trend of coal prices with some anxiety he went on to stress that where coal formed so large a proportion of their traffic it was clear that the coalfields and the railway could prosper only in unison. There was, nevertheless, a limit to the price they were prepared to pay for coal. Every shilling increase in price per ton meant an additional cost to the G.W.R. of over £100,000 per year, and while it was recognised that some increase in the price of coal was right, the recent increases had placed a very substantial extra burden on the finances of the Company.

Quite apart from the cost of hauling coal to the locomotive depots in the West of England the physical nature of the routes made electrification a welcome prospect. The severity of the gradients west of Newton Abbot imposed a very severe limitation upon the overall speeds that could be maintained. The curvature of the line largely precluded any compensation for slow hill-climbing by running fast on the favourable stretches. But with electrification some substantial improvement in uphill speeds could reasonably be expected, with an appreciable acceleration of journey times. As indicating the problem the G.W.R. was up against in coal prices the following figures were quoted at the time Messrs. Merz and McLellan were commissioned to prepare the electrification scheme:

Average Net Selling Prices per ton of coal at pit head.

Year	Price per ton
1934	12s. 11d.
1935	13s. 0d.
1936	14s. 0d.

By September 1937 the price had risen to 17s. 1.47d., representing an increase over 1934 of no less than 32 per cent. At the time the project was launched it was thought that not all the branches would be electrified, but as the elimination of steam was thought to be an essential part of the scheme those branches not electrified would be diesel worked, to avoid the necessity of maintaining any steam depots west of Taunton. At the time, amid certain misgivings as to the economic justification for the scheme, 'The Railway Gazette' pointed to the experience of the Swedish State Railways, on which electrification had been found to give very substantially greater practical economies than had been expected. As a result the conversion from steam to electric traction had been extended on a much wider scale than was originally proposed, and always with increasing benefits, not only in economy but in improved traffic facilities.

The report of the consulting engineers was published in May 1939 and was extremely interesting in its frank analysis of steam and electric costs and attributes. The order issued by the Ministry of Transport in 1932 required the railway companies, when electrifying any section of their line, to adopt the direct current system, with collection from a third rail at 750 volts, or from an overhead line at 1,500 volts, or, with the Minister's sanction at 3,000 volts. The consultants were satisfied that on all practical and economic grounds the overhead system was preferable for the Taunton –Penzance line, and for a variety of reasons, they based their estimates on the use of current at a pressure of 3,000 volts. Very careful examination of the line however, showed that owing to the unusually high proportion of curved to straight track, shorter spans than normal would be required between the structures carrying the overhead wire on 61 per cent. of the route, in order to maintain the conductors in their proper position over the centre of the track. This would have involved additional cost, while the installation of the overhead conductors would also have necessitated fairly heavy expenditure in raising bridges, re-siting water columns and signals, and so on. So far as electric locomotives were concerned, the engineers considered it would have been more economical to provide a small number of locomotives suitable for the heaviest passenger and freight trains, and three lighter and less powerful types for other purposes. Altogether it was estimated that about 164 electric locomotives would have been required which, for various reasons, would have replaced

Table I.—ESTIMATE OF CAPITAL EXPENDITURE ON ELECTRIFICATION

Item	Description	Amount, including overhead charges	
1	Overhead line equipment of 450 miles of single-track running lines and 133 miles of sidings, including bonding of the rails, cable connections, supervisory and telephone lines ..	£	£ 1,556,100
2	Alterations to ways and works:—		
	(a) Bridges, water columns and loading gauges ..	59,400	
	(b) Track alterations near Taunton and Newton Abbot ..	70,000	
	(c) Telegraph and telephone circuits	50,000	
	(d) Signal and telegraph poles ..	35,000	
	(e) Track circuits and A.T.C. ..	53,200	
	(f) Capstans, including supply arrangements ..	22,000	289,600
3	Alterations to running sheds and repair shops		105,000
4	Substations and switch cabins ..		475,600
5	Electric locomotives and multiple unit train equipments ..		2,554,000
6	Spare parts for electric locomotives and train equipments, substations and overhead line equipment ..		153,500
			5,133,800
	Less:		
7	Credit value of released steam locomotives ..	726,000	
8	Credit value of coal wagons, coal stock, steam locomotive spare parts ..	46,700	772,700
	Net capital expenditure excluding expenditure, if any, in connection with the supply of power ..		4,361,100

only almost the same number of steam locomotives. The net capital cost of electrifying the lines mentioned was estimated at over £4,000,000, while the balance of saving in working costs available for interest on the net capital expenditure was calculated to work out at less than one per cent. The investigations thus revealed that the section of line was not particularly suited to electrification by reason of its physical characteristics, the nature of the traffic and the wide variation between winter and summer traffic density; while the high cost of electric locomotives was another adverse factor.

The actual estimates are given in the accompanying tables, 1, 2, and 3. So far as the last mentioned is concerned, the amounts for depreciation were calculated on a sinking fund basis on an agreed life, it being assumed

Table II.—COMPARATIVE ESTIMATES OF ANNUAL WORKING COSTS, STEAM AND ELECTRIC

Item	Description	Steam	Electric
		£	£
1	Locomotive coal, including freight ..	157,480	—
2	Electric power, delivered to the substations	—	202,610
3	Oil fuel for train heating	—	7,043
4	Water	7,477	152
5	Lubricants, stores, clothing and miscellaneous	12,439	6,420
6	Footplate staff	206,140	109,297
7	Locomotive preparation, maintenance and repairs	155,251	80,500
8	Superintendence	9,495	7,940
9	Maintenance of engine sheds etc.	3,879	2,140
10	National insurance	21,452	14,500
11	Maintenance and operation of overhead line equipment, and substations	—	41,100
12	Additional maintenance of railway telegraph, telephone and other installations	—	1,375
		573,577	473,077

Saving in annual working costs due to electrification £100,500

that the payments would accumulate with compound interest at 3 per cent. In each case allowance was made for the residual value of the asset. Deducting the net total of £67,786 per annum from the saving in working costs of £100,500 there was a balance of £32,714 available for interest. This however represented no more than 0.75 per cent. of the net capital expenditure, and in face of such a small anticipated return the G.W.R. Board somewhat naturally decided not to proceed with the scheme.

The electrification 'exercise' was a pleasant diversion, in a period of depression, in almost every sense. Financially, the year 1938 was one of the worst ever. This could be attributed in large measure to the uncertainties of the International situation, because although the large programme in re-armament was providing a fillip to the heavy industries in many areas, there was generally a very severe recession in trade. Despite the needs of re-armament the production of pig iron and steel

Table III.—CAPITAL CHARGES ON ELECTRIFICATION EXPENDITURE

Item	Description	Amount
		£
1	Depreciation on overhead line equipment ..	25,500
2	Depreciation on substations and switch cabins	9,415
3	Depreciation of locomotives:— .. .. Electric .. .. .. £42,600 Steam £12,000 	30,600
4	Additional depreciation on railway telegraph, telephone and other installations	2,271
	Total net depreciation	67,786
	Balance of saving in working cost available for interest on net capital expenditure .. Equal to	32,714 0.75 per cent

ingots in Monmouthshire and South Wales decreased by 864,900 tons as compared with 1937—equivalent to no less than 32.9 per cent. As if this were not bad enough, the Great Western suffered badly from domestic mishaps. Just at the period of the peak August traffic severe thunderstorms in South Devon caused serious flooding and damage to the line, to say nothing of traffic dislocation in the Torquay, Newton Abbot, Teignmouth area. Then there were the two disastrous fires in the power signal boxes at Paddington Arrival Box, and Westbourne Bridge. The prompt way in which these latter emergencies were met were in some degree prophetic of the action that became proverbial in the face of enemy air attack in the years that were to follow.

The beginnings of the great scheme for Air Raid Precautions were set in motion on the G.W.R. some years before the International situation welled up to crisis point. It was developed and supervised by the Superintendent of the Line, and a special section was formed to carry out the training of the staff, and the planning of A.R.P. schemes. It was decided that the best way of training the recruits was by instructors drawn from the railway staff. With great care suitable men were selected and sent for a course of instruction at the Home Office Air Raid Precautions School. Then in April 1938 officers of the Company, heads of departments, and sections, members of the clerical staff, and all grades of the traffic, goods, engineering and other departments, attended the first class for the training of G.W.R. staff at Paddington. It was all kept rather quiet, because many men and women liked to feel that they were training only in wise precautions, and that war was not yet inevitable, but also for a reason that Collie Knox has expressed more picturesquely:

> The classes went on every week all through 1938 and 1939, and no one talked about them much at home or in the local 'pub'. The reason for this damping down . . . for this almost ashamed silence on the part of men who were up and doing the while the snorers snored more loudly than ever is obvious. At that time any man who spent his time off 'playing about with hoses and pumps' was judged to be partially demented. He was more often than not an object of affectionate scorn and bantering ridicule. The A.R.P. started its career amid an atmosphere of music-hall jokes and bantering pity.

In the meantime more positive precautions were undertaken. Preparations were made to protect from blast vulnerable features of the lineside equipment. If a signalbox suffered a direct hit there was not much that could be done about it; but a bomb falling in the vicinity could by its blast blow in windows of signalboxes and relay rooms, and cause a lot of damage without seriously interfering with the structure. Consequently much was done to protect windows behind which vital apparatus was located. At first time permitted of nothing more lasting than sandbags, but later many of these windows were bricked up. Stores were built up of supplies likely to be needed for repair work, and to meet the mounting expense the Board, on January 20, 1939, approved an expenditure of £500,000 on A.R.P. At that stage Government funds were to be made available to finance it; but there was a clause in the agreement that if war did eventuate, and the railways were brought under the Government control, the G.W.R. would pay back up to 50 per cent. of the cost. In 1939 a substantial traffic had developed in the transport of the small 'home' air raid shelters, many of the components of which were made in South Wales.

As early as January 29, 1939 arrangements in the London area had been developed to the extent of carrying out a full test exercise in the early hours of a Sunday morning. Between 1.0 a.m. and 4.0 a.m. a 'black-out' was staged, covering the passenger and goods stations, the three miles of running and carriage lines as far as Old Oak Common, and the locomotive depot and the marshalling yards at that point. Lighting throughout the area was drastically reduced; searchlight signals were fitted with extra long shields to prevent the rays being seen from above, and the battery of floodlights at Old Oak Common was replaced by restricted lighting in the yard, offices, and locomotive sheds. All trains passing through the area had blinds drawn and locomotives carried special covering over the engine cabs to prevent the light from the fire-boxes being seen. During the test, work proceeded normally, and there were no delays to trains. At Paddington the company's A.R.P. scheme was tried out, and fire, decontamination, first aid, and rescue squads operated under realistic conditions. Volunteers from the company's staff acted as casualties, and dummies were used in the staged fire exercises in connection with which the Paddington Auxiliary Brigade was called out. During the 'black-out', aerial observation was kept and a special train run between Paddington and Old Oak Common to test restricted train lighting arrangements. The test was carried out in full accordance with schedule. It was preliminary work of this kind that enabled men and women of the G.W.R. to go into action with confidence when the bombs really began to fall.

XV

The War Years : Phase One

Studying the tactics of aggression pursued by the Axis countries in one *coup* after another, and having regard to the speed of military aircraft of that period it was generally assumed that any major war would open with a sudden attack by air, at the utmost speed, to deal a crippling blow at the enemy in the first hours of conflict. The British A.R.P. services both railway, civilian, and other administrations had been trained to deal with such an emergency; casualties were expected to be heavy, and the use of poison gas was anticipated. For many months prior to the actual outbreak of war careful consideration had been given to the evacuation of school children from London and other large cities, because it was then expected that the greatest weight of aerial bombardment would be directed upon the largest centres of population. Plans for large-scale evacuation were therefore drawn up, involving the closest co-operation between school authorities, the railways, and numerous local authorities in the dispersal areas. The plans were completed to the finest details, with due regard to the fact that more than 100,000 children had to be conveyed out of London alone, and that some of this task might well have to be performed under actual air attack.

During the last week of August 1939 the International situation deteriorated so rapidly that the Government decided to commence the evacuation of children on September 1st. Early the same morning Germany attacked Poland in the 'Blitzkrieg' style that our own A.R.P. services had been trained to expect, and also on that same momentous day the Minister of Transport made an Order taking control of the main line railways of Great Britain, of the London Passenger Transport Board, and of certain smaller railway companies that had lain outside the Grouping scheme of 1922. Before recalling many of the achievements of the Great Western Railway during World War II it is important also to refer to the circumstances in which Government control was assumed. On August 24, 1939 the Emergency Powers (Defence) Act, 1939 received the Royal Assent, and Regulation No. 69 issued in pursuance of the Act laid down that:

The Ministry of Transport may by order take control of such railway undertakings as may be specified in the order; and an order made under this regulation in relation to any railway undertaking shall operate as a requirement:
(a) that any property from time to time held by the undertakers for the purposes of the undertaking (other than currency, gold, securities, or negotiable instruments) shall be placed at the disposal of the Minister in accordance with any directions which may be given by him or on his behalf while the order is in force; and (b) that the undertaking shall be carried on in accordance with any directions which may be so given while the order is in force.

Inevitably one makes comparisons with what transpired in 1914. Then, no special Act was passed enabling the take-over to be effected. An Act of 1871, passed at the time of the Franco-Prussian War, provided that:

> When Her Majesty, by order in Council declares that an emergency has arisen in which it is expedient for the public service that Her Majesty's Government shall have control over the railroads in the United Kingdom, or any of them, the Secretary of State may, by warrant, under his hand, empower any person or persons named in such warrant to take possession in the name or on behalf of Her Majesty of any railroad in the United Kingdom, and of the plant belonging thereto.

As in 1914 executive responsibility for running the railways was vested in The Railway Executive Committee. Sir Ralph Wedgwood, recently retired from the high office of Chief General Manager of the L.N.E.R. was Chairman, and the other members of the Committee were the General Managers of the four main line railways and Mr. Frank Pick of the London Passenger Transport Board. This take-over by the Government was of course wholly in the national interest, and the unification of control became all the more vital when the war suddenly took a much more serious turn in May 1940. But the plain fact was that in the wartime emergency a vast amount of private property had been taken over, for the duration, and the shareholders naturally wondered what compensation would be paid to them by the Government for the use of their property. In the meantime the first months of the war involved the railway staffs in many unusual tasks. At the outbreak of war the following chief officers of the Great Western Railway were holding office:

Chairman	Viscount Horne
General Manager	Sir James Milne
Secretary	F. R. E. Davis
Chief Accountant	C. R. Dashwood
Superintendent of the Line	F. R. Potter
Chief Goods Manager	A. Maynard
Chief Engineer	R. Carpmael
Chief Mechanical Engineer	C. B. Collett
Signal and Telegraph Engineer	F. H. D. Page

During the war years there were four changes among the executive officers above, as follows:

January 1940;	Chief Engineer: A. S. Quartermaine
January 1941;	Superintendent of the Line: Gilbert Matthews
July 1941;	Chief Mechanical Engineer: F. W. Hawksworth
July 1942;	Chief Goods Manager: F. W. Lampitt

The great initial task was the evacuation of the children, and the heaviest share of this fell to the Great Western. The country districts of Wessex and the Far West were regarded as relatively safe, and the majority of the reception areas lay between Reading and Penzance. The order for the evacuation was given on Thursday August 31, and so completely were the plans in readiness that the first special train left Ealing Broadway for the West at 8.30 a.m. next morning. This station was chosen as the principal concentration point and rail head for the G.W.R. system because of its connection with the District and Central London lines of London Transport, and it was a remarkable feat of organisation to provide a constant flow of passengers to Ealing Broadway, and to convey them away by train without any congestion, either of passengers waiting for trains, or trains waiting for passengers. In the first two days the evacuees were schoolchildren accompanied by teachers; on the remaining days they were mainly mothers with children, and miscellaneous groups. The success of the heaviest part of the scheme—the schoolchildren—rested on complete control from school to billet. The sustained and systematic 'feed' on which the railway relied for the smooth functioning of its own evacuation services was secured by a careful, and rehearsed, timing of the journey from the school to station. Tickets were issued before leaving school, and the progress of the scheme was so co-ordinated that the evacuees arrived at their entraining stations in complete train-loads, and 15 min. before the departure time of their allotted train.

The general plan was for every train to be made up to twelve coaches and to provide accommodation for 800 passengers. The trains were interchangeable, and it was found that 50 train-sets would be required to carry through the programme. The stock was drawn from many parts of the system. It was concentrated at West London, Old Oak Common, and Acton, at which depots it was marshalled and prepared according to plan. The emergency timetable specified the times at which the empty trains should leave the depots for the entraining point, where provision had been made for them to be stabled in sequence ready to draw into the station for loading up. The preparation of the timetable involved the timing of 64 trains, 60 of them from Ealing Broadway—as a standard programme to be applied to each of the four days of the evacuation. The working was 8.30 a.m. to 5.30 p.m. and trains were planned to leave at 9 min. intervals through the whole period. The actual service was based on the requirements as disclosed by the progress of the evacuation, and varied from 58 trains, with 44,032 passengers, on the first day, to the 28 trains which carried 17,796 passengers on the fourth day. During the evacuation period Ealing Broadway station was entirely closed to ordinary passengers between 8 a.m. and 5.30 p.m. The special trains were queued up on the down relief, and the down goods lines between Acton and Ealing, and with the children arriving marvellously according to plan the specials were able to draw into the down relief line platform at Ealing Broadway, load up, and follow each other with complete precision. The down relief line was monopolised thus during the period of evacuation, and all other traffic ran over the main lines. Ordinary local trains were restricted to one per hour, and omitting a stop at Ealing Broadway. The main line service was much restricted, and all trains carried special headcodes. The down express passenger trains passing Ealing during the time of the evacuation were:

8.40 a.m.	Birmingham (via Oxford)
9.00 a.m.	South Wales
9.45 a.m.	Birmingham (via Oxford)
10.00 a.m.	Penzance
11.30 a.m.	South Wales
12.00 noon	Penzance
1.15 p.m.	Birkenhead (via Oxford)
1.30 p.m.	Penzance
3.15 p.m.	Truro
3.40 p.m.	South Wales
4.00 p.m.	Birkenhead (via Oxford)
5.15 p.m.	Bristol
5.30 p.m.	Worcester
5.55 p.m.	South Wales
6.15 p.m.	Plymouth
6.35 p.m.	Cheltenham

So far as the evacuation trains were concerned the timing was so arranged that coaches working outwards up to mid-day on short-distance trains should be returned empty to Acton yard for use on further evacuation specials later in the same day. The timetable also specified times for the return of long-distance stock so that it should be ready for the resumption of the evacuation early the following morning. All evacuation trains bore numbered identity labels. They were booked at express passenger speeds, and to run non-stop to destination except where it was necessary to make intermediate calls for locomotive purposes. Staff was increased and turns of duty extended, especially on the third day of the evacuation which fell on a Sunday; and extended working of many signal boxes and control offices was necessary to cope with the flow of trains.

The evacuation programme at reception stations was set in motion by the receipt of a wire from the entraining point. This gave the departure time of the train and the approximate number of evacuees it carried. It was then the duty of the stationmaster to advise the local reception officer and road transport officials so that the final feeding and billeting arrangements might be made. Excellent work was done at reception stations, where the staff and voluntary helpers were required to deal with anything up to 800 evacuees, and to superintend their transfer to distribution centres and road vehicles. As far as possible, all trains were cleaned and re-equipped at reception stations before return to the London division, and additional staff was drafted on to work where needed. During the four days over which the London scheme was operated, 163 trains were run and 112,994 evacuees were carried. The train-working arrangements were complicated by the services programmed for ordinary passengers. At the week-end, particularly, these services were heavily taxed by the returning holiday traffic from the West and the considerable pressure of unofficial evacuees. Apart from the London area, the G.W.R. was concerned in the evacuation from Birmingham and Smethwick, and from Birkenhead, Liverpool, and Bootle. In addition, the company was called upon to provide numerous specials for Government departments during the same period. On the evacuation trains engines of the 'Star', 'Castle', 'King', 'Hall', and 'Grange' classes were used on the longer distance workings, while the trains to Reading, Oxford, and so on, were mostly worked by 2-6-2 suburban tank engines of the '61XX' class.

The drastically reduced train service run during the period of the evacuation was continued until Sunday September 24, and on the following day there came into operation the first full war timetable, completely printed in the usual book form on sale to the public at the then-standard price of sixpence. The expected aerial attacks had not come, but the severity of the railway service curtailments, and the extent of the decelerations were clearly intended to provide for some recovery in the event of serious damage to parts of the line. The institution of this first war timetable naturally invoked comparisons with the services provided during World War I. The outstanding difference between 1939 and 1918 was that the service operated at the end of World War I was the result of a gradual curtailment, and then of deceleration. The Cornish Riviera Express, for example, was still running at pre-war speed, though with vastly increased loads until the winter of 1916. In 1939 the evacuation, and the expectance of aerial attack led to an immediate and drastic deceleration. The maximum start-to-stop average speed of any express train was laid down at 45 m.p.h., while at first all West of England trains ran via Bristol, and made stops at Chippenham and Bath. Restaurant and sleeping cars were cut out altogether. The accompanying table compares the facilities available to the public in October 1918, October 1938 and October 1939, and the severity of the decelerations are certainly emphasised.

With the exception of the Cardiff service from London, which was equal to that of 1918, and the Worcester service which was faster, all the services were slower, the fastest time to and from Plymouth, in particular, was 45 min. slower than that of 1918, and 1 hr. 40 min. slower than that of 1938, while the average times similarly were 47 min. slower than 1918, and 1 hr. 42 min. slower than 1938. One reason for the substantial deceleration to and from Plymouth and Penzance was that no day trains at first used the Westbury route, all the West of England services being over the Bristol route, which is 20 miles longer, and involved stops at Chippenham, Bath and Bristol. The only regular weekday express using the Westbury line was the 1.15 a.m. night train from Paddington to Penzance, which also, incidentally, then made the longest non-stop run on the system —Paddington–Taunton, 142.7 miles in 3hr. 5 min. at 46.3 m.p.h. That speed of 45 to 47 m.p.h. from start to stop was the limit in the new emergency timetable, and compared with a normal fastest schedule of 71.4 m.p.h. (the Cheltenham Flyer). In that respect the new timetable was

G.W.R. EMERGENCY MAIN LINE TIMETABLE, OCTOBER, 1939

FASTEST AND AVERAGE TIMES AND FREQUENCY OF SERVICE BETWEEN PADDINGTON AND VARIOUS PROVINCIAL CENTRES IN 1918, 1938 and 1939

London and:—	Distance	Fastest Time			No. of Trains Daily			Average Time			Average Deceleration 1938–1939	
	miles	Oct., 1918 h. m.	Oct., 1938 h. m.	Oct., 1939 h. m.	Oct., 1918	Oct., 1938	Oct., 1939	Oct., 1918 h. m.	Oct., 1938 h. m.	Oct., 1939 h. m.	h. m.	per cent.
Oxford	63.5	1 18	1 00	1 28	14	26	20	1 30	1 20	1 39	0 19	24
Birmingham	110.6	2 30	2 00	2 33	10	14	8	2 46	2 05	2 51	0 46	37
Bristol	118.3	2 15	1 45	2 35	16	20	14	2 45	2 15	2 58	0 43	32
Worcester	120.4	3 06	2 10	3 06	8	12	8	3 41	2 37	3 20	0 43	27
Cardiff	145.1	3 10	2 41	3 15	10	14	8	3 23	2 55	3 23	0 28	16
Plymouth (N'th Rd.)	225.5*	5 00	4 05	5 45	8	12	9	5 39	4 44	6 26	1 42	36
Penzance	305.0†	7 55	6 30	8 35	6	9	6	9 11	7 18	9 35	2 17	31

* Via Bristol, 245.9 miles, in 1939   † Via Bristol, 325.4 miles in 1939

Plate 39. SHIPPING SUPPLIES TO RUSSIA

Cable being loaded at Barry, May 1946

Electrical equipment loading at Barry, November 1946

Plate 40. WARTIME 2-8-0s ON THE G.W.R.

Standard '28XX' class 2-8-0 No. 2884

Stanier '8F' 2-8-0 No. 8400 built at Swindon

American Austerity 2-8-0 No. 1604

considerably more drastic in its slowing down than that of the latter part of 1918, when, for example, the modified down Cornishman ran the 95.6 miles from Paddington to Westbury in 107 min., at 53.6 m.p.h., and there were other schedules up to 54.4 m.p.h. in speed, when the fastest peacetime booking had been 59.2 m.p.h. As a result of its higher booked speed, and of taking the Westbury route, the 10.15 a.m. down in 1918 reached Plymouth North Road at 3.15 p.m., whereas the 10.30 a.m. down of September 1939 from Paddington was not due in Plymouth till 4.40 p.m.; normally the 10.30 a.m. Cornish Riviera Express reached Plymouth at 2.35 p.m.

As far as possible, departures from Paddington in the new timetable were retained at times to which passengers were accustomed, such as 10.30 a.m., 1.15, 4.15, and 6.30 p.m. to Bristol and the West of England; 8.55 a.m., 1.55, 5.55 and 7.55 p.m. to South Wales, and 9.10 a.m., 2.10 and 6.10 p.m. to Birmingham and the North; but the considerable gaps in this list, as compared with the normal departures, are obvious. Thus the 10.30 a.m. had to carry the passengers previously using the 10.0 a.m. Bristolian, the 10.30 Cornish Riviera Express and the 11.15 a.m. to Bristol and Weston-super-Mare; similarly the 1.15 p.m. incorporated the 12 noon Torbay Limited, the 1.15 p.m. to Bristol and Weston, and the 1.40 p.m. to Penzance; and the 4.15 p.m. combined the 3.30 p.m. to Plymouth, the 4.15 p.m. to Bristol, and the 5.5 p.m. to Plymouth. There were corresponding combinations in the up direction. Among curious effects of the re-organisation was that a station like Chippenham got a service to and from Paddington not far short of normal. Owing to diversion of the West of England expresses from the Westbury route, although certain Weymouth trains still travelled via Newbury, a number of previous Weymouth connections were made at Chippenham, West of England expresses being stopped for the purpose. In the emergency timetable fourteen daily services between Paddington and Chippenham averaged 2 hr. 20 min. in journey, as against sixteen trains averaging 1 hr. 59 min. normally.

As regards cross-country trains, the service between Birmingham and the West of England via Stratford-upon-Avon and Cheltenham, as well as that between Birmingham and South Wales by the same route, was entirely suspended. The North to West service via Shrewsbury and Hereford was cut down to one day, one evening, and one night train in each direction connecting the L.M.S.R. main line at Crewe with Bristol and the West of England. The Birmingham and South Wales service was maintained by way of Malvern and Hereford. All through services to and from the Southern Railway via Basingstoke, via Reading, and via Salisbury were suspended, as well as those to and from the L.N.E.R. via Banbury, with the exception of one L.N.E.R. night service in each direction, which worked to and from Swindon. In contrast to the main line curtailments, very little alteration was made to the normal London suburban services. Until after about 7 p.m., these were practically normal, with a minor amount of slowing down of trains running the longer distances to the outer suburban area. Reading still had most of its excellent non-stop service to and from Paddington, though there the travelling time was increased from the 39 to 40 min. of the normal timetable to a general figure of 47 min. for the 36 miles. In 1918 the time allowed was 43 min. On the country branches, although certain cancellations were made, and the times of other trains were altered to connect with altered times of main line-trains, services in general were well maintained, and the normal times of the majority of the trains, especially those radiating from the various centres like Birmingham, Wolverhampton, Bristol, Cardiff, Newport, and Plymouth, were very little altered. The reduction of branch services could be taken to average not more than 10 to 20 per cent. of the trains, and of local suburban services from 5 to 10 per cent.

From October 16 however, the Railway Executive Committee gave permission for restaurant cars to be restored on a limited number of trains. On the Great Western this amounted to 28 weekday and 10 Sunday services. A fortnight later the Cornish Riviera Express was restored to its normal route via Westbury, and scheduled to run non-stop between Paddington and Exeter. In these abnormal circumstances the Great Western regained the record for the longest non-stop run in Great Britain, though the average speed of only 48.4 m.p.h. did not involve any exceptional locomotive work. At the same time the original wartime 10.30 a.m. down from Paddington, which ran via Bristol, was changed to 10.35 a.m. and reached Penzance at 7.40 p.m. Quite apart from speed, railway travel in the early days of the war was rendered very trying by the imposition of the 'black-out'. No one questioned the urgent necessity for maintaining this, but with carriages in their pre-war condition the mere drawing of the blinds did not provide sufficient obscuration, and the majority of compartments had no more than a miserably dim light. When dining cars were restored, on October 16, it was possible to have full lighting inside, through the simple expedient of painting a broad band of black paint on the glass adjacent to the framing, and this was subsequently applied generally. This made travelling in the black-out tolerable.

A measure of 'black-out' was also applied to locomotives. Those having side-windowed cabs had steel plates fitted over those windows, and tarpaulins were in some cases stretched from the cab roof to the front of the tenders. Drivers and firemen, in common with other men whose duties took them on the line, as well as signalmen, carried steel helmets as a protection against bomb splinters and flying debris, and were also issued with a civil defence type of gas mask. The hastily erected sandbag protection on vulnerable structures and areas was rapidly replaced by massively built blast-walls, and all the engineering departments gave special attention to the building up of supplies of spares, located at 'strategic' points ready for use in repair of air raid damage. In common with many businesses, for the continuance of communication and control it was considered advisable to move headquarters out of London at the beginning of the war, and six country houses lying west of Reading were duly adapted to accommodate departments temporarily evacuated from Paddington. The war-time emergency headquarters of the Company was located at Beenham Grange, Aldermaston, and provided the offices for the General Manager, the Secretary, and the Solicitor. Other houses taken over were:

Crookham House, Thatcham:	Chief Goods Manager
Hyde End House, Midgham:	Chief Accountant
Wharf House, Padworth:	The Surveyor
Wasing Place, Midgham:	Chief Accountant's department, for routine matters.
The Gables, Cholsey:	Registration Office

In passing I must mention that four of these one-time 'stately-homes' were buildings of great character and charm, particularly Hyde End House, and Wasing Place, which were Georgian. Beenham Grange was a large Victorian mansion, while Wharf House was a large cottage residence in the most beautiful surroundings. It is to be feared however that those temporarily transferred there had little time or inclination to appreciate the qualities of the houses themselves! Beenham Grange would be known to locomotive enthusiasts in that there existed a Great Western 4-6-0 named after it.

In the early days of the war the strategy of the Allied high command was based on the anticipation of a long drawn out campaign along the eastern frontier of France, similar to that experienced in 1914-8, and after the despatch of the British Expeditionary Force arrangements were quickly made to provide locomotive power for hauling of military trains behind the front. It was originally intended to use 2-8-0 engines of Great Central design, many of which had served overseas with the Railway Operating Division in World War I. A total of 350 of these engines was to be withdrawn from British railway service, 300 from the L.N.E.R. and 50 from the Great Western. It was later decided not to use these ex-Great Central engines; instead orders were placed for a large number of Stanier 2-8-0s of the L.M.S.R. type, but modified to include the Westinghouse brake and other continental features. In addition to these 2-8-0s however the Government requisitioned 100 Great Western 0-6-0 tender engines of the celebrated 'Dean goods' type. Some were reconditioned at Swindon, and others at Eastleigh. They were fitted with the Westinghouse brake, and painted black with the letters W.D. on the tenders. Many of these engines had seen service overseas in World War I. On account of their light axle loading these engines were particularly acceptable for general overseas service.

During all these operational and engineering works arising from the onset of war negotiations were in progress with the Government concerning the principles on which compensation would be paid to the shareholders during the period of Government control. While no one would question for a moment the need for centralised control of so essential a national service as the railways it must not be forgotten that in 1939 these priceless assets were private property. The proprietors were not merely a few rich men with many thousands of pounds' worth of stock, but also a very large number of small investors, whose property was commandeered in the national interest. It was a strange position so far as all railway shareholders were concerned. The companies had fought their way through the lean years of the 1930s, and year by year at the various Annual General Meetings the shareholders had accepted very small dividends so that funds could continue to be devoted to the upkeep and modernisation of the plant, to provide the finest possible service. There had never been any question of whittling down the standards of service in order to provide better dividends. The Great Western had been better than most in the way of dividends, and it was only in the altogether abnormal year of 1938 that less than 3 per cent. was paid on the ordinary stock. Then, when war came and railway installations, rolling stock, and organisation was ready to perform the greatest tasks in their history control was taken out of the hands of the owners. It was the more disconcerting, because the circumstances of war and the need to restrict the use of imported oil fuel meant that much of the traffic that had been lost to road haulage in the 1930's would have been thrown back on to the railways. There was every chance that the railways would be doing business on a bigger scale than ever before, but not under the full control of their own managements.

There was naturally much anxiety as to how payment would be made to the companies for services rendered, and that anxiety increased as weeks went by in the late autumn of 1939, and no word was forthcoming from the Minister of Transport. By mid-November various disquieting rumours were in circulation, of sufficient substance for 'The Railway Gazette' to publish a long leading article under the title 'Compensation or Nationalisation?' It was pointed out that in contrast to the circumstances in which the railways were taken over in 1914, the Act permitting the take-over in 1939 was not limited in its duration, and the delay in reaching a settlement on which terms of compensation could be made public added to the uneasiness. This important difference doubtless lent colour to the suggestions of those who felt that the situation in 1939 would result in nationalisation, as indeed had already been suggested in some daily newspapers. There were rumours of deep differences of opinion between the Ministry of Transport and the Treasury on one hand, and between the main line railways and the London Passenger Transport Board. At the same time it was appreciated that if the special traffic carried in war-time were paid for on a commercial basis the prosperity of the companies would be increased to such an extent as to encourage demands for higher wages at a time when every effort was being made to check the spiral of inflation. The general feeling of uncertainty was increased by the fact that since the beginning of Government control no weekly traffic returns had been published, and consequently there were no official indications of traffic trends.

The problem was discussed in some detail at the Annual General Meeting of the British Railways Stockholders Union, held on December 15, 1939. By that time no settlement had been made, but the Union passed a resolution laying down certain principles on which it would accept compensation for services rendered.

1. That the average of nett profits covering the last three years (unless it were possible to exclude 1938 as a crisis year) should be accompanied by a suitable and adequate percentage addition covering three things:

   (a) general trade improvement over the slump conditions of 1938.

   (b) Improvement due to wartime traffic both before and after the declaration of war. This might be regarded as acceptable in determining both the minimum compensation and also the dividends for the period from the outbreak of war to the end of the calendar year.

2. That any final arrangement should, subject to the minimum mentioned above, fully reflect all wartime increases in traffic, after provision had been made in the rates schedule for all increased working expenses.

At this same meeting it was particularly noted that since the outbreak of war merchandise and mineral traffic on the Great Western had increased by 47 per cent. compared with the same weeks in 1938. Although no official figures for traffic as a whole were forthcoming it was obvious to the most casual observer that the railways generally were being required to carry far heavier traffic than had been enjoyed for some years past, and this made all the more irritable the sense of uncertainty of the financial arrangements with the Government. The situation as it existed at the end of 1939 was aptly summed up in a leading article in 'The Railway Gazette' of January 19, 1940, under the Heading,

'NO SETTLEMENT YET'

The prolonged delay in arriving at agreement on the terms of State financial arrangement with the railways for the control of their systems during the war having for some time been causing inconvenience and irritation has now become a factor of financial loss to the stockholders. It has now become necessary for the directors of the G.W.R. and of the L.N.E.R. to announce that they have to defer consideration of final dividend payments, in view of the impossibility of striking balances while negotiations with the Government are still in progress. The urgency of evolving an acceptable plan to the parties before this stage was reached has been emphasised in 'The Railway Gazette' in recent weeks. Now it would appear that in addition to the financial disability which will be imposed upon large numbers of railway stockholders, many of them people with small means to whom regularity of their too-often meagre dividends is of great importance, the companies will have to hold their annual meetings within the limits of time allowed by the Acts under which they are constituted, and then adjourn until such time as sufficient data are available to enable business to be concluded. In most cases the provisional dates which the companies have announced for the holding of their meetings have been the latest permitted. Thus the Great Western, which is required to hold its meeting in February, has selected the 28th day of that month for the purpose; similarly, the L.M.S.R. has until March 15 and has announced that date. Although the accounting period of each of the companies ended with the calendar year, the financial officers of the lines cannot prepare final accounts until negotiations are concluded. This, of course, is an essential first step to deciding the amount of any dividend, while no actual payment of a dividend is valid unless approved in general meeting. The delay in payment of dividends will be directly related to the time when agreement upon compensation is reached. In the meantime, the market for the stocks has suffered from the uncertainty and quotations have tended to fall away.

Criticism is now being bestowed upon both the Treasury and the railway companies for the impasse which has been reached. In an endeavour to bring the matter to final settlement 'The Financial Times' urges the submission of the case to arbitration. The desirability of that course is open to question; but it might be a satisfactory solution in the case of some outstanding points which are delaying the whole settlement. Resort to an independent ruling may become necessary if the matters at issue are of such magnitude that they are insoluble by direct negotiation or if they involve a decision upon principles which the parties are unwilling to make. But if a large measure of agreement has been reached, and on the one hand the Treasury and Ministry of Transport, and on the other the four main-line companies and London Transport are unanimous in their respective viewpoints it should prove possible to agree a compromise formula by direct negotiation. That would appear preferable on all counts to making the compensation award a matter of controversy and subjecting one side or the other to an outside judgment. In view of the importance of the work which the railways are performing and the necessary closeness of their relations with the Government, it is desirable that there should be the maximum co-operation and the minimum cause for friction between the parties.

The month of January 1940 can be said to have marked the end of Phase One of the war, so far as the Great Western Railway was concerned. It was a phase of apprehension, preparing for the worst it was thought the enemy could then do, evacuation of children from large cities, and evacuation of staffs from London, working in the dark in more senses than one —for to the physical blackout at night there was the psychological blackout of uncertainty over future finance. Added to this the new year brought some of the most severe winter weather experienced for many years, though for security reasons the full extent of the blockages of the lines and the delays being experienced were not related until some time afterwards. Then on February 7, 1940, the Minister of Transport was at last able to clear the air by announcing in the House of Commons that the long-awaited agreement between the Government and the companies had at last been reached, and that a White Paper would be circulated on the following day. The full text of this, which had such an important bearing upon railway fortunes during the critical years that were to follow, is contained in one of the appendices to this book. Its implications, particularly as they affected the Great Western, are discussed in the next chapter.

XVI

The Years of Endurance

1940-1941

In opening an account of the part played by the Great Western Railway in the two most critical years ever experienced by this old country it may at first sight be a little inappropriate to refer at some length to the position of the railway shareholders. The White Paper issued on February 7, 1940, announcing the terms of agreement between the four main-line companies, the London Transport Board and the Government did not escape criticism, and in certain quarters it was felt that the agreement left the way wide open for the railway shareholders to profiteer at the expense of the taxpayers in time of crisis. In Great Britain railways generally have always been fair game for the critics, and to the press was being rapidly added the criticism of broadcasting commentators. The spell of favourable comment on Great Western affairs referred to in earlier chapters of this book had long since passed, and the company shared with the other three the lukewarm, and often hostile press that prevailed. It was therefore somewhat natural that to some critics the idea that railway shareholders should at last stand a chance of getting a reasonable dividend was altogether abhorrent. On the other hand the true position of the railway shareholder, and one that is scarcely ever appreciated in reference to the preparedness of the Great Western and other British railways for war, was admirably expressed by Lord Horne at the Annual General Meeting of the company, on February 28, 1940.

After a reference to the nature of the enemy against whom we were engaged, and to the terrifying consequences of a German victory Lord Horne said:

Our thoughts, therefore, and all our efforts—until the overmastering task of achieving victory is completed—must be directed to playing our part in the mechanism of war. I hope it will not be regarded as overweening vanity if I venture to suggest that in this respect railway shareholders already deserve well of the nation. Through many years of great discouragement and often with little or no return on their hard-won savings, they have not only kept in existence an essential part of the country's war machine, but at considerable sacrifice to themselves, they have preserved it in a condition to perform with perfect smoothness the infinite tasks which our war effort has thrown upon it. If the shareholders had insisted upon dividends rather than a high standard of maintenance and renewals, the Government would now have been faced with the necessity of large expenditure—for without efficient railways the war could not be fought. Happily, it stands to the credit of the British railways that they compare in efficiency with any other railway in the world and that they have been maintained in peacetime in a condition which renders them adequate to the needs of the nation in war.

During the lean years of the 1930s Great Western shareholders had been more fortunate than most, and with the upsurge in traffic in the latter part of 1939 they would have been justified in expecting a better dividend than the 3½ per cent actually paid; but the Company was then bound by the agreement made with the Government, and at that stage nothing more was permitted. The address of Lord Horne on February 28 was of outstanding interest because it revealed something of the nature of the negotiations that had taken place between the railways and the Government between the outbreak of war and the issuing of the White Paper on February 7. He told how, towards the end of 1937, the railway companies had been asked to outline their proposals in regard to the financial arrangements which should be adopted if and when emergency arose and the railways were again taken over by the Government, although at that time it was never anticipated that we should be involved in another war. In these circumstances the railway companies naturally founded their claim upon the Standard Revenue which was recognised by Parliament in the Railways Act of 1921 as being the reasonable level of income which, in the public interest, the railway companies should be able to earn. While it is true that since the Act was passed none of the companies had ever earned its full Standard Revenue, this was largely due to unregulated competition from road transport which the Government had been taking steps to remedy. Moreover, it was obvious from the experience of the first world war that the Companies during any war period would be called upon to deal with greatly increased traffics and that, under the provisions of the Railways Act relating to the fixation of charges, they would without any doubt be in a position to earn their Standard Revenues.

The railway companies submitted their views to the Minister of Transport in May, 1938, but little progress was made until July, 1939, when they received the first definite proposal of the Government. This proposal was that the companies should be given a guarantee of pre-emergency profits plus some addition by way of retention by the companies of a share in any increased profits actually earned, up to a maximum—the remainder being taken by the Government.

It appeared to the companies to be wrong in principle that any part of the compensation payable to the companies should be dependent on net earnings when the control of expenditure was taken out of their hands. It also appeared to them to be unjustifiable that the Government should participate in earnings already limited by Statute and that the companies' share of such earnings might be further diminished if the Excess Profits Tax was to be applied. They could not therefore regard the Government's proposal as affording a satisfactory or equitable basis for settlement. As an alternative the companies suggested a guarantee of their average net revenues for an agreed pre-emergency period—to be supplemented by an addition which would reflect in each year any increase in gross receipts not arising from higher charges.

Later it was stated that the pre-emergency profits which the Government had in mind were the average net revenues of the companies for the years 1936 to 1938 inclusive. The companies, however, pointed out that 1938 was on all hands recognised as having been an abnormally bad year, and that in framing their alternative proposal they had contemplated that the Government's guarantee would be based on their average net revenues for the years 1935, 1936 and 1937.

On November 8, 1939 the Minister of Transport intimated that the Government was unable to accept the alternative proposal of the companies on the ground that they, the companies, would have no direct financial interest in the management of their undertakings and no incentive to keep down their expenditure. Moreover, the Government could not agree to the exclusion of the year 1938. At the same time the Minister outlined in greater detail, and with certain modifications, the terms of compensation proposed by the Government, a new feature being that the companies would be required to pool their financial interests with those of the London Passenger Transport Board. This proposal was strongly resisted by the companies. It was pointed out that the transport board were interested only in the London passenger suburban passenger traffic, which had suffered a very heavy decline. The result of the suggested pool would be to shift the chief burden of this decline from the shoulders of the London Passenger Transport Board on to those of the main line companies who would have to make good out of their increased freight receipts the losses of the London Passenger Transport Board on passengers. On that matter, however, the Minister was obdurate and on January 16, 1940, the companies were informed that in the view of the Government it was an essential condition of any settlement that the London Passenger Transport Board should be included in the general pool of net revenue. At the same time it was further stipulated that the financial transactions involved in the requisitioning by the Government of privately-owned wagons must be brought within the control account. This meant throwing an unknown liability upon the companies, since neither the terms of compensation nor the payments to be made for wagons when used for domestic or storage purposes had been settled.

In view of these new considerations, however, the Government indicated that they would be prepared to modify the terms of their original proposal in certain respects—the main alterations being an offer to guarantee to the companies yearly payments equal to their average net revenues for the years 1935 to 1937 inclusive, instead of the years 1936 to 1938, and at the same time to raise the level at which the Government would begin to participate in the net earnings of the companies and the transport board. It was reiterated that the Government considered it necessary that the companies should have a direct financial interest in the expenses of working the railways; some inducement to see that charges were maintained at an economic level; and a direct concern in the amount secured by way of net revenue.

The companies were compelled, therefore, to consider the Government's revised offer in the light of the decisions thus conveyed to them. They recognised that during the period of war, restrictions and obligations which in normal conditions they would strongly resist might have to be accepted in the national interest. They felt bound to record, however, their considered view that their own proposals would have provided a simple, sound, and equitable basis for a settlement, and would have obviated many of the difficulties and objections both practical and political involved in a scheme the central feature of which was a pool of net receipts and a partnership or quasi-partnership with the Government with whom would rest the control of policy.

The main line railways and the L.P.T.B. were unanimous in regarding the amended offer of the Government as a reasonable basis for a settlement —purely as a financial arrangement—and the price of railway stocks rose somewhat on publication of the terms. But just as it had fallen to the Great Western Chairman to give so clear and full account of the negotiations that took place prior to the agreement, so it fell to a prominent Great Western shareholder, Mr. Ashley Brown, to summarise the effect of the agreement on railway shareholders. He said that a section of the press —fortunately small, but with influence on the company's employees— had devoted considerable space to the statement that the Government had presented railway stockholders with something like £100,000,000. Never, he supposed, was a statement more misleading or more deliberately mischievous. Of course stocks had risen. To some extent the rise was that of debenture and guaranteed stocks keeping pace with other gilt-edged securities. With regard to other stock, so far as he could ascertain, it had been bought by the stockholders many years previously at somewhere between 70 and 114. Before agreement was reached it had fallen to 10. It rose during the course of discussions to 20. Could any sane man say that the rise to 20 of stock purchased probably at 70 or 80 represented a gain to the holders? 'We cannot make it too clear', he said, 'that the recent rise has not been a gain to the stockholders; at the very best it has been a mitigation of their loss.'

At the same time there were many people, railway servants and otherwise, who were already looking beyond the situation prevailing in the war years, and their looking ahead was fraught with some apprehension. There were, in 1940, many men who considered that the Railways Act of 1921, which produced the Grouping, was the first regular step towards railway nationalisation, and they feared that the agreement of February 1940 could well prove to be the second. At that time there seemed no doubt that in the event of nationalisation being raised in definite form later, the amount agreed voluntarily by the companies as their wartime revenues would be cited, should it become necessary to agree a capitalised revenue, as the capital value of the assets of the companies. Superficially at least the agreement, by treating the railway companies and the transport board as one for the purposes of the guaranteed revenue, and the Minister's statement that operation was to be under unified control, fostered the principle of what some prefer to call "unification".

The proportions of the 'pool' were as follows:

Great Western Railway	16 per cent.
London Midland & Scottish Railway	34 per cent
London & North Eastern Railway	23 per cent.
London Passenger Transport Board	11 per cent.
Southern Railway	16 per cent.

How these proportions would work out at various stages of increase in revenue were analysed in a most interesting tabulation prepared by 'The Railway Gazette', setting out the ascending conditions of pooling and payment, until each of the five concerns involved had reached its Standard Revenue, and therefore by the terms of the agreement was not entitled to a greater share of the earned revenue, regardless of the traffic it was carrying. As was to be expected, the Great Western, on the basis of its results for the years 1935, 1936 and 1937, began with much the best dividend on its ordinary stock. Its maximum share from the pool was fixed at £8,500,000, and this was reached when the total earnings were £60,300,000. After that the G.W.R. would not benefit financially and the maximum dividend on its ordinary shares was limited to 8.1 per cent.

One could go on for many pages discussing points arising from this interesting analysis but it is time to leave railway finance and to pass on to some of the more physical effects of the war. At the time of the Great Western Annual General Meeting, and during the time all the discussion and criticism of the White Paper was in progress, the war was still 'phoney', so far as the great majority of British civilians were concerned. There had not been any definite attack on targets in this country, and many of the evacuees so dramatically conveyed from London and other large cities in September 1939 had returned to their former homes. In the minds of eminent railway leaders like Lord Horne however there was no doubt that the most desperate reckoning with the enemy was soon to come. And indeed it befell that the marvellously fine summer of 1940 was one that will remain forever in the minds of those who lived through it. The campaign on the Western front, when it did start, instead of lasting three or four years as expected, was all over in a month, and the British Expeditionary Force stranded by the capitulation of its allies was huddled almost defenceless on the beaches of Dunkirk. Never before was the marvellous talent for improvisation in emergency, so characteristic of the British nation, displayed more vividly than in the days that followed. The assembly of that motley and amazing Armada of ships of all shapes and sizes: the coolness and courage of all concerned, and the positive ferry services performed by some of the most unlikely ships has many times been told. Here I am particularly concerned with the deeds of Great Western ships. Readers of a younger generation may wonder what ships of the Great Western were doing at Dunkirk at all; but in that grave hour ships of relatively shallow draught from all British coastal

waters were pressed into service, and the Fishguard–Rosslare packet
steamers performed heroic work alongside ships from the Firth of Clyde,
and beside Great Western steamers from the Channel Islands service.

The Great Western ships mainly concerned with the Dunkirk evacuation
were the *St. Andrew* and the *St. David*, from the Irish service, both converted to hospital ships; the *St. Julien*, from the Channel Islands service,
also a hospital ship; and the *St Helier* and the *Roebuck*, from the Channel
Islands service, converted to transports. All except the *Roebuck*, which
was a cargo boat normally engaged in the carrying of potatoes and other
produce from the Channel Islands, were cross-channel packets with a
tonnage of around 2000, turbine driven, and capable of speeds of around
18 knots. The *St. Julien*, on one of her peacetime trips leaving Weymouth
is shown in a photograph reproduced on Plate 31. One is accustomed
to read in railway literature of the names of drivers and firemen who make
fast and successful runs on the line. It is therefore appropriate to set down
here the names of the Captains of the ships who made so many dramatic
'runs' to and from Dunkirk.

St. Andrew	Capt. J. W. Reed
St. David	Capt. Joy, later commanded by Capt. Mendus
St. Helier	Capt. Pitman
St. Julien	Capt. Richardson

The most extraordinary thing about the Great Western ships concerned
at Dunkirk was that despite the bombing and machine gunning they
received from enemy aircraft, and the intense difficulty of navigation in
the wreck infested approaches and harbour at Dunkirk, not a single
casualty occurred in any of the ships. As I shall show in a moment this
was not because they sought 'easy' or 'safe' tasks. The hospital ships
in particular, though carrying huge red crosses were very heavily attacked.
Fortunately none of them received a direct bomb hit; but there were
many near-misses, and some collisions with other craft in the crowded
waters. There was no question of escort, or taking pilots to get into a
harbour strange to them. Some measure of 'traffic control' was exercised
by naval vessels at times, but ships coming in had to find berths as best
they could alongside the heavily bombed quays, and it was no mean feat
of seamanship to bring a vessel of the size of the *St. David* or the *St. Julien*
into an inferno such as Dunkirk presented from May 23 onwards.

The *St. Andrew* and the *St. David* were together involved in an operation
which in its hazards and confusion exemplified both the circumstances and
the spirit in which the Dunkirk evacuation was effected. The *St. David*
had experienced a very rough time of it, so much so that the Second
Engineer had a 'black-out' of memory, disappeared, and later turned up
at Fishguard, while Captain Joy collapsed, and was invalided on shore.
The Chief Officer, Mendus by name, immediately took command, and
on May 31, they arrived once again off Dunkirk. Despite the brilliant

weather of that cloudless May the port was hidden under a pall of smoke and fire, and it was extremely difficult to see what was happening inside the harbour. A signal was made from the shore to stand off for the time being, as the *St. Andrew* was in what was left of the harbour, and was embarking stretcher and cot cases. 'Standing off' meant the ship was lying outside exposed to every enemy air attack, and her huge red crosses seemed to mark her out as a specially favoured target. At one moment a magnetic mine exploded less than 100ft. from her bows, and she was lifted high in the water. About this time the *St. Andrew* signalled to her to come in and take over, but owing to the smoke and fire that signal was not seen on the *St. David*. The Captain after waiting for what seemed like eternity tried to get into the harbour himself; once within hailing distance he tried to attract attention, but out of the smoke and confusion no response came, and even a ship with the intrepid record of the *St. David* could not, without orders, try to force a way through the oily black smokescreen that masked the entrance to the harbour. So the Master and his crew had to suffer the most grievous disappointment of having to return to Dover without having entered Dunkirk, on their third trip.

In the meantime the *St. Andrew*, inside the harbour, had been engaged in operations which 26 years later read like some outrageous stretch of a lunatic's imagination. Many of the quaysides had been blown away; the harbour itself was an archipelago of partly sunken ships, and alongside what remained of the quays were ships of all kinds embarking troops who could walk. The *St. Andrew* had come in to take on the seriously wounded. As she came in a destroyer instructed the Master to berth where he could find room. This was no small task in itself, in such conditions. It was like trying to find parking space for one's car, except that bombing and machine gunning was almost continuous, and that so much shipping was on the move in those fantastic conditions that collisions were almost inevitable. Having finally manoeuvred into a berth the *St. Andrew* was instructed to move to another part of the harbour where, they were told, there were ambulances waiting with casualties to embark. With difficulty amid all the dense smoke and confusion the *St. Andrew* moved across, only to find that the ambulances had been bombed, and all the remaining occupants were dead. Moving again, the ship got to another fragment of quay where many casualties were waiting. The crew seeing the situation quickly improvised a gangway, and every man of them acted as stretcher bearers, carrying scores of wounded men on board, in the midst of a particularly heavy air raid, and amidst all the turmoil of uninjured men, and walking cases trying to embark on other ships.

Dusk was falling, and the *St. Andrew* wished to get her precious freight away from Dunkirk before the tide got too low. It was then that she tried to signal to the *St. David*, waiting outside, to come in and take her place, embark the rest of the wounded and sail at daybreak. But as previously mentioned, that signal was never seen. The *St. Andrew* sailed, in pitch darkness, save from the fires on land, and with no aids to navigation.

The sea was alive with hundreds of small craft, none carrying lights, and full to overflowing with rescued soldiers. There was great danger of running some of them down in the darkness. But to sailors like those of the *St. Andrew* superb seamanship is second nature, and no accident occurred, and the ship reached Dover safely. Captain Reed subsequently reported how his officers and men had been exposed to great danger; but in face of it thousands of wounded men were evacuated in these nightmare conditions. Had it not been so, they would have been left to die where they lay on the piers. And amid all this there was the miracle that not a single casualty befell any one of the ship's company, nor to any of the men they rescued.

The *St. Helier* was fitted out as a troopship, and she was involved off the French coast even before the main body of the B.E.F. had been driven into the Dunkirk perimeter. On May 22, she was directed to Calais, while that place was still being defended; but on arrival, greeted as usual by enemy bombers, she found the place deserted, and returned to Dover for orders. Then began an incredible series of trips across the Channel, first on May 23, then on May 25, and again on May 30. As a troopship the *St. Helier* was armed, modestly it is true, but on her May 25 trip she escorted the two Great Western hospital ships *St. Andrew* and *St. Julien* and came in for some heavy bombing. Although all these ships suffered superficial damage they all escaped direct hits, though the situation was indescribably 'uncomfortable'. The *St. Helier* was conveying 1,500 to 2,000 troops from Dunkirk to Dover every trip. On May 31 she arrived at Dunkirk for the fifth time, and in the process of evacuating another 1,600 troops from the quays she was involved in two slight collisions with other craft. On her sixth trip, Saturday June 1, she was asked to load stretcher cases, although not designated a hospital ship. But designations counted for nought at this stage, and she lay alongside the quay for seven hours, during absolutely continuous air raids. Once the stretcher cases were safely embarked the rest of the ship was filled with troops and off they went once again for Dover. Shells straddled her course; the glare of fires on land lit up the sea, so that the ship seemed to those on the bridge to be steaming through fire.

By that time the evacuation was nearing its end. The harbour at Dunkirk was becoming impassable, and the survivors were being embarked from the beaches. On Sunday morning June 2 a Naval Commander and ten ratings were put aboard the *St. Helier*, in case help was needed in taking troops off the beaches, and so she came to Dunkirk for the last and seventh time. Her almost incredible saga was ended by taking on board the very last remnants of the British Expeditionary Force, more than 2,000 men—a great honour for an indomitable ship. In all she conveyed more than 10,000 men of the Allied armies. On her last trip she was very difficult to manoeuvre, having been holed at the fore-end, and it was with difficulty that she made her way from Folkestone to Southampton. It was during this hazardous last voyage to comparative safety that the Chief Engineer told the Master not to worry, and that he and his men would keep going as long as the ship continued to float the right way up!

Once the troops were rescued from the beaches of Dunkirk and landed in England their dispersal to camps in many parts of the country was a major railway operation. In this however the lion's share of the work fell upon the Southern Railway in marshalling the trains at Dover, and conveying them to various junctions with the other railways. Mercifully, the various strategic points in this great railway operation were not attacked by the enemy, or the task would have been made infinitely more difficult, and costly in lives. The collapse of the Western Front, and the presence of the enemy throughout the length of the French channel coast needless to say altered the entire strategic plan that had been developed by the Allies, and would appear to have made redundant a small, but important piece of inter-railway connection at Reading. Previously the connection between the Great Western and the Southern had been by the steeply graded line diverging from the Great Western immediately to the east of Reading station. The lay-out was rather cramped, and its use had hitherto been confined largely to the working of through express passenger trains from the Great Western system to destinations on the Kent Coast. It was not ideally equipped for heavy freight traffic. To feed supplies to the Channel Ports plans for a new junction were prepared, further east, where there was room to provide siding accommodation for freight trains, and the equipping of this new 'junction' was in hand in the early spring of 1940. To avoid the necessity of building a new signalbox a small miniature lever power frame, with all-electric interlocking, was installed at Reading East Main signalbox, and all the new points and signals at the junction were electrically operated. I had a hand in this work myself. At that time Westinghouse had not previously supplied semaphore signals to the Great Western, and because of the urgency we had to use the nearest thing to Great Western standards for which we had patterns. As a result a number of the posts at Reading new junction had pinnacles of Great Central pattern!

Once the campaign in Western Europe was over a major attack and invasion of Great Britain became expected daily. But a summer of almost unbroken sunshine passed with little more than sporadic raiding. Nevertheless, in the course of some of these raids Great Western lines and stations were hit, and one of the first of such instances was at Newton Abbot, where considerable damage was done to the station and rolling stock. In view of the evacuation from London in the first days of the war it is somewhat ironical to reflect that where raiding did begin, albeit on no more than a minor scale at first, some of the greatest damage was done in areas originally considered to be 'safe'. By the late summer of 1940 the loading of passenger trains was very much on the increase. The number of services personnel travelling on postings or leave was becoming large, and regular trains were crowded. My own wartime journeys were mainly confined to occasional trips over the West to North route via the Severn Tunnel, and trains like the 7.15 p.m. north mail out of Bristol were packed every day of the week. Within my own field of observation some remarkably good locomotive work was done during that anxious summer, and one of my own most vivid memories is of a particularly fast run made one night by the engine *Usk Castle* when from Abergavenny northwards we were running through a continuous 'Alert'. Day after day there were air raid warnings in Bristol and Plymouth, with the enemy continuously probing our defences with no more than isolated planes; but in the early autumn the Battle of Britain opened in earnest, and men of the Great Western who had toiled already in several major operations of war transport then had the experience of carrying on railway duties under air bombardment. At the same time there were no sharply concentrated attacks on railway targets in this country such as the Royal Air Force delivered against specific German railway targets. The bombs fell on railway property in the course of attacks on the towns and cities themselves, when the strategy of the enemy seemed to be to try and break the morale of the civilian population rather than to destroy railway plant, or other installations engaged directly upon war work.

Even as it was, the 'Blitz' was bad enough, and in the history of the Great Western Railway, and its men and women, some notable incidents need to be recalled. One of the worst in London did not actually occur on Great Western property, but it was the result of a direct hit by a large high explosive bomb on Praed Street, Inner Circle station. But it was the Great Western A.R.P. folk who dealt with it, and magnificently they did it too. The bomb fell at 11.23 p.m. on October 13, 1940, when that Underground station was crowded, and immediately the Paddington A.R.P. went into action, in conditions indescribably difficult. In the semi-darkness of a blacked-out station, amid falling masonry and splintered woodwork and an atmosphere thick with dust and fumes, these Great Western men and women plunged down to the succour of those below. The platforms were strewn with the dead and dying; the cries of the wounded were heartbreaking, and yet in the incredibly short time of *twenty-seven minutes* all the seriously injured had been brought out, dealt with at the railway Casualty Clearing Station, and sent off to hospital by ambulance. The civil defence personnel could not have done it alone. Many other railwaymen, passengers and police immediately volunteered as stretcher bearers, leaving the highly trained railway ambulance men and women to tend the injured. That Casuality Clearing Station at Paddington had, up to December 31 1940, alone treated 3,367 civilians and 792 men and women of the Services. A typical requisition for stores, that should go down in history was:

1,000	miles of bandages	125,000	rolls of boric lint
52	miles of sticking plaster	3	tons of petroleum jelly
165,000	sterilised dressings	3,500	bottles of castor oil.
150,000	packets of cotton wool		

Plate 41. SOUTH WALES DOCKS

Port Talbot: loading steel into a Russian vessel

S/S *Esperance Bay* and *Larges Bay* at Cardiff, November 1943

Plate 42. PADDINGTON STATION CLOSED

The queues in Eastbourne Terrace waiting to enter the station to join West of England trains

Some deeds of great gallantry were enacted in the normally unromantic areas of the shunting yards. Incendiary bombs were bad enough among offices and the homes of the people; but in the war years marshalling yards frequently included loads of ammunition, shells and our own bombs, and if such a load were detonated the destruction could have been extremely serious. It was in some of these prosaic areas that the men with the shunter's pole covered themselves with glory. They proved themselves railwaymen to their finger-tips acting with the same sense of responsibility and self-reliance as signalmen, and all grades of enginemen when an emergency had to be faced. There was a remarkable case at Birkenhead, during one of the Merseyside Blitzes, when incendiary bombs fell on a train loaded with high explosive bombs. Fortunately the contents were covered with sheeting and in the wagon concerned this sheeting caught fire. The incendiaries had gone through the sheeting and were wedged amongst 250 lb. bombs. A shunter named Tunna then displayed sublime courage in dealing with this desperate situation. The ammunition train was ready to leave the yard, and was awaiting 'line clear'. Running to the engine he got water and threw it on the burning wagon; but when this failed to extinguish the incendiary bomb he climbed up, tore the sheeting off, and tried a stirrup pump. But the blaze was too fierce; there was nothing for it but to get that one incendiary bomb out. He used his shunter's pole to force two large bombs apart and then, with his bare hands he lifted the incendiary out and threw it out of harm's way. The driver and fireman of the train also played their part in this heroic action carrying water, and helping with the stirrup pump—for even when the incendiary had been thrown clear the 250 lb. bombs in the wagon had by that time become dangerously hot. Tunna won the George Cross for his work that night, when there were two B.E.M.s and a George Medal also won by G.W.R. men in the Birkenhead yard.

In the yards up and down the line men, and women, worked calmly through the most hair-raising incidents of fire and high explosive, and the number of times utter devastation from the explosion of ammunition trains was avoided were legion. An instance where the railwayman's sense of responsibility came to the fore in the height of a severe raid needs special mention. Many men and women were getting accustomed to dealing with incendiary bombs by the early months of 1941, and even, as in the Birkenhead case, of separating them from our own bombs. In the cold light of retrospect however one could not helping asking what could be done if incendiary bombs fell into a truck-load of pigs! The immediate thought that comes to mind is, to let the pigs out and leave the wagon to burn. This situation occurred at a relatively small goods station, where wagons and goods sheds contained high explosives and oil. The man in charge was no more senior than a parcels porter, and the incident of the pigs occurred on the third successive night of heavy 'blitz'. The animals were in frenzy, and if released would run madly about, and many of them would have been lost. This parcels porter, F. J. Harris by name, had, even in this emergency, the highest regard for his railway duty. To those helping with the fires all around them he said: 'We can't let those blue-pencil pigs out of those trucks. They are in the Company's care and we must not lose them.' So he took the infinitely harder alternative of getting amongst those shrieking pigs and putting the fire-bombs out.

The exploits of the Fishguard–Rosslare packet-steamers *St. Andrew* and *St. David* at Dunkirk have already been mentioned. Their sister ship, the *St. Patrick* was still engaged on her normal run, though in 1940–1 this did not mean that the conditions were normal. Far from it: she had twice been attacked by enemy aircraft, and on one occasion a member of the crew had been killed. Then came her last run, eastbound on a May morning, and at that time of the year she was approaching Fishguard in broad daylight, after the overnight voyage from Rosslare. Just off Strumble Head she was attacked and hit by several bombs; many of the passengers were killed outright, and the ship sank so quickly that there was no time to lower lifeboats. Among many acts of courage and fortitude, amid the confusion that followed, there was one that stands out—that of a stewardess, Miss May Owen. How, in the light of fires that immediately broke out in the ship she got a number of terrified women passengers to the one lifeboat that was being launched, struggling up perilously tilting gangways, and breaking a door down in the process, was one story; but she had with her also an hysterical woman, who had lost her lifebelt. This one must obviously be her special care; but by this time the ship was sinking so rapidly that the only way to avoid being drawn down with it was to jump clear. This Miss Owen did, taking the hysterical woman with her. How this intrepid stewardess managed to survive the frenzied clutches of her companion, and keep her afloat—without a lifebelt!— for more than two hours is a story in itself. Like the epics of Shunter Tunna, and Parcels Porter Harris, it was just another of the brave deeds of Great Western men and women in those years of endurance. Miss Owen was awarded the George Medal, and also the Lloyd's War Medal for Bravery.

XVII

War Years : The Middle Phases

At the height of the 'blitz' the Company was unfortunate in sustaining a bad accident to a passenger train. This was not the result of direct enemy action, though so far as personnel was concerned it was undoubtedly a consequence of it. To those who did not live through it the constant strain under which men and women existed in that winter of 1940–1 may be a little difficult to imagine. Without fail railwaymen rose to great heights of endeavour, endurance, and outright bravery when faced with emergencies; but for every one of those incidents, many of which did not 'hit the headlines', there were thousands of men and women going stoically about their work on the railway, and through all this trying period the Great Western reputation for safety in operation was, with this one tragic exception, fully maintained. In reviewing this incident it is nevertheless important to recall that it was not only the men and women on the line who were involved in the 'blitz'. Everyone was in it and one can imagine the feelings of trainmen going out on a long night's duty knowing that an air-raid on their home town was highly probable before the night was out. Many of the regular double-home turns originated from centres subject to some of the heaviest bombing, such as London, Plymouth, and Swansea. The driver of the 9.50 p.m. express from Paddington to the West of England on the night of November 4, 1940, was an Old Oak man, and his home had been damaged, and subsequent events revealed that strain on him had reached almost to breaking point.

The train as usual was a very heavy one, and worked by a 'King' class engine. It was routed via Bath and Bristol, and did a great deal of roadside work. Traffic delays were frequent at that period, and on the night in question the train arrived at Taunton 68 min. late. The 12.50 a.m. newspaper train which ran via Westbury had however made a punctual run, and was scheduled to pass Taunton without stopping. The signalman then decided to give the newspaper train a clear run through ahead of the 9.50, and despatch the latter on the relief line, crossing it over to the main line at Norton Fitzwarren in the wake of the newspaper train. This was a very logical and practical course to take, which it was hoped would cause the minimum of delay. If the 9.50 had been allowed to take its normal route at Taunton West, on the main line, it would have blocked the newspaper train, and by reason of the disparity in weight of the two trains checked it throughout the ascent to Whiteball Tunnel. There would then have been two trains running late instead of one. When the 9.50 was given the 'right-away' from Taunton, however, with all around him blacked out—though with signals showing clearly—the driver made the fatal assumption that he was taking the normal route of the train, namely from the down relief line platform through the cross-over road on to the down main, whereas he was signalled and travelling on the down relief line.

The signals at the west end of Taunton were a conspicuous and well-displayed group, and in normal circumstances would admit of no misunderstanding; but to this unfortunate driver's first mistake the layout of the line and its signalling between Taunton and Norton Fitzwarren did nothing to correct his quite wrong impression that he was travelling on the down main line. The signals for the latter line, of which there were several intermediately in the two miles between the two stations, were all located on the right hand side of the track, and all were showing clear, for the newspaper train which was coming up rapidly. His own signals, at precisely corresponding locations were on the left hand side, and as each one was approached the 'all-clear' ring of the A.T.C. bell was received in the cab. From his usual stance on the right hand side of the engine the driver was observing the main line signals, all at clear, thinking they were his own. Approaching Norton Fitzwarren however his own signals were adverse, because the cross-over to the main line which he was eventually to take could not be set until the newspaper train was clear. The relief line signals cautioned him to be prepared to stop at the station. The A.T.C. warning siren sounded in the cab, and this the unfortunate driver, still observing the main line signals, must have acknowledged and thus forestalled the automatic brake application. At this moment he was overtaken by the newspaper train running at about 60 m.p.h., and he came to a sudden and belated realisation that he was not on the line he had imagined himself to be. He was then travelling at about 45 m.p.h., and it was too late to avoid disaster. The train ran through the catch points protecting the cross-over to the down main; the engine overturned on to soft ground, and was no more than slightly damaged, but the wreck of the train was very serious. The six leading coaches, all crowded, were badly smashed up, and 27 people were killed and 56 seriously injured. The engine had turned over on its left-hand side and although the driver was almost unhurt, to add to this unfortunate man's burden his fireman was killed.

The Great Western Railway had a remarkable freedom from serious accidents, and while this would to a very great extent be attributed to the excellence of its operating arrangements and to the high standard of maintenance of rolling stock and signalling, it also reflected upon the diligence of the staff, and their high regard for safety in working. There were times also when the critical factors fell on the safe side, and the Great Western was generally considered to have enjoyed a certain amount of good luck as well. This was definitely the case at Norton Fitzwarren in November 1940. Bad though that accident was it could have been infinitely worse had the respective running times of the two expresses varied by less than a minute in the wrong direction. If the 9.50 had been running earlier by a matter of 15 to 20 secs., and the newspaper train later by a similar amount, the wreck at the catch points would have occurred right in the path of the fast-running newspaper train, and with spreadeagled and telescoped carriages strewn across both relief and main lines the inevitable collision would have been terrifying in its results. As it was the newspaper train just, but only just got clear. The 'nearmiss' was 'near' enough however for something to strike the rear van of the newspaper train as it passed the engine of the 9.50 just as the derailment took place. The guard stopped the train in the open country just to the west of Victory Siding. He told the driver of the blow that had struck the van, but they could find nothing apparently wrong and proceeded to Wellington where they stopped for a thorough examination. It was only then that they learned how narrowly they had avoided the wreck of the 9.50.

*   *   *

The Nazi attack on Russia in the summer of 1941 was accompanied by a great lessening of air attack on this country, and the chances of invasion were lessened. But even before this relief careful thought had been given to improvements in the train service, particularly towards punctuality. The Norton Fitzwarren accident stemmed originally from the altered running arrangements made at Taunton because of the late running of the 9.50 p.m. from Paddington, and although it was not a point of criticism in the subsequent enquiry it was the one factor from which all else followed. With a view to encouraging the recovery of lost time whenever possible the Great Western, as early in the war as April 1941, relaxed the maximum speed limit from 60 to 75 m.p.h. This in itself was a fine testimony to the condition of the track, in the prevailing circumstances; but definite instructions were printed in the working timetables operative from May 5, 1941, to the effect that drivers must run to sharper timings than standard if their trains were running late. Some examples of the effect of this instruction are set out in the accompanying table. In the event of late running average speeds of around 54 m.p.h. were required on non-stop runs between Paddington and Taunton, Paddington and Exeter, and Paddington and Bath, providing recovery margins of 10 to 20 min. on long runs. Actually, with locomotives in good condition, considerably better times even than these were possible without exceeding the new 75 m.p.h. limit. By that time in the war however train loads were very heavy. A large proportion of the increasing strength of the armed forces was still stationed in this country, and trains were crowded with personnel travelling on numerous duties and leave. Although the civilian population was continually exhorted not to travel unless it was absolutely necessary, there were times when some 'break' was essential, and the railway was then the only means of travel for the great majority. Despite this the demand for travel was at times embarrassing, and dangerous, in that very large numbers of persons congregated at stations at the same time, for the few trains scheduled, and by so doing constituted an immense risk of heavy casualties. The normal method of dealing with extra pressure of this kind was to run the more popular trains in duplicate, and this was done with many Great Western services in the war. The midday service to Bath and Bristol was a case in point, being regularly worked in two trains of 14 to 15 coaches each, running about 10 min.

RECOVERY TIMES: MAY 5, 1941 ONWARDS

FROM	Distance	Normal		Revised		Recovery Margin
		Sch.	Av. sp.	Sch.	Av. sp.	
	Miles	min.	m.p.h.	min.	m.p.h.	min.
Paddington–Exeter	173.5	210	49.6	193	53.9	17
Exeter–Paddington	173.5	215	48.4	191	54.5	24
Paddington–Taunton	142.9	180	47.6	159	53.9	21
Paddington–Newport	133.4	165	48.5	151	53.0	14
Paddington–Bath	106.9	130	49.3	118	54.3	12
Reading–Newport	97.4	121	48.3	112	52.2	9
Leamington–Paddington	87.3	118	44.4	107	49.0	11
Swindon–Paddington	77.3	95	48.8	86	53.9	9
Reading–Bath	70.9	88	48.3	79	53.8	9
Paddington–Banbury	67.5	90	45.0	83	48.8	7
Banbury–Paddington	67.5	95	42.6	83	48.8	12
Reading–Chippenham	58.0	72	48.3	65	53.5	7
Didcot–Paddington	53.1	70	45.5	60	53.1	10
Chippenham–Didcot	40.9	53	46.5	47	52.2	6

behind each other. In the summer of 1941, however, in view of the relative freedom from air attack and the desire of many people to get some relief from the strain of wartime London, a special announcement was made from Paddington that commencing on Saturday July 26th, and on each Saturday until August 29th, additional trains would run as follows:

> 9.35 a.m. for the Weymouth line, Taunton, Minehead and
> and 2.15 p.m. Barnstaple branches.
>
> 12 noon for the Torquay line
>
> 3.30 p.m. for the Weymouth line, Taunton, Exeter, Teignmouth, Newton Abbot, Torquay line and Plymouth.

It was good to see such old favourites as the Torbay Limited, and the 3.30 p.m. West of England expresses restored, albeit at much reduced speed and on Saturdays only, and for five weeks only at that. It was nevertheless evidence of good railway management to deal with the traffic offered. Though an attempt had been made to spread the load over the working day at Paddington, the situation on the Saturday before Bank Holiday was such that the wartime Cornish Riviera Express had to be run in *five* sections. The actual loading of this train, and of the special extra trains just mentioned were:

	Number of Passengers
9.35 a.m. extra, Taunton and Minehead	346
10.30 a.m. Cornish Riviera,	
1st part for Penzance	743
2nd part for Penzance	1089
3rd part for Paignton	1000
4th part for Exeter and Kingswear	800
5th part for Newton Abbot	890
10.35 a.m. ex-Paddington (via Bristol)	
1st part for Bristol	276
2nd part for Penzance	1000
12 noon extra, for Kingswear	500
2.15 p.m. extra, for Minehead	581
3.30 p.m. extra, for Plymouth	233

The above statistics are most interesting in showing that the public had not paid much attention to the special announcement of extra trains, but had preferred to pack into the earlier service which they knew of old, rather than wait until afternoon for the extras at 12 noon and 3.30 p.m.

In October 1941, in view of the Government's decision to introduce legislation placing all public utility undertakings upon the same basis as regards war damage, and in pursuance of the policy announced in the Budget Speech of minimising the impact of increased costs of transport upon the prices of essential goods and services the Government agreed with the four main line railways, and with the London Passenger Transport Board upon an important revision of the financial arrangement concluded in February 1940. In a White Paper issued in October 1941 it was stated that fixed annual payments were to be made to the five undertakings, and in future the net results of the 'pool' would be for the account of the Government who would receive any surplus and make good any deficiency. The fixed annual payments provided for were:

	£
Great Western Railway Co.	6,670,603
London Midland & Scottish Railway Co.	14,749,698
London & North Eastern Railway Co.	10,136,355
Southern Railway Co.	6,607,639
London Passenger Transport Board	4,835,705
	£43,000,000

On October 17, 1941 "The Railway Gazette" had a long editorial article that very aptly summarised both the new agreement itself, and reaction to it. The following is the full text:

The revised financial agreement between the Government and the controlled railways has escaped attack and criticism no more than the predecessor it is designed to replace. Certain sections of the community, always vocal in these matters, have not disguised their disappointment that the Government has decided not to adopt the advice they have given so freely and with so little practical knowledge, to nationalise the transport system of the country. The new agreement, which provides for renting the railways by the State, has also been criticised on the grounds that its terms are unduly generous to the transport systems. How little substance there is in these protestations is easy to see if one is prepared to delve far enough into the facts of the case, to divest one's mind of prejudice, and to approach the problem from the basis of equity. On this basis the original agreement by no means can be judged generous to the proprietors of the railways; nor can the second. At best it assures a very meagre return upon the capital which has been invested in the undertakings and without which, allied to the patience which, perforce, has been exercised by a long-suffering body of stockholders, the railways of this country could not have reached their present high standard of efficiency, which has contributed so greatly to the successful prosecution of the war.

Of recent years there has been all too prevalent an idea that the standard revenue which was fixed by the Railways Act, 1921, as fair and reasonable and in the public interest is beyond the possibility of attainment—that the £51,359,000 at which it now stands has become but a mythical figure. It should be remembered that Parliament considered the attainment of that standard revenue was so expedient in the public interest that it placed a duty on the Railway Rates Tribunal to fix charges so as to enable a company to earn its standard revenue. Although it is a fact that Parliament's object was not attained in the case of all the railway companies, this has been due very largely to acute and unrelegated competition by road interests. There can be no doubt that in present circumstances the railway companies could earn their standard revenues, and this much has been admitted by responsible ministers; in fact, although no figures have been published, it is believed that certain companies have achieved their standard since the outbreak of war. Moreover, the use made now of the capital provided by the railways is much greater than in the period before the war, and includes the use of assets which then were operated at a loss, but were continued in use to meet conditions which now exist. Taking into consideration the relative service of the capital of the London Passenger Transport Board, a total of £56,853,000 would be required as the total standard revenue of the whole of the undertakings, and it is this figure which should be borne in mind when comparisons are made with the fixed annual net revenue of the five major parties in the revised arrangements which provide for a rental of £43,000,000 in addition to the net revenue from certain excluded items.

It must not be overlooked that in agreeing to the revised agreement, the main detail of which were outlined in 'The Railway Gazette' of October 3, the railway companies have made considerable sacrifices. There can be no doubt that in this they were influenced by two main factors; these were that the national interest in the present emergency had to be paramount, and that ordinary commercial considerations, within reasonable limits, had to be subordinated to that interest; and that although the fixed annual payment of £43,000,000 could not be taken as representing the existing or potential earning capacity of the undertakings—there can be no doubt that the earnings, even for 1941 so far, have been proportionately much in excess of the fixed payment—they could not leave out of consideration the fact that conditions might arise which would substantially affect earning capacity, such as, for example, an invasion of this country or a decline in traffics towards the end of control. In agreeing to the new arrangements the railways and the transport board have foregone the substantial sum due to them as a result of the considerable lag which arose from the fact that under the old agreement fares and charges were not adjusted promptly to meet increases in working costs. Moreover the controlled undertakings have given up the pooling arrangement, under which at least some of them would have received their standard revenue, and are also giving up the right to charge as revenue expenditure, the cost of restoring war damage up to a maximum of £10,000,000 a year, and to recover that cost through increased charges.

On the other hand the undertakings will receive the annual payment of £43,000,000 during the whole period of control irrespective of what contingencies might arise, and they will retain for their own account the sums charged against the pool account in 1940 in respect of the cost of restoring war damage. There can be no doubt that on balance the arrangement cannot be viewed as particulary favourable financially to the railways and London Transport, nor can it be suggested that the £43,000,000 is a subsidy to the railway. On the contrary, the railways are subsidising the Government at the present time, for even at the present level of charges there can be no doubt that the £43,000,000 will be substantially exceeded. It has to be remembered that the railways and the board are very large undertakings; the gross expenditure of the pool in 1940 to operate these undertakings for war purposes was £203,500,000, and the annual labour bill is over £150,000,000; the capital spent on providing the undertakings is £1,300,000,000. These figures put the £43,000,000 rental, which incidentally includes the revenue from ancillary businesses, in its proper perspective which is that it is a return of under 3½ per cent. on the capital.

It is all to the good that the new financial arrangements make more definite provision for maintenance than those which were in operation during the last war by providing for meeting arrears in maintenance both during and at the end of control; they will avoid many of the difficulties which arose at the end of the last war on this account. As has been pointed out already in 'The Railway Gazette' of September 5, 'there is little ground for the view, in some quarters that under the new agreement there will be no further increases in charges. The agreement is apparently worded with some care on the point and refers to 'minimising the impact' of increased costs of transport on the prices of essential goods and services. There can be no question of the desirability that charges should be raised against Government Departments concerned, even if only on some broad basis, as if they are not, there must not only be a tendency to extravagance, but failure to do so would severely deplete the revenues of the companies. Although ostensibly this would be the concern of the Government, since it is receiving revenues against making the fixed payment, there is another point to be considered; this is that if railway revenues are seriously depleted a cry may be raised that the Government is subsidising the railways, when on a true basis the reverse is the case. It would be helpful if a record were to be kept of variations in costs of labour and materials for each year of control, and if the Government were to continue to publish an annual statement giving the financial results of the controlled undertakings and recording the effects of the variations in these costs.

On the results of the year 1940 the Great Western had been able to pay a dividend of four per cent. on the ordinary shares, and this same dividend was paid in 1941. But the Company was the most fortunate of all the concerns involved in the financial agreements of 1940 and 1941, because of its position in the three years 1935, 1936 and 1937. Although it is carrying the story forward two years the basic position was asserted at the Annual General Meeting in 1943 when Mr. Ashley Brown, a prominent shareholder, referred to the plight of those whose savings were invested in other railways. Instancing the L.N.E.R. in particular he said: 'These stockholders had maintained their company in a state of the highest efficiency for many years by the sacrifice of their dividends, and now when the company was earning record profits and carrying record traffic, the Government had confiscated every halfpenny which would otherwise have passed into dividends'. As Mr. Ashley Brown had said earlier at the Great Western meeting: '. . . it was very difficult for stockholders in this favoured company to realise precisely all that this war agreement meant to some stockholders in some other companies'.

Reverting for a moment to the year 1940, the Company sustained a grievous loss in September by the death of the Chairman, Viscount Horne. He had been a director for nearly 18 years, and Chairman for the last seven of those. It was no light task to follow so outstanding a Chairman as Viscount Churchill, but Lord Horne brought all his remarkable qualities, his world-wide experience in business, and his tremendous personality to bear upon the task, and his success was absolute. He was succeeded by Mr. Charles J. Hambro, a Vice-Chairman since 1934, and a member of a famous banking house. During 1940 also two other prominent members of the board had to resign on taking up important

Ministerial positions in the Government. These two directors were Lord Portal, who subsequently returned to the Great Western Railway to become its last Chairman, and Mr. Harold Macmillan who succeeded Sir Anthony Eden as Prime Minister. Among chief officers of the Company Mr. F. R. Potter retired from the position of Superintendent of the Line, and was succeeded by Mr. Gilbert Matthews, as from January 1941. Another change proposed by the new Chairman could however not immediately be put into effect. He had proposed that the General Manager, Sir James Milne, should become a member of the board. While this created a precedent so far as the Company was concerned his fellow directors agreed readily enough, and a Bill was in preparation to give the necessary legal sanction when a difficulty arose over Sir James Milne's membership of the wartime Railway Executive Committee. The Minister of Transport intimated that he could not see his way to accepting a director of the G.W.R. as a member of the R.E.C. In the circumstances, as soon as his election to the Great Western Board was ratified he had to resign, formally, in order to retain his membership of the R.E.C. which was vital in wartime. His seat on the Great Western board was kept vacant until conditions permitted him to be re-elected.

*   *   *

Transport of freight and munitions of war towards the south coast had been a major concern of all British railways since 1939 and since the evacuation from Dunkirk plans were being perfected for the build-up of supply routes for an army that would eventually re-enter the Continent of Europe. The Japanese attack on Pearl Harbour and the entry of the U.S.A. into the war ensured that massive American reinforcements would be available to assist the forces already marshalled in Great Britain and the plans for improvement of railway facilities were pushed rapidly ahead. Great Western developments in this overall plan fell into three broad categories:

1. The provision of additional running loops and extensions to existing loops on double track main lines.

2. The lengthening of passing loops on certain north to south secondary lines, which were single-tracked, to permit of the handling of lengthy freight trains.

3. Main line quadrupling.

In the last mentioned category an important scheme was illustrated and described in 'The Railway Gazette' of March 20, 1942, though at that time, for security reasons, its location was not revealed. From the photographs and plans it could be identified as the section between Severn Tunnel Junction and the outskirts of Newport. This section was then carrying a very heavy traffic from the north and from South Wales, and the existence of only two running lines between these two centres was causing

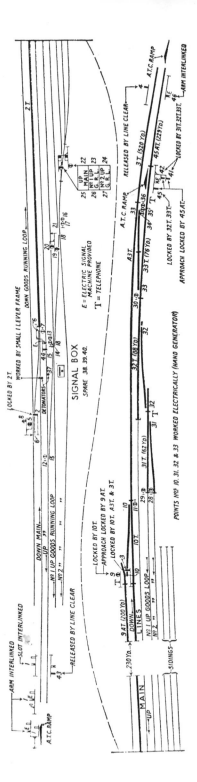

DETECTION

No.	NORMAL	REVERSE
9		10 [10]
11		10
12		15
13	18	
14		18
16		21
17	21	
19	15	
20		15
22		15 18
23	15	
24	18	
25		15 18
26	15	
27	18	
28		32

ELECTRICAL DETECTION SHEWN [ ]

No.	NORMAL	REVERSE
29		32
30		33
34		31 32 33
35	31	32
36	32	33
41		31 [31] 32 [32]
42	31 [31]	
45	32 [32]	
5		6
7		6
8	6	

SUBSIDIARY LIGHTS

RED	9 13 14 16 17 19 20 (22 23 24) (25 26 27) 28
WHITE	29 30 5 7 8 / 12 34 35 36 11

REPEATERS

LEVER Nos. Etc.

TYPE		
FLAG	I	3 4 46 9
ARM	2	(41 42 45)
LAMP	II	(3 4 41 42 45 46 9)
SPECIAL	I	DISTANT
	I	INTERMEDIATE DISTANT
	I	INNER DISTANT
	4	INNER DISTANT

Fig. 21. Diagram of layout with running loops and hand-generator points typical of a number on the GWR.

congestion. The work of quadrupling was carried out in the remarkably short time of 6½ months from the date of authorisation of the scheme. The work involved 8½ miles of route, and included the reconstruction of two intermediate stations, Magor and Llanwern, much excavation and embankment work, the extension of a number of overbridges to span four tracks instead of two, the laying in of cross-over roads at three points intermediately, to facilitate crossing freight and other trains from main to relief lines and vice versa. So far as permanent way changes were concerned, in addition to the laying in of the plain line on the new section there was considerable point and crossing work at each end, together with new signalling.

The provision of new, or longer running loops was made extensively on the West to North route, via the Severn Tunnel, and numerous stations between Pontypool Road and Shrewsbury were so equipped. In the design of these new layouts it was desirable, in the prevailing shortage of manpower, to avoid using any additional staff. Yet the lengthening of existing loops, and the putting in of new ones to accommodate maximum length freight trains necessitated the placing of certain points beyond the limit of 350 yds. for mechanical working. Additional signal boxes and signalmen were avoided by use of the hand-generator system, which enabled the long distance points to be worked efficiently and economically without accumulators or other sources of power. The accompanying plan shows the signalling arrangements at a typical location. As in the case of the main line quadrupling between Severn Tunnel Junction and Newport the original descriptions of this work preserved a wartime anonymity; but in actual fact the majority of stations between Pontypool Road and Shrewsbury were so equipped, with variation of the typical layout illustrated to suit the local conditions. On the single tracked Didcot, Newbury and Southampton line the crossing loops were lengthened, and and again hand generator operation was used for the long distance points.

At midsummer 1941 the veteran Chief Mechanical Engineer, Charles B. Collett, retired. He was then 70 years of age, and had served the Company nobly during 19 momentous years of office. One has only to look back through the chronicles of Swindon works to appreciate the success of his work: the 'Castle' class engines; the triumphs of the locomotive exchanges of 1925 and 1926; the production of the 'Kings', and the record running of the Cheltenham Flyer, in 1932. But above all there was the remarkably high standard of constructional and repair work in all the main workshops—not only Swindon, but Caerphilly, Wolverhampton and the light repairs performed at major running centres like Old Oak Common and Newton Abbot. At the time of his retirement there was a general disposition to regard the 'Castle' as Collett's greatest engine design, though time was to show, particularly after nationalisation, that the 'King', fully developed, was an outstanding engine for its size and weight. There is a further significance in this, for Collett's successor, F. W. Hawksworth, was Chief Locomotive Draughtsman at the time the

'King' was designed, and all the detail work was his direct responsibility. Hawksworth had the misfortune in some respects of taking office at a time when new engine designing was drastically limited by war conditions. A man of Hawksworth's training and long experience would naturally look forward to the time when he could develop designs of his own, to meet the ever-increasing, and ever-changing demands of traffic, and some consideration was given to the design of an express passenger locomotive much larger and more powerful than the 'King' class; but authority to build even a prototype was not forthcoming. Instead by Government order, Swindon had to build 2-8-0 freight engines of L.M.S.R. design for general service on the British railways.

So far as the personalia of Great Western locomotives was concerned a pleasant gesture was made by renaming some of the 'Castle' class engines after British aircraft types that had won undying fame in the Battle of Britain. It is worth setting out on record these names, and the engines to which they were applied:

No.	Name	No.	Name
5071	*Spitfire*	5077	*Fairey Battle*
5072	*Hurricane*	5078	*Beaufort*
5073	*Blenheim*	5079	*Lysander*
5074	*Hampden*	5080	*Defiant*
5075	*Wellington*	5081	*Lockheed Hudson*
5076	*Gladiator*	5082	*Swordfish*

The names displaced were subsequently used again when construction of the 'Castle' class was resumed after the war. As economy measures during the war the style of painting of passenger engines and of carriages was greatly simplified. Engines were turned out in plain green, with the polished safety valve bonnets and chimney caps painted over. The cream upper panels of main line coaches disappeared, and carriages were painted chocolate all over instead of the previous two-tone scheme. New engines of the 'Hall' class built for mixed-traffic during the war were turned out without names, to avoid using brass in the large nameplates traditional on the G.W.R. Nevertheless, that 'pride in the job' so treasured from end to end of the line found some ways of expressing itself, even in the austere circumstances of wartime, and at some sheds engines working the principal express passenger turns had the paint carefully removed from their bright parts, and continued to take the road in much of their old splendour. It must be added of course that such adornment of engines was not done at the expense of more essential tasks. It was done at sheds where the standards of all-round maintenance were very high.

The year 1942 marked an anniversary which would have been the subject of much celebration and reminiscent pageantry in normal times, for May 22 marked the 50th anniversary of the final conversion of the broad gauge. I have described elsewhere*, in some detail, the remarkable feat of organisation that enabled the whole line between Exeter and Truro to be converted in a single week-end, 171 route miles in all, including the branches from Newton Abbot to Kingswear, and from Truro to Falmouth. At the time of the 50th anniversary of the conversion there was on the Great Western board a director whose service dated back to broad gauge days. This was Sir Watkin Williams-Wynn Bt. who was first elected to the board in 1885. His directorship recalls an interesting item of early Great Western history, in that the owner of Wynnstay, under the North Wales Mineral Railway Act of 1845, had the right to appoint a director to the Great Western board. Sir Watkin's uncle was a director, but it is of special note that at one time he resigned his seat and nominated Daniel Gooch as his successor. This was in 1865. But another director retired at the same time and Sir Watkin the elder then rejoined the board. The Sir Watkin who was on the board in 1942 was elected when he succeeded to the baronetcy in 1885. He was then only 25 years of age, and his term of office, extending to his retirement in 1943, covered the periods of seven Chairmen, and eight General Managers. Here indeed, in Sir Watkin, was a link with the very earliest days of the G.W.R., for he sat on the board for four years under the Chairmanship of Sir Daniel Gooch. When Sir Watkin retired in 1943 he was 83 years of age, yet still so alert and well preserved that he might have been taken for ten years younger. At different times three Great Western locomotives had been named after the family. There was a 2-2-2 of the narrow gauge 'Sir Daniel' class, engine No. 471 named *Sir Watkin*, built in 1869. Then came a Dean 4-4-0 of the 'Badminton' class, No. 3311 named after the family seat, *Wynnstay*. This engine was later incorporated in the 'Flower' class and numbered 4119. Finally there was a 'Bulldog' class 4-4-0, No. 3375 *Sir Watkin Wynn*, which was still running at the time of his retirement from the board.

It was certainly a far cry from the broad gauge, and from the days when the little 2-2-2 *Sir Watkin* ran on the north main line of the G.W.R. to the late autumn of 1942, for it was then that the first American-built 'Austerity' 2-8-0s began to arrive in Britain, which in their stark functionalism represented the very antithesis of the early Great Western designs. The first of them was formally handed over to Lord Leathers, Minister of War Transport, by Colonel Norman H. Ryan, Acting Chief of Transportation Corps, American Army, at a ceremony at Paddington on December 11, 1942. The front of the engine was decorated with the Union Jack and the Stars and Stripes, and while the locomotive itself looked very strange in British eyes it, as the first of a large class, was received gratefully enough. Engines of this type were soon familiar objects on British railways. After some early running on the L.N.E.R. by a few engines of the type the entire batch was allocated to the Great Western Railway. Their stay in Britain was not expected to be more than brief,

---

* Great Western Railway in the 19th Century.   *Published by Ian Allan*

because their ultimate sphere of activity was intended to be on military railways when the long-planned invasion of the European mainland had been achieved.

XVIII

The War—To V.E. Day

The arrival of American troops in Great Britain, and the working of American locomotives on British metals as the outward signs of the vast material reinforcements that were pouring in, was a reassurance to the British people that the eventual outcome of the war was no longer in doubt. But with that reassurance came the realisation that many cherished individualities of old were gradually, but very definitely slipping away. This was particularly so on the Great Western Railway. Under ministerial order the chief mechanical engineer, at Swindon, could no longer build the locomotives he desired, and the regulations surrounding the working of passenger trains involved many frustrations for dedicated railwaymen, such as those of the Great Western. Nevertheless despite the many signs of change a tremendous effort was being put into the build-up of railway facilities that would assist the allied armies in launching the assault that was to prove the knock-out blow to the Nazi régime.

Reference has been made in earlier chapters to the important signalling works carried out to provide for running additional and longer freight trains on routes leading towards the south coast. In addition to this work, a number of new connections were put in to facilitate exchange of traffic between the G.W.R. and its neighbours, and maps are now shown illustrating some of the more interesting of these wartime works. They are important as indicating some of the overall planning of railway facilities that had to be carried out by the wartime Railway Executive Committee. In the ordinary way an enormous amount of north–south traffic passed through the heart of London, over the City Widened lines of the former Metropolitan Railway, and over the East London Line. Equally, traffic over the West London line, and over the North and South West Junction Railway, coming from the Great Western and the L.M.S. Railways was heavy. It was imperative to provide for alternative routes to the Southern Railway, not only to relieve congestion in London, but to avoid complete standstill in the event of serious enemy action.

It was therefore agreed that traffic for the South Eastern section of the Southern, from the Great Northern and Great Eastern sections of the L.N.E.R., and from the Midland and L.N.W. sections of the L.M.S.R. would be routed via Sandy, Bedford, Bletchley, and Oxford to the G.W.R., and thence on to the South Eastern line at Reading. The signalling of the new junction at Reading has been mentioned in an earlier chapter. A plan of the connections is shown herewith. In addition it was necessary to improve running conditions at Oxford, and a new

Plate 43. FREIGHT TRAFFIC

Train hauled by two American austerity 2-8-0s

Ex- R.O.D. Great Central type 2-8-0 on down train near Teignmouth

Up coal train leaving the Severn Tunnel hauled by 2-6-2 and 2-8-0 tank locomotives

Plate 44

Viscount Portal
Chairman 1944-1947

Gilbert Matthews
Superintendent of the Line 1941-1947

F. W. Hawksworth
Chief Mechanical Engineer 1941-1947

Sir Allan Quartermaine
Chief Engineer 1940-1947

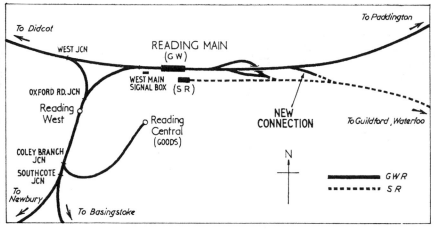

Fig. 22. New wartime connections built at Government expense, at Reading . . .

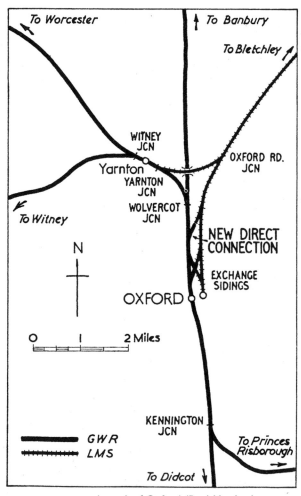

. . . and north of Oxford (Pool Meadow).

junction, as illustrated, was laid in to provide for direct running off the former L.N.W.R. line, instead of the indirect layout at the existing exchange sidings. The new junction at Reading was brought into use as early in the war as June 1st, 1941, and by its existence an alternative route was available to the G.W.R. South Lambeth depot and to Battersea Power House, should the West London line be put out of action. Traffic from the G.W.R. and the G.C. section of the L.N.E.R. using the West London line to reach the Brighton section of the Southern could be diverted via Banbury, Oxford, Winchester and Eastleigh to enter the Brighton section at Fratton.

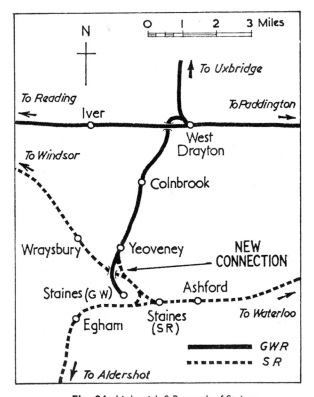

Fig. 24. Link with S.R. north of Staines.

Another small, but vital connection was put in between the G.W.R. single line branch from West Drayton to Staines, and the Southern Railway Windsor line, at Staines itself, as shown in the accompanying plan. This new link was brought into service in September 1940, primarily to provide an alternative route to the West London line for heavy freight traffic passing south from the G.W. and L.N.E.R. Joint line via High Wycombe. When this connection was available arrangements were made for Southern Railway locomotives to take over the haulage of these trains at Northolt Junction and then to proceed via the Greenford loop to Hanwell and West Drayton, thence over the Staines branch, and by the new connection via Virginia Water, and Guildford to Redhill. Traffic over this new connection was at times heavy. Trains from the north were brought into Northolt by powerful L.N.E.R. 2–8–0 locomotives; but the roundabout, though vital route to the Southern precluded the use of locomotives of equivalent power, on account of weight limitations, and in general some remarshalling had to be carried out at Northolt to make up three Southern trains for every two arriving from the north.

In the West of England the Great Western branch to Tavistock and Launceston proved of vital importance, not only during the intense air attacks on the Plymouth area in April and May 1941, but in the preparations for D-day. The accompanying map shows the layout of Great Western and Southern lines in this area during the war period. The new connection at St. Budeaux was one of the early provisions for alternative routes, and was opened in March 1941, but it was Lydford that was to prove, perhaps a little unexpectedly, of the utmost importance in the months immediately following. There the Great Western and Southern stations are alongside, and a short exchange connection existed between the two. Otherwise, although the old L.S.W.R. main line and the G.W.R. Launceston branch ran cheek by jowl down the valley for some 6½ miles to Tavistock there was no other physical connection. During the very severe bombing of the Plymouth area during April and May 1941, there were many occasions when the lines were damaged, and to all intent and purposes the Great Western and Southern " pooled " their tracks, and shared timetables. At one time when the G.W.R. was blocked the Southern was running far more Great Western trains over its line than its own.

All this took place before the new connection, shown on the map, had been put in at Launceston. Some such alternative route workings were: G.W.R. trains from Cornwall via Bodmin Road, Bodmin, Wadebridge and Okehampton to Exeter; G.W.R. trains running from Exeter to Plymouth via Okehampton, and the St. Budeaux link; Southern trains using the G.W.R. line between Lydford and Plymouth; and Southern trains running between Exeter and Plymouth via Newton Abbot and Totnes. The provision for alternative route working in emergency was carried to the extent of enginemen of both companies learning each others roads between Exeter and Plymouth. Certain local trains on each route were regularly worked by engines of the other company, and this practice was continued after the war. Things were made difficult from the Great Western point of view, because limitation of axle loading over Meldon Viaduct precluded the use of any larger locomotives than the standard 2–6–0 tender engines. In preparation for D-day two new

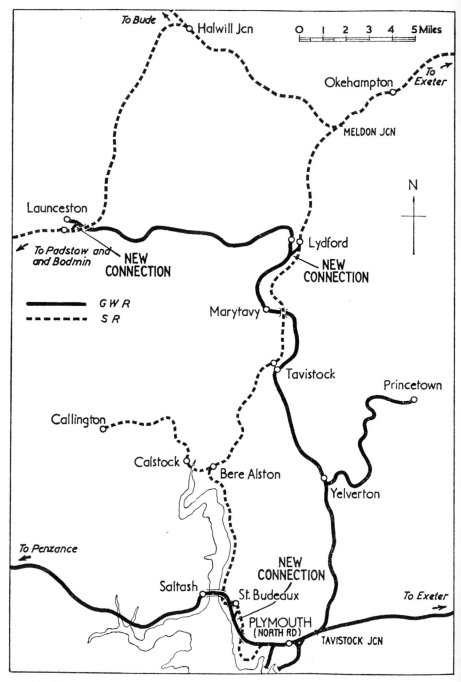

Fig. 25. The three wartime connections with the Southern in the West Country.

connections between the two companies' lines were put at Lydford (November 15th, 1943) and Launceston (September 22nd, 1943).

The improvement of the Didcot, Newbury and Southampton line was another important wartime project, and reference to the signalling works in connection with the lengthening of the loops has already been made. It was not until after the end of the war that the full extent of the work was revealed, and the fact that the line had been temporarily closed to enable it to be done. Although the line connected two important main routes, it did not carry a heavy traffic in pre-war days, but was required to form a wartime north-south communication of importance. When it was built, some 60 years ago, the formation and bridges were made sufficiently wide to accommodate double tracks, although a single track only was laid. Subsequently, weathering of the banks took place, and the accumulation of consequent deposits became overgrown, with the result that from time to time the track had been slewed towards the centre of the formation to obtain the clearances required by new standards. particularly under arched overbridges. Accordingly it would not have been possible to lay an additional track throughout the entire length without considerable adjustment of formation, and it was decided to allow part of it to remain single track, and to increase the carrying capacity by additional crossing facilities and other improvements such as lengthening loops from 300 yd. to 550 yd.

By reason of these engineering works, the passenger service on the whole line from Didcot, through Newbury to Winchester (Cheese Hill) was suspended on Tuesday August 4th, 1942. A passenger road service, with strictly limited accommodation, was provided by railway-associated buses in lieu of the rail service. Passengers were picked up and set down only at stations and halts, and tickets were required to be taken at the station booking office in the usual way. Rail service was restored on March 8th, 1943. The 18-mile section from Didcot to Newbury was doubled throughout and brought into use as double line on April 18th, 1943. From Enborne junction at Newbury the line was doubled for a length of two miles to Woodhay, and opened on March 8th, 1943, but on the 23 miles thence to Winchester additional passing places and lengthened loops sufficed. At Worthy Down, near Winchester, an entirely new single-line connection for up traffic was made with the main line of the Southern Railway where the latter crosses the G.W.R. on an overbridge, and brought into service on May 5th, 1943. The new connecting line of about a mile in length ran through a large new cutting over a new embankment and bridge.

Two other wartime connections in Wessex may be briefly mentioned, and these are shown in the accompanying diagrams. The first two were wholly Great Western, and provided for direct running from the Corsham direction to the Melksham–Trowbridge line at Thingley Junction, and for direct running from this line to the Sturt and Westbury cut-off. At Thingley Junction the formation already existed, and the work involved

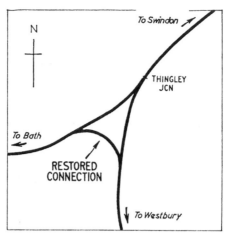

Fig. 26. Restored east to south spur at Thingley, near Chippenham.

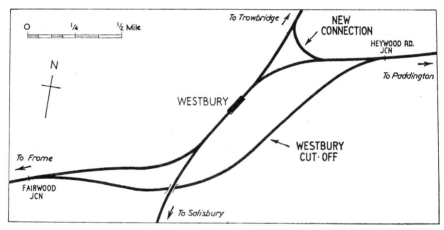

Fig. 27. New north to east spur at Westbury (Wilts.).

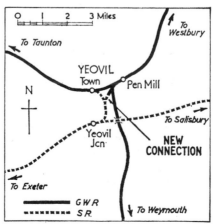

Fig. 28. New G.W. to Southern link at Yeovil.

the relaying of track on a former spur, but at Westbury a new line had to be built. The remaining item to be mentioned among these wartime works was a connection put in to provide through running between the Great Western and Southern at Yeovil, as shown in the accompanying map. This was brought into service in October 1943. It is important to appreciate that all these new connections were made at Government expense, and were Government and not railway property, although coming within the jurisdiction and management of the railway companies concerned. There were, of course, others elsewhere in the country; but the Great Western, in its vital role of feeder-line to the Southern and the South Coast ports had more than any other company.

The war years were a time of great activity and anxiety in all the engineering departments of the G.W.R., and from the outset it was realised that the question of alternatives for timber would need early consideration, if new timber was to be retained only for main line purposes, and second-hand sleepers were to be released for Government work and Army operational purposes. Some experience had been obtained with concrete sleepers during World War I. In 1917–18 various types of transverse and pot-sleepers were tried on the Taunton Division, but failures occurred almost as soon as they were put in the track. Then 36 transverse sleepers 8ft. × 8ft. × 6in. deep were put in the Barnstaple Branch and of these, six lasted two years, six for seven years, 12 for nine years, and the remaining 12 were removed after 14 years for reasons other than failure. In this track the sleepers had been subjected to traffic at 30 m.p.h. at a density of 14 trains a day. Circular concrete pots, connected by tie bars, were tried in a goods loop at Taunton with flat-bottom rails and were subjected to traffic at 10 m.p.h. at a density of 40 trains a day. Although cracks appeared in these pots, the test was not altogether unsatisfactory but, as the timber position had improved, the use of concrete as a substitute was not pursued.

The results of these previous trials were re-examined in the light of the new emergency, and it was decided to confine attention to the pot, or block type for use in sidings and goods loops. The Great Western development during wartime is extremely interesting, despite its limited field of application, for it is the block type concrete sleeper with steel connecting bar that has become the standard for the heaviest main line traffic on some Continental European railways operating very fast trains. On the G.W.R. the design produced was that shown as Type A, which had a domical recess on the underside, a cage reinforcement of 5/16 in. dia. steel bar, recessed chairbolt washers on the underside, a $\frac{1}{2}$in. elm pad as a cushion between the chair and concrete and in which the $\frac{7}{8}$in. dia. chairbolts were symmetrically spaced in the pot. The mix of concrete was 1 : 1$\frac{1}{2}$: 3, using granite aggregate and rapid hardening cement. Pots were made with the chairbolt holings 12 in. and 11 in. centres to suit either G.W.R. " oo ". or B.S. 95 chairs. In the first stages of laying in these pots, timber sleepers were used on each side of the joints

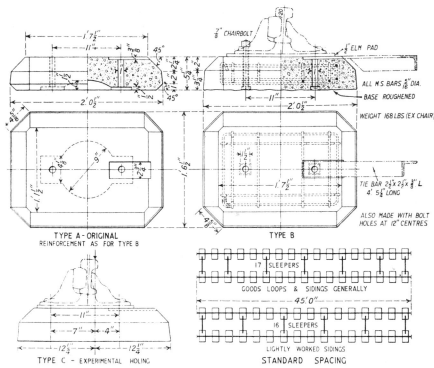

Fig. 29. Development of concrete sleepers, introduced to alleviate the timber shortage.

and every third pair of pots was tied by a $2\frac{1}{2}$ in. $\times$ $2\frac{1}{2}$ in. $\times$ $\frac{3}{8}$ in. angle by means of the inner chairbolts. The pots had a small chamfer on the lower edge to facilitate handling. In one case, after some little time in the track, it was found that several pots had cracked through the bolt holes and, although the mass was held together by the reinforcement and it was not at that time necessary to remove them from the track, several were removed for subjection to test. The pots were mounted on supports giving a 9 in. clear span and a vertical load was applied to a piece of rail keyed in the chair.

Subsequent amendments (Type B) were made to the design and practice, as follow:

(a) The domical recess was omitted and a roughened base used.

(b) The ribbed washer was dispensed with and a recess provided for the head of the chair bolt.

(c) Felt pads were substituted for the elm, and satisfactory tests were made without any cushion at all between chair and concrete, but as G.W.R. chairs have serrated bases a felt pad was considered desirable to facilitate even bearing.

(d) Elm and felt pads were supplied with one round and one elongated hole to suit either 11 in. or 12 in. holing, thus avoiding special ordering.

(e) Timber sleepers at the joints were omitted and angle tie bars used exclusively.

From the above it will be seen that 100 per cent. saving in timber had been effected.

It was found that there was a tendency for pots to tip inwards with a resultant tightening of gauge. Consideration was given to this and it was decided to make some pots with the bolt holes slightly eccentrically disposed in the length of the pot, so that the line of thrust from the rail came through the centre of the pot. This resulted in a slightly longer projection of the pot on the four-foot side (see Type C) which contributed to stability. A number of this type of pot was laid in track adjacent to the Type B pots, but the test result was negative, as no trouble was experienced on this side with either type.

Pot sleepers got a better bearing on ashes, but they were also used successfully with stone ballast. Discretion was used as to the employment of pot sleepers on new embankments, but little trouble was experienced on new banks up to 10 ft. depth. To conserve crossing timber, experiments were carried out using pot sleepers instead of timber for that portion of turnouts between the heel of the switch and leg of the crossing. The width of a standard pot was found to prohibit the full use of this type, and so a smaller block was designed which alternated with the standard. The standard blocks were tied with angle bars and the smaller blocks were left free. By the spring of 1943 pot sleepers were being manufactured on the G.W.R. at the rate of 5,000 per week, and by that time well over half a million were in service.

Another interesting example of the expedients used under the stress of war conditions concerned the methods of wagon repair. With the intensification of the war effort, and the continued expansion of railway traffic the need to keep a maximum number of wagons in service was acute. By efficient arrangements for discharging and loading the turn-round times were kept to a minimum, but wear and tear is continuous, and the methods used for repair were examined critically with a view to minimising the time each wagon was out of service. At Swindon the wagon shop had its own electrically-operated sawmill, and it was near a timber store. It was equipped to build 4,500 new wagons a year, and repair some 20,000 wagons in the same period. The great majority of wagons coming in for repair during the war years included a large amount of wood work. As a wartime economy measure open wagons were not repainted or re-lettered after repair, and thinner hardwood boards were used for replacement of worn or damaged flooring or sheeting. Where thinner side boards were introduced packing pieces were inserted beneath the steel tie bars to compensate for the difference in thickness between the original and replacement timbers. By intensive organisation it was found possible at Swindon to step up the output of repaired wagons to more than 500 per week.

In locomotive construction, under the direction of the new chief mechanical engineer, Mr. F. W. Hawksworth, a notable departure from traditional Great Western practice was made in a series of new 4-6-0 locomotives of the 'Hall' class, turned out in 1944. One of the major constructional features of the Churchward 2-cylinder locomotives, which had been followed in all variants and wheel arrangements from the classic prototypes of 1903–5 had been the casting of the saddle for supporting the front end of the boiler integral with the cylinders. The two halves, each one including one complete cylinder, were bolted together on the centre line of the engine, and these castings were supported on forged steel extensions bolted to the main frames. This arrangement was not without its disadvantages, and in the new engines of 1944 Hawksworth adopted a more conventional design, carrying the main frame plates through to the buffer beam. The cylinders were cast separately from the smokebox saddle, and were bolted to the frames, with a fabricated stiffener between the frames themselves. This stiffener was extended upwards to form the smokebox saddle. Hawksworth also abandoned the traditional Churchward type of bar-frame bogie, and used instead a plate-frame design. Another variant was the inclusion of a larger superheater, of a new type, providing 314.6 sq. ft. of heating surface, as compared with the 262.62 sq. ft. of the standard Swindon No. 3 superheater which had been used without variation on all 4-6-0 and 2-8-0 locomotives having the standard No. 1 boiler, over a period of nearly 35 years. Although from the motive power point of view the new engines were little more than additions to a numerous standard class, in detail design they represented a notable development, calculated to keep Great Western locomotive power abreast of the changing circumstances of train operation.

The new engines were designated '6959 class', after the running number of the first of the series. They were originally turned out in unlined black, but with the coat of arms on the tender, between the initials G.W.; and they were unnamed. From the outset they did excellent work on the road. I was doing some footplate work at the time and the running inspectors whom I met all considered they were just that little better than the original 'Halls'. They were put into passenger work, and generally worked turn and turn about with 'Castle' class engines, though designated 'mixed-traffic'. At that time of course the schedules of express passenger trains were considerably slower than those of pre-war years, though the '6959' class had a fine turn of speed, and ran freely up to a maximum of 75 to 80 m.p.h. In these engines, his first new design, Mr. Hawksworth scored a complete success, and in his readiness to depart from Swindon traditions, particularly in the matter of superheating, he took the first steps towards the interesting developments of later years.

Another mechanical engineering development of the war years was the introduction of a new type of balanced girder turntable, to obviate some of the disadvantages inherent in the older standard type, which was supported on a fixed centre post, and revolved on a cup and ball bearing. The heavy locomotives then in use and the great weight concentrated on the central pivot of the balanced-girder type turntable necessitated very large concrete foundations, and the main girders needed to be of sufficient strength throughout to sustain the load without too much deflection at their ends. These considerations necessarily increased the cost, and the problem of finding a less expensive, but satisfactory, turntable, had been constantly under review by the company's mechanical engineers with the result that the "Mundt" patent turntable was given a practical trial.

This type of turntable was used on many of the European railways and was specially designed by an engineer named Mundt, of the Netherlands Railways, to deal with the heavy locomotives used on the transcontinental services. It differed from the G.W.R. balanced turntable in that the central pivot carried only part of the weight of the engine and tender being turned; most of the load was borne by the turntable wheels. By distributing the weight over three points in that way, instead of concentrating it on the centre post, the central concrete foundations did not need to be so large, and lighter and less costly girders could be used for the engine cradle. Although the heavy load on the track rail involves considerably more effort for turning, this, to a large extent, was off-set by the use of ball-bearings on the turntable wheels and a special ball-race on the centre bearing. Two men at the hand turning gear could turn a full load quite comfortably.

The year 1943 saw the war effort working up to its maximum intensity. Women were employed in a great diversity of duties, and by that time in the war no fewer than 16,000 were serving the G.W.R. Many of these tasks were a repetition of those that women had done so well in World War I, ranging from engine and carriage cleaners to guards and ticket collectors; but a novelty was the use of waitresses on the few dining cars that were then operating. One of the most unusual and successful tasks undertaken by women was however the parcels "flying squad". These women travelling porters were stationed at Paddington, Bath, Birkenhead, Birmingham, Bristol, Cardiff, Carmarthen, Chester, Didcot, Exeter, Hereford, Newport (Mon.), Newton Abbot, Oxford, Pembroke, Plymouth, Shrewsbury, Swansea, Swindon, Taunton, Trowbridge, Westbury (Wilts.), Weymouth, Whitland, Wolverhampton, and Worcester. Every day their duties took them over wide areas, often covering several counties, and involving some 250 miles of train travel. Their special duty was to see that every package loaded at the starting station and everywhere else *en route* went into the right van on the right train, in the exact spot in that van to suit the destination, so that the pile of parcels

for each place lay handy by the most convenient door ready to be unloaded the moment the train stopped. They formed part of the company's
intensified campaign to combat the combined difficulties created by wartime traffic volume and wartime staff shortage, and to avert delays,
damage, and losses due to over-carrying, short-carrying, missed connections,
mis-transfers, and hurried handling. Each girl first directed the loading
of traffic at her home station. She then travelled in the guard's van,
and worked in turn for each of the twenty or thirty station-masters at
whose platforms the train stopped. Moreover, all the time the train
was running between stations she passed from van to van through the
connecting gangways adjusting the stowage of the load. The timekeeping
of over 300 of the busiest regular trains was improved by the "flying
squad".

Another notable effort to speed up the handling of freight was the
use of volunteer labour at weekends for unloading wagons. At one week-
end in October 1943 no fewer than 27,000 wagons were so dealt with, and
volunteer spare time labour largely contributed to this result. The
volunteers, who came from many walks of life were paid the appropriate
rate for the job, and they included butchers, grocers, greengrocers,
dustmen, road-sweepers, insurance agents, commercial travellers,
university students, women clerks and housewives. It was all in the
spirit of the times—all or nothing.

An important item of preparation for the forthcoming assault on the
mainland of Europe was the provision of ambulance trains for the
American Army. These trains of which the first were provided by the
Great Western Railway, were manned by American staff, and to enable
them to be used on the Continent as well as in Great Britain they were
fitted with the Westinghouse brake. Special sidings were laid out on
the north side of the main line, at Shrivenham, Wilts., where casualties
were unloaded. The trains themselves were mostly worked by L.N.E.R.
Class 'B 12/3' 4-6-0s, which as an ex-Great Eastern type were fitted with
the Westinghouse brake. As they had to be prepared to go anywhere,
almost at a moment's notice the locomotives and trains were manned
on the caboose system, with relief men always available. On heavily
graded routes the train engines frequently needed assisting by engines
from the local companies. Existing passenger vehicles were stripped and
re-arranged as ward cars. The first of these ambulance trains was handed
over on March 25th, 1943, by Mr. Hawksworth to Brigadier General
P. R. Hawley, Chief Surgeon of the American forces in Great Britain.

Amid all the intensity of the war effort and the strain under which
railwaymen and women were constantly working it would have been
surprising if there had not been accidents. The remarkable thing is that
there were so few. One of particular interest happened to an American-
built 2-8-0 'Austerity' engine, at Honeybourne, while working a freight
train from Banbury to Margam. It was typical of working conditions
at the time that the engine was prepared at Banbury and worked to

Leamington by one driver; another relieved him for the next 15 miles to Stratford-on-Avon, and a third crew then took charge. It was these latter men who sustained the unfortunate accident at Honeybourne, just before midnight on November 17th, 1943. Unfamiliarity with the working of the American steam valve to the water gauge, and the fact that the latter could show a false level in the glass if the valve was not fully opened, led to the uncovering of the firebox crown, and its eventual collapse. The partial explosion that followed severely scalded the fireman, though in the darkness and confusion on the footplate following the accident neither he nor his driver realised how seriously the unfortunate man had been injured. It was typical of the times that despite his injuries he walked nearly a mile to Honeybourne East Loop signal box to report the accident. There he received most efficient first aid treatment from the signalman; but it was of no avail, and he died later on November 18. As a result of this accident notices were posted at the sheds where the U.S.A. engines were stationed impressing upon footplate men the necessity of ensuring that the steam valves were fully open.

Another incident of an unusual nature took place in the Plymouth district on December 8th, 1942, though for security reasons details were not made public until some 18 months later. A farmer's wife, Mrs. Steer, of Wivelscombe Farm near Saltash, was driving slowly home through the blackout shortly after 11 p.m., and had crossed the railway by the private road that leads to the seaward side of the line over the top of Wivelscombe Tunnel when she felt the ground falling away and sliding sideways beneath her car. In the darkness it was an eerie experience, and having stopped her car she found that a 20-yard length of the road had sunk about 4 ft. and that cracks were opening in the ground all around her. By that time in the war the people of Plymouth and its surroundings were used to 'alarms and excursions' of all kinds, and far from being seized with panic Mrs. Steer's first thought was for the safety of the railway which ran nearby, in a deep cutting leading out of Wivelscombe Tunnel towards Saltash. Immediately, but not without some difficulty, she made her way to the nearest telephone and reported her discovery and fears to the G.W.R. telephone exchange at Plymouth. So promptly had her action been taken that the engineering and traffic departments were alerted before midnight, and arrangements were made at once to 'freeze' all traffic movements over the line. An up goods train was stopped at St. Germans, west of the slip, but otherwise there were no trains caught in the area.

The immediate task was to find out how the railway was affected. Only by a very long detour could the site be reached by road, as the Tamar ferries were not then running at so late an hour. One of the civil engineers therefore took a locomotive and proceeded, to find, in the darkness, a great bulge of rock on the down side of the cutting, obstructing the down line. But the up line was clear, and the waiting goods train was allowed to proceed at dead slow speed past the slip.

Single line working, at 5 m.p.h. was authorised from that time until
10.15 a.m. on the following morning, but then having seen the full
extent of the disturbance the line was completely closed until certain
precautionary measures were taken by the Chief Civil Engineer's department. At once the arrangements for alternative routing, perfected during
the 'blitz' period of April and May 1941, were put into force. Certain
trains were diverted via the North Cornwall line of the Southern Railway,
while in other cases passengers were conveyed between St. Germans and
Saltash by bus. An enormous amount of rock was involved in the slip
and the Engineer's department feared that complete blockage of the
cutting might occur at any moment. The remarkable thing was that the
slip had been caused not by earth movement but by the falling over of
the vertical strata of rock formation. Apart from the ultimate need for
complete clearing of the line the first point was to ascertain how stable
the ground was in the area of the slip, and blasting was decided upon.
It was thought that a heavy explosion would show whether further falls of
rock, or movement of the earth, were imminent. Less than 48 hours after
the occurrence of the slip, a heavy charge of ammonal was exploded,
and although there was some shaking it was found that the position
was a great deal more stable than had at first been thought.

With the possibility of further slips seeming to be remote all efforts
were turned to clearing the line. Single-line working was restored for
goods trains on the evening of December 10th, at 5 m.p.h., but traffic
could pass only in the night, because the up line was required in daylight,
for engineering department wagons in use for clearance purposes.
Although the line was thus reopened, albeit on a much reduced scale,
single-line working was involved over a section of four miles, and the delays
to traffic would have been considerable. Accordingly a short single-line
section extending only past the site of the slip was made. Crossover roads
were put in at each end; signal boxes were installed, with electric token
instruments at each end. Materials held in readiness for the repair of
air raid damage were used, and all the signalling and permanent way
work was completed by December 18th. Normal traffic could then pass
over the line, subject only to the delay involved in traversing the short
single-line section past the slip. The extent of the slip will be appreciated
from the fact that it took 4½ months to clear the obstruction. Double
line working was restored on May 2nd, 1943, at 5 m.p.h. A fortnight later
the speed restriction was removed from the up line, but it was retained on
the down line for several months more. In all 9,000 cu. yd. of material
had to be removed. The engineering and geological problems involved in
the investigations and repair work were fascinating in themselves; but
the dramatic nature of the discovery of the slip in the first place, by
Mrs. Steer, and the speed with which remedial action was taken lifted
the entire incident completely out of the ordinary.

With the coming of the year 1944 arrangements for the mass-invasion of
the European mainland were approaching completion. The restrictions on

civilian travel were tightened considerably, and in readiness for the actual period when troop movements and transport of munitions to the south-coast ports of embarkation would be at their height the strictest instructions were issued by the Ministry of War Transport that no extra passenger trains were to be run, and that no existing trains were to have their accommodation increased by the addition of extra coaches. The civilian population was exhorted to 'stay-put', and leave the railways free to handle the huge volume of military traffic. It was also anticipated that once the invasion started large scale bombing of this country would recommence, and it was doubly necessary to have the railways as free as possible to make dispositions for alternative routing, without having to consider civilian traffic moving, in the month of June, for holiday purposes. It was a logical and wise provision, in view of events that could then be foreseen. Unfortunately however things turned out differently, and slowness in reaction to the changed circumstances led to one of the most dangerous situations faced by the Great Western Railway at any time during the war.

The public was braced to the highest pitch of readiness and enthusiasm by the time D-day actually came, and after the first hours of intense anxiety, and news of the success of the landings in Normandy came through, one could sense a lifting of the tension, particularly as no resumption of air raiding immediately commenced. But then, totally unexpected by the great mass of the people, there began the 'flying bomb' attack on the London area, which continued day and night. This was a new and altogether more grim experience than anything that had gone before. The Battle of Britain, in 1940, had been fought by day; the winter 'blitz' of 1940-41 by night. In both cases there had been some intermediate respite; but with the 'flying bombs' the 'alerts' were continuous for days on end. It was not long before people got to know that the area under assault was fairly limited, and it was a natural reaction that many desired to get their families out of the danger zone, and to areas where they themselves could at least sleep peacefully at night, even though their day's business in the London area was fraught with continual danger. The result was an unprecedented descent on Paddington. 'The Railway Gazette' described the situation vividly in a leading article:

For the first time in its history Paddington station had to be closed for three hours last Saturday morning, the platforms and 'Lawn' being packed with would-be travellers. Soon approaches were densely crowded, and bookings had to be suspended from the Underground and tubes to prevent more passengers emerging from the subways and adding to the crowds in the main line station. There was similar congestion at Euston and Waterloo and other stations, but not quite to the same extent as at Paddington. It is regrettable that, notwithstanding its competence in other directions, the Ministry of War Transport has not shone in its dealings with passenger rail travel. The same trouble has occurred at every holiday period during the war. Whilst refusing consistently to take any step to ration travel, it failed to give the railways a free hand to cope with any situation that might arise. It has contented itself with appeals and admonitions regarding unnecessary travel, apparently hoping that a Government Department could accomplish what no one else has succeeded in doing, namely, getting a quart into a pint pot.

The 'Daily Mail' was even more forthright:

The Government gets no congratulations for the way it is handling the flying-bomb warning system or the rush to the railways.

For the first time in its history Paddington Station was closed (on Saturday) for some hours. The crowds were so large that they had to be controlled by mounted police. We hesitate to think what the casualty list might have been had a flying bomb landed there.

This problem has cropped up every year, and every year the authorities have appeared to be bankrupt of ideas to solve it. Their only expedient has been to announce that no extra facilities will be made available to the travelling public.

Behind this unprecedented state of affairs, during which enormous queues formed up on both pavements of Eastbourne Terrace, was of course the Ministerial order that no extra coaches were to be provided. As the situation developed repeated appeals were made to the Minister of War Transport, in person, for some relaxation of the order, and at first none was forthcoming. In the meantime the men of the Great Western, as practical railwaymen, had decided quickly enough how to cope with such an emergency. Engine crews were called out, locomotives prepared and trains of empty coaches marshalled at Old Oak Common. Still, however, they had no authorisation to use them. Further appeals were made to the Ministry, pointing out the appalling casualties that would result if a flying bomb should fall on such a densely packed multitude as that crowded in the station. Still the attitude remained completely obdurate, and it continued so until Sir James Milne threatened to take the matter to still higher authority than the Ministry of War Transport. Only then did someone from the Ministry come to Paddington to see for himself. Authority to run extra trains was given quickly enough then, and the men of the Great Western cleared the vast crowds in record time. The G.W.R. was no more than slightly affected by actual damage from flying bombs; but in traffic working it was more severely pressed than any other company.

Plate 45. 'CASTLE' ENGINES AT SPEED

The pre-war Bristolian taking water at Goring: engine No. 5070 *Sir Daniel Gooch*

A.T.C. special near Twyford, 12th October 1947 at 86 mph: engine No. 5056 *Earl of Powis*

Plate 46. OIL-BURNING LOCOMOTIVES

4-6-0 No. 5091 *Cleeve Abbey*

2-8-0 No. 2872

4-6-0 No. 5955 *Garth Hall*

XIX

'Sour Apple Harvest'

I have lifted the resounding phrase titling this chapter from John Buchan, who used it to describe the situation that developed in Great Britain after World War I. It was certainly most appropriate to the situation in which the railways of this country found themselves from 1945 onwards. By the winter of 1944–45, although there were still many perils of war to be endured it was clear that at last we were winning, and Victory was becoming only a matter of time. In many organisations throughout the country the thoughts of top management were turning to post-war reconstruction, and the presence of so many Americans amongst us naturally led to a good deal of re-thinking around problems that were unsolved at the time war broke out, more than five years earlier. The railways came in for much attention in this respect. The acute discomforts of travelling, the slowness, the delays, and the total lack of amenities were unfortunately ingrained in the public mind, and to the great majority of persons the responsibility for this state of affairs was thought to rest entirely on the shoulders of the railway companies themselves. The extent to which they had been controlled and restricted in the national interest by the Ministry of War Transport was scarcely appreciated at all. Under Government order they had been compelled to make do with old rolling stock and fixed equipment. No responsible railwayman doubted the absolute necessity for such restrictions, though there were times, as during the flying-bomb attacks when they yearned for more freedom of action in dealing with immediate crises, such as the one that led to the closing of Paddington on that memorable Saturday in August 1944.

Covertly and overtly a great deal was discussed about the future of the railways, quite apart from any political influences that might develop after the end of hostilities. There were many railwaymen of high status who felt that the unification of control that had been exercised by the Railway Executive Committee during the war held out so many advantages that it should be continued in peace-time under some new organisation of railway management. It is however no secret that the top management and chief executive officers of the Great Western Railway were very much against any such unification. There was more to it than a mere love of isolationism. Certainly officers of other companies were apt to exclaim, in exasperation, that the 'broad gauge' mentality still prevailed on the G.W.R.; and in a sense it still did! The company had a way of doing things differently from everyone else, and it rejoiced in the knowledge that it had, in many respects, that little 'extra' that the others had not got. There was the continued use, as an immutable standard, of the lower-quadrant type of semaphore signal; the use of a higher degree of vacuum for the braking system; right-hand drive on locomotives; and above all, a widely-installed and very effective form of automatic train control. Some of these features could not be classed as 'extras'—in fact others would regard them with disfavour; but in the braking system, and in its A.T.C. the G.W.R. held two aces. So far as the unification of railways was concerned, it was not that there was any unwillingness to share outstanding features with others; there was always the spectre of what had happened to the broad gauge. Standards could unfortunately be established, on the grounds of cost and expediency, at an average level rather than at the best that was available.

Out on the line during the winter of 1944–45 the standards of running were remarkably good, seeing how men and equipment had been worked almost to the limit in the years leading up to D-day. My regular journeys took me from Chippenham to London and to Oswestry, and in addition I had the privilege of making some runs on the footplate of 'Castle' engines on the double-home turns between Newton Abbot and Shrewsbury, in each case on the morning North and West through expresses. A few impressions of the northbound run on the 9.45 a.m. train from Newton Abbot are worth recalling, not so much in regard to the performance of the locomotive, which was impeccable, but in the traffic working. Three other expresses were leaving just ahead of us: the 9.20 and 9.28 a.m. for Paddington, both worked by 'King' class engines, and our own train was proceeded by a relief running as far as Bristol. As was to be expected this latter train did most of the roadside work, and with vast numbers of passengers presenting themselves its stops were accordingly prolonged. On a line with station facilities such as those of the Great Western the practice of trying to run two trains at comparatively short headway can lead to serious unpunctuality. At most of the intermediate stops only one platform road was available, and we were checked or dead-stopped outside every stopping station. Our initial lateness of 2½ min. on leaving Newton Abbot had increased to 21½ min. by the time we reached Bristol, entirely due to the train in front spending excess time at stations. At this particular time of the day the traffic was too dense for the capacity of the line. There was nevertheless nothing that could be done about it in wartime. The running of a relief train at all was something of a concession, and that train had to run as close as possible to the path of the regular train. North of Bristol we could have looked forward to some recovery of the lost time, on schedules considerably easier than those of peacetime and with no relief train ahead; but we became involved in the congestion of freight traffic through the Severn Tunnel, and lost a further 16 min. between Stapleton Road and Pontypool Road alone. By this time our lateness had grown to 42 min., but by some excellent running over the remaining part of the journey the arrival in Shrewsbury was only 31 min. late.

Turning now from traffic working to affairs of management, at the end of the year 1943 a veteran figure of the Great Western Railway retired, Lord Palmer of Reading, who had been a director since August 1898, and Deputy Chairman since July 1906. Ernest Palmer was the son of one of the founders of the famous Reading biscuit manufacturing firm of Huntley & Palmers Ltd., and for most of his life he took the deepest interest in the affairs of the Great Western Railway. He was created a Baronet in 1916, and elevated to the Peerage in 1933. He served as deputy to four successive Chairmen, Alfred Baldwin, Lord Churchill, Lord Horne and Sir Charles Hambro. It will probably come as a surprise to most readers to learn that his peerage was conferred not in connection with biscuits or railways, but for his services to music. He was a devoted patron of that art and made many princely gifts towards the encouragement of British music and British composers. Locomotive enthusiasts will know that G.W.R. engine No. 2975 of the 'Saint' class was named after him.

Another important change on the board of directors took place early in 1945 when Sir Charles Hambro, in consequence of other commitments, resigned from the Chairmanship, though continuing to serve on the board. The directors thereupon invited Viscount Portal of Laverstoke to fill the office of Chairman. Lord Portal originally joined the board in December 1927, but in September 1940, on his appointment as an additional Parliamentary Secretary to the Ministry of Supply, he had of course to resign his directorship. He was subsequently Minister of Works from 1942 to 1944. On relinquishing the latter post he rejoined the board of the G.W.R., and in the following year he became Chairman— the last Chairman indeed, of the Company.

Financially, the effect of the Railway Control Agreement was to limit the net revenue in each of the later war years mainly to the fixed annual payment due under that agreement; and despite the vast traffic conveyed it was not possible to pay a dividend of more than $4\frac{1}{2}$ per cent. on the ordinary stock in both 1944 and 1945, as a result of the working in the previous years. One of the most damaging effects of the war was the progressive decline in standards of maintenance, in track, rolling stock and fixed equipment. This was not due to any planned dilution of effort, but simply to scarcity of labour and materials. At the end of 1943 there were accumulated arrears of work of about £13,000,000. Translated into actual physical work there was an arrears in complete renewal of the permanent way equivalent to the amount of work that would normally be done in 15 months, while the arrears in locomotive renewals represented a normal two-years building programme. In passenger carriage construction the arrears were equivalent to about three years normal renewal work.

As early as the Annual General Meeting of March 1944, the speech of Sir Edward Cadogan, deputising on that occasion for Sir Charles Hambro, already indicated some uneasiness on the part of the board as to the likely developments in railway legislation when the war was over; though at that stage the chief anxiety was that the railways should receive 'the square deal', in respect to road traffic, for which they had petitioned so persistently in days before the war. A year later, Sir Charles Hambro, presiding as Chairman for the last time, referred more particularly to the status of the companies themselves, because the advocates of change were by that time becoming somewhat voluble. He said:

> The achievements of the railways in meeting the unprecedented demands made on them during the war are an eloquent tribute to the efficiency of their organisations and to the high pre-war standard at which their lines and equipment were maintained. If, as I assume, the sole object of any change would be to ensure the most efficient and economic use of all forms of transport in meeting the requirements of the users, I would emphasise that, as our records show, we have hitherto been able to meet all reasonable demands by the users, and there is no reason for thinking we shall be unable to do so in future. Our view therefore is that the main-line railways should continue as four separate entities and that co-ordination of all forms of internal transport should be effected in such a way as to secure to users, as far as practicable, a free choice of alternative facilities, with competition on a fair basis. It is along these lines that we are proceeding with our post-war plans.

At this meeting Sir Charles quoted figures of the Great Western 'Roll of Honour' for service in the war, up to the time of the meeting. Of 15,000 members of the staff serving in the Forces, or in whole-time Civil Defence the casualties known were:

444 killed in action, or died of wounds or disease.
155 reported missing
271 prisoners of war, or interned in neutral countries.

The awards for war service were:

George Cross	1
C.B.E.	1
O.B.E.	4
M.B.E.	21
George Medal	7
British Empire Medal	55
Commendations	24

As soon as possible after the total Allied victory in Europe a General Election was held in Great Britain, but as for all men in the forces overseas the vote was a postal one the result was not known until many weeks afterwards. Then there was returned to power, with a huge majority, a Labour Government committed to bringing about State control of the coalmines, transport, and the iron and steel industry. At once a degree of uncertainty was introduced into business generally, because there was widespread apprehension as to the ultimate intentions of the Labour Party, particularly among those people most likely to be affected. At the same time it must not be imagined that a desire for railway nationalisation was purely an idealogical plank in the programme of a particular party. During the war, because of the complete cessation of holidays abroad, and virtual abolition of private motoring, more people than ever before had experience of railway travel. There were young schoolchildren who had never been in a train before, and the business man deprived of the use of his car, and compelled to travel by train, crowded, hungry, and often late was not in a mood to sympathise with the problems of higher railway management. Not a few felt that nationalisation would be a good thing, because shortcomings could be openly debated in Parliament and appropriate action secured. Opinion polls taken at this time showed a fairly consistent verdict of 60 per cent. in favour of nationalisation; only 25 to 30 per cent. definitely against, and the balance specified as 'don't know'.

If the result of the General Election caused uncertainty and apprehension at home, the effect abroad was stunning. At VE day the prestige of Great Britain had never stood higher. The fortitude of the people during the years of endurance had then been crowned by magnificent feats of arms, while the Prime Minister ranked as a world hero. And then, overnight as it were, this great leader was virtually dismissed by the British electorate! At home the changed situation was accepted as a twist in political history; to the vast majority of people abroad it was utterly incomprehensible, and there is no doubt it markedly influenced the part Britain could play in the immediate post-war world. We had spent to the limit in financing the war effort; now assistance was needed as the work of rehabilitation was about to commence, and it was soon evident that many obstacles were to be laid in our path. They ranged from the covert 'brush-off', and excessively hard bargaining, to the open derision of certain unfriendly organs of the foreign press in which John Bull was represented as a humbug begging on his knees for charity. As a result the country as a whole began a descent into an era of unprecedented austerity. All internal reconstruction was subjugated to the needs of the export trade, and the proud wartime slogan 'Britain can take it', was parodied into 'Britain can lump it'!

Whatever the political climate of the day might be, the spring and summer of 1946 saw some welcome improvements and acceleration of train services on the G.W.R. The through trains from Wolverhampton and Birmingham to Devon and Cornwall, via the North Warwick line and Stratford-on-Avon were restored, with through locomotive working between Wolverhampton and Newton Abbot—actually through from Paignton in the up direction. There was a notable acceleration of the Bristol services, with the 11.15 a.m. and 1.15 p.m. departures restored to a non-stop run from Paddington to Bath, and with a fast new train at 5.5 p.m., also non-stop to Bath, there was quite a lavish provision of excellent trains all running the 106.9 miles in 115 min. start-to-stop—55.8 m.p.h. Another innovation was the putting on of a new and much faster down morning train from London to Bristol at 9.5 a.m. calling only at Reading and detaching a slip portion at Bath. Lastly, regarding the Bristol service, the time-honoured 6.30 p.m. was accelerated to cover the 94 miles to Chippenham non-stop in 101 min., an average speed of 55.8 m.p.h. start to stop. The continuing presence of large units of the Admiralty administration and engineering staff at Bath provided a considerably increased amount of business travel between London and the 'Queen City' and no doubt influenced the preferential treatment given in this first post-war batch of improved services. Another service restored was the night Postal special between Paddington and Penzance running via Bristol, as previously. The inaugural down train on October 1, 1945 was worked by engine No. 6019 *King Henry V*, and this led 'Modern Transport' to comment felicitously: 'Once more into the breach, dear friends'!

By the summer of 1946 the G.W.R. had 21 daily runs of 100 miles or more made non-stop, and this number was increased to no fewer than 43 on Saturdays. The daily runs were:

100-MILE RUNS MADE DAILY

Route	Distance miles	No. of Runs	Fastest		
			Train	Time min.	Speed m.p.h.
Paddington–Plymouth	225.5	2	10.30 a.m. down	270	50.1
Paddington–Exeter	173.5	2	12 noon down	190	54.8
Paddington–Taunton	142.7	4	11 a.m. down	156	54.8
Paddington–Newport	133.6	7	8.50 a.m. down	155	51.7
Paddington–Bath	106.9	5	1.15 p.m. down	115	55.8
Taunton–Reading	106.7	1	1.48 p.m. up	122	52.5

On Saturdays there were runs between Paddington and Brent; Paddington and Torquay; Paddington and Newton Abbot; Paddington and Teignmouth, in addition to many additional runs over the routes already covered in the weekday 100-mile runs. Of the 100-mile non-stop runs made in Great Britain during the summer of 1946 the Great Western were, on the average, much the fastest. The majority of the long non-stop L.M.S.R. runs were made on relatively slow night trains, while of the L.N.E.R. collection more than half were made between Kings Cross and Grantham, with a fastest average of 54.1 m.p.h.

It was gratifying to observe also that in general the new services proved of no difficulty to the locomotive department. The major express passenger classes, 'Stars', 'Castles', and 'Kings', had been well-maintained during the war years, and some of the individual engine performances that I noted personally in the summer and autumn of 1946 were fully up to pre-war standards. By hard running when necessary, efficiently made, drivers were not long in showing that they had time in hand on the new schedules. It was most gratifying to record, because the recovery towards pre-war standards was, in its first phases, much more rapid than in the first year of peace after World War I. Nevertheless, while these selected trains were giving a good account of themselves the general position in the locomotive department was far from reassuring. Coal was becoming a major problem. The heavy hand of Government control was seriously affecting supplies made available to the railways generally, and during the winter of 1945 the Great Western decided to equip a number of locomotives for oil firing. Some further details of this interesting project are given in a subsequent chapter, dealing with locomotive matters generally; but in broad outline the scheme, while aiming at a substantial saving in the use of coal, was launched at first as a limited objective. Eighteen heavy mineral engines of the '28XX' class were scheduled for conversion, and intended for working through the South Wales area. The scheme included the construction of oil fuelling depots at Llanelly, and Severn Tunnel Junction.

It may seem very strange that a once-rich coal producing area like South Wales should have been the scene of the first oil-firing project on the G.W.R.; but it was one of the paradoxes of the austerity era in post-war Britain that the coal situation was most acute from the railway point of view in South Wales. The best coal was being exported, and in 1947 the local railways were running on American coal—an astonishing situation having regard to the past history of railways like the Barry, the Rhymney and the Taff Vale. To revert to the oil-firing of Great Western locomotives however, the subsequent equipping of certain 4-6-0s of the 'Hall' and 'Castles' was an experiment towards another regional oil-firing scheme. Just as the West of England lines had been chosen in pre-war years for an examination of the prospects of electrification, because of the cost of transporting coal to Taunton and beyond, so, in 1946, there was a broad conception of making Cornwall an oil-fired area to the exclusion of all coal burning engines. Some of the most interesting trials of 'Castle' and 'Hall' class engines took place from Laira shed, Plymouth, and these are referred to in the next chapter. The essence of the Great Western scheme was that it was limited in its extent; but at a time when shortage of fuel was already becoming a source of embarrassment to the Government the project was so applauded by the Minister of Transport that he authorised the main line railways to proceed as quickly as possible with the conversion of 1217 locomotives from coal to oil-firing. It is well known however that after many locomotives had been converted, and vast sums of money spent on fuelling plants, the whole scheme ended in a colossal fiasco, simply because there was not enough foreign exchange available to purchase the oil!

This is anticipating somewhat, but coal shortage generally was a major difficulty as the country as a whole entered upon the terrible winter of 1946–47. We had a first taste of what was to come even before Christmas, when snow fell heavily, and train services were disrupted;

but the real onslaught came at the end of January. In a very few days there was widespread dislocation. So far as actual snow blockages went the Great Western suffered most severely on the lines fringing Dartmoor and in the Brecknock Beacons; but even on such relatively straightforward lines as that between Paddington and Bristol there were some extraordinary incidents. There was the night when ice and snow caused a succession of block failures, and the 9.50 p.m. down Penzance sleeper crawled into Chippenham just after 8 o'clock next morning; but an experience with the 7.45 a.m. from Bristol to Paddington could have been equally disastrous to traffic working had the men on the train not taken some pretty resolute action. It was a positively Arctic morning, but they had started well, and east of Swindon despite the weather, they were running practically on time. Then suddenly between Shrivenham and Uffington the brakes went on and the train was brought to a stop. A serious vacuum leakage had occurred on one of the leading coaches and no immediate repairs could be made. Snow was lying 8 to 10 in. deep, and it was freezing hard. There was nothing for it but to detach the coach on which the failure had occurred. The brakes had to be released by hand on each coach, since against such a leakage the locomotive ejector was quite impotent. Several brake blocks had become frozen to the wheels and had to be released by the fireman's pick. Ultimately, after proceeding cautiously to Uffington, with only the locomotive brake available, the coach was detached. To the lasting credit of all concerned the train was no more than an hour late on arrival at Paddington.

At that particular time most passengers took such incidents quite stoically, though one occasionally heard complaints of railway inefficiency. In those extremes of weather I recall only too well how, even if there was plenty of heat on, the icy winds seemed to discover the minutest cracks or gaps round the windows and set up a whirling draught inside; how rugs and overcoats were of little avail, and how snow drove in through the corridor connections between the coaches. As for the dining car crews their work was beyond praise, even though they had the most frugal of meals to serve. I remember particularly the conductor who worked the 11.15 a.m. down from Paddington and the 5.25 p.m. up from Bristol, and the serio-comic flourish with which, night after night, he announced 'Saute of whalemeat, gentlemen'! There was a memorable night at Paddington when the engine of the 6.30 p.m. down failed in the platform and the train could not start. Finding a relief engine was no easy task in the depths of the glacial period, when many workings were disorganised. But the dining car crew set to work as if nothing unusual was happening—or not happening!—and they were cheerfully calling passengers for the *third* dinner before the train finally got away.

During this period frozen water troughs were a common occurrence, and it was then shown that despite the untoward conditions the working efficiency of Great Western locomotives remained as high as ever. Non-stop runs were regularly made over the 94 miles between Paddington and Chippenham without taking water intermediately. On the fearful afternoon of February 21, with a blizzard raging and visibility just about *nil* for most of the distance the 12 noon from Bristol to Paddington, with a 450-ton load, was worked up non-stop from Chippenham in $113\frac{1}{2}$ min. The driver went cautiously from the start, and took 27 min. for the 16.7 miles to Swindon; but after that the remaining 77.3 miles were covered in $86\frac{1}{2}$ min. Quite apart from getting a clear road in such conditions this journey emphasised the tremendous value of the A.T.C. apparatus. At Paddington the driver told me that for most of the distance he could see nothing at all, and was relying entirely upon the audible cab signals. What could be done in clear weather, despite frozen water troughs was shown on another run with the same train and load, when the 94 miles from Chippenham to Paddington were covered in $101\frac{1}{2}$ min. even though adverse signals at one point caused a loss of about 4 min. 'Castle' class engines were used on both these notable journeys.

The adventures of passenger trains during this period of extreme weather, though the most vivid memory for most people, were however set against one of the most serious fuel shortages this country has ever known. How the coal crisis developed was a complicated story, but at one time it reached the stage that the arrival of a coal train in London had the same kind of publicity, on radio, that a convoy battling its way into Malta received during the war. And the Great Western, having maintained its normal services with a fair degree of punctuality during the winter, was forced in the spring to make some drastic cuts in express train services to save coal. This particular phase of austerity saw the withdrawal of the Cornish Riviera Express above all trains, and the transfer of its traffic to the 11 a.m. down. In some respects one could regard this withdrawal as a gesture, because the 11 a.m. had frequently to be duplicated, and when I made a footplate journey on a Saturday in early summer it was run in *six* parts.

Despite the very great difficulties arising from the exceptional weather of the 1945–46 winter the financial results for the year were such as to make possible the best dividend for a long time, namely 5 per cent. on the ordinary shares. But the shadow of nationalisation hung over all the proceedings. In the previous autumn, on November 19th, in the House of Commons, the Lord President of the Council, Mr. Herbert Morrison, had announced that it was the intention of the Government during the life of the present Parliament to introduce measures designed to bring transport services essential to the economic well-being of the nation under public ownership and control. He stated that powers would be taken to bring under national ownership the railways, canals, and long-distance road-haulage services, and indicated that consideration would be given to various alternatives for bringing road passenger services and dock and harbour authorities within the scope of the national scheme.

In his speech to the shareholders at the Annual General Meeting on
March 6th, 1946, Viscount Portal commented thus:

The Lord President of the Council, when broadcasting to America last August, is
reported to have said: 'There is only one justification for either nationalisation or
private enterprise—that is efficient service in the interest of the nation. If only nationalisation will secure this result then we must nationalise. But if private enterprise can do
it, well, then, let private enterprise remain.' If this is to be the test, neither the record
of the railway companies nor the experience of nationalisation of railways in other
countries would justifiy the policy which the Government propose to adopt.

Both under peace and wartime conditions the achievements of the British railways
can be looked on with pride and satisfaction. Even the severest critics of the railways
acknowledge that the policy of preparedness pursued by the companies in the period
before the war proved of inestimable value in the trying years which followed. The
railways certainly could not have met the heavy demands made upon them during the
war if they had not been well organised and their lines and equipment maintained at
a high standard.

Our main difficulties at the present time are largely the result of our inability to obtain
during the six war years the necessary labour and materials to maintain our undertaking at the pre-war level, and if, during the long periods of depression which preceded
the war the railways had allowed their undertakings to depreciate to the same extent
as was inevitable in the war years, the results might well have been disastrous.

The working of the railways during the war period has evoked the warmest tributes
from the former Prime Minister, the heads of all service departments, the present and
former Ministers of War Transport and other Government departments, and it is hardly
likely that anyone would now question the efficiency of the service given by the railways
in the furtherance of the war effort.

We feel we can fairly claim to have fulfilled our primary duty, which is to give
efficient services to the public under both peace and wartime conditions, and that in
this respect we have observed the conditions which the Lord President of the Council
has stated would justify the Government in allowing any industry to remain in the
hands of private enterprise. If so, there is surely even greater justification in considering
the position of a statutory undertaking like ours.

Interjecting a point here about the war effort of the Company, in his
statement Lord Portal gave the final figures for casualties in this country.
During the war, while on company's service the totals were 68 killed and
241 injured, while 88 members of the staff were killed and 255 injured
while off duty—an impressive and tragic record.

The long expected Bill for bringing the country's inland transport
services under public ownership was introduced in Parliament on
November 28th, 1946, by Mr. Alfred Barnes, the Minister of Transport,
and with such a majority as the Labour Government possessed the end
of the privately-owned main line railways of Great Britain became no
more than a matter of time. It was clear that no argument could deflect
the Government from its course, and the subsequent debates centred
around the proposals for the new administrative organisation, and the
amount of compensation to be paid to the stockholders. Against such
massive strength in the House of Commons the Conservative opposition
could put up little more than a rearguard action, yet during the committee
stages of the Bill its clauses were bitterly and acrimoniously contested.
One particular incident must specially be mentioned here, as indicating
something of the irresponsible talk indulged in by Ministers of the Crown,
in support of the nationalisation project. During the second reading of
the Bill, on December 17th, 1946, Mr. Hugh Dalton, Chancellor of the

Exchequer, attempted to justify the Government's proposals for the acquisition of railway stockholdings, and then added:

This railway system of ours is a very poor bag of assets. The permanent way is badly worn. The rolling stock is in a state of great dilapidation. The railways are a disgrace to the country. The railway stations and their equipment are a disgrace to the country.

Reading such remarks now, after appreciating the service the railways rendered during the war, and the recovery that the Great Western in particular was making in 1946, leaves one rather bereft of words and it was not surprising that such a speech caused intense indignation and resentment among railwaymen of all grades. For so exalted a Cabinet Minister to stigmatise the railways as 'a disgrace' was regarded as a piece of effrontery, though unfortunately the sentiments aroused, bitter though they were, could not stay the progress of the Bill through Parliament. Indeed the Bill received positively farcical treatment in Standing Committee. Under the timetable insisted upon by the Government it was necessary to omit no less than 37 clauses and 7 schedules from discussion of any kind, and to pass over many others in haste. Only three days were allocated to the Report stage, in which the Minister of Transport tabled 176 more Government amendments, in addition to the 245 inserted during the Committee stage. As 'The Railway Gazette' commented on May 2nd, 1947:

The Bill, therefore, which affects profoundly the commercial and private life of the whole nation, has been hurried through the House of Commons in a manner which has precluded it from receiving the consideration which, in normal times, would have been accorded a far less controversial measure.

It is now expected that the Bill will receive its Third Reading next week and will be sent to the House of Lords before Whitsuntide. It seems unlikely that the Upper House will insist on amendments to the Bill which would involve a crisis between the two chambers, but there is every reason for hoping that the peers will revise with especial care a measure which has been the subject of such scant courtesy and reasoned thought in the House of Commons.

Eventually the Bill received the Royal Assent on August 6th, 1947, establishing the British Transport Commission for the purpose of a publicly-owned system of inland transport, other than by air. The vesting date was fixed as January 1st, 1948, and in this way the end of the Great Western Railway Company, together with the other privately-owned main line railways of Great Britain was finally sealed. In the last years of its existence however, the old company had a fine record of technical achievements to its credit, and there are some notable engineering works to be recorded in the succeeding chapter of this book.

XX

Engineering Prowess

1945-1947

Certain commentators, whose observations of contemporary practice could not have been much more than superficial, tended to give the impression that in locomotive matters things were almost stagnant on the G.W.R. in the period now under review. Taking the most cursory of views one could agree that this was so, and enthusiasts whose partisan sentiments lay elsewhere than with Swindon suggested that the apparent stagnation was due to one of two things: either that the drawing office was completely bereft of new ideas, or that the department was still resting on the laurels it had won in the late nineteen-twenties, when Great Western locomotive affairs both in practice and performance were substantially ahead of every other company. The 'County' class 4-6-0, produced in 1945, included some features that were then considered retrograde in certain quarters, if not actually obsolete, and when construction recommenced, in 1946, of engines of the 'Castle' class—altered only in certain details from the original design of 1923—the critics were confirmed in their assertion that Swindon was bereft of new ideas. Actually, of course, the period 1945-47 was one of great activity in the locomotive department, and some of the points then evolved were to play a notable part in the steam locomotive practice of the nationalised British Railways. It was my good fortune to see a good deal of this important work at first hand.

The senior officers on Mr. Hawksworth's staff who were mainly involved, most of whom I came to know personally were:

F. C. Hall	Principal Assistant to C.M.E.
W. N. Pellow	Locomotive Running Superintendent and Outdoor Assistant to C.M.E.
K. J. Cook	Locomotive Works Manager
H. Randle	Carriage and Wagon Works Manager
F. C. Mattingly	Chief Draughtsman
A. W. J. Dymond	Assistant to the C.M.E.

Two others, a little lower down the chain of command at that time, but who had already played an important part were C. T. Roberts, then Assistant Locomotive Works Manager, and S. O. Ell, who was in charge of locomotive testing. It was a strong team under Hawksworth, composed entirely of men who had spent their entire working lives in the service of the Great Western, and one of my clearest recollections of the pleasant times I spent in their company is of their enthusiasm and complete devotion to the G.W.R. Many of them were clearly concerned as to how the changes imposed by politics upon the railway industry would affect their futures; but this did not influence their belief in the rightness of the engineering policies that had been hammered out at Swindon, nor of the changes that Hawksworth was then gradually introducing.

The first entirely new engine design produced under Mr. Hawksworth's direction was the powerful mixed-traffic 'County' class 4-6-0, introduced in the summer of 1945. These engines were at first regarded as a development of the improved 'Hall' class, with a high nominal tractive effort of 32,580 lb. at 85 per cent. boiler pressure. But the new engines included some rather unusual features, such as the high boiler pressure of 280 lb. per sq. in., and a wheel diameter that was new to Great Western practice, namely 6 ft. 3 in. The boiler was not an existing standard, but in other respects traditional practice was followed in the use of two cylinders $18\frac{1}{2}$ in. diameter by 30 in. stroke, and the Stephenson link motion, inside. The arrangement of engine and bogie framing was the same as on the improved 'Hall' 4-6-0s. The tender was a new design, with tanks produced entirely by welding. The smooth, straight sides were something quite novel on the G.W.R. In an earlier chapter I made reference to the proposals for a very powerful 'Pacific' engine, which, in war conditions it was not possible to build. After the war it was hoped that opportunity would come to build the 4-6-2 and in the 'County', two features of the proposed new express passenger engine were incorporated, namely a boiler pressure of 280 lb. per sq. in., and 6 ft. 3 in. coupled wheels.

Taken at its face value, without any regard for the longer-term planning behind these two features, the 'County' was a useful addition to the Great Western motive power stud. At first the steaming of the new boiler was not entirely satisfactory; but in the year 1945 there were many British locomotives, the reputation of which had been impeccable in pre-war years, that were steaming indifferently all too often. The 'Counties' had that capacity for rapid acceleration that characterised all Great Western 4-6-0s, and with such a high nominal tractive effort as 32,580 lb. the acceleration was often very spectacular. In continuous running at express speed however the 'Counties' showed no advantage over the 'Castles'. The former engines were at their best on hilly roads, as on the Cornish main line, and on the Chester road north of Wolverhampton. From the footplate I recorded much excellent work with them, particularly with very heavy trains between Wolverhampton and Shrewsbury.

Building of the 'Castles' was resumed in 1946 with a batch of ten new engines numbered 5098–9, and 7000 to 7007. On these the boiler was modified to include a 3-row superheater of new design, instead of the traditional Churchward type used on the 'Castles' since their first introduction in 1923. The first two of the new engines, 5098 *Clifford Castle* and 5099 *Compton Castle* had the previous standard form of hydrostatic sight-feed lubricator, under the control of the driver; but later engines of the class had mechanical lubricators. The actual superheating surface was no more than slightly increased, from 262 to 295 sq. ft.; but the modified disposition of the tubes, and improved gas flow circuit made these new engines very free in steaming, despite the frequent incidence of poor coal. Hawksworth was definitely feeling his way towards a higher degree of superheat, and in 1947 two existing engines were modified to have much larger superheaters, with four rows of elements. These were the 'Castle' No. 5049 *Earl of Plymouth*, and engine No. 6022 *King Edward III*. I rode both these engines, and the 'King' in particular gave some excellent results.

The resumption of 'Castle' building in 1946, needs a further word of comment, in view of the misinterpretation that was put upon it in certain quarters at the time. The other British main line railways were then all involved in substantial developments. The work of Thompson and then Peppercorn on the L.N.E.R. had been to build larger and more powerful 'Pacifics' even than those of Sir Nigel Gresley. The L.M.S.R. in extending the work of Sir William Stanier was putting on rocking grates, roller-bearing axle boxes, and self-cleaning smokeboxes, while on the Southern O. V. S. Bulleid was turning out his air-smoothed 'Pacifics'—packed with novel features—at a high rate of construction. Against all this activity elsewhere the Great Western was content to build more 'Castles' no more than slightly changed in detail from a 1923 design. But Paddington had no desire to prolong the working of the Brobdingnagian loads of wartime a day more than was absolutely necessary. Postwar timetables already showed a trend towards the policy of 'lighter trains and more of them'. For this kind of work the 'Castles' were still second-to-none among British locomotives of their power class, and with the design proved up to the hilt, and the engines themselves extremely popular with their crews and economical in running costs there was every justification for building more of them.

Reverting to the changes in superheating generally it was however not so much in the modernisation of existing engine designs to meet changed requirement—important though that was—but in the development of methods for the precise assessment of engine performance that the Hawksworth régime has such a distinguished place in British locomotive history. For some time past it had been felt that traditional methods of testing left much to be desired. Runs made out on the road with the dynamometer car, whether on service or special trains, were inevitably subject to all the incidental hindrances of ordinary railway working: signal checks; temporary speed restrictions; variations in wind and weather, and the technique of individual engine crews. Even when the actual coal and water consumption was related to the work done on the drawbar there were wide inconsistencies in the results. One has only to compare the basic coal consumption figures for engines 4074 *Caldicot Castle*, and 5000 *Launceston Castle* in dynamometer car runs conducted in 1924 and 1926 respectively when the coal consumptions were 2.83 and 3.86 lb. per drawbar horse-power hour. The increase of 36 per cent. in the latter case was far greater than could be accounted for by the difference in calorific value of the coals used. If one analysed the respective circumstances down to fundamentals there is no doubt that the performance of the two locomotives would be revealed as near enough equal; but the traditional methods of testing revealed wide variations, and therefore by inference, must have permitted some serious anomalies.

At Swindon, shortly after the war, work was initiated to establish reliable means of obtaining the principal boiler relations for any locomotive, so that the indicated horsepower could be reliably related to the steam and the coal rates. With the modernised test plant runs were made, up to the maximum output, at constant speed with various types of locomotive, and satisfactory thermodynamic analyses obtained. But work on a test plant has a degree of artificiality about it, in that the locomotives are being tested in conditions that never prevail in service—that is running at constant speed. On the L.M.S.R. just after the war an attempt was made to inter-relate test house and road testing by use of a specially designed dynamometer car, and mobile test units which hold the speed of a locomotive constant at any desired rate while running over an undulating track. But this in a way was carrying the artificiality still further. At Swindon it was felt that the true aim must be to link the thermodynamic performance of the engine with the natural variable speed running normally experienced in service. Data were available from pre-war studies of locomotive performance on various routes, and this indicated that most of the daily work of express passenger engines was done, or could be done at constant steam rates. It will be appreciated that this would be an advantage from every point of view, in that the fireman would be working uniformly and the boiler steaming at a relatively constant rate, and so efficiently.

From this point onwards the yardstick of testing became not constant speed, but a constant steam rate. Apparatus was designed to assist the driver in keeping the steam rate constant on runs on the test plant, and then tests were made on the road, at the variable speeds of service trains, but at the same time with strictly controlled steam rates. It was found that if a locomotive was steamed on the test plant at, say, 25,000 lb. per hour, and all the principal boiler relations established, exactly the same coal consumption was recorded in a road test, *at variable speed*, if care was taken to keep the steam rate precisely constant. The testing procedure built up under the supervision of S. O. Ell was without a doubt the most comprehensive and accurate yet applied to steam locomotives, and it succeeded in eliminating the discrepancies between test results taken at various times to such an extent that the performance of engine classes such as the 'Castles', 'Halls' and 'Kings' could be used for planning new train schedules. If, for example, the traffic department wished to book a train at 60 m.p.h. start-to-stop from Paddington to Newport the testing section could tell them, in a very short time, the maximum load that could reliably be taken with a 'Castle' class engine. Schedules were re-planned so as to include point-to-point times along the route which would give a relatively constant steam rate. At the same time allowances were built into the new schedules to provide for some recovery margin against the effect of temporary speed restrictions, or signal checks.

The full analysis of the performance of individual engines on the stationary plant revealed the varying basic coal consumptions corresponding to different steam rates. Hitherto, it had been vaguely thought that a 'Castle', for example, should yield a coal consumption of about 3 lb. per drawbar horsepower hour. Test results carried out with the precision that Ell's work demanded showed that the coal per drawbar horsepower varied considerably with the steam rate. The steam rate indeed became the datum line, as it were, against which all other factors of the performance were related. Apart from any scientific results however, the spectacle of such engines as 'Kings' and 'Castles' working at high speed and high steam rates on the stationary plant at Swindon was thrilling beyond measure. When I was first privileged to witness the plant in action, examination of various types of superheaters was in progress. There were three varieties of 'Castles', and especially good results were obtained with the first of the 3-row superheater type, No. 5098 *Clifford Castle*. Later I saw the first 'King' to be fitted with a 4-row superheater running at a road speed of 70 m.p.h. on the plant. After nationalisation the test procedure developed at Swindon was examined most carefully by the engineers of the newly-formed Railway Executive, and the principle of Controlled Road Testing —that is at variable speed, and steam rate kept absolutely constant—was adopted as a national standard.

Reference has already been made to the introduction of oil-firing. By the autumn of 1946 the earliest passenger engines to be equipped were in service, though in logging their performance from the train little difference could be noted from the normal work of both 'Castles' and 'Halls'. In the following summer however I made a number of journeys on the footplate on both the Paddington–Bristol main line, and in Cornwall, and some very interesting observations resulted. In relation to the loads hauled the Cornish main line must be one of the hardest in the country. 'Castle' and 'County' class 4-6-os were required to haul loads of over 400 tons up gradients including lengthy stretches of 1 in 60; speed was limited to a maximum of 60 m.p.h. throughout from the Royal Albert Bridge, Saltash, to Penzance, so that slow hard work on the banks could not be compensated for by fast running downhill. Furthermore the principle of working at a constant steam rate could be practised only on the adverse stretches, because all the downhill running had necessarily to be made with steam shut off. The demands upon the boiler were thus subject to the widest variation, and fuel consumption was consequently heavy. One could appreciate the intention of making Cornwall an all oil-fired area, because it was an area where the coal consumption per train mile was inordinately heavy, and there were optimum savings to be realised

Plate 47. POST-WAR EXPRESSES

The Up Cornish Riviera Express ready to leave Penzance; engine No. 5915 *Trentham Hall*

Birkenhead–Paddington express near Saltney Junction, Chester; engine No. 1017
County of Hereford

Plate 48. THE FIRST GAS-TURBINE LOCOMOTIVE

On 6.35 p.m. Paddington–Cheltenham express near Reading

On 3.30 p.m. Paddington–Penzance express at Cowley Bridge Junction, Exeter

by a change from coal to oil firing. The following table shows a comparison between working on the Bristol main line and in Cornwall:

G.W.R. OIL-FIRED 'CASTLE' WORKING

Engine No. Load gross behind tender, tons	5039 375	5079 365 to Truro 325 to Penzance	5079 365
Route	Paddington to Bristol	Plymouth to Penzance	Penzance to Plymouth
Length of trip, miles	118.3	79.5	79.5
Total time of trip	138¼ min.	135½ min.	150½ min.
Water consumption, galls.	3600	2900	2700
Oil consumption, galls.	340	380	370
Water per train mile	30.4	36.5	34.0
Oil per train mile	2.88	4.78	4.65
Evaporation: gall. water/gall. oil	10.5	7.6	7.3
Ratio 'A': percentage of total time in which engine was steamed	85%	56%	47%
Evaporation: Ratio 'A'	0.124	0.135	0.155
Overall speed of trip, m.p.h.	51.4	35.2	31.7

The experience of the war years with different coal, and the developments in different parts of the world towards non-steam locomotives led to the interesting experiment with gas-turbine propulsion initiated by Mr. Hawksworth in 1946. The outstanding success of Sir Frank Whittle's jet-propulsion aero-engine had turned the attention of engineers towards means for utilising the same principles for rail traction purposes; but actually the first gas-turbine locomotive preceded Whittle's historic development by several years. The former was ordered in 1939 by the Swiss Federal Railways from the firm of Brown-Boveri of Baden. Hawksworth had a great personal interest in Swiss railways, and was very familiar with their motive power problems from much experience on the footplate; and as soon as possible after the war he travelled to Basle, with A. W. J. Dymond, to examine the 2200 h.p. machine that by that time had several years of service to its credit. It was, in effect, an electric locomotive in which the drive for the motors was provided by the gas turbine. In this, of course, it differed from the Whittle engine, in which all the power generated was devoted, through the agency of the compressor, towards production of the jet. The fact that the Great Western became interested in gas turbine locomotives just when attention elsewhere was being concentrated upon the diesel might be taken as yet another example of the Great Western determination to be different from everyone else; but Hawksworth had initiated a project that could have had far greater consequences than the mere following of a fashion in motive power that had become very popular in the U.S.A.

His interest in the gas turbine in 1946, and the purchase of a Swiss locomotive for trial purposes had in it something of an echo of Great

Western affairs in 1903 when Churchward's interest in the de Glehn compound 'Atlantics' led to the purchase of the *La France*, and all the development that came from it. Had the old Company continued in existence and Swindon works been allowed to continue in their own way one could have foreseen a careful development of the gas turbine locomotive from a foreign prototype to a standard and wholly indigenous product, using, moreover, British coal instead of imported oil. The prospect of a coal-fired gas turbine locomotive was more than a vague dream at the time the Brown-Boveri locomotive was on order, and it was this prospect as much as any other that stimulated interest in the gas turbine when the decision was taken to experiment with non-steam locomotives of high power for express passenger service. In addition to the Brown-Boveri engine, a second gas turbine locomotive of even greater power was ordered as a result of a decision taken jointly by the Great Western Railway and the Metropolitan-Vickers Electrical Co. Ltd. to investigate the possibilities of applying to rail traction the technique which the latter firm had acquired during the war in perfecting aircraft jet engines. The project as designed from 1946 onward differed considerably from the original intention, as advances in gas turbine knowledge had taken place since the initiation of the joint scheme.

Neither of these experimental locomotives No. 18000 from Brown-Boveri, and No. 18100 from Metropolitan Vickers was delivered until the end of 1949, and although at that time Hawksworth was still in the chair at Swindon he was no longer solely responsible to a General Manager and Board of Directors at Paddington, but instead to The Railway Executive, at 222, Marylebone Road. Although a great deal of trial and regular running was made with both locomotives the experiment lay completely outside the policy formulated by the nationalised British Railways, and naturally did not have the interest and backing that it undoubtedly would have had if the Great Western Railway had continued in existence. Both locomotives had the ill-luck to be dogged with troubles lying outside the main experiment. There were difficulties with the traction motors, and particularly with the oil-fired steam heating boilers, which made the engines very unpopular with travellers in the winter months when they were on the Plymouth run. As motive power units both locomotives did some extremely fine work, and showed clearly what might have been done had the authority been given for development work to continue at top pressure. As it was the effort gradually tailed off until eventually both locomotives were withdrawn. A very interesting paper covering the design, construction and running experiences with these two locomotives was read before the Institution of Locomotive Engineers by A. W. J. Dymond, in 1953.

The final point to be recorded containing Great Western engineering matters is of Automatic Train Control rather than locomotive design. Reference has been made in earlier chapters to the policy of retaining, even in colour-light signalled areas, the aspects associated with two-position lower quadrant semaphore signalling. After the war however plans were drawn up for certain re-signalling schemes in which true multi-aspect signalling was to be incorporated, with four-aspect signals providing the same aspects as extensively used on the Southern and London and North Eastern Railways. The problem arose as to how the standard Great Western system of automatic train control could be linked in with the proposed multi-aspect signals. The existing audible warning at an adverse distant signal, with the blood-curdling wail of the vacuum siren starting up was a most arrestive indication. With four-aspect signalling this would have been the second warning, whereas on a train running at high speed it is the first, corresponding to the first sight of a 'double-yellow', that is perhaps the most important. With some ingenuity the signal department had rearranged the electrical and mechanical apparatus at the lineside, and in the cab, to give a 'double-hoot' on the audible cab signal, to correspond with the 'double-yellow' of the wayside signal.

It was one of those devices which could sound most attractive in theory, but which sometimes fail the practical test. On Sunday October 12th, 1947 however the development work had progressed to the stage when it could be demonstrated to the technical press, and on that afternoon the senior officers gathered for what I believe was the last railway field-day enjoyed by the old Company. Inspecting Officers of the Ministry of Transport, high officers of other railways, as well as the press, were invited. I was privileged to accompany the test train, and a superb exhibition it proved to be. Under the prevailing circumstances speed was limited to 75 m.p.h., but to give the system a thorough test at the higher speeds anticipated in later years the up main line between Reading and Maidenhead was fettled up to permit of unlimited speed. The test train consisted of the dynamometer car, for registering the drawbar pull of the locomotive and providing a continuous record of the speed; two of the special Ocean traffic saloon carriages for the Company's officers and their guests, and a brake van including some demonstration apparatus. The engine chosen was a 'Castle' class 4-6-0, the *Earl of Powis*, No. 5056. The 'course' for the high speed test was just short of 12 miles long, but unfortunately from the viewpoint of making records the 75 m.p.h. limit had to be observed through Twyford station when five miles on our way. Consequently the distance in which a really high speed might be attained was restricted to the six miles between Twyford and the western signals of Maidenhead station.

So that the audible signals received in the engine cab might be heard by all travelling in the train a system of loud speakers had been fitted up, and as we got under way from Reading we heard clearly the short loud ring of the bell each time we passed a clear signal, and an observer on the engine announced the speed. We passed through Twyford at slightly over the stipulated speed, and then the engine was opened out. I was recording the speed with a split-second chronograph, and succeeding miles were covered at 83.4 m.p.h., 87.3, 90.5, 93.3 and finally 95.2 m.p.h. Then came a fine demonstration of the 'double-hoot', the brakes were fully applied, and we rode smoothly to a stop at Maidenhead station. The maximum speed attained as registered in the dynamometer car was 96.4 m.p.h. and at that high speed the extremely smooth riding of the coaches was a tribute to the excellent condition of the permanent way no less than to the quality of workmanship put into the coaches themselves. The afternoon was primarily a 'party' for the recently appointed Signal and Telegraph Engineer, A. W. Woodbridge, who had succeeded F. H. D. Page in that office in the previous April. F. W. Hawksworth rode in the dynamometer car, while among other high officers A. S. Quartermaine, the Chief Engineer, and Gilbert Matthews, Superintendent of the Line, rode in the saloons. Among the distinguished visitors present were J. A. Kay, Editor of The Railway Gazette, and that well-known signal engineer and author T. S. Lascelles. On a beautiful afternoon of mellow autumn sunshine it was a pleasant and impressive engineering finale to the independent days of the Great Western Railway.

XXI

The G.W.R. and
The Nationalised Railways

In the foregoing chapters the story of the G.W.R. in the 25 years of the grouping era has been told. Its end was made inevitable by the result of the General Election of 1945, but while nationalisation was very unwelcome to a great many railwaymen, and to many others who were friendly to the railways, it is not altogether out of place to try and visualise what might have happened if the four main line railways of Great Britain had remained as private companies from the year 1948 onwards. Nothing political short of a general embargo on production for the home market would have checked the enormous upsurge in private motoring, nor in the development of long distance road haulage. The conditions that led to the 'Square Deal' campaign of 1938 would have been intensified, and with the upward spiral of wages and prices it would seem that nothing could have saved the companies from plain bankruptcy. The nationalised railways have not proved viable, and their huge deficits are a charge on the exchequer. With railways still as ever, an essential service, a very difficult situation for privately-owned companies might have arisen in the economic conditions that pressed so inexorably upon the country as a whole. It is one thing for Parliament to accept the deficit of a nationalised industry; it would have been quite another to try and extract a large subsidy for an essential, though bankrupt private industry.

The Great Western ended its days as a going concern, and its final dividend was 5 per cent. on the ordinary shares. This, of course, did not represent the true results of the traffic conveyed, because operating was still under Government control until the end. In theory the make-up of the nationalised British Railways was hoped to be a synthesis of all that was best from the constituent companies; but amalgamations rarely work out that way, and now that British Railways have been operating for 20 years it is interesting to look back and see the extent of the Great Western contribution to the common cause. At the time of the setting up of the British Transport Commission, and subordinate to it, the Railway Executive, there was only one ex-G.W.R. man on either body, Mr. David Blee, the former Chief Goods Manager, who became the member of the Railway Executive responsible for commercial matters. Of the original seven full-time members there was one each from the G.W.R., the L.M.S.R., and the Southern; two from the L.N.E.R., and two non-railwaymen, though of the latter Mr. W. P. Allen, representing

Trade Union interests, had at one time been an engine driver. The chairmanship of the Railway Executive was actually offered to Sir James Milne, who was by many years the senior of the former General Managers; but it was generally known that he in common with most Great Western men was so out of sympathy with the whole business of nationalisation that he declined. The post went to Sir Eustace Missenden, formerly General Manager of the Southern.

The two appointments to the Railway Executive that had perhaps the greatest influence on future management in what became the Western Region of British Railways were those of Mr. V. M. Barrington-Ward of the L.N.E.R. as member responsible for operation, and of Mr. R. A. Riddles, the member responsible for mechanical and electrical engineering. On the L.N.E.R., the Southern, North Eastern and Scottish Areas had been allowed almost complete autonomy in their traffic working arrangements, and there had been a persistent cleavage of opinion between the Southern Area and the others on the methods of recording and regulation in the train control offices. Barrington-Ward, in the Southern Area favoured the L.M.S.R. method, rather than the graphic records used in the North Eastern and Scottish Areas, and after nationalisation there was a gradual infiltration of Midland methods. The most important difference from the Great Western point of view was that the responsibility for locomotive running was transferred from the Chief Mechanical Engineer to the Operating Department. At one time all railways placed the responsibility for locomotive running under the Chief Mechanical Engineer, or Locomotive Superintendent as he was known on some railways. It had the great advantage that the man who built and maintained the locomotives also had to run them, whereas in the system introduced on the Midland Railway in 1907 the Operating Department had everyone concerned with the running of trains under their control. Either way there was a division of responsibility; but the older method, of which the Great Western remained the only exponent in 1947, worked well enough under the organisation that had prevailed at Swindon for so many years.

The change was not made at once. Hawksworth remained in control, though of course reporting to Railway Executive headquarters for matters of future policy, and W. N. Pellow, as Locomotive Running Superintendent still continued to report to Hawksworth. It was only when the latter engineer retired, on December 31st, 1949, that the new organisation was brought into play, and the former Chief Mechanical Engineer's department was split into three sections, Locomotive Construction and maintenance, under K. J. Cook; Carriage and Wagon construction and maintenance, under H. Randle, and Locomotive Running, under W. N. Pellow, who from that time onwards was responsible to the Operating Superintendent. The organisation of British Railways has been changed considerably in the intervening years, and it is no part of this final chapter to record, or comment upon those changes; but in the course of them Great Western men took responsibilities far afield. K. J. Cook later became

Chief Mechanical and Electrical Engineer of both Eastern and North Eastern Regions, with his headquarters at Doncaster; Randle became Carriage and Wagon Engineer of the London Midland and Scottish Region, at Derby; still later, C. T. Roberts became Chief Mechanical and Electrical Engineer of the Scottish Region. The influence of Swindon thus spread in many directions.

At first, however, Swindon cut a rather poor figure in British Railways locomotive matters, at any rate so far as outside observers could see. Little more than three months after vesting date the Railway Executive announced that an extensive programme of locomotive interchange running was to be carried out between locomotives of express passenger, mixed traffic and heavy freight classes, from all the former companies and over a variety of routes. Strange though it may seem, the Great Western was penalised from the outset. Because of structure gauge clearances the Swindon engines were prohibited from running on any lines of the former L.M.S.R., and also from the Waterloo–Exeter section of the Southern. The engines chosen for competitive running were the 'King', in the heavy express passenger class, the 'Hall' in the mixed traffic class, and the '28XX' 2-8-0 among the freight engines. Although having slightly larger cylinders the 'King' was no wider across the outside cylinder cleadings than the 'Castle'—8 ft. $11\frac{1}{2}$ in., and only $\frac{1}{2}$ in. wider than the 'Star'; and at first it might have seemed strange that the 'Castle' could have been accepted for trial running between Euston and Carlisle in 1926 while the 'King' was prohibited in 1948. But the circumstances of the 1926 interchange trials were very different from those of 1948, and it is generally understood that there had been one or two 'near-misses' with platform facings and so on, during the running of *Launceston Castle*. So it befell that the only 'foreign' running made by Great Western engines in 1948 was between Kings Cross and Leeds by one of the 'Kings'; between Marylebone and Manchester by one of the latest Hawksworth type 'Halls', and between Peterborough and Hornsey by a '28XX' class 2-8-0.

Remembering 1925 some observers expected to see some highly spectacular running, and when none materialised those same observers jumped to the facile conclusion that somehow or other Great Western engines had deteriorated, to a pale shade of their old selves. The 'King' on the Great Northern line and the 'Hall' on the Great Central were both worked by the same driver; a staid and essentially 'safe' man, but one who in the competitive spirit of the hour did not impress. It was the same when running on home metals. In 1948 there was no Sir Felix Pole, determined that the G.W.R. should be utterly pre-eminent. At high level no great interest was taken in the contest. It was not altogether to be wondered at when, as a locomotive inspector put it to me, 'There were so many "thou shalt nots" and a man of Mr. Hawksworth's standing had to ask permission from the Railway Executive to ride in his own dynamometer car!' This is no place to dwell upon the actual results, which in terms of coal consumption per drawbar horsepower hour put the Great Western locomotives well down from the top of the list. There were several factors that contributed to this disappointing result, and much improved working was revealed when certain of the trials were repeated in the autumn using the soft Welsh coal for which the engines were designed, instead of the hard East Midlands variety selected for general usage in the main series of trials.

As the mechanical engineering staff of the Railway Executive got down to the task of producing a new range of standard steam locomotives for British Railways the finer points of Swindon practice, both in design, construction and testing were brought out, and gradually the locomotive practice of the Great Western began to take its lawful place in contributing to the common weal of the nationalised railways. In design, by far the greatest contribution was that of the boiler. In this respect the contribution was also shared by the L.M.S.R. When he became Chief Mechanical Engineer of the latter railway W. A. Stanier had taken Churchward's classic boiler practice, in its entirety, and in the light of experience on the L.M.S.R. some of the details were subsequently changed. The British Railways' standard boilers, with the exception of those on the 'Pacific' engines were a synthesis of the development work of two ardent disciples of Churchward: Stanier on the L.M.S.R. and Hawksworth, on the Great Western.

The other great contribution from Swindon was the practice of engine testing, using the controlled road testing system, as perfected by S. O. Ell. Many 'foreign' classes of locomotives came to Swindon to be tested, and the method was applied by the dynamometer car testing staff of the former L.M.S.R. to some maximum output trials of a most spectacular kind over the far-famed Settle and Carlisle line. The principle of testing at a constant steam rate could not, however, be applied throughout a run from Carlisle to Skipton, and vice versa. There is such a disparity in the physical character of the line north and south of the Aisgill-Blea Moor tableland that constant speed testing had to be confined to the uphill sections. The Great Western system was also successfully applied to diesel-electric and diesel-hydraulic locomotives, while some particularly interesting analyses were made of the capacity of the rebuilt 'Merchant Navy' class 4-6-2s of the Southern Region entirely by dynamometer car.

At the time of nationalisation there were considerable differences of opinion among railwaymen outside the ranks of the former G.W.R. as to the form the British Standard form of automatic train control should take. It was not by any means agreed that an audible warning system based upon the distant signal was the most suitable form for British Railways. Certain interests were pressing hard for more sophisticated methods. There was a trial, on the L.N.E.R. line, of continuous inductive cab signalling. In the meantime the Great Western installation was complete over the entire main line network. The chief objection to it, outside the G.W.R., was the contact ramp, which it was thought could become inoperative in conditions of ice and snow. Against this the actual record of the G.W.R. apparatus was one showing a very high degree of reliability. Eventually after a great deal of discussion the *principle* of the G.W.R. system was accepted in its entirety; but it was laid down that the pick-up was to be inductive, as in the experimental installation put down on the L.M.S.R. Southend line before World War II. It was some time before the new system for British Railways reached the stage of of a prototype installation, but now it is well established; and although it differs greatly in detail, in principle it is unchanged from the system worked out on the G.W.R. before World War I and described by W. A. Stanier in a paper to the Institution of Electrical Engineers read in December, 1914.

*   *   *

During the winter of 1947–8, pending the removal of my home from Bushey to the West Country, I was living at a small private hotel near Chippenham station—near enough to hear all the trains, but not near enough for them to be a disturbance at night. I have never been one for going to bed early, and I frequently used to hear the West of England postal special dash through around midnight. On New Year's Eve, 1947 I was preparing for bed, feeling, like many another supporter of the old railways, a little disconsolate. I had little heart in letting in this particular New Year; and then, just on midnight the 'Postal' approached. Whether the driver was in a spirit of *joie de vivre*, or whether he was a particularly ardent supporter of nationalisation I do not know, but he sounded the most tremendous and prolonged fanfare on the whistle, punctuating it with several short blasts to add momentarily to the melodious New Year bells of Chippenham. For good or ill, he had, in that fanfare, left the Great Western behind forever, and was continuing at 70 m.p.h. into the era of British Railways.

The last weeks of 1947 had been marked by many valedictory speeches, some sad, some retrospective, and some looking anxiously into the future. The other three main line railways each had 25 years of corporate existence behind them, and a varied and distinguished history before that to be seen in the records of their constituents. The Great Western had existed for 112 years, and many a reference to this long span was made in the expressions of regret, mingled with pride, that marked many utterances from senior officers at that time. The last issue of the Great Western Railway Magazine, December, 1947, contained messages to the staff from the Chairman, Viscount Portal, and from the General Manager, Sir James Milne. Both wrote of the future as much as of the past, and Sir James in particular, spoke from his long experience of railway management when he said:

> Every possible effort will be needed to make the new administration a success, and I know that, in the duties entrusted to you, you will worthily uphold the traditions which have so long been associated with the name of our great company.

The retirement of Sir James Milne, at the relatively early age of 64 was much commented upon, and with the end of the company itself, it is interesting to recall the names of his predecessors, and their spans of office. The post of General Manager was created in 1863, when Charles Saunders retired from the position of chief executive officer, and in the ensuing 84 years there were eight general managers. The span of Sir James Milne's tenure, 18½ years, was surpassed only by the first holder of the office, James Grierson, though in those early days the General Manager was more of a predecessor to the later post of Superintendent of the Line, in that the engineering officers reported directly to the Board, and not through the General Manager. The eight holders of the title may be recalled thus:

James Grierson	Oct. 1863–Oct. 1887
Henry Lambert	Oct. 1887–July 1896
Sir Joseph Wilkinson	July 1896–June 1903
Sir James Inglis	June 1903–Dec. 1911
Frank Potter	Jan. 1912–July 1919
Charles Aldington	Aug. 1919–June 1921
Sir Felix Pole	June 1921–July 1929
Sir James Milne	July 1929–Dec. 1947

In the new organisation the title of General Manager fell for some time into disuse, though it has since been revived, with the added dignity and responsibility that in the various Regions of British Railways the General Manager is the Chairman of the Regional Board. In 1948 however, the chief executive officers of the Regions were designated Chief Regional Officer, and as such Mr. K. W. C. Grand, the former Assistant General Manager of the Great Western Railway took office on January 1st, 1948. The final curtain did not fall until two months later, and then on March 5th, 1948, the Final General Meeting of the Great Western Railway Company was held at the Great Western Royal Hotel, Paddington station, with Viscount Portal, the last Chairman, presiding. It was the shortest General Meeting in the history of the company, and lasted barely 20 minutes. There were no resolutions to be put before the proprietors: nothing but details of the final pay-out, and some very brief speeches of farewell. In round figures the final dividend on the ordinary stock was 7¼ per cent. The exact figure was 7·282158, and was the result of a decision to distribute an additional £574,000 that had been made available. In the first years of Government control during the war, before the revision of the agreement to provide for a fixed annual sum, the revenue of the company had been estimated. The Transport Bill precluded the distribution of certain profits based on the estimated revenue, and in 1946 a sum of £542,540 had been taken into the accounts, but not distributed. Similarly, in 1947 a further sum of £31,640 had been taken in. At the end of 1947, with the ending of the company's existence, it was agreed that the sum of these amounts could be distributed, and the final dividend was based on the total revenue made up from the following sources:

1. The fixed annual sum received during the later years of Government control.

2. Net revenue from undertakings excluded from the control arrangements.

3. Profit on realisation of investments.

4. Add, the revenue arising from the exact ascertainment of the company's revenue previously estimated for the years prior to 1941 when the Control Agreement was amended to provide for the fixed annual sum.

And with this brief meeting the Great Western Railway Company came formally to an end.

APPENDIX I

MAKE-UP OF THE NEW G.W.R.–JANUARY 1923

CONSTITUENT COMPANIES   MILES

	MILES
Great Western Railway	3005
Barry Railway	68
Cambrian Railways	$295\frac{1}{4}$
Cardiff Railway	$11\frac{3}{4}$
Rhymney Railway	51
Taff Vale Railway	$124\frac{1}{2}$
Alexandra (Newport and South Wales) Docks and Railway	$10\frac{1}{4}$

SUBSIDIARY COMPANIES

(a) Independently worked

Brecon & Merthyr Tydfil Junction	$59\frac{3}{4}$
Burry Port & Gwendreath Valley	21
Cleobury Mortimer & Ditton Priors	12
Llanelly & Mynydd Mawr	13
Midland & South Western Junction	$63\frac{1}{4}$
Neath & Brecon	40

(b) Semi-independent lines: worked by G.W.R. but possessing separate rolling stock

Port Talbot Railway & Docks	35
Rhondda & Swansea Bay	29

(c) Non-working companies:

1. Originally leased to or worked by the G.W.R.

Didcot, Newbury & Southampton	$42\frac{3}{4}$
Exeter Railway	$8\frac{3}{4}$
Forest of Dean Central	5
Gwendreath Valley	3
Lampeter, Aberayron & New Quay Light	12
Liskeard & Looe	9
Princetown	$10\frac{1}{2}$
Ross & Monmouth	$12\frac{1}{2}$
Teign Valley	$7\frac{3}{4}$
West Somerset	$14\frac{1}{2}$

2. Originally leased to, or worked by the Taff Vale Railway

Penarth Extension	$1\frac{1}{4}$
Penarth Harbour, Dock & Railway	$9\frac{1}{4}$

3. Originally leased to, or worked by the Cambrian Railways

Mawddwy	$6\frac{3}{4}$
Van	$6\frac{3}{4}$
Welshpool & Llanfair Light	$9\frac{1}{4}$
Wrexham & Ellesmere	$12\frac{3}{4}$

4. Originally leased or worked by the Port Talbot Railway & Docks

South Wales Mineral	13

5. Originally leased or worked by the Barry Railway Vale of Glamorgan

	$20\frac{3}{4}$

JOINT RAILWAYS MILES

(a) Now wholly comprised in the G.W.R.
Quakers Yard and Merthyr 6
Taff Bargoed 11

(b) Jointly with the L.M.S.R.
Birkenhead 56½
Brecon & Merthyr & L.N.W. Joint 6
Brynmawr & Western Valleys 1¼
Clee Hill 6
Clifton Extension 9
Halesowen 6
Nantybwch & Rhymney 3
Severn & Wye 39
Shrewsbury & Hereford 82¾
Tenbury 5
West London 2¼
Wrexham & Minera.. 3

(c) Jointly with L.M.S.R. & Southern
West London Extension 5¼
(quarter share)

(d) Jointly with the L.N.E.R.
Great Western & Great Central Joint 41

(e) Jointly with the Southern
Easton & Church Hope 3½
Weymouth & Portland 5½

(f) Jointly with the Metropolitan
Hammersmith & City 3

(g) Jointly with the G.S. & W.R. (Ireland)
Fishguard & Rosslare Railways & Harbours 107

APPENDIX II

DIRECTORATE OF THE NEW G.W.R.–JANUARY 1923

From the Great Western Railway:

Viscount Churchill (Chairman)
Sir Ernest Palmer, Bart. (Deputy Chairman)
Lord Barrymore
Frank Bibby, Esq.
T. Robbins Bolitho, Esq.
Sir Aubrey Brocklebank, Bart.
F. W. Grierson, Esq.
Lord Inchcape
J. F. Mason, Esq.
F. B. Mildmay, Esq.
Charles Mortimer, Esq.
Sir H. B. Robertson
J. Shaw, Esq. (also Alexandra Docks)
G. A. Wills, Esq.
J. W. Wilson, Esq.
Sir W. W. Watkin-Wynn
Lieut.-Col. Sir H. A. Yorke (also Alexandra Docks)

From the Barry Railway:
Earl of Plymouth

From the Cambrian Railways:
Lieut.-Col. David Davies (also Barry Railway)

From the Cardiff Railway:
Lord Glanely (also Rhymney Railway)

From the Rhymney Railway:
W. Heward Bell, Esq.

From the Taff Vale Railway:
G. Birkley Forrester, Esq.

From the Alexandra (Newport & South Wales) Docks and Railways:
Sir H. Mather Jackson, Bart. (also Rhymney Railway)

APPENDIX III

AN OBITUARY NOTICE FROM THE 'TIMES'
4th JANUARY 1934

LORD CHURCHILL

The Court, Business and Politics

We regret to announce that Viscount Churchill died yesterday of pneumonia at his Scottish seat, Langlee House, Galashiels, at the age of 69.

In the course of a distinguished career he had held high office at Court, and as the head of the Ascot Office at St. James's Palace, which deals with applications for tickets for the Royal Enclosure, he was well known to racegoers. He had been a soldier, a Conservative Whip in the House of Lords, and in the City was a familiar figure to many; but he will be longest remembered by the conspicuous business ability he showed as chairman of the Great Western Railway Company, an office which he filled for 25 years with the greatest satisfaction to both passengers and shareholders.

His death was quite unexpected to all but this closest friends, as he had been in London just before Christmas, and was out riding a few days ago. He became suddenly indisposed and pneumonia developed.

The Right Hon. Victor Albert Francis Charles Spencer, first Viscount and third Baron Churchill, a Prince of the Holy Roman Empire, was born on October 23rd, 1864, the only son of the second baron, whom he succeeded in 1886. After being educated at Eton, where he was in Miss Evans's Dame's House, and the Rev. James Leigh Joynes was his tutor, he passed into the Royal Military College, Sandhurst. In 1884 he received a commission in the Coldstream Guards, retiring as a subaltern in 1889. From 1876 to 1881 he had been a Page of Honour to Queen Victoria, of whom he was a godson, and in 1889 he was appointed a Lord-in-Waiting, continuing in that office until 1892. He was again a Lord-in-Waiting to Her Majesty from 1895 to her death in 1901, and from that year until 1905 he was a Lord-in-Waiting to King Edward. He held numerous other Court appointments, among them being Master of the Buckhounds in 1900 and Lord Chamberlain in 1902, and at the Coronation of King George he was Master of the Robes. In 1902 he was created a viscount, and in the same year was raised to G.C.V.O., having been made K.C.V.O. in 1900. Lord Churchill was also the recipient of many foreign decorations, the chief of them being the Grand Crosses of the Prussian Order of the Red Eagle, the Prussian Crown (in brilliants) the Portuguese Order of Jesus Christ, the Crown of Italy, the Dutch Order of Orange of Nassau, and the Redeemer of Greece.

In politics the late peer gave good service to the Conservative Party as Whip in the House of Lords for many years. During the war he served at home and in France with the rank of Colonel. He was an honorary member of the Jockey Club.

To the railway world in general his unexpected death will come as a severe shock, but it will be particularly keenly felt by the Great Western Railway. Ever since 1908 he had been the guiding hand for this, one of the world's most famous railway systems. Both he and Lady Churchill had been well known to so many of the nearly 100,000 Great Western employees that his loss will be felt in a personal sense by many hundreds of them. It was only a little over a week ago that Lady Churchill opened the Christmas festivities at Paddington, and few then could have foreseen the severe loss that she and the Great Western were soon to share.

When Lord Churchill first became the chairman of the board of the Great Western the company was only just entering on its era of greatest prosperity, for the shorter and more direct line to Taunton and the West of England had not long been opened. The quicker route between Birmingham and Bristol was opened the same year, and the shorter route to Birmingham from London, avoiding Reading and Oxford, was only opened in 1910. Thus Lord Churchill during his period of office benefited by the carefully thought out plans of his predecessors, who had to overcome the troubles due to Brunel's unwise choice of the broad gauge, but equally he will pass on to his successors a railway property which, for its physical efficiency and potential earning capacity, in times of reasonably good trade, is probably unexcelled by any other large railway system in the world.

Heavily hit by the War period with its attendant worries and tribulations, followed by the period of post-War reconstruction, and, later, by almost 10 years of trade depression, the Great Western Railway has, thanks largely to the wise guidance of its chairman, come through the abnormal conditions of the last 20 years almost unscathed. Even in 1932 the company succeeded in paying three per cent. on its Ordinary share capital.

It was largely due to the power Lord Churchill possessed of inculcating in all the staff a spirit of high enterprise and strong *esprit de corps* that the company of which he was so fond, and in whose interests he was so immersed, can lay claim to its leadership of a world-wide industry. The duty of a railway chairman is to guide a great organisation in safe financial courses, and to encourage the initiative and progressive spirit to be discovered in a widely scattered staff. In the achievement of both these objects Lord Churchill could claim great credit.

The Great Western Railway of future years will be a monument to his chairmanship, and no monument would have pleased him better. It is indeed sad that he should have passed away so soon after it became known that the Great Western's fortunes had improved materially over the preceding year.

Lord Churchill's City interests included the chairmanship of the British Overseas Bank. Of this bank, which was established in 1919, he had been chairman for 10 years and his speeches at the bank's annual meetings provided a useful commentary on the state of international trade and of conditions in some of those countries, such as Poland, where the bank is especially interested. He was also a member of the board of the Peninsular and Oriental Steam Navigation Company the British India Steam Navigation Company, and the Grand Union Canal Company. In the City he possessed a high reputation for conscientious attention to the work of the boards of directors with which he was associated.

In 1887 he married Lady Verena Lowther, daughter of the third Earl of Lonsdale, by whom he had a son, Major the Hon. Victor Spencer, born in 1890, who succeeds as second Viscount; and two daughters—the Hon. Mrs. Cecil Brassey and the Hon. Mrs. Alick Tod. An elder son died in infancy. Major Spencer has no son, and there is therefore no heir to the new peer's viscountcy but his first cousin once removed Captain A. S. J. Monro-Spencer, becomes heir-presumptive to the barony.

Lord Churchill married, secondly, in 1927 Christine McRae, daughter of Mr. William Sinclair, by whom he had a daughter, Sarah, born in 1931.

APPENDIX IV

GOVERNMENT CONTROL OF RAILWAYS

Under The Railway Control Order, 1939 (S.R. & O. 1939 No. 1197).

OUTLINE OF FINANCIAL ARRANGEMENTS BETWEEN THE MINISTER OF TRANSPORT, THE FOUR AMALGAMATED RAILWAY COMPANIES, AND THE LONDON PASSENGER TRANSPORT BOARD.

1. As from September 1st, 1939, the date upon which the Government assumed control, the revenue receipts and expenses of the controlled undertakings will be pooled and the resultant net revenue for each accounting period will be appropriated in accordance with the arrangements set out below.

2. There will be paid out of the pool to each of the controlled undertakings a minimum sum which, in the case of

(a) each of the railway companies will be the average of its net revenue for the years 1935, 1936, and 1937;

(b) the board will be the net revenue for the year ended June 30th, 1939;

adjusted as may be necessary for interest on capital issued or redeemed subsequent to the basic period. These payments (amounting to £40 millions*) will be guaranteed by His Majesty's Government and are referred to as the guaranteed net revenues. They will accrue to the controlled undertakings approximately in the following proportions:—

	Per cent.
London Midland & Scottish Railway Company	34
London & North Eastern Railway Company ..	23
Great Western Railway Company	16
Southern Railway Company	16
London Passenger Transport Board	11
	100

3. After the payment of the guaranteed net revenues any balance in the pool, up to an amount of £3½ millions*, will be paid to the controlled undertakings in proportion to their respective guaranteed net revenues.

4. If the net revenue in the pool exceeds the sum of the amounts payable to the controlled undertakings under paragraphs 2 and 3 (£43½ millions*) then, until the sum paid to them reaches £56 millions*, being the estimated sum required to bring the net revenues of the controlled undertakings up to their standard revenues, one half of the excess over £43½ millions will be paid to the Exchequer and the other half will be paid to the controlled undertakings in proportion to their respective guaranteed net revenues: Provided that if the share of any of the controlled undertakings, together with its net revenue from other sources, would result in that undertaking exceeding its standard revenue, the excess will be paid to the other controlled undertakings in proportion to their respective guaranteed net revenues, but so that in any case the total net revenue accruing to a controlled undertaking shall not exceed its standard revenue. Standard revenue means in relation to a railway company the standard revenue ascertained

*These figures are approximate only.

245

under the Railways Act, 1921, with allowances for additional capital as provided by that Act and in relation to the board means the net revenue necessary to enable the board to pay the standard rate of interest on its 'C' stock.

5. Any net revenue in the pool remaining after the controlled undertakings have received their standard revenues on the basis laid down in the preceding paragraph will be paid to the Exchequer.

6. In ascertaining the net revenue of a railway company there shall be excluded any net revenue derived from investments in road transport undertakings and from ownership of and investments in railways in Northern Ireland or Eire. Net revenue in relation to the board means the whole of the net revenue of the board ascertained in accordance with the statutory form of railway accounts.

(NOTE.—Pursuant to the provisions of section 40 of the Civil Defence Act, 1939, repayments will fall to be made by the railway companies to the Exchequer of one-half of the grants made for air-raid precautionary measures if net revenues accrue to them in excess of their respective guaranteed net revenues, and by the board if net revenue accrue to it in excess of its average net revenue for the years ended June 30th, 1937, 1938, and 1939 inclusive.)

7. After December 31st, 1939, the London Passenger Pooling Scheme will be suspended and any guarantees dependent upon the pool established by that scheme will, during the period of suspension, be related to the pool to be established under these financial arrangements.

8. For the period of control ended December 31st, 1939, the Exchequer will contribute a sum equal to the amount by which the guaranteed net revenue of the board for that period exceeds the net revenue which accrued to the board after the operation of the London Passenger Pooling Scheme during that period. This contribution will form part of the net revenue of the pool. As between the board and the Exchequer there will also be payments so as to adjust the net revenue of the board for the six months ended December 31st, 1939, to the amount of £2,430,000, being the estimated net revenue for the corresponding period of the previous year.

9. Provision will be made (among other matters) for :—

(a) the standardisation of charges for maintenance (including renewals) on the basis of the average of the charges made in the basic period, subject to adjustment for altered conditions;

(b) the cost of restoring war damage up to a maximum of £10 millions in any full year (and pro rata for part of a year) to be charged to revenue expenditure when the damage occurs;

(c) the revenue receipts and expenditure in respect of the requisitioning by the Minister of Transport of privately-owned wagons to be included in the revenue receipts and expenditure of the controlled undertakings.

10. Rates, fares, and charges will be adjusted to meet variations in working costs and certain other conditions arising from the war, and machinery will be provided to this end.

11. The Minister of Transport or the railway companies and the board jointly may, after the end of the year 1940, propose revision of these arrangements for any cause of a major character and, if agreed, the arrangements shall be revised accordingly.

12. These arrangements have been agreed between the Government, the railway companies, and the board on the understanding that it will be open to certain other controlled railway companies to become parties to the arrangements on similar terms.

APPENDIX V

NEW LINES OPENED BY GREAT WESTERN RAILWAY
1923–1947

13 May 1925   Dunstall Park to Brettell Lane for passenger and goods traffic, including Tettenhall, Compton, Penn, Wombourn, Himley, Gornal, Pensnett, Bromley and Brockmoor stations or halts. 12 miles.

13 July 1925   Shifnal to Madeley Court reopened. 4 miles. Passenger and Goods.

11 July 1927   Penar Branch, stations Oakdale, Penmaen, and Treowen. (Previously colliery line.) Passenger and mineral.

APPENDIX VI

LIST OF NEW STATIONS AND HALTS

1st January, 1923 to 31st December, 1947

Date		Station	Halt
	1923	Heathfield (Pembs.)	
1 Dec.	1924	Iver	
13 July	1925		Coed Ely
23 Dec.	1926		Ham Green Platform (Pill)
20 Sept.	1926		South Greenford
,,			Long Ashton (Bedminster)
,,			North Filton
,,			Ashton Gate (reopened)
,,			Fleur de Lys (Pengam)
,,			Pentwynmawr (Crumlin H.L.)
,,			Park Hall (Gobowen)
May	1927	Whitchurch (Bristol)	
14 May	1927	Horfield	
11 July	1927		Aberthaw L.L. (reopened)
,,			St. Athan Road (reopened)
,,			St. Mary Church Road (reopened)
,,			Stanwell Moor & Poyle (Staines)
,,			Christian Malford
,,			Treowen (Crumlin H.L.)
,,			Penmawr & Oakdale
,,			Glascoed (Usk)
,,			Llandogo (Tintern)
,,			Whitebrook (St. Briavels)
,,			Port Sunlight (Spital)
Apr.	1928		Pentrefelin (Morriston)
June	1928		Cutnall Green
,,			Nightingale Valley
,,			Pilning L.L.
,,			Sampford Peverell
,,			Sebastopol
,,			Alphington
,,			Bolham
,,			Brimley
,,			Cross Hands
,,			Donyatt
,,			Dunsford
,,			Garneddwen
,,			Glanyrafon
,,			Goodrington Sands
,,			Halberton
,,			Ilton
,,			King Tor
,,			New Passage
,,			Pontypool, Blaendare Road
,,			Thorney
,			Wainfelin

Date	Station	Halt
July 1928		Westbury on Severn
,,		West Exe
Nov. 1928		Harefield
,,		Morris Cowley
,,		Creech St. Michael
,,		Castlebythe (Puncheston)
,,		Wootton Rivers
,,		Lyng (Athelney)
,,		Beulah
,,		Hayles Abbey
Mar. 1929		Burn (Up Exe)
,,	Oldfield Park	
		Oaksey (Kemble)
		Pans Lane (Patney)
		Coldharbour (Culm Valley)
Apr. 1929		Chalvey (Slough)
Nov. 1929		Monks Risborough
,,		Blaisdon (Grange Court)
,,		Weston under Penyard (Ross)
,,		New Inn Bridge (Puncheston)
,,		Martell Bridge (Castlebythe)
,,		Llandanwg (Harlech)
7 Dec. 1929		Olmarch (Pont Llanio)
1 Jan. 1930		Martoll Bridge (Puncheston)
June 1930		Mill Lane (Box)
,,		Burlish (Bewdley)
,,		Ellerdine (Peplow)
,,		Pencarreg (Lampeter)
6 Apr. 1931		Tackley (Heyford)
20 July 1931		Perranporth Beach
Apr. 1933		Llanstephan
6 May 1933		Stratford-upon-Avon Racecourse
29 Jan. 1934		New Dale (Ketley)
1 Feb. 1934		Wynnville (Ruabon)
12 Mar. 1934		Green Bank (Coalbrookdale)
14 Apr. 1934		Trawsfynydd Lake
30 Apr. 1934		Birches & Bilbrook (Codsall)
4 Jun. 1934		Llys (Garneddwen)
11 Jun. 1934		Wyre (Pershore)
9 July 1934		Tutshill (Chepstow)
,,		Trelewis (Treharris)
4 Aug. 1934		Cound (Berrington (Severn Valley))
22 Sept. 1934		Haughton (Rednal)
3 Nov. 1934		Plas-y-court (Westbury, Salop.)
8 Feb. 1935		Dolserau (Dolgelly)
18 Mar. 1935		Abertafol (Penhelig)
27 July 1935		Trehowell (Chirk)
17 Aug. 1935		Coole Pilate (Audlem)
17 Sept. 1935		Little Drayton (Tern Hill)
21 Sept. 1935		Bonwm (Corwen)
23 Sept. 1935		Alltddu (Tregaron)
7 Dec. 1935		Westwood (Much Wenlock)
14 Dec. 1935		Lower Cwmtwrch
2 Mar. 1936		Ingra Tor (Burrator)
6 Mar. 1936		Ketley Town (Wellington (Salop))

Date	Station	Halt
9 Mar. 1936		Cassington (Oxford)
4 Apr. 1936		Easthope (Longville)
4 May 1936		Parcyrhun (Tirydail)
18 May 1936		Astwood (Worcester Shrub H.)
6 July 1936		Whitlock's End (Shirley)
31 May 1937		Heolgerrig (Merthyr)
1 June 1937		Dilton Marsh (Westbury)
21 June 1937		Dorton (Brill)
5 July 1937		Furze Platt
8 Nov. 1937		Mickleton (Honeybourne)
4 Apr. 1938		Liddaton (Lydford)
11 Apr. 1938		Carreghofa
13 Mar 1939		Bryncelynog (Cwm Prysor)

Total number of halts opened up to and including 13th March 1939 is 401.
Stations opened for passenger and goods traffic. Halts probably for passenger only, but no information available.

APPENDIX VII

BRANCH LINES CLOSED. 1923–1947

All branches closed for passenger service only except where stated.

Date	*Line*	*Mileage*	*Remarks*
21 Sept. 1925	Limpley Stoke–Hallatrow	11½	
June 1926	Garnant–Gwaun-cae-Gurwen	1¼	
5 Dec. 1927	Old Hill–Halesowen	1½	
8 July 1929	Moreton in Marsh–Shipston on Stour	9	
,,	St. Blazey–Fowey	4	
14 Apr. 1930	Rhymney Lower–New Tredegar	2	
5 May 1930	Cowbridge–Aberthaw	5¾	
7 July 1930	Plymouth–Yealmpton	10¼	
,,	Cinderford–Drybrook Halt	1½	
22 Sept. 1930	Bridport–West Bay	2	
,,	Blackmill–Gilfach Goch	4½	
,,	Cymmer Corrwg–Glyn Corrwg	2¾	
,,	Port Talbot Jn.–Tonmawr Jn.	6	Closed to goods only
1 Jan. 1931	Dinas Mawddwy–Cemmes Rd.	6¾	
,,	Rhos Junc.–Rhos	4¼	
,,	Wrexham–Moss Platform	3¼	
,,	Croesnewydd–Berwig Halt	6¾	
9 Feb. 1931	Abermule–Kerry	3¾	
20 July 1931	Coryton–Rhydyfelin Halt	5½	Closed completely
14 Sept. 1931	Congresbury–Blagdon	6¾	
12 Sept. 1932	Maesteg–Pontyrhyll	5	
,,	Pontypridd–Nelson & Llancaiach	6	
,,	Ystradgynlais–Colbren Junc.	4¾	
12 Oct. 1932	Wolverhampton–Stourbridge Junc.	12	(via Wombourn)
16 July 1933	Dauntsey–Great Somerford	2¾	Closed completely
11 Sept. 1933	Port Talbot–Maesteg (Neath Rd.)	5	
,,	Swansea–Jersey Marine	3½	(Swansea Riverside)
16 Sept. 1935	Neath (Canal Side)–Court Sart	1½	
28 Sept. 1936	Swansea East Dock–Neath	8½	
5 Feb. 1940	Lostwithiel–Fowey	5¼	
3 May 1942	Southall–Brentford	3½	
		156¾	
Also			
1 Jan. 1931	Machynlleth–Corris	6½	Narrow gauge 2 ft. 3 in.
9 Feb. 1931	Welshpool–Llanfair Caereinion	9	Narrow gauge 2 ft. 6 in.
18 May 1940	Weston, Clevedon & Portishead		
4 Nov. 1940	Van Railway		(Goods only)

APPENDIX VIII

LIST OF STATIONS AND HALTS CLOSED BY THE G.W.R.

1st January, 1923 to 13th December, 1947

Name	Closed to Passengers	Goods	Closed entirely
Abbeydore	15 Dec. 1941		
Aberangell	1 Jan. 1931		
Aberffrwd	31 Aug. 1939	26 Sept. 1937	
reopened	23 July 1945		
Abersychan	5 May 1941		
Aberthaw Low Level	5 May 1930	1 Nov. 1932	1 Nov. 1932
Abertysswg	14 Apr. 1930		14 Apr. 1930
Almeley	1 July 1940	1 July 1940	1 July 1940
Aston Cantelow Halt	25 Sept. 1939		
Astwood Halt	25 Sept. 1939		25 Sept. 1939
Bacton	15 Dec. 1941		
Baglan Sands Halt	25 Sept. 1939		25 Sept. 1939
Baldwin's Halt	11 Sept. 1933		11 Sept. 1933
Basingstoke	1 Jan. 1932		
Beulah Halt	25 Oct. 1937		25 Oct. 1937
Billacombe	6 Oct. 1947		
Black Lion Crssg. Hlt.	22 Sept. 1924		22 Sept. 1924
Brampford & Speke		1 Oct. 1923	
Brentford	4 May 1942		
Brentham Halt	30 June 1947		
Bridport East St.	22 Sept. 1930		22 Sept. 1930
Bridport West Bay	22 Sept. 1930		
Briton Ferry Road	28 Sept. 1936		28 Sept. 1936
Briton Ferry West	8 July 1935		
Brixton Road	6 Oct. 1947		
Brockmoor Halt	31 Oct. 1932		31 Oct. 1932
Bromley Halt	31 Oct. 1932		31 Oct. 1932
Brymbo W. Crssg. Hlt.	1 Jan. 1931		1 Jan. 1931
Bryn (Port Talbot)	11 Sept. 1933		
Burbage		10 Nov. 1947	10 Nov. 1947
Burngullow	14 Sept. 1931		
Burrington	14 Sept. 1931		
Camerton	21 Sept. 1925		
Capel Bangor (Cambr)	31 Aug. 1939	25 Sept. 1937	
reopened	23 July 1945		
Cardiff Parade (Rhy)	15 Apr. 1928		15 Apr. 1928
Cardiff Queen St. (Taff)		30 Mar. 1925	
Cardonnel Halt	28 Sept. 1936		28 Sept. 1936
Carmarthen Junc.	27 Sept. 1926		
Castlebythe Halt	25 Oct. 1937		25 Oct. 1937
Castle Caereinion (Camb)	9 Feb. 1931		
Cemmaes (Cambrian)	1 Jan. 1931		
Clifford	15 Dec. 1941		
Clifton Maybank		7 June 1937	7 June 1937

Name	Closed to Passengers	Goods	Closed entirely
Coed Poeth	1 Jan. 1931		
Combe Hay Halt	21 Sept. 1925		21 Sept. 1925
Compton Halt	31 Oct. 1932		31 Oct. 1932
Coombes Holloway Hlt.	5 Dec. 1927		5 Dec. 1927
Cottage Siding (Taff)		Feb. 1933	Feb. 1933
Cwmaman		Jan. 1936	Jan. 1936
Cwmaman Colliery Hlt.	22 Sept. 1924		22 Sept. 1924
Cwmaman Crossing Hlt.	22 Sept. 1934		22 Sept. 1924
Cwmdu (Port Talbot)	12 Sept. 1932		
Cwmffrwdoer	5 May 1941		
Cwmneol	22 Sept. 1924		22 Sept. 1924
Cyfronydd (Cambrian)	9 Feb. 1931		
Danygraig Halt	28 Sept. 1936		28 Sept. 1936
Dare Junc.		1 Sept. 1939	1 Sept. 1939
Defiance Platform	27 Oct. 1930		27 Oct. 1930
Dinas Mawddwy (Camb)	1 Jan. 1931		
Dolarddyn Crossing	9 Feb. 1931		9 Feb. 1931
Dorstone	15 Dec. 1941		
Drybrook Halt	7 July 1930		7 July 1930
Dunkerton	21 Sept. 1925	21 Sept. 1925	21 Sept. 1925
Dunkerton Colly. Halt	21 Sept. 1925		21 Sept. 1925
East Dock	28 Sept. 1936		28 Sept. 1936
Elburton Crossing	6 Oct. 1947		6 Oct. 1947
Ford Halt	6 Oct. 1941		6 Oct. 1941
Garth & Van Road		4 Nov. 1940	4 Nov. 1940
Gatewen Halt	1 Jan. 1931		1 Jan. 1931
Gilfach Goch	22 Sept. 1930		
Glanrafon (Cambrian)	31 Aug. 1939		31 Aug. 1939
Glanyllyn (Cardiff)	20 July 1931	20 July 1931	20 July 1931
Glyntaff Halt	5 May 1930		5 May 1930
Godreaman Halt	22 Sept. 1924		22 Sept. 1924
Golant Halt	1 Jan. 1940		1 Jan. 1940
Golden Hill Platform	5 Feb. 1940		5 Feb. 1940
Golfa (Cambrian Rlys.)	9 Feb. 1931	9 Feb. 1931	9 Feb. 1931
Gornal Halt	31 Oct. 1932		31 Oct. 1932
Gors-y-Garnant Halt	4 May 1926		4 May 1926
Great Alne	25 Sept. 1939	25 Sept. 1939	25 Sept. 1939
Great Somerford Halt	17 July 1933		17 July 1933
Green's Siding	15 Dec. 1941		
Gwaun-cae-Gurwen Halt	4 May 1926		4 May 1926
Gwersyllt Hill Halt	1 Jan. 1931		1 Jan. 1931
Halesowen	5 Dec. 1927		
Hendreforgan	22 Sept. 1930	1 Jan. 1931	1 Jan. 1931
Heniarth (Cambr)	9 Feb. 1931		
Himley	31 Oct. 1932		
Kerry (Cambrian)	9 Feb. 1931		
Laira Halt	7 July 1930		7 July 1930
Langford	14 Sept. 1931		
Legacy	1 Jan. 1931		
Letterston	25 Oct. 1937		
Lipson Vale Halt	23 Mar. 1942		23 Mar. 1942
Llanbadarn (Cambrian)	31 Aug. 1939		
Llandavey Halt	4 Oct. 1947		4 Oct. 1947

Name	Closed to Passengers	Goods	Closed entirely
Llanfabon Road Halt (Taff)	12 Sept. 1932		12 Sept. 1932
Llanfair Caereinion (Cam) ..	9 Feb. 1931		
Llangyfelach	22 Sept. 1924		
Llanycefn	25 Oct. 1937		
Lletty Brongu (Port Tbt) ..	12 Sept. 1932		
Long Ashton	6 Oct. 1941		6 Oct. 1941
Longdon Road	8 July 1929	1 June 1941	1 June 1941
Lyonshall	1 July 1940	1 July 1940	1 July 1940
Madeley (Salop)	21 Sept. 1925		
Maenclochog	25 Oct. 1937		
Maesteg (Neath Road) (Port Tbt)	11 Sept. 1933		
Mallwyd (Cambrian) ..	1 Jan. 1931		1 Jan. 1931
Marlborough High Level ..	6 Mar. 1933		
Martell Bridge Halt	25 Oct. 1937		25 Oct. 1937
Mary Tavy	11 Aug. 1940		
Mickleton Halt	6 Oct. 1941		6 Oct. 1941
Millbay	23 Apr. 1941		
Monkton Combe	21 Sept. 1925		
Moss Platform	1 Jan. 1931		1 Jan. 1931
Mutley	3 July 1939		3 July 1939
Nailbridge Halt	7 July 1930		7 July 1930
Nantgarw (Cardiff)	20 July 1931		20 July 1931
Neath Abbey	28 Sept. 1936		
Nelson (Glam) (Taff V.) ..	12 Sept. 1932		
New Inn Bridge Halt ..	25 Oct. 1937		25 Oct. 1937
Newquay Harbour		1926	1926
Nightingale Valley Hlt. ..	23 Sept. 1929		23 Sept. 1929
North Acton	30 June 1947		30 June 1947
Oakdale Halt	12 Sept. 1932		12 Sept. 1932
Old Oak Lane Halt	30 June 1947		30 June 1947
Oswestry	7 July 1924*		
Park Royal	26 Sept. 1937		
Park Royal West Halt ..	30 June 1947		30 June 1947
Paulton Halt	21 Sept. 1925		21 Sept. 1925
Penn Halt	31 Oct. 1932		31 Oct. 1932
Penmaen Halt	25 Sept. 1939		25 Sept. 1939
Pensnett Halt	31 Oct. 1932		31 Oct. 1932
Penstrowedd Siding (Cam) ..		31 May 1937	31 May 1937
Pentre Broughton Halt ..	1 Jan. 1931		1 Jan. 1931
Pentre Piod Halt	5 May 1941		5 May 1941
Pentresaeson Halt	1 Jan. 1931		1 Jan. 1931
Pentwyn Halt	5 May 1941		5 May 1941
Perivale Halt	30 June 1947		30 June 1947
Peterchurch	15 Dec. 1941		
Plas Power	1 Jan. 1931		
Pont Lliw	22 Sept. 1924		
Pontypridd, Craig (Barry) ..	10 July 1930		10 July 1930
Portbury Shipyard	26 Mar. 1923		26 Mar. 1923
Portreath		1 Jan. 1936	1 Jan. 1936
Puncheston	25 Oct. 1937		

* Former Great Western Station. Cambrian Station not closed.

Name	Closed to Passengers	Goods	Closed entirely
Pwllglas (Cambrian) ..		4 Nov. 1940	4 Nov. 1940
Radford Halt	21 Sept. 1925		21 Sept. 1925
Rattery Siding		1 Sept. 1938	1 Sept. 1938
Red Housing Siding (Camb)		4 Nov. 1940	4 Nov. 1940
Red Lion Crossing Halt ..	4 May 1926		4 May 1926
Rheidol Falls (Cambrian) ..	31 Aug. 1939		
Rhiwfron (Cambrian) ..	31 Aug. 1939	26 Sept. 1937	
Rhos	1 Jan. 1931		
Rhostyllen	1 Jan. 1931		
Rhydyfelin Halt (Cardiff) ..	20 July 1931		20 July 1931
St. Blazey	21 Sept. 1925		
Shipston-on-Stour	8 July 1929		
South Harefield Halt (GW & GC)	1 Oct. 1931		1 Oct. 1931
South Rhondda		1 Mar. 1930	1 Mar. 1930
Steam Mills Crossing Halt ..	7 July 1930		7 July 1930
Steer Point	6 Oct. 1947		
Stretton-on-Fosse	8 July 1929	1 June 1941	1 June 1941
Sylfaen Halt (Cambrian) ..	9 Feb. 1931		9 Feb. 1931
Tettenhall	31 Oct. 1932		
The Lodge Halt	1 Jan. 1931		1 Jan. 1931
Tongwynlais (Cardiff Rly.) ..	20 July 1931	20 July 1931	20 July 1931
Trecynon		1 Sept. 1939	1 Sept. 1939
Treforest High Level (Barry)	10 July 1930	1 Sept. 1930	1 Sept. 1930
Trewythan Siding (Cambrian)		4 Nov. 1940	4 Nov. 1940
Troedyrhiw Garth		1 Aug. 1947	
Trumper's Crossing Halt ..	1 Feb. 1926		1 Feb. 1926
Upper Boat (Cardiff) ..	20 July 1931	20 July 1931	20 July 1931
Uxbridge High St.	1 Sept. 1939		
Vicarage Crossing Halt ..	1 Jan. 1931		1 Jan. 1931
Vowchurch	15 Dec. 1941		
Wainfelin Halt	5 May 1941		5 May 1941
Welshpool Raven Sq. (Cam)	9 Feb. 1931		9 Feb. 1931
Welshpool Seven Stars ..	9 Feb. 1931		9 Feb. 1931
Westbrook	15 Dec. 1941		
Weymouth Quay	25 July 1940	May 1942	May 1942
Whimsey Halt	7 July 1930		7 July 1930
Wombourn	31 Oct. 1932		
Wrington	14 Sept. 1931		
Yealmpton	6 Oct. 1947		

APPENDIX IX

STANDARD LOCOMOTIVES at December 31st, 1947

Wheel Arrgt.	Class	Duty	Cyls. No.	No. of Engines in class
4-4-0	'Bulldog'	Light pass.	2 inside	43
4-4-0	'Dukedog'	Light pass.	2 inside	30
4-6-0	'Saint'	Exp. pass.	2 outside	47
4-6-0	'Hall'	Mixed	2 outside	281*
4-6-0	'Grange'	Mixed	2 outside	80
4-6-0	'Manor'	Light pass.	2 outside	20*
4-6-0	'County'	Heavy mixed	2 outside	30
4-6-0	'Star'	Exp. pass.	4	47
4-6-0	'Castle'	Exp. pass.	4	141*
4-6-0	'King'	Heavy Exp. Pass.	4	30
2-6-0	'43XX'	Mixed	2 outside	101
2-8-0	'28XX'	Heavy Freight	2 outside	167
2-8-0	'47XX'	Heavy mixed	2 outside	9
0-6-0	Dean goods	Light goods	2 inside	50
0-6-0	'2251'	Light goods	2 inside	118
0-4-2T	'4800'	Light pass.	2 inside	95
0-6-0PT	'5400'	Light pass.	2 inside	94
0-6-0PT	Pannier tank	Mixed shunting	2 inside	810*
2-6-2T	'3150'	Heavy tank	2 outside	33
2-6-2T	'5100'	Suburban tank	2 outside	220
2-8-0T	'4200'	Mineral tank	2 outside	151
2-8-2T	'7200'	Mineral tank	2 outside	54
2-6-2T	'45XX'	Fast branch tank	2 outside	175
0-6-2T	'56XX'	South Wales tank	2 inside	200
0-6-0PT	'94XX'	Shunting tank	2 inside	10*

* Further engines of this class built after Nationalisation.

APPENDIX X

CHAIRMEN AND CHIEF OFFICERS OF THE G.W.R.

CHAIRMEN:

Benjamin Shaw	Sept. 1835–Oct. 1837
William A. Sims	Oct. 1837–Nov. 1839
Charles Russell	Nov. 1839–Aug. 1855
Rt. Hon. S. Walpole	Aug. 1855–Feb. 1856
Viscount Barrington	Feb. 1856–May 1857
Hon. F. G. B. Ponsonby	May 1857–Feb. 1859
Lord Shelburne	Feb. 1859–Feb. 1863
Rt. Hon. S. Walpole	Feb. 1863–Aug. 1863
Richard Potter	Aug. 1863–Nov. 1865
Sir Daniel Gooch	Nov. 1865–Oct. 1889
F. G. Saunders	Oct. 1889–July 1895
Viscount Emlyn	July 1895–Mar. 1905
Alfred Baldwin	Mar. 1905–Feb. 1908
Viscount Churchill	Feb. 1908–Jan. 1934
Viscount Horne	Jan. 1934–Sept. 1940
Sir Charles J. Hambro	Sept. 1940–Feb. 1945
Viscount Portal	Feb. 1945–Dec. 1947

GENERAL MANAGERS:

James Grierson	Oct. 1863–Oct. 1887
Henry Lambert	Oct. 1887–July 1896
Sir Joseph Wilkinson	July 1896–June 1903
Sir James Inglis	June 1903–Dec. 1911
Frank Potter	Jan. 1912–July 1919
Charles Aldington	Aug. 1919–June 1921
Sir Felix Pole	June 1921–July 1929
Sir James Milne	July 1929–Dec. 1947

SECRETARIES:

William Tothill	
(Bristol Committee)	Jan. 1833–Oct. 1835
Charles A. Saunders	
(London Committee)	Oct. 1833–Nov. 1840
Secretary and General Superintendent of the Line	Nov. 1840–Sept. 1863
Capt. T. J. Chapman	
(Bristol Committee)	Oct. 1835–May 1837
Thomas Osler	
(Bristol Committee)	May 1837–Feb. 1843*
W. Stevenson	
(Financial Secretary)	Oct. 1863–Dec. 1866*
F. G. Saunders	Oct. 1863–June 1886
J. D. Higgins	June 1886–April 1892
G. K. Mills	May 1892–June 1910
A. E. Bolter	July 1910–Jan. 1926
F. R. E. Davis	Jan. 1926–Dec. 1947

* Office abolished

SUPERINTENDENTS OF THE LINE:

G. N. Tyrrell	Feb. 1864–June 1888
N. J. Burlinson	July 1888–April 1894
T. I. Allen	April 1894–Dec. 1903
J. Morris	Jan. 1904–Jan. 1911
Charles Aldington	Jan. 1911–Mar. 1919
R. H. Nicholls	Mar. 1919–Dec. 1932
H. L. Wilkinson	Jan. 1933–Aug. 1936
F. R. Potter	Aug. 1936–Dec. 1940
Gilbert Matthews	Jan. 1941–Dec. 1947

CHIEF GOODS MANAGERS[1]:

W. L. Newcombe	April 1856–Sept. 1857
James Grierson	Sept. 1857–Oct. 1863
John Grant	Sept. 1863–Mar. 1879
Henry Lambert	April 1879–Oct. 1887
J. L. Wilkinson	May 1888–Jan. 1896
L. Wilkinson (Maiden)[2]	Jan. 1896–May 1904
T. H. Rendell	May 1904–Mar. 1912
C. A. Roberts	Feb. 1912–July 1921
E. Lowther	July 1921–Feb. 1924
E. Ford	Feb. 1924–Mar. 1931
A. Maynard	Mar. 1931–July 1942
F. W. Lampitt	July 1942–Feb. 1946
David Blee	Mar. 1946–Dec. 1947

[1] There had been a 'Goods Manager' from 1850.

[2] Mr. Wilkinson took the name 'Maiden' while in office to avoid confusion with Sir J. L. Wilkinson, the General Manager.

ENGINEERS AND CHIEF ENGINEERS:

I. K. Brunel	Mar. 1835–Sept. 1859
T. H. Bertram	Sept. 1859–April 1860
Michael Lane	April 1860–Mar. 1868
W. G. Owen	Mar. 1868–Mar. 1885
L. Trench	Mar. 1891–Sept. 1892
J. C. Inglis	Oct. 1892–June 1904
W. W. Grierson[3]	Jan. 1904–Dec. 1923
J. C. Lloyd ⎱ Joint W. Waddell ⎰	Jan. 1924–Dec. 1925
J. C. Lloyd	Jan. 1926–Jan. 1929
R. Carpmael	Jan. 1929–Dec. 1939
A. S. Quartermaine	Jan. 1940–Dec. 1947

[3] The title became Chief Engineer in July 1916.

CHIEF MECHANICAL ENGINEERS:

Daniel Gooch (Loco. Supt.)	Aug. 1837–Oct. 1864
Joseph Armstrong (Loco. and Carriage Supt.)	Jan. 1864–June 1877
William Dean (Loco. and Carriage Supt.)	June 1877–June 1902
G. J. Churchward[4]	June 1902–Dec. 1921
C. B. Collett	Jan. 1922–July 1941
F. W. Hawksworth	July 1941–Dec. 1947

[4] The title became Chief Mechanical Engineer in 1916.

SIGNAL ENGINEERS:

T. Blackall* ..	1885–June 1893
A. T. Blackall	.. Aug. 1897–June 1923
R. J. Insell ..	.. June 1923–Mar. 1928
C. M. Jacobs	.. April 1928–Feb. 1936
F. H. D. Page	.. Feb. 1936–April 1947
A. W. Woodbridge ..	.. April 1947–Dec. 1947

* From date of retirement of Mr. T. Blackall in 1893 until appointment of Mr. A. T. Blackall in 1897 the Signal department was in charge of Mr. W. Dean, the Loco-Superintendent.

Index

Accidents:
  Aisgill (Midland Rly) 28
  Charfield (L.M.S.R.), 29
  Honeybourne—boiler explosion, 208
  Midgham—derailment, 60
  Norton Fitzwarren, 183 et seq.
  Signal box fires, Paddington, 156
  Wivelscombe landslip, 209 et seq.
Air Raid precautions:
  Black-out, carriages and engines 166
  Blast protection, 157
  Casualty clearing station at
    Paddington, 180
  Country houses, Wartime H.Q. 167
  Exercise at Paddington, 157
  Launching of Scheme, 156
Air Services (passenger 107) et seq.
Aldershot, through carriages to Fish-
  guard, 6
Alexandra (Newport & South Wales)
  Docks & Railway, 2
Amalgamations, 2, 213
Ambulance trains, 208
Annual General Meetings:
  1924, 13
  1925, 21
  1927, 75
  1929, 81
  1932, 106, 148
  1933, 109
  1938, 150
  1940, 171
  1944, 215
  1945, 216
  1946, 222
Automatic Train Control, 27 et seq., 93,
  184, 230, 236

Baldwin, Mrs. Stanley, 118
Baltimore and Ohio Railroad, 58
Barry Railway, 2, 14, 34
Bishops Road Station, 96
Brakes, G.W.R. version of auto-vacu-
  um, 27, 236
Brecon & Merthyr Tydfil Junc. Rly, 2,
  34
Bridges, strength of, 56
Bristol, 98, 99
Bristolian, The, high speed train, 116

British Empire Exhibition, 58
Broad gauge anniversary, 193-4
Broad gauge mentality, 213

Cadoxton, new sidings, 4
Caerphilly Works:
  engine repairing, 129
  rebuilding of shops, 10, 125
Cambrian Railways, 2
Cardiff, City of, rating, 35
  ,,   Docks, 4
  ,,   Railway, 2, 34
  ,,   Station rebuilding, 97, 100, 101
  ,,   Valleys Division, 3
Centenaries:
  Baltimore and Ohio, 58
  Great Western, 114 et seq.
Cheltenham Flyer, 5, 71, 107, 133 et seq.
Chepstow Racecourse, 43
Churchill, Viscount, 2, 6, 13, 14, 20, 75,
  77, 81, 106, 113, 114, 148, 215
Churchward, G. J. death of, 111
Coaches, 32 et seq. 121, 193
Coal crisis: 1926, 48 et seq., 53
            1947, 221
Cogload Junc. remodelling, 92, 94
Compensation, during Govt. Control:
  General, 169
  The first agreement (1940), 170
  Account of negotiations, 172
  Revised agreement, 187 et seq., 215
Constituent Companies (1923), 2
Cornish Riviera Express, 45 et seq., 52,
  56, 61, 90, 121, 142, 221
Costs: proposed new lines, 6-9
       electrification, 154-156

Didcot, Newbury & Southampton line,
  29, 201
Diesel traction, 107, 111 et seq.
Directors:
  Baldwin, Alfred, 118, 215
  Baldwin, Stanley, 20
  Barrymore, Lord, 2
  Bolitho, Robbins, 2
  Brocklebank, Sir Aubrey, 55
  Churchill, Viscount, 2, 6, 13, 14, 20,
    75, 77, 81, 106, 113, 148, 215

Directors—*cont.*
  Hambro, Sir Charles, 189, 215
  Horne, Viscount, 115 *et seq.*, 171, 189
  Macmillan, Harold, 190
  Mortimer, Charles, 2
  Palmer, Lord, 2, 215
  Portal, Viscount, 215, 222, 237
  Watkin-Wynn, Sir, 2, 194
  Yorke, Col. Sir Arthur, 2
Dividends:
  1923, 13
  1924, 21
  1927, 75
  1928, 81
  1931, 106
  1932, 109
  1940, 172
  1944–5, 215
  1947, 238
  Comparison with other railways, 86
  South Wales lines, 34
Docks organisation (1923), 2
Dunkirk, evacuation from, 175 *et seq.*

Electrification of West of England lines,
    152
  Estimate of capital needed, 154
  Comparison steam v. electric, 155
  Capital charges, 156
Evacuation of children (London 1939),
    161 *et seq.*
Exeter Railway, 4 *et seq.*
Expenses in operation, 75

Flying Bomb attacks, 211
Forest of Dean Central Railway, 4 *et seq.*
Freight services, 72
Freight train names, 72 *et seq.*
Frome, 89

General Meeting, the last, 238
Glacial winter (1946–7), 220 *et seq.*

'Helping Hand' fund, 59
Heywood Road Junction, 90
Horne, Viscount, 115, 150, 171, 189

Instanter couplings, 105
Interchange loco. trials:
  with L.N.E.R., 45 *et seq.*, 53
  with L.M.S.R., 54
  under B.R., 235

Irish services:
  restoration, 6
  Killarney day trips, 43

'King' class locomotives, 55 *et seq.*, 122

Launceston, new wartime junction, 200
Locomotives, G.W.R.
  classes: 'Castle', 11, 55, 225
           'County', 225
           'Hall', 206
           'King', 55, 122
           South Wales, 41 *et seq.*
           War 0–6–0, 167
  engineering: boilers, 23, 125
               coal consumption, 25,
                 27, 46, 122
               cylinders and valves, 24
               dynamometer car, 25,
                 26, 226
               frame design, 206
               oil firing, 219 *et seq.*,
                 228, 229
               optical lining up, 123
                 et seq.
               performance (post-
                 war), 218
  Gas turbine, 229
  Individual:
    Caerphilly Castle, 11, 58
    Caldicot Castle, 15, 25, 46 *et seq.*
    King George V, 58, 117
    Launceston Castle, 54, 57, 107
    Lord of the Isles, 20
    Manorbier Castle, 133
    Pembroke Castle, 19
    Pendennis Castle, 58
    Queen Adelaide, 19
    Saint Bartholomew, 6
    The Great Bear, 19
    Tregenna Castle, 133
    Viscount Churchill, 20
    Windsor Castle, 14
    Named after aircraft, 193
    Pacific proposed, 225
    Publicity, 11, 46 *et seq.*
    War, interworking with Southern,
      199
Locomotives, other than G.W.R.:
  American Austerity 2–8–0, 194
  L.M.S.R. *Royal Scot*, 58
  L.N.E.R. Gresley Pacific, 45 *et seq.*
  Southern, *Lord Nelson*, 55, 57
Lydford, new wartime junction, 200

Maintenance, wartime arrears of, 215
Maps and plans:
  Automatic Train Control, in 1930, 93
  Bristol new signalling, 98, 99
  Caerphilly Works, 130
  Cardiff Disrtict, 36
  Cardiff new signalling, 100, 101
  Fairford–Cirencester line (proposed), 7
  Launceston, new junction, 200
  Lydford, new junction, 200
  Mathry Rd.–St. Davids (proposed), 8
  New Radnor–Trawscoed (proposed), 9
  Oxford, new junction, 197
  Paddington, before and after rebuilding, 95
  Reading, new junction, 197
  St. Budeaux, new junction, 200
  South Wales, map in 1923, 3
  Staines, new junction, 198
  Swansea Docks, 83
  Thingley Junction, 202
  Westbury (and Frome) by-passes, 91
  Westbury, new east curve, 202
  Wolverhampton Works, 130
  Yeovil, new junction, 202
Masters, of ships at Dunkirk, 176
Mauretania specials, 18, 19
Men, and women of G.W.R.:
  Cook, Fireman A., 15
  Dumas, C. K., 27
  Flewellyn, Inspector G. H., 15
  Harris, Parcels porter, 181
  Owen, Stewardess May, 182
  Pearce, W. H., 27
  Rowe, Driver E., 15
  Tunna, Shunter (*George Cross*), 181
  Helping Hand Fund, 59
  Volunteer labour, in wartime, 208
  War casualties, 216, 222
  War honours, 216
  Women in war service, 207

Nationalisation:
  Bill, introduced by A. Barnes, 222
  Dalton, H. speech in Parliament, 223
  Hurried measure, 223
  Loco. Interchange trials, 235
  Morrison, H. Speech, 221
  Opinion polls, 217
  Railway executive, 233
  Re-organisation, 234

New lines, proposed,
  Bishops Castle–Montgomery, 9
  Bridgwater–Watchet, 9
  Fairford–Cirencester, 6, 7
  Mathry Rd.–St. Davids, 6
  New Radnor–Trawscoed, 7
  Pwllheli–Nevin, 9
Newport, 4, 30
Newton Abbot,
  air raid damage, 179
  station rebuilding, 10
New Works:
  1923 programme, 9 *et seq.*
  Bristol remodelling, 98, 99
  Cardiff remodelling, 100, 101
  Paddington enlargements, 95
  Taunton, widening, 92
  Westbury (and Frome) by-pass lines 89

Ocean traffic, at Plymouth, 18 *et seq.*
Officers, senior, G.W.R.:
  Auld, J., 4, 14, 111
  Blackwell, A. T., 29
  Blee, D., 233
  Churchward, G. J., 56, 111, 122, 206
  Collett, C.B., 14, 25, 56, 122, 192
  Cook, K. J., 224, 234
  Dannatt, E. H., 4
  Dymond, A. W. J., 224, 229
  Ell, S. O., 224, 236
  Ford, E., 105
  Grand, K. W. C., 238
  Grierson, W. W., 13
  Hall, F. C., 224
  Hannington, R. A. G., 59
  Hawksworth, F. W., 59, 192, 206, 208, 224, 227, 232, 234,
  Hurry-Riches, C. T., 4
  Inglis, Sir James, 56, 238
  Insell, R. J., 29
  Lloyd, J. C., 13, 56
  Matthews, G., 190, 232
  Mattingly, F. C., 224
  Maynard, A., 105
  Milne, Sir James, 14, 86, 190, 212, 236
  Nicholls, R. H., 110
  Page, F. H. D., 232
  Potter, Frank, 160
  Potter, F. R., 111, 190
  Quartermaine, Sir Allan, 232
  Randle, H., 224
  Roberts, C. T., 224, 235
  Stanier, Sir William, 14, 60, 111, 236

Officers, senior, G.W.R.—*cont.*
 Vickery, J. H., 4
 Waddell, W., 4, 13
 Wilkinson, H. C., 110
 Woodbridge, A. W., 232

Paddington:
 Modernisation, 95
 closed, (flying bomb attacks), 211 *et seq.*
Parliamentary:
 General Election 1923, 11
 General Election 1924, 20, 148
 Labour Government 1929, 87
 Loans and Guarantees (1929) Act, 88
 National Govt. 1931, 106
 Emergency powers (Defence) Act 1939, 159
 Compensation agreement 1940, 171
 Revised agreement, 187 *et seq.*, 215
 General Election 1954, 216
 Nationalisation bill, 221 *et seq.*
Personalities:
 Allen, Cecil J., 61, 132
 Baker, Humphrey, 132
 Baldwin, Stanley, 48
 Bromley, John, 48, 76
 Brown, Ashley, 189
 Cook, A. J., 48
 Ferreira, L. M. G., 29
 Hungerford, Ed., 58
 Lowe, A. C. W., 23
 Pringle, Col. Sir John, 28
 Steer, Mrs., 209
 Stevens, W. J., 13
 Thomas, J. H., 47 *et seq.*, 76, 87
 Wallace, Capt. Euan, 151
 Willard, Daniel, 58
Pole, Sir Felix J. C.:
 General references, 114, 120, 235
 Engine design, 56
 General strike, 49 *et seq.*
 Interchange loco. trials, 45
 Knighthood, 13
 Negotiations *re* wages, 76
 Reduction in wages, 47
 Resignation, 84
 South Wales, co-ordination in, 4, 35
 Systematised train departures, 15
'Poor Bag of Assets' (Dalton speech), 223
Prince of Wales, H.R.H. at Centenary Banquet 1935, 117 *et seq.*

Race specials, 73 *et seq.*
Racecourse station (Chepstow), 43
Railcars, diesel, 111 *et seq.*
Rails, 33
Railway Executive Committee (1939), 160
Restrictions in management, 213 *et seq.*
Rhymney Railway, 2, 4, 10, 34, 35
Road Competition, 20
Road services, 78, 79, 80, 82
Rogerstone yard, 4
Royal Commission on Transport, 82, 148
Royal Visit to Swindon, 1924, 14

Severn Tunnel, Conveyance of cars, 42
Shakespeare Express, 79
Ships (G.W.R.) at Dunkirk, 176–182
Signalling:
 Block working, 103
 Bristol alterations, 98, 99
 Cardiff alterations, 100–101
 Colour light principles, 97 *et seq.*
 Power locking frames, 103
 Precautions in block working, 31
 Reading new junction, 179
 Route working, 30
 Upper quadrant signalling, 29, 102
 Wartime loop lines, 191
South Wales:
 Coal handling, 4, 37
 Co-ordination, 34 *et seq.*
 Developments, 13
 Dock business, in 1933, 113
 Export of coal, for steam locos. 4, 35
 Loading of ships, 38
 Mining Industry dispute, 45
 Modernising locomotives, 41
 Position in 1929, 81
 Recession in Trade, 1931, 106
 Re-organisation of railways, 4
 Tinplate trade, 104
 20-ton Wagons, 37, 43
Speed:
 Cheltenham Flyer, 6, 132
 Ocean Mails, 18, 19
Square Deal campaign, 148 *et seq.*
Steam, alternatives to, 107
Strikes:
 Coal dispute, 1926, 48 *et seq.*, 53
 General strike, 49 *et seq.*
 Terms of settlement, 52
Swansea docks, 83
Swindon:
 day excursions, 61

Swindon—*cont.*
engine building, 131
optical lining up, 123
Royal visit, 14
Testing plant, 131 *et seq.*

Taff Vale Railway, 2, 4, 34
Taunton, new works, 92
Thingley Junction, 201, 202
Trade Unions:
Negotiations *re* lower wages, 76
Railwaymen and the coal dispute, 47
Reduction in expenses, 47
Traffic recession, 105 *et seq.*
Train services:
Birmingham in 1¾hr. investigation,
141
Bristolian, The, 116
Cheltenham Flyer, 71, 84, 133 *et seq.*
Cornish Riviera Express (*q.v.*)
Curtailments, 1947, 221
Emergency service during evacuation, 1939, 162 *et seq.*
Express diesels, Cardiff & Birmingham, 112
Extra holiday trains, 1941, 186–7
Freight trains, 72 *et seq.*
'Grand National' special, 74
Passenger travel analysis, 1924, 15
Post-war restorations, 217
Shakespeare Express, 79
Slip coach services, 67
Swindon 5/- excursions, 61
Systematic departure times, 1924, 15
et seq.
Torquay Pullman, 71, 104
Zenith of passenger services, 135 *et seq.*
Tabulations:
Daily non-stops 100 miles or more
1927, 66
Express services from London 1928,
144
Fastest times from London 1914 and
1927, 65
Long non-stop runs, 143
Mileage comparison with other railways, 139, 140
Recovery times, 186
Runs at 58 mp.h. start to stop: 1927,
68
Runs at 58 m.p.h. start to stop: 1938,
137
Services between provincial towns,
146

Tabulations—*cont.*
100-mile runs daily in 1946, 218
Turntables, 207

Unemployment, relief of:
A.T.C., extension of, 94
Bristol reconstruction, 97
Cardiff reconstruction, 97
G.W.R. proposals of works, 87 *et seq.*
Paddington modernisation, 96
Taunton, widening etc., 92 *et seq.*
Westbury (and Frome) by-passes, 89
et seq.
Unification, railway, 213, 216, 217

Wagons:
'Instanter' couplings, 105
'Mink G', 105
War-time repair methods, 205, 206
20-ton coal, 37 *et seq.*, 104
War conditions and incidents:
Air raids:
Birkenhead, 181
Fishguard steamer, 182
London area, 183
Newton Abbot, 179
Praed Street, 180
Air raid precautions, 156 *et seq.*
Alternative routings, 196
Ambulance trains, 208
Arrears of maintenance, 215
Austerity painting (coaches and
engines), 193
Austerity U.S.A. locomotives, 194,
208
Black-out conditions, 166
Casualties, 216
Concrete 'pot' sleepers, 203 *et seq.*
Dunkirk evacuation, 175
Emergency headquarters, 167
Engines for overseas, 167
Engines, Swindon built L.M.S. type,
193
Evacuation of children, 161 *et seq.*
Extra holiday trains, 1941, 186–7
Flying bomb attacks, 211 *et seq.*
Inter-working, G.W. & S.R. locos.,
199
Junctions, new for wartime:
Launceston, 200
Lydford, 200
Oxford, 197
Reading, 179, 197
St. Budeaux, 199, 200

War conditions and incidents—*cont.*
  Junctions, new for wartime—*cont.*
    Staines, 198
    Thingley Junction, 202
    Westbury, east curve, 202
    Yeovil, 202
  Making up lost time, 185
  New lines, Newport-Severn Tunnel, 190
  Recovery times, 186
  Train running, 214 *et seq.*
  Travel conditions, 214

War conditions and incidents—*cont.*
  Volunteer labour, 208
  Wagon repair methods, 205, 206
  Women in wartime work, 207, 208
Westbury, by-pass line, 89
  ,,   new wartime junction, 202
Winchester, Cheese Hill, 29
Wivelscombe, Landslip, 209 *et seq.*
World Record, 'Cheltenham Flyer', 133 *et seq.*
Wolverhampton, works reconstruction, 127 *et seq.*

Index to Illustrations

	Plate
Air raid Damage:	
Birmingham	37
Bristol, Booking Office ..	37
„ Coaches outside ..	35
Paddington	36
Air Raid Precautions:	
Ambulance	34
Evacuation of children.. ..	35
Home Guard & C.D. parade ..	34
Air Services	13
Austerity locos from U.S.A.	
2–8–0 being landed at Cardiff	38
2–8–0 general view	40
2–8–0 on freight train	43
0–6–0T being landed	38
Buses	12
Centenary film, scenes from ..	18
Coat of Arms	1
Diesel Railcars	20
Docks:	
Barry	39
Cardiff (crane)	33
„ (steamers)	41
Millbay, Plymouth	7
Newport	9
Penarth	9
Port Talbot	3
Port Talbot	41
Swansea	3
Freight trains:	
Near Teignmouth	43
Leaving Severn Tunnel ..	43
Gas Turbine locomotive ..	48
General Strike:	
Unloading milk at Paddington	6
Volunteer woman driver ..	6

	Plate
Locomotives:	
King George V in U.S.A. ..	8
King George III	32
King Henry VII (streamlined)	22
King Edward VIII (wartime style)	32
Manorbier Castle (streamlined)	22
Cleeve Abbey (oil fired)	46
Garth Hall (oil fired)	46
Arlington Grange	22
2–8–0 No. 2884	40
2–8–0 No. 2872 (oil fired) ..	46
South Wales tank types ..	11
Tank engine variety	25
L.M.S. type 2–8–0 built	
Swindon	40
Locomotive Works:	
Caerphilly, boiler shop.. ..	5
„ erecting shop ..	10
„ wheel shop ..	10
„ heavy machine shop	26
Swindon, Royal visit	5
„ Test plant	27
Wolverhampton General View	19
„ Erecting shop	19
Paddington station closed ..	42
Passenger trains:	
Up Bristolian, engine 5070 ..	45
A.T.C. Special, engine 5056 ..	45
Up Cornish Riviera, engine	
5915	47
Birkenhead–Paddington engine	
1017	47
Personalities:	
Carpmael, Raymond ..	16
Churchill, Viscount	2
Collett, C. B.	2
Hawksworth, F. W. ..	44
Horne, Viscount	16
Lloyd, J. C.	16
Matthews, Gilbert	44
Milne, Sir James	16
Nicholls, R. H.	2
Pole, Sir Felix J. C.	2
Portal, Viscount	44
Quartermaine, Sir Allan ..	44

	Plate					Plate
Signalling:		Station reconstructions:				
Bristol, Temple Meads East Box	23	Bristol	..	..	..	.. 14
Reading, signalbox interior ..	23	Bristol	..	..	..	.. 21
Searchlight signals Cardiff ..	15	Newton Abbot		..	.. 21
Semaphore signals, Reading ..	15	Newton Abbot		..	.. 29
Square Deal	30	Swansea		..	.. 29
		Taunton		..	.. 17
Stations: exteriors		Steamers ..	..	..	.. 31
Leamington Spa	24				
Newport, (Mon).	24	Wagons ..	..	..	.. 4